A COMPLETE GUIDE

COSTA RICA

Malpais and Santa Teresa have some of the world's most beautiful beaches.

FIRST EDITION

COSTA RICA

Great Destinations Central America

With Excursions to Nicaragua & Panama

Paige R. Penland

The Countryman Press
Woodstock, Vermont

I'd like to dedicate this book to my mom, Wanda Olson, for enabling my travel addiction since childhood; for repeatedly storing sagging boxes of old Lowrider magazines and sweaters now years out of style while I traipse across the tropics; for providing me with a permanent mailing address and the occasional undeserved deposit into my emptied checking account; and for visiting me in both Costa Rica and Nicaragua (braving choppy Lake Nicaragua in a tiny lancha to visit Isla Ometepe) over the years. Perhaps Panama is next! I love you, mom.

ISBN 978-1-58157-097-7

Cover photo © Kerrick James
Interior photos by the author unless otherwise specified
Book design by Bodenweber Design
Page composition by Chelsea Cloeter
Maps by Mapping Specialists Ltd., Madison, WI, © The Countryman Press

Published by The Countryman Press, P.O. Box 748, Woodstock, Vermont 05091

Distributed by W. W. Norton & Company, Inc., 500 Fifth Avenue, New York, NY 10110

Manufactured in the United States of America

10 9 8 7 6 5 4 3 2 1

GREAT DESTINATIONS TRAVEL GUIDEBOOK SERIES

Recommended by *National Geographic Traveler* and *Travel + Leisure* magazines

[A] CRISP AND CRITICAL APPROACH, FOR TRAVELERS WHO WANT TO LIVE LIKE LOCALS. —*USA Today*

Great Destinations™ guidebooks are known for their comprehensive, critical coverage of regions of extraordinary cultural interest and natural beauty. The authors in this series are professional travel writers who have lived for many years in the regions they describe. Each title in this series is continuously updated with each printing to ensure accurate and timely information. All the books contain more than one hundred photographs and maps.

Current titles available:

The Adirondack Book

Atlanta

Austin, San Antonio
  & the Texas Hill Country

The Berkshire Book

Bermuda

Big Sur, Monterey Bay
  & Gold Coast Wine Country

Cape Canaveral, Cocoa Beach
  & Florida's Space Coast

The Charleston, Savannah
  & Coastal Islands Book

The Chesapeake Bay Book

The Coast of Maine Book

Colorado's Classic Mountain Towns

Costa Rica: Great Destinations
  Central America

The Finger Lakes Book

The Four Corners Region

Galveston, South Padre Island
  & the Texas Gulf Coast

The Hamptons Book

Hawaii's Big Island

Honolulu & Oahu:
  Great Destinations Hawaii

The Jersey Shore: Atlantic City to Cape May

Kauai: Great Destinations Hawaii

Lake Tahoe & Reno

Los Cabos & Baja California Sur:
  Great Destinations Mexico

Maui: Great Destinations Hawaii

Michigan's Upper Peninsula

Montreal & Quebec City:
  Great Destinations Canada

The Nantucket Book

The Napa & Sonoma Book

North Carolina's Outer Banks
  & the Crystal Coast

Palm Beach, Fort Lauderdale, Miami
  & the Florida Keys

Palm Springs & Desert Resorts

Phoenix, Scottsdale, Sedona
  & Central Arizona

Playa del Carmen, Tulum & the Riviera Maya:
  Great Destinations Mexico

Salt Lake City, Park City, Provo
  & Utah's High Country Resorts

San Diego & Tijuana

San Juan, Vieques & Culebra:
  Great Destinations Puerto Rico

San Miguel de Allende & Guanajuato:
  Great Destinations Mexico

The Santa Fe & Taos Book

The Sarasota, Sanibel Island & Naples Book

The Seattle & Vancouver Book

The Shenandoah Valley Book

Touring East Coast Wine Country

Washington, D.C., and Northern Virginia

Yellowstone & Grand Teton National Parks
  and Jackson Hole

Yosemite & the Southern Sierra Nevada

If you are traveling to, moving to, residing in, or just interested in any (or all!) of these enchanting regions, a Great Destinations guidebook is a superior companion. Honest and painstakingly critical, full of information only a local can provide, Great Destinations guidebooks give you all the practical knowledge you need to enjoy the best of each region. Why not own them all?

The Golfo Dulce, or Sweet Gulf, from the Osa Peninsula

Contents

Acknowledgments

There are so many people without whom this book would not have been possible, beginning with Kim Grant, who first contacted me about the gig, and the gracious, flexible, and supportive editorial staff at The Countryman Press, including Kermit Hummel and Jennifer Thompson, as well as diligent copyeditor Collette Leonard. Thanks also go out to my mom, Wanda Olson, for keeping an eye on my business back in the United States, and my sister Beth, for her help with research.

Many others have helped me out on my journey, including everyone at Scotland Apartments (www.hotels.co.cr/scotland.html) in San José for keeping the Internet up and running. Special thanks to Beto Lizarraga and Jaime Peligro in Guanacaste; Nadene, Camillo, and Ann in Nicaragua; Jefe, with information on the Río San Juan; Vera and Edgart, with those Atlantic updates; and of course my neighbors and friends here in San José, who have kept me going: Jim, Anthony, Jesse, Tom, Barry, Jules, Diana, Kyle Alex, Manfred, Dexter, Carlos, and Jason. And to everyone who I've forgotten, many thanks and *pura vida*!

Introduction

One has to wonder—while threading the orchid-clad understory of an ancient cloud forest, or admiring the tenacity of ten thousand green turtles nesting on some gray and untouched beach—is it possible? Could we really preserve Eden? The answer to that ancient question could be as simple as *pura vida*.

This is the unofficial slogan of Costa Rica, and you'll hear it every day, in place of "hello," "goodbye," or "I'm doing very well, thanks for asking." Literally, it means "pure life," and in this place where schools of hammerhead sharks swirl unmolested in chilly plankton-rich waters, and one quarter of the world's bees buzz through the endangered dry tropical forest, it seems quite literal indeed.

Costa Rica is one of those rare places where *la naturaleza* is valued more than gold, again, literally: One mine was shut down as this book went to press, despite record gold prices, for polluting a rarely visited wildlife refuge. Cold metal glitters, to be sure, but have you ever seen a misty sky full of rainbows, or a flock of red and blue macaws, reflected in every dewdrop that clings to a living bouquet?

You can. For the engine upon which Eden turns is ecotourism; there is simply no way that this tiny, resource-poor country will realize its ambition to preserve paradise without guests like you. Thus, the land's serene and smiling caretakers, with their legendary hospitality, have opened their arms to all who want to see what they've accomplished, whether on an inspiring walkabout through untried rain forest, or the elegant opulence of a gauze-and-teak bungalow overlooking a pristine white-sand beach.

Why not accept their invitation? This is paradise, after all, where you might immerse yourself in some of the world's most stunning white water, or perhaps a healing hot spring, from which you'll watch lava streak red and golden through the night. Lend your own individuality, for a moment, to our planet's most intense riot of biodiversity, amidst colorful corals beneath the Caribbean Sea, or surrounded by the kaleidoscope of life that is the Osa Peninsula.

Or just relax into that warm Costa Rican welcome, resting assured in your comfortable hammock that the philosophy of *pura vida* requires taking time to slow down, and enjoy all that the pure life has to offer.

THE WAY THIS BOOK WORKS

This book covers the entire country of Costa Rica, which I have divided into six destination chapters. The chapter about San José, the nation's capital, also covers the suburbs of Aserri, Ciudad Colón, Escazú, Los Yoses, San Pedro, and Santa Ana. The Central Valley, which surrounds San José, includes the misty mountain towns of Alajuela (home to Juan Santamaría International Airport), Cartago, Heredia, Orosí, Sarchí, and Turrialba, as well as natural attractions such as Poás and Irazú National Parks.

The Northern Zone takes in several of Costa Rica's most famous attractions, including Arenal Volcano and the cloud forests of Monteverde, as well as the less toured region of Sarapiquí. Continuing northeast, the "Guanacaste and Nicoya Peninsula" chapter details the Papagayo Peninsula, Playas del Coco, Montezuma, Sámara, Tamarindo, and the provincial capital, Liberia, home to Daniel Oduber Quiros International Airport.

Heading south along the West Coast, the "Central Pacific Coast and the Osa Peninsula" chapter takes in such popular spots as Dominical, Jacó, Manuel Antonio National Park, Quepos, and the Osa Peninsula, home to Corcovado National Park. Finally, "The Caribbean Coast" includes Barra del Colorado, Cahuita, Tortuguero, and fabulously festive Puerto Viejo de Talamanca.

I've also included four possible side trips to neighboring countries, easily arranged as a side trip from Costa Rica, and perfect for those who need to take a three-day "visa vacation" to renew their tourist visa. Southwest Nicaragua centers on Granada, one of the first European cities in the Americas, while the Río San Juan is one of the world's iconic riverboat rides. If you'd rather head east to Panama, I've included the pretty mountain town of Boquete and sultry Caribbean islands of Bocas del Toro.

Other chapters deal with the history, culture, and environment of the fascinating country of Costa Rica, as well as information about lodging, dining, transportation, and the nitty-gritty for planning your trip.

A series of indexes at the back of the book provide easy access to information. The first, a standard index, lists entries and subjects in alphabetical order. Next, hotels, bed-and-breakfasts, and nature lodges are categorized by price. Restaurants are organized into two separate indexes: one by price, one by type of cuisine.

Favorites

In addition to listing the finest hotels, bed-and-breakfasts, and nature lodges, as well as the best restaurants and attractions, I've added a ★ next to places that are personal favorites.

Price Codes

Cost of lodging is based on an average per-room, double-occupancy rate at peak season (December through April). Costa Rica's 16.39 percent tax and gratuities are not included.

Rates are often reduced during Green Season (May through November). An **asterisk** (*) denotes that a full breakfast is included with the room price.

Dining prices are based on the cost of a dinner entrée with a non-alcoholic drink, not including the 13 percent taxes and 10 percent gratuity added to the cost of almost all restaurant meals (except for the very cheapest *sodas*). Menus note whether or not their listed prices include this hefty 23 percent total surcharge, some listing two sets of prices.

Code	Lodging	Dining
Inexpensive (\$)	Up to \$50	Up to \$5
Moderate (\$\$)	\$50 to \$100	\$5 to \$10
Expensive (\$\$\$)	\$100 to \$200	\$10 to \$20
Very Expensive (\$\$\$\$)	\$200 and up	\$20 or more

Tourist Information

Costa Rica has the best-developed tourist infrastructure in Central America, with an excellent network of public and private tourism bureaus. Almost any tour operator or hotel can arrange transportation, accommodations, and a variety of guided tours, so ask. Before you go, however, peruse the online resources I've included at the beginning of each destination chapter, and throughout the planning chapter. Or check out these great general Web sites offering all sorts of wonderful ideas.

Central America.com (centralamerica.com/cr) Excellent private site with information about Costa Rica and Central America.

Costa Rica Maps (www.maptak.com) Comprehensive selection of online maps, many interactive, can be downloaded to your WAP cell phone.

Costa Rica Tourism (www.tourism.co.cr) Sprawling Web site with information, articles, and up-to-date listings for the entire country.

Costa Rica Info (www.infocostarica.com) Portal with scores of links to tourism-related businesses.

★ **Ministry of Tourism** (www.visitcostarica.com) Costa Rica's official Web site welcomes you "with open arms" and a quite comprehensive list of attractions, accommodations, tour operators, and other services, as well as articles and press releases.

The Real Costa Rica (www.therealcostarica.com) Information and insight from a long-time expatriate, Tim.

★ **Tico Times** (www.ticotimes.net) English-language weekly is a great way to keep up with the latest goings-on.

Wiki Costa Rica (wikicostarica.com) Your new favorite country has its own Wikipedia: Read and, after your vacation, contribute.

1

History and Culture

Natural history and human history seem more peacefully intertwined in Costa Rica than elsewhere on the planet. Perhaps because it is so resource poor, it has rarely attracted the attention of envious empires, and remained a quiet backwater through the rise and fall of the Aztec and Inca civilizations, as well as throughout the Spanish incursion.

Its relatively gentle history is just one reason why the residents of the "Rich Coast" have in modern times been able to preserve Costa Rica's real jewels: emerald forests, sapphire seas, and ruby-throated hummingbirds. But the philosophy of *pura vida*, shored up by a political system based on equality, democracy, and nonviolence, has given Costa Ricans the tools to preserve one of the world's most important national park systems. They've used them.

Natural History

Perhaps 150 million years ago, the super continent of Pangaea began to buckle, rending itself into Europe and Africa, then releasing North America, and finally South America, into a sea of magma that would slowly carry these last to the far side of the planet. The Americas were then two great islands apart, separated by the ancient Sea of Tethys, where the manatee was born. Each continent expanded as the climate cooled and water receded, offering itself over the eons to mammals that filled a void left behind by the fall of the dinosaur kingdom, some 65 million years ago. Camelids (llamas), horses, and giant sloths would eventually roam the south, while primates, bats, and saber-toothed tigers patrolled the north.

Then, around 50 million years ago, at the bottom of the sea between them, two relatively tiny tectonic plates came together in a collision of volcanic proportions. As the Caribbean Plate began to subsume smaller Cocos Plate, an undersea archipelago erupted, breaking the water's surface as a crescent of fuming islands several million years later. It would take another 40 million years for this arc of fire to connect the great continents in the land bridge we now call Central America.

As the isthmus emerged, it divided the oceans and interrupted the world's currents, perhaps causing the first Arctic ice caps to form, and the waters to farther recede. The creatures of the south and north, perhaps driven from the poles by this new and fearsome cold, quickly moved to colonize a new land. Between ten and twenty thousand years ago, they were followed by yet another species, similar to native monkeys but better armed, called *Homo sapiens*.

Mysterious granite spheres were left behind by Costa Rica's indigenous people.

Ecosystems Ecology

The dramatic topography of Costa Rica, carved by this collision, has given rise to a dozen different ecosystems that carpet the country with life. Mountain ranges topping 3,000 meters (10,000 feet), including the mighty Talamanca and Cordillera Central, as well as a string of more than one hundred volcanoes tracing the ancient fault line, rise to sudden cloud-forested heights from humid rain forest lowlands and dry tropical savannah below. The country's position on the land bridge between the continents, as well as a sultry, Neotropical climate that comfortably cradles new life, have all conspired to shelter a remarkable amount of biodiversity.

Despite its tiny size, only .03 percent of the Earth's surface, this marvelously varied land is home to more than 500,000 species, including more than 300,000 insects, 12,000 plants, 237 mammals, 360 amphibians, and 850 species of birds (more than twice as many as the United States and Canada combined) that represent some 4 percent of species worldwide. It would be impossible to include a comprehensive survey of the creatures here, but dozens of books detailing the denizens of these rich ecosystems have been written (see Suggested Reading). But here are a few of their worlds, well worth visiting yourself.

Cloud Forests

On well-watered tropical mountains rising above 1,500 meters (5,000 feet), a chill and humid ecosystem called the cloud forest arises. Much of the time a veil of mist obscures the rich forests, where the trees themselves are covered with different mosses, bromeliads, and epiphytes. Many of these plants, some parasitic but most self-sufficient, cover each

Costa Rica's excellent public school system contributes to the 96 percent literacy rate.

outstretched limb with cisterns of rainwater, where frogs and other creatures come to lay their eggs. Beneath the thick upper canopy are descending levels of green, from huge Jurassic ferns to tiny orchids, many pollinated by bats and hummingbirds. All of these conspire with the fog to obscure the sight of wildlife, including the much-sought-after resplendent quetzal, though even on the mistiest days you may hear the echoes of howler monkeys and three-wattled bellbirds in the clouds.

The most famous of these surround Monteverde, where three massive cloud forest preserves are crisscrossed with developed hiking trails, hanging bridges, canopy tours, and other aerial adventures. But you can escape the crowds and meander through the clouds at other heights, including Los Angeles Cloud Forest, with a beautiful lodge; Bosque de la Paz, surrounded by several simple *cabinas* and one of the country's best luxury hotels; atop volcanoes including Tenorio, Poás, and Irazú; and in Quetzales National Park, with several comfortable lodges in neighboring Santa María de Dota.

Coral Reefs

This delicate, undersea ecosystem may be the world's most threatened, as poorly understood climate changes, called global warming by the majority of the world's scientists, subtly alter the chemistry of the seas. The euphemism is "bleaching," rendering the world's corals, massive gardens of life, white and lifeless beneath the waves. It is a holocaust that not even Costa Rica's conservationists can quell.

Regardless, Costa Rica's Cahuita National Park remains a wonderful sight to behold, a place that some argue is actually more biodiverse, meter for meter, than the Osa Peninsula. Snorkeling and diving trips here and at the neighboring Gandoca-Manzanillo reefs can be arranged from any of the region's beach towns. Though Pacific reefs are perhaps less spectacular in their variety, they offer wonderful diving and snorkeling along the Central

Pacific, most prominently off the coast of Manuel Antonio National Park and Bellena National Park, as well as more threatened sites that can be seen from the Nicoya Peninsula.

Dry Tropical Forest

This is the most rare ecosystem in the Americas, as its beautiful hardwoods are easily felled, and relatively rich soils converted to farms and ranches. But where it remains, it makes for wonderful hiking and relatively easy wildlife watching, thanks to wide-open spaces between the trees. Its most striking tree is not a tree at all: The strangler fig (called *matapalo*, or "killer branch," in Spanish) is born in an unlucky host tree's branches, from which it sends great tentacles to the ground that will eventually encase its host in a living, buttressed sarcophagus. These woods are also unlike rainier forests, where nutrients are immediately bound up by living beings, leaving the soil almost barren. Instead, the dry tropical forest loses its leaves at the beginning of the dry season, as temperate forests will when winter arrives. The carpet of leaves is mulched into the soil, enriching it for future growth—or human settlement.

Guanacaste preserves the world's largest remaining tracts of this rare biome, which now surrounds Costa Rica's most luxurious hotels, atop the Papagayo Peninsula, and covers, unmolested, the Santa Elena Peninsula, wholly preserved as Santa Rosa National Park. This is just part of the Guanacaste Preservation Area, also home to caverns, kitesurfing, and several climbable volcanoes, where Rincón de la Vieja offers excellent trails through dry tropics. Any Guanacaste hotel or operator can arrange hikes and other adventures, or you can commune with the forest more closely at several nature lodges.

Mangrove Forests

Home to manatees and bull sharks, huge flocks of waterfowl and enormous tarpon, mangrove forests mark the boundary between the oceans and fresh water. Though the trees may seem similar, with specially adapted roots allowing them to colonize this ever-shifting tidal realm, different species (black, white, red, tea, and buttonwood) are descended from wholly different lineages, all working together to protect Costa Rica's fragile shores. Indeed, the Northern Caribbean is shielded from tropical storms not by coral, as most coasts are, but by this endangered ecosystem.

Hiking through the mangroves is at best a muddy proposition, so most people arrange boat tours through the wilderness. The easiest access is from Tortuguero and the other towns of the Northern Caribbean, along the Río Sierpe into the Osa Peninsula, and between Golfito and Zancudo.

Tropical Rain Forest

This ancient ecosystem was the world's most widespread in the age of the dinosaurs, when all was moist and warm. The rain forest remains home to the greatest species diversity of any biome on Earth, covering 5 percent of the Earth, but called home by more than half of all species. Perpetually hot and humid, there are endless layers of green in the rain forest. The crown of a marvelous ceiba, called the *kapok*, or "tree of life" by indigenous Costa Ricans who once revered its buttressed bulk, can top 60 meters (200 feet). Unlike forests of northern climes, where only a few species will dominate thousands of square kilometers, an astounding assortment of moss- and bromeliad-covered trees can be discovered within a few short steps.

There are many ways into the rain forest, the most accessible near Arenal, where hanging bridges can be found. Canopy tours, dozens of guided hikes, and river floats can be arranged. Also, in Sarapiquí a handful of lodges and research stations offer opportunities for exploration. The Caribbean side includes some of the rainiest spots on Earth, enjoyed on the canal trip to Tortuguero, or a hike in Cahuita National Park. Though the Central Pacific offers several rain-forested havens such as Manuel Antonio National Park, the prize goes to the Osa Peninsula, an almost untouched rain forest with more species per square meter than anywhere else on Earth. All these spots can be seen on great guided tours, as well as some of the country's best lodging.

Public Policy

Costa Rica's rampant wildlife is administrated by the powerful Ministry of Environment and Energy (MINAE), and its sub-ministry, the National System of Conservation Areas (SINAC). The system includes more than 160 protected areas, including 26 national parks, all connected by growing, mixed-use conservation areas guarding important wildlife corridors. More than 28 percent of Costa Rica is preserved in one way or another.

Conservation efforts began in the 1950s, spurred on as often by eco-conscious expatriates and foreign scientists as by Costa Rican activists, when such dramatic spots such as Irazú Volcano were first set aside. As international interest grew, funding from all over the world allowed preservationists to purchase and protect vast tracts of primary forest, most famously in Monteverde. Resistance from many residents of this once impoverished nation, who had traditionally relied on farming, logging, hunting, and harvesting to sustain their families, melted as ecotourism became the country's most important industry.

Today Costa Ricans (Ticos) are proud of their conservation efforts, and the quest to conserve continues. New national parks and wildlife refuges are added to the tally almost annually. Tree-planting campaigns have reforested the countryside: In 1987, forests covered 21 percent of the country; today, 51 percent of Costa Rica has it made in the shade. Private companies, such as Nature Air, have voluntarily gone carbon neutral. The country's Blue Flag Program, which rewards clean, protected beaches with this coveted banner, has spurred beach communities to institute exemplary protection programs. Meanwhile, the National Biodiversity Institute, INBio (www.inbio.ar.cr) is compiling Costa Rica's vast genetic library to create a searchable online catalog with more than 3 million examples of Costa Rica's 500,000 species.

When President Oscar Arias was re-elected in 2006, he called upon Costa Rica to become "a country at peace with nature." His plan includes efforts to conserve biological diversity, improve environmental quality, manage water resources, and help study and alleviate climate change. His administration has also begun enforcing environmental regulations more stringently, shutting down resorts and rescinding blue flags, despite the economic cost. In 2008 Costa Rica was ranked fifth of 149 countries on the Environmental Performance Index by the World Economic Forum in Davos—the only non-European nation to break the top five.

These impressive accomplishments hinge upon one fickle industry, however: ecotourism. Although the country has begun to diversify the economic importance of its protected areas, your eco-dollar (or eco-euro) is still key to supporting the conservation efforts of this tiny, idealistic country. The Costa Rican Tourist Board (ICT) has enacted the Certified Sustainable Tourism (CST) program, which evaluates and certifies hotels and tour operators based on sustainability and community support. Businesses are ranked with one to five "leaves" (five being the very difficult-to-reach pinnacle of eco-consciousness), which signify their accomplishments protecting natural and human resources. I've included CST rankings for hotels throughout the book, but search their online directory (www.turismo-sostenible.co.cr) for the most recent inductees.

SOCIAL HISTORY

Famed for its commitments to democracy, freedom, conservation, and peace, this most unusual of nations has achieved a standard of living unrivaled in Central America, and boasts longer life spans and higher literacy rates than even the United States. Many Costa Ricans will point to the abolition of the military in 1949 as the source of their success, as this freed up resources for health care and education. But one must also take into account Costa Rica's long history as a relatively egalitarian agricultural society, as well as the influence of idealistic and effective leaders who, for all their imperfections, are the envy of any nation.

The Original Costa Ricans

The first remains of human habitation in Costa Rica, found near Turrialba, date to between 10,000 B.C. and 12,000 B.C., a small collection of spearheads that reveals quite a lot. Some are very typical of South American hunters, while others have a fishtail barb (a rather advanced technology for the era), almost identical to points used in Clovis, New Mexico, around the same time. The land bridge of Central America connected the great human cultures of north and south, and Costa Rica is apparently where they met.

You might expect that bloody clashes characterized the meeting of these notoriously warlike cultures, which would go on to build such well-armed civilizations as the Olmec, Aztec, Maya, and Inca empires. But there is little evidence that this was the case. They apparently did not build fortresses, one reason why Costa Rica lacks the awesome fortified ruins of Mexico and Peru.

Some 96 percent of Costa Rica's energy comes from renewable sources, such as the Miravalles Geothermal Project.

Evidence of the first permanent human settlements, dating to around 3,000 B.C., is found in Guanacaste and Southwest Nicaragua. Called the Chorotega people by Spanish chroniclers, they were probably descended from the Olmecs of southeastern Mexico. They made fine pottery prized throughout Costa Rica, and carved elaborate *metates* (corn grinders) and huge, mysterious granite spheres, fine examples of which are displayed at the National Museum in San José. Their beautiful polished jade, carved from stones that were probably imported from Guatemala, can be appreciated at the Jade Museum in San José.

The population increased dramatically around 800 A.D., concurrent with the fall of the Classic Mayan Empire. Ceramics became more colorful and sculptural, and Ticos for the first time took to the seas. Body painting, tattooing, and piercing became popular all over the country.

The Central Highlands and Caribbean Coast were populated by people connected by language, culture, and a yuca-based diet to the Amazon region of South America. Regularly used by hunting parties from the south as early as 5,000 B.C., the region's first permanent settlements, dated to 1,500 B.C., are found near Turrialba, and can be explored at Guayabo Archaeological Monument. After being introduced to corn by their neighbors in Guanacaste, their populations exploded, spreading settlements throughout the Central Valley and Caribbean Coast. They maintained connections to the Amazon and Andes, from whom they adopted musical instruments, ceramic styles, and crops like beans and sweet potatoes. Circular buildings called *palenques*, common in Colombia and Ecuador, became popular around 500 A.D.; you can see (or stay in) reproductions at the Centro Neotrópico in Sarapiquí.

A third, less complex, culture arose along the South Pacific, where infertile soils precluded widespread agriculture. Culturally connected to Chiripí Province of Panama, the

Costa Rica recycles!

first evidence of permanent settlement dates to only 1,000 B.C. By 500 A.D., there were sev-eral small settlements characterized by distinctive incised, or "scarified" pottery, and tools used to ingest coca leaf. Remote from other Costa Rican cultures, these mysterious people were apparently influenced more by seafaring traders who stopped in the calm and pro-tected waters of the Golfo Dulce.

Today, there are about 65,000 indigenous Costa Ricans (1.7 percent of the population), about 40 percent of whom live on the Caribbean Coast and Talamanca Mountains. There are 22 indigenous reservations, the largest (having 11,000 residents) is the Bribri of Limón. Communities are characterized by endemic poverty and political disenfranchise-ment; Indians were only given the right to vote in 1990. Thanks to political activism and international aid, however, these groups are increasing their power and influence, and have successfully sued for the return of illegally appropriated land. You can visit the Bribri and other Talamanca communities from Cahuita and Puerto Viejo on the Caribbean Coast, and arrange trips to meet the Malekú from the Arenal area, or Borucas on the Central Pacific. A great spot to see Chorotega pottery made the old-fashioned way is in the tiny town of Guaitíl on the Nicoya Peninsula. April 19th is Indigenous People's Day.

Enter the Spaniards

In 1502, on his fourth voyage to the New World, an exhausted Christopher Columbus landed on Isla Uvita, just off the shores of Puerto Limón. The locals offered him a warm welcome, presenting the aging explorer with gold jewelry. Columbus thus christened the land *Costa Rica*, "Rich Coast," and went on to spend two years stranded on Jamaica before his final return to Spain.

In 1506 the first Spanish expedition set out to penetrate the fabled Rich Coast. This time, however, the locals mounted heavy resistance to the would-be conquistadors, who turned back empty-handed. The Spanish would eventually begin settling Central America from the dryer Pacific Coast. The first successful incursion began in 1522, led by a young and untried explorer named Gil González Dávila, who "discovered" the port of Puntarenas, and towns of Nicoya and Santa Cruz.

After a long and arduous period of Spanish settlement near Puntarenas, the capital city of Cartago was founded in 1563. Costa Rica was administrated as part of the Spanish Viceroyalty of Guatamala, which also included El Salvador, Honduras, and Nicaragua. It was the farthest province from the capital, resource poor, and sparsely populated—by any measure a backwater. Though there were certainly wealthy families who exercised dispro-portionate political power, they simply could not amass the vast riches of the Spanish elite in wealthier regions. The result was a relatively egalitarian agricultural community, quite peaceful in its unimportance.

In 1808 the Costa Rican economy got a serious jolt. Coffee was introduced from Cuba: Cheap to grow, easy to ship, and famously addictive, it soon became the most important crop in the country. Europeans, in particular Germans, arrived to sow the cool highlands with the "golden bean." Prosperous for the first time, the Spanish-bred elite were finally elevated to a position of power and wealth that their brethren elsewhere in the empire had enjoyed for centuries.

Then, in October 1821, the provincial government received word that the Spanish Empire had fallen in Central America. Mexico had issued its declaration of independence in the name of the entire region; it had taken a month for news to make it to Cartago. Sud-denly, Costa Rica was free.

On Their Own

The newly moneyed upper class was divided about how to deal with their newfound independence. The Spanish old guard wanted to keep power consolidated with the conservative institutions of Spain, joining the Mexican Empire but retaining authoritarian political structures and the influence of the Catholic Church. Reformers, who often had a mixed racial heritage that had barred them from Spanish high society, wanted to build a democracy as part of the Federal Republic of Central America.

The four major cities of the Central Valley took sides. Conservative Cartago and Heredia wanted to join Mexico, while liberal San José and Alajuela were ready to fight for the Republic. Militias met halfway between Cartago and San José, where the republicans handily won. On April 5, 1823, they declared San José the new capital and Costa Rica a member of the Federal Republic. Juan Mora Fernández was made the first head of state, and he immediately got down to business: minting coins, designing a flag, and, most importantly, streamlining the shipment of coffee.

Though the battle ended quickly in Costa Rica, the rest of Central America was collapsing into protracted civil war. These brutal conflicts inspired the Nicaraguan Province of Guanacaste to petition peaceful Costa Rica for membership. After the matter was put to a vote, Guanacaste was annexed on July 25, 1824. The provincial capital changed its name to Liberia, where you can still attend one of the country's best parties every Annexation Day.

The Federal Republic of Central America effectively disbanded in 1938, but Costa Rica barely missed a beat. The *cafetaleros* (coffee barons) were building a vibrant capitalist economy, inviting foreign investment and encouraging development including roads, telegraphs, and electricity. These wealthy and powerful landowners also used their influence to support, or topple, presidents of their choosing.

Presidents like José María Castro Madriz, who instituted freedom of the press and founded the first girl's high school, were forced to resign by the *cafetaleros*. Yet even their undemocratically selected replacements, in this case business-friendly coffee exporter Juan Rafael Mora Porras, earned illustrious spots in the history books.

Though sabers had rattled along the border between Costa Rica and Nicaragua in the decades since Guanacaste's secession, in 1856 Costa Rica was invaded by Nicaraguan "President" William Walker, a Tennessee-born mercenary funded by pro-slavery businesspeople and politicians in the United States. President Mora wasted no time assembling a militia, and quietly surrounded Walker's troops at Hacienda Santa Rosa in Guanacaste. After a battle that lasted only minutes, the Americans collapsed into retreat. Mora chased Walker all the way to Rivas, Nicaragua, where a decisive battle was won by the ultimate sacrifice of drummer boy Juan Santamaría, who ran through a hail of bullets to successfully set Walker's position on fire.

Though Walker escaped the burning mansion, he would eventually die in front of a Honduran firing squad, his name unremembered in his native land. But you can visit a museum dedicated to his defeat in Santa Rosa National Park. Juan Santamaría is still revered as Costa Rica's only real national hero, with a holiday and international airport named in his honor. And, as for President Mora, he became quite the social democrat, fighting for the poor, for which the coffee barons eventually ousted him.

Later, General Tomás Miguel Guardia would help organize a military coup against Mora's unpopular replacement, and subsequently implement the 1871 Constitution, which relaxed restrictions on voting (paving the way for the country's first truly democratic elections), abolished the death penalty, and challenged the influence of *cafetaleros*.

Since the 1800s, coffee has been one of Costa Rica's most important exports.

Banana Republic

In 1871, General Tomás Miguel Guardia hired three brash young New York brothers, the Keiths, to do the impossible: Build a railroad to transport coffee through the steaming jungles to the Caribbean Port of Limón.

Though working conditions were brutal, the worst part was the disease: malaria, yellow fever, dengue, and dysentery. Two of the Keith brothers succumbed before the first 50 kilometers (31 miles) of track were laid, as did hundreds of railroad workers. But the last remaining brother, Minor Cooper Keith, would not give up. When funding for the massively over-budget project ran out in 1882, he even borrowed £1.2 million from British investors. As continued incentive, the Costa Ricans did give Keith some 800,000 acres of tax-free land along the railroad, which Keith planted with an unusual imported fruit, bananas, providing cheap food for his workforce.

The railroad was finally completed in 1890, in massive debt. Coffee couldn't fill the railcars fast enough, so the ever-clever Keith decided to ship a boatload of bananas to New Orleans, where they were a hit. Bananas soon replaced coffee as Costa Rica's most important export, and Keith began acquiring massive holdings across the country and Latin America. His company, United Fruit, would become one of the most influential in the hemisphere, a fascinating story told in *Bananas! How the United Fruit Company Shaped the World* by Peter Chapman.

Despite the thriving economy, it was an era of turmoil for Costa Rica. In 1917, War Minister Federico Tinoco established a short-lived military dictatorship; after he was overthrown, the Communist Party began agitating for revolution. Instead, the outraged populace elected left-wing President Rafael Angél Calderón, who instituted Costa Rica's socialized health care system, as well as an eight-hour workday and minimum wage.

Calderón, however, was loath to leave power. After he "invalidated" the 1948 elections, the winner, Otilio Ulate, helplessly conceded the presidency. The people were not so quick to accept defeat, however, and turned to utopian "farmer-socialist" José Figueres to lead the fight.

Born in Alajuela to Spanish immigrants, Figueres' colorful career included dropping out of MIT (he claimed to have learned more in the Boston Public Library), training an insurgent army on the Caribbean Coast, and running a unionized coffee and hemp farm in Terrazú, which he named *La Lucha Sin Fin* (The Fight Without End).

When the country needed a troublemaker, it didn't have to look far. With widespread support, Figueres took control of the National Liberation Army and handily defeated both the Costa Rican military and a Communist insurgency, a 44-day civil war that left 2,000 people dead, the bloodiest event in recorded Costa Rican history.

Though he would eventually hand the presidency to Ulate, Figueres took power for 18 months and implemented a new constitution, which abolished the military, nationalized the banks, gave women and blacks the right to vote, blacks the freedom to travel, and allowed Jewish war refugees to work legally, all part of "reforms that completely changed the physiognomy of the country, building a more human revolution than that of Cuba," as Figueres explained in 1981. Though he stepped down in 1949 as promised, he would return to power democratically in 1953 and 1970, during which time he would make an enemy of Nicaragua's ruling family, the Somozas.

War and Peace

Fiercely critical of U.S. involvement in Central American affairs (despite working with the CIA himself on occasion), Figueres was particularly outspoken against the U.S.-backed Somozas, who had held power undemocratically since 1936. Somoza accused Figueres of backing a 1954 attack on the Nicaraguan government by anti-Somoza exiles, which was probably true, and in turn financed a violent 1955 bid by exiled Costa Rican President Calderón to return to power. Both attacks failed, but the enmity intensified.

Throughout the 1970s, Figueres supported the Nicaragua revolution against the Somozas, led by a group who called themselves the Sandinistas. When they successfully overthrew President Anastasio Somoza Debayle, Figueres cheered. The United States was less enthusiastic.

Beginning as early as 1981, the United States began actively supporting the Contras, a loose anti-Sandinista coalition. Although the U.S. Congress specifically forbade the Reagan administration to use public funds to "overthrow the Nicaraguan government," Reagan massively increased funding to both Costa Rica and Honduras, used to train and supply Contra forces.

Costa Rican President Luis Alberto Monge was pressured into allowing the construction of as many as nine bases on Tico territory; Liberia's airport was originally developed as part of the effort. By this time, El Salvador and Honduras had been dragged into the fighting, while the ongoing civil war in Guatemala had taken a turn for the worse—genocide. The superpowers were playing out their bloody endgame between "communism" and "capitalism," and Central America was paying the price. In 1986, Costa Rica elected President Oscar Arias Sánchez, who had run on a platform of neutrality.

A small man with big ideas, Arias called upon the five Central American presidents to sign a peace treaty. It required each leader to arrange peace talks, open the press, schedule democratic elections, and stop accepting weapons and training from outside parties—specifically, the United States and Soviet Union. It seemed so quixotic, these Esquipulus Accords, but then the windmills fell on their own: The U.S.S.R. collapsed, and could no longer afford to ship arms abroad, while the Reagan administration's illegal antics—using profits from illegal arms sales to the Islamic Republic of Iran to fund the Contras—were revealed, and ended, with the discovery of the Iran-Contra Affair.

Without arms dealers the battles stopped, and by 1993, peace reigned in Central America for the first time in generations. You can see President Arias' Nobel Peace Prize at the National Museum, or visit the tiny Museum of Peace in San José, where Nicaraguan President Violeta Chamorro presented a gun cut in two to Arias. The plaque does not indicate whether the gun was used by the Contras, for which two of Chamorro's children fought, or by the Sandinistas, which her other two children supported.

The end of Central America's wars also encouraged what was about to become Costa Rica's most important industry, tourism.

WELCOME TO SUNNY COSTA RICA!

Already internationally recognized for its commitment to conservation, Costa Rica was suddenly attracting increasing numbers of ecotourists from all over the world. Birders, hikers, surfers, and scientists came for the broad beaches, erupting volcanoes, and wildlife-rich forests, with well-known areas like Monteverde hosting 100,000 tourists per year by the late 1990s. They were followed by less adventurous visitors, lured here by tales of wonderful wildlife and world-class hospitality in the stable, peaceful democracy.

The Costa Ricans are no slouches when it comes to marketing. The government created the National Tourism Institute (ICT) to spread the word, while taking even stricter measures to protect its wildlife. Though the government remained mired in the usual swamps of scandal and corruption (three former presidents have been jailed in recent years), the nation has been buoyed by ecotourism and other former investment, most importantly Intel's construction of a Pentium processor plant in 1998.

The most contentious issue today is Central American Free Trade Agreement (CAFTA, or TLC in Spanish), which has been enthusiastically resisted by Costa Rica even as every other country in the region signed on. In 2006 former President Oscar Arias used his influence to amend the constitution, allowing him to serve a second term, then run for office on a platform of implementing CAFTA, arguing that "when goods don't cross borders, armies will."

He narrowly won reelection, but anti-CAFTA forces, with slogans like, "Don't sell my country," continued to resist. In the end, it was probably Arias' solemn promise to pull out of the agreement if it hurt Costa Rica that convinced voters to approve the agreement. But realistically, there's no turning back. State-run monopolies, criticized on all quarters for their inefficiency though they have been the backbone of the Costa Rican economy for decades, will now be opened to international competition.

At the same time, the Arias administration severed a six-decade relationship with Taiwan, instead opening full diplomatic relations with China, which has since lavished upon the tropical nation at least $40 million in aid money, as well as tantalizing discussion of a $6 billion expansion of the Puerto Limón oil refinery. Foreign investment continues to pour in from all over the world, primarily from the $1.9 billion per year tourism industry; 2007 saw a 10 percent jump in visitors.

2

Planning Your Trip

Costa Rica is probably the easiest country in Latin America to navigate independently, with an excellent network of public and private transport, as well as helpful hotel and tour desks (often operating in fluent English) eager to arrange transportation, tours, lodging, and so much more.

Ticos and *Ticas*, as Costa Ricans call themselves, usually try their best to be polite and helpful in every situation. This "Tico hospitality" is more than just professionalism. Costa Ricans prize playing well with others above almost any other trait; confrontation is both avoided and scorned. Anyone who loses his or her temper also loses face. Even raising your voice can earn you a reputation as someone with an "ugly personality," causing people to avoid your company.

The very best way to guarantee good service, even more so than tipping well (though that helps), is to keep your cool and stay friendly, no matter what the situation. Begin each interaction with a smile and *buenos dias*, rather than a demand, and you'll be amazed at how much more quickly your complaints are addressed and your requests made real. Heck, you may even break down that barrier of polite professionalism with a bit of basic courtesy, and make a few real friends in your travels.

One Week

Though Costa Rica is a small country, about the size of West Virginia, rough roads and other obstacles conspire to make travel time consuming. If you've only got a week, choose one section of the country, and relax.

Culture Lover

Book a historic hotel in central San José and explore the museums, perhaps indulging in a walking tour. Take a day trip or two to see Arenal Volcano, the Peace Waterfalls, or a coffee plantation, and be back in time for a night on the town or fine meal. Then head into the Central Valley where you can visit Orosí's church, museum, and ruins; Sarchí's woodworking studios; or Guayabo National Archaeological Monument. Bed-and-breakfasts and fine hotels abound, as do hot springs, white-water rafting opportunities, and national parks.

Exploring the Osa

After spending a day or two in San José or the Central Valley, take a bus or plane to the Osa Peninsula. Drake's Bay and Puerto Jiménez are both great places to begin. If you aren't up

Sometimes, drivers will need to share the road.

for the two-day hike across Corcovado National Park, arrange day hikes, snorkel tours, and boat trips instead, being sure to allow a couple of days for R & R on those beautiful beaches.

Lindo Guanacaste

Fly into Liberia and explore the colonial town that evening, arranging a tour to Rincón de la Vieja or other area national parks the next day (or two). Next, pick a beach and relax: How about friendly Sámara, or plush Papagayo, or maybe festive Tamarindo?

Lush Caribbean

After a detour through wilderness-rich Sarapiquí, take a riverboat through the canals to Tortuguero. Explore the jungles and watch the sea turtles, then get a boat to Puerto Limón and choose your beach town: mellow Cahuita, fun Puerto Viejo de Talamanco, or one of the luxurious hotels along the beaches toward Manzanillo.

Pacific Promenade

Head straight from the airport to Jacó, the closest beach to the capital, and find accommodations either slumming it at an in-town lodge or relaxing in some divine suite at Villa Caletas or Los Sueños. From there, catch a boat to the pristine beaches of the Southern Nicoya, or head south to famed Manuel Antonio National Park, with snorkeling, boating, and tanning opportunities aplenty. Farther south you'll also find beaches with fewer tourists.

TWO WEEKS

With two weeks to spare, you can mix and match: Combine either the Caribbean or Pacific Coast tours with the Culture Lovers trip around the Central Valley, or with a trip to Arenal and Monteverde in the Northern Zone. You could easily combine the Pacific Promenade and Exploring Osa tours as well. Or, go farther afield.

Guanacaste and Southwest Nicaragua

After an extended Guanacaste tour, head north to Nicaragua and visit Granada, the oldest European city in the Americas, perhaps with a side trip to Ometepe Island.

The Whole Caribbean

Begin in Puerto Viejo de Sarapiquí, where you can arrange boat tours of Nicaragua's Río San Juan and Solentiname Islands. Spend time in Tortuguero with the turtles, or Barra del Colorado, with excellent sportfishing, then head to the South Caribbean's coastal party towns. From there cross the border to Bocas del Toro, Panama, an island archipelago with great diving and more.

ONE MONTH

(Now you're talking.)

Action and Adventure

Begin in the Central Valley, climbing Cerro Chirripó or Barva Volcano, spotting quetzals in Dota, or white-water rafting near Turrialba. Hit the Pacific for a week of surfing, perhaps Dominical or Playa Zancudo, with wilder waves, or more manageable surf around Jacó and Hermosa. Grab a boat to the Southern Nicoya to explore Curú and Cabo Blanco, then work your way north (perhaps on the almost impassable coastal road?) to see turtles nesting in Ostional. Next, it's diving with the bull sharks near Playas del Coco, or hiking at Rincón de la Vieja and Santa Rosa National Parks. Finish up with a flight to the Caribbean, where you can arrange jungle tours and treks to Panama.

Costa Rica's Greatest Hits

Begin with San José's museums and nightlife, then into the Central Valley for the Culture Lover's tour. From there, it's a few days exploring Arenal, and up to Monteverde to hike the cloud forests. Continue on to Guanacaste, perhaps with a side trip to Southwest Nicaragua, and pick a few spectacular beaches or volcanoes to explore. Continue south along the coast, stopping at some of the Central Pacific's festive beach towns, then trek across the Osa Peninsula. Return to San José through the mountains, perhaps stopping in Dota for coffee and quetzals, and head east for wildlife watching in Sarapiquí, turtles in Tortuguero, and finally relaxation on the Southern Caribbean.

GETTING THERE AND AROUND

A Note about Addresses

Streets are rarely given names or numbers, and even in cities like San José, which does have a convenient system of numbered *calles* (streets) and *avenidas* (avenues), locals may

Costa Rica Statistics

Area: 51,100 square kilometers (19,730 square miles)

Coastline: 1,290 kilometers (802 miles)

Population: 4,133,884 (July 2007)

Percent protected: 28 percent

Percent of energy from renewable resources: 96 percent

Goal for Costa Rica to go carbon-neutral: 2021

Average age of visitors: 43

Number of visitors in 2007: 1.9 million

Percent with a university degree: 80 percent

Percent traveling as a couple: 33 percent

Percent traveling alone: 29.4 percent

still prefer traditional addresses. These usually use directionals from a local landmark, resulting in addresses that look like this: *Del correo, 200m norte, 50m este* (200m north and 50m east of the post office). Even if you have no idea what an address means, any cab driver or local can help figure it out for you.

Be aware that "100m" means one block (not precisely 100 meters), and that reference points may no longer exist, such as the long gone Coca-Cola bottling plant from which many San José addresses are given. Usually, however, directions are given from the central park (*parque central*) or church (*iglesia*), in the city center. Directionals are usually cardinal, *norte*, *sur*, *este*, and *oeste* (north, south, east, and west), but may also use *derecha* (right) and *izquierda* (left), as well as *frente* (across from).

Entry Requirements for International Visitors

Regulations for international visitors vary from country to country, with citizens of the United States, Canada, and most English-speaking nations given an automatic 90- or 30-day visa. The Embassy of Costa Rica (www.costarica-embassy.org/consular/visa) has specific country-by-country information in English. In general, visitors must have a valid passport with one blank page, and can be asked to show an onward ticket and proof of sufficient funds (a credit card usually does the trick). Extensions are possible, but inconvenient. Instead, most long-term visitors leave the country for a 72-hour "visa vacation," and have their visas automatically renewed at the border. The Side Trips chapter covers great destinations in Panama and Nicaragua for such vacations.

Air

Costa Rica has two major international airports: **Juan Santamaría International Airport** (SJO; 506-2437-2400), located 16 kilometers (10 miles) from San José, in the town of Alajuela; and **Daniel Oduber International Airport** (LIR; 506-2668-1010; www.liberiacostaricaairport.net), 12 kilometers (7 miles) west of Liberia. SJO is the most convenient airport for visitors to the Caribbean, Central Valley, Central Pacific, and Osa Peninsula; while LIR is a better choice for Guanacaste and the Nicoya Peninsula. Both have direct flights to the United States and around the country, but SJO has more connections to Europe and the rest of Latin America.

Domestic Flights

Both the national airline, **Sansa Air** (506-2290-4100; www.flysansa.com), and privately-owned **Nature Air** (506-2299-6025; www.natureair.com) offer inexpensive flights throughout the country. The major hubs are in San José (both the international airport and

An impressive network of inexpensive public buses keeps Costa Rica connected.

smaller **Tobias Bolaños Airport**) and Liberia. Other airports serve Arenal (La Fortuna), Drake Bay, Barra del Colorado, Jacó, Golfito, Liberia, Limón, Nosara, Palmar Sur, Puerto Jiménez, Punta Islita, Quepos, Sámara, Tamarindo, Tambor, and Tortuguero. Nature Air also serves Panamá City and Bocas del Toro, Panama. They plan to serve Granada, Nicaragua, in the future, so check. Charter planes and helicopters can be arranged through **Paradise Air** (506-2231-0938, 877-412-0877 USA and Canada; www.flywithparadise.com) or **Air Costa Rica** (506-2296-8591; www.flyaircostarica.com).

Public Bus

A safe and convenient network of buses connects Costa Rica and Central America. The main hub is San José, with a dozen different bus stations serving various destinations. This book does not give comprehensive bus information, but your hotel or any tour desk can give you details, or check out **The Bus Schedule** (www.thebusschedule.com) or **Avenida Central** (www.avenidacentral.com) online.

City buses are very basic, often refurbished school buses from the United States, and can be confusing to use at first, especially for non-Spanish speakers. If you're used to public transport or speak some Spanish, your hotel and almost any passerby can help you navigate any city system.

Intercity buses are more comfortable, with safe luggage storage (though I keep my computer and valuables with me, in a small backpack), reclining seats, and really loud movies, but no bathroom; they stop every three hours or so. Buy tickets at least one day in advance.

International buses are even nicer, with air-conditioning and rest rooms. They also make crossing the borders a breeze. ★**Tica Bus** (506-2221-8954; www.ticabus.com) serves all of Central America and Southern Mexico.

Private Shuttles

Private shuttle companies offer fast, direct service between major tourist destinations in clean, air-conditioned minibuses, which pick you up at your hotel. Costs are about triple that of a regular bus. Make reservations at least one day in advance through any hotel or tour office, or contact these companies directly.

Interbus (506-2283-5573; www.interbusonline.com) Largest and most popular company offering countrywide service.

Grayline Fantasy Bus (506-2232-3681; www.graylinecostarica.com) Plush buses offer comfy countrywide service, plus buses to Nicaragua.

Shuttle Me (506-2294-7670; www.shuttleme.co.cr) Runs between San José and many major destinations.

Tour Bus Shuttle Service (506-2642-0919; www.montezumaexpeditions.com) The Nicoya Peninsula specialists.

Turiverde (506-2645-5855; www.turiverdetransfer.com) Runs between Monteverde and Guanacaste.

Quality Transfers (506-2645-6263; www.qualitytransferscr.com) Runs between Monteverde and other tourist destinations.

Taxis

Taxis are an excellent option for getting around cities, and between them. Even if you rent a car, it's worth taking taxis at night, particularly in San José. Always make sure that taxis are official; most are red, and have yellow triangles on the door, "taxi" signs on top, or other external markings. Taxi drivers should display identification and have the meter running (they start at 465). If the meter appears to be off, ask innocently, *"La maría no está funcionando?"* ("The meter isn't working?") Pirate taxis, or unlicensed private cars, can be cheaper for Ticos, but may take ruthless advantage of tourists. Have your hotel call an official cab for you.

Your hotel can also arrange private taxis between cities, which can be very reasonable, about $60 per 100 kilometers (62 miles), though costs vary widely. Arrange fares beforehand. To make complaints about official taxis, call 1-800-TRANSITO, or fill out the form at www.mopt.go.cr/quejas.html.

Boats and Ferries

Destinations on the northern Caribbean Coast, including Tortuguero, are accessible only by boat or plane; details are covered in the Caribbean Coast chapter. The Northern Zone has boat service between Puerto Viejo de Sarapiquí and the Caribbean, a river system that also serves the Los Chiles border crossing with Nicaragua, with continuing boat service to the Río San Juan and Lake Nicaragua.

Convenient car ferries connect Puntarenas with the Southern Nicoya while passenger ferries run between Golfito and Puerto Jiménez. Private boats run between Jacó and Montezuma.

Rental Cars

There are more than a dozen car rental companies in Costa Rica, any of which can pick you up at the airport or your hotel. You must have a valid drivers license from your home country, a credit card, and for most companies, be at least 25 years old. Online quotes may not include taxes and mandatory insurance (18 percent of base fees), so check. Insurance is skeletal; there's a $1,500 deductible and many potential disasters aren't even covered. Make reservations in advance during the high season, when four-wheel-drive cars are in large demand.

In addition to regular rental companies such as **Europecar** (www.europecar.co.cr) and **Thrifty** (www.costarica.thrifty.com), unusual options include **Mapache** (www.mapache .com), certified carbon neutral; **Nature Rovers** (www.naturerovers.com), renting groovy vintage Range Rovers; and **Premium Transport Services** (www.premiumcostarica.com) with upscale rides.

Driving can be a challenge in Costa Rica, and if you plan to do any exploring at all, it's worth renting a four-wheel drive. Many roads are unpaved, or have epic potholes. During the rainy season, ask locally about driving conditions, as paved roads wash out, dirt roads turn into soupy quagmires, and rivers rise, rendering some spots inaccessible.

Costa Rican drivers are fearless, and will pass on blind curves in pouring rain. Don't be tempted—you're on vacation, remember? Instead, simply schedule a couple of extra hours between destinations, just in case you're caught behind that slow moving truck.

Police may pull you over for speeding or "bad driving." Tickets are *never* paid on the spot; this is done conveniently through your rental car company. However, corrupt cops may ask for an illegal bribe, which often costs more than the actual ticket. I recommend taking the ticket. Rental cars are also targeted by thieves; see Crime, below.

CLIMATE

Though Costa Rica is a small country, its dramatic topography and dual coasts give rise to several microclimates. In general, there are two seasons: The dry season, called *verano* (summer), from December through May; and the rainy season, or *invierno* (winter), June through November. Most visitors come during dry season, when you can expect hot, sunny days and big crowds.

The rainy season (rebranded as the "green season") can be wet, with regular showers in the afternoons starting by early June, graduating to almost constant rain through September and October. Hotel costs drop by as much as 25 percent, and major attractions are much less crowded. Guanacaste enjoys sunnier weather than the rest of the country, while the Caribbean Coast, where it rains year round, usually experiences a "mini dry season" in late September.

Though Costa Rica's climate is mild overall, expect scorching days in Guanacaste in March and April, and chilly weather year round at higher elevations, including San José, the Central Valley, and Monteverde.

LODGING

Costs fluctuate with the seasons, particularly in popular beach towns. This book gives normal high season rates, which drop perhaps 25 percent during rainy season

Many bridges in Costa Rica are one-way; ceda el paso *means "yield."*

(May–November). Rates can double around Christmas and New Year's, as well as *Semana Santa* (Easter Week), when beach hotels fill weeks in advance. Hotels are charged a 9.309 percent "merchant fee" for credit cards, and may offer a discount for cash.

This book lists many wonderful lodging options, but there's no need to limit yourself. Here are some great Web sites worth perusing:

★ **Actuar** (www.actuarcostarica.com) Community-conscious collection of basic hotels and sustainable ecolodges.

Adventure Hotels of Costa Rica (www.adventurehotelsofcostarica.com) Midrange to expensive hotels vary wildly in quality; double check with a trip advisor.

Association of Small Costa Rican Hotels (www.asociacionpequenoshotelscr.com) Tico-owned, midrange hotels.

★ **Charming + Nature Hotels of Costa Rica** (www.charminghotels.net) Excellent selection of midrange to upscale hotels, including several bed-and-breakfasts.

Sustainable Tourism Program (CST; www.turismo-sostenible.co.cr) A federal program awards one to five "leaves" to hotels based on eco-consciousness, and lets you search by price and location here.

Costa Rica Hotels (www.costaricahotelsite.com) More than 1,300 hotel listings.

★ **Holland Hotels Costa Rica** (www.hollandhotelscr.com) Eclectic collection of Dutch-owned hotels includes some real gems.

★ **Small Distinctive Hotels** (www.distinctivehotels.com) Costa Rica's most exclusive and
beautiful boutique properties.

Vacation Rentals by Owner (www.vrbo.com/vacation-rentals/central-america/costa-rica)
Largest list of Costa Rican vacation rentals online.

Restaurants and Food Purveyors

Traditional Costa Rican cuisine tends to be a bit bland (not at all like Mexican cuisine), but
is nevertheless delicious, filling, and healthy. The unofficial national dish is a set plate
called a *casado*, literally meaning "married," as this is what a married man should theoretically be served for lunch. Rice, beans, and a couple of deli-style salads accompany your
choice of meat, usually pork chops, stewed beef or chicken, or seafood. At breakfast, left-
over rice and beans are fried together with the holy trinity of Tico cuisine (onion, cilantro,
and sweet red pepper) to make *gallo pinto*, literally "spotted rooster," often served with
eggs, soft white cheese, and perhaps *natilla,* a mild sour cream. You'll usually find hot sauce
or salsa Lizano, a locally made vegetable sauce, on the table to spice things up.

If you'll be having coffee with that, it may be made in a *chorreador*, by pouring hot water
through a suspended cloth "sock" filled with ground coffee. Or try a *fresco*, also called a *natural*, made of fruit blended with sugar, ice, and your choice of water or milk. Ask for it *sin
azucar* (without sugar) if you find them too sweet.

The classic Costa Rican eatery is called a *soda,* simple, family-run restaurants serving a
limited menu of inexpensive typical dishes for around $2 to $6. But you can definitely go
upscale, and a wide variety of international cuisine is available in tourist towns like
Tamarindo and Puerto Viejo de Talamanca, as well as San José.

Tap water is treated and safe to drink in major inland cities. Water in beach towns usually is not. If there's heavy flooding, stick to *agua en botella* (bottled water) no matter where
you are. Most tourist restaurants use purified water to make ice, but if you aren't sure, ask
for drinks *sin hielo* (without ice).

The humble casado *is Costa Rica's delicious and nutritious typical meal.*

SHOPPING

Name brand clothing, electronics, camping supplies, and other imported items are available in San José, but are much more expensive than in the United States or Europe. If you are on the tall or heavy side, or wear shoes larger than size 44 (U.S. men's 10), it will be difficult to find clothing in your size. If you're in a pinch, stores selling secondhand clothing from the United States will have larger sizes. (Ask for *ropa Americana*).

Although Costa Rica lacks the rich handicraft traditions of Guatemala or Mexico, you can find beautiful handmade hammocks, jewelry, and wood carvings, as well as the usual souvenirs, such as T-shirts, towels, and very pretty sarongs. The souvenir everyone will appreciate, however, is coffee, available in any grocery store, or for a few dollars more at the San José Airport. **Britt Coffee** (www.cafebritt.com) is the most popular, but look for export-quality **Dota** (www.coopedota.com) and **Monteverde** (www.monteverde.com) beans as well. Household brands such as ★**Coffee 1820** are less expensive and often just as good.

Prime shopping destinations include Sarchí in the Central Valley, famed for its woodwork and fine furniture; and Giuatíl, in Guanacaste, with a pottery tradition dating to pre-Columbian times. The town of Masaya, Nicaragua, covered in the Southwest Nicaragua side trip, boasts one of Central America's best craft markets.

PRACTICAL MATTERS

Emergency numbers should have English-speaking operators available.

Accident Report: 800-800-8000
Emergency Services: 911
Highway Patrol: 117
International Collect Calls: 175
International Directory Assistance: 124
International Operator: 116
Local Directory Assistance: 113
National Collect Calls: 110
Pharmacy location and information: 800-2200-2020
Poison Control: 506-2223-1028
Police: 911, 117, 127, 506-2222-1365
Red Cross: 128
Traffic Police: 506-2222-9330

CRIME

Although Costa Rica is a relatively safe country, tourists are targeted for theft, particularly in San José and major beach towns. Pickpockets and car break-ins are the most popular ways to rip you off, but armed muggings (in broad daylight) are increasingly common.

Though you can reduce your chances of being robbed by staying alert, dressing simply, avoiding illegal drugs, using guarded parking, and taking taxis at night, take a few preliminary precautions just in case. Write down passport and credit/debit card numbers and store them in your E-mail, along with your bank's international phone number. **American Express** (506-2295-9494), **Diner's Club** (506-2257-7878), and **Mastercard/Visa** (506-2257-0155) all have offices in San José. The U.S. Embassy (506-2232-7944; sanjose.us

Potholes can form overnight on Costa Rica's back roads.

embassy.gov; Pavas, San José) can advise U.S. citizens—or find other embassies at **Embassy World** (www.embassyworld.com).

After arriving, make photocopies of your passport, including the entry stamp, and carry this instead of the original whenever possible. Your valuables are always safer in the hotel. I travel with my cards and passport in a money belt, and a bit of spending money in a wallet, which I will cheerfully surrender if I'm ever mugged. I also stash $100 in different pieces of luggage. Photos can be burned onto CDs at any Internet café, so thieves can't snatch your memories.

Rental cars are targets for break-ins. Always unload the car immediately after arriving at your hotel, and use guarded parking where available. You can often pay street guards or local businesses a few dollars to keep an eye on your vehicle. *Never, ever* leave your packed car unsupervised while you take a short walk or quick dip in the ocean.

If you get a flat tire immediately after leaving a parking area, have a fender bender in traffic, or are told by another motorist that something is wrong with your car, be aware that this might be a setup for theft. If possible, keep driving until you reach a safe, populated area. If not, keep a close eye on your belongings, as the latest scam is to rob people while they're watching a "good Samaritan" change the tire.

If you are the victim of a crime, call the police at 911, or visit the local police department. They probably won't help recover stolen property, but they will fill out a police report and offer other assistance. Larger cities have a Judicial Investigation Bureau (OIJ) office that can help with legal advice, or contact **San José Victim's Assistance Office** (506-2295-3271; victimadelito@poder-judicial.go.cr; Judicial Building, San José). To make a complaint against a hotel or travel agency, contact the **Claims Area of the Costa Rica Tourist Board** (506-2223-1733 x238; San José, Av 4, Calles 5 & 7).

HOSPITALS AND CLINICS

Costa Rica offers excellent health care, often ranked higher than the United States'. You can visit any clinic in the country, without an appointment, and receive low-cost health care. Most traveler's insurance is accepted at Costa Rica's three best hospitals, all located in San José: ★**Clínica Bíblica** (506-2522-1000; www.clinicabiblica.com; Calle Central, Av 14 & 16), **CIMA** (506-2208-1000; www.hospitalsanjose.net; Escazú), and **Clínica Católica** (506-2246-3000; Barrio Guadelupe). Other hospitals and clinics include:

CENTRAL VALLEY
Hospital Max Peralta (506-2550-1999; Cartago)
Hospital San Rafael (506-2436-1001; Alajuela)
Hospital San Vicente de Paúl (506-2261-0091; Heredia)

GUANACASTE AND NICOYA
Hospital de la Anexión (506-2685-8400; Nicoya)
Hospital Dr. Enrique Baltodano (506-2666-0011; Liberia)
Hospital Mons. Victor Manuel (506-2663-0033; Puntarenas)
Playas del Coco Clinica Ebais (Playas del Coco; 506-2670-0987)
Tamarindo-Villa Real Clinic (Tamarindo; 506-2653-0611)

CENTRAL PACIFIC AND OSO PENINSULA
Hospital Max Teran (Quepos, 506-2777-0922)
Jacó Clinica Ebais (Jacó; 506-2643-3667)

CARIBBEAN
Hospital Tony Facio (506-2758-2222; Puerto Limón)

MEDICAL VACATIONS

Costa Rica's excellent health care and relatively low costs (about 25 percent of U.S. prices) have helped build a medical tourism boom, with around 15 percent of visitors having work done. Bariatric medicine, dental work, joint replacement, LASIK, and cosmetic surgery are all popular. Several hotels and tour operators organize medical vacations, including English-speaking doctors and accommodations that provide follow-up care. While you should definitely do your own research, here are some Web sites to get you started:

Clínica Biblíca Medical Tourism (800-503-5358; www.hospitalbiblicamedicaltourism .com) Costa Rica's best hospital offers English-language site with information on doctors, accommodations, and more.
Medical Tourism of Costa Rica (267-886-3888 USA; www.medicaltourismofcostarica .com) Lists doctors, procedures, and costs.

Surgical Specialists in Costa Rica (www.costarica-surgeons.com) Lists medical practitioners and their resumes.

Plastic surgery is the big draw, and several hotels and tour companies can arrange doctors, follow-up care, and more. These include:

Ariva Costa Rica (www.arivacostarica.com) Free information on "board certified" plastic surgeons, dentists, and doctors, plus exhaustive links.

Chetica Ranch (506-2268-6133; www.cheticaranch.com; Escazú) Comfortable retreat designed with post-op comfort in mind.

Las Cumbres (506-2228-1011; 866-644-2705 USA; www.recoveryretreatsincostarica.com) Recovery retreat with wonderful views.

Destination Pura Vida (506-2339-4387; www.destinationpuravida.com) Arranges plastic surgery and dental vacations.

Health Costa Rica (www.healthcostarica.com) Procedures, accommodations, and more.

Paradise Inn (506-2252-3530; 786-228-9148 USA; www.paradisecosmeticinn.com; Escazú) Plush hotel can organize any surgery, and offers nice rooms and medical spa services.

MONEY, TAXES, AND TIPPING

Costa Rica's official currency is the colón (¢), which has for years hovered around ¢500 to US$1 exchange rate; check the most recent rates online. Coins, which are large and heavy, come in 5, 10, 25, 100, and 500 colón increments. Bills come in 1000, 2000, 5000, and 10,000 colón increments; ¢5000 bills are often clumsily counterfeited, so familiarize yourself with the details of that bill. Dollars are widely accepted, but you may receive poor rates; I do most transactions in colones. Many prices, particularly hotels, are quoted in dollars.

Traveler's checks are difficult to use; I recommend avoiding them altogether. ATM machines are widely available, and usually give competitive exchange rates, though they may charge hefty transaction fees. Visa/Plus debit cards are more widely accepted than Mastercard. Most credit cards are widely accepted, but businesses are charged stiff fees for using them, which they may have to pass on to you.

There is no sales tax. Hotels charge a 16.3 percent tax, which may be waived if you pay cash. Restaurants charge 13 percent tax and usually a 10 percent tip. If the 10 percent gratuity is included, there's technically no need to tip your server, though that would still be very nice.

Costa Rica is a tipping country. You should always tip tour guides a few dollars, as that's part of their salary. Others who help you out—hailing taxes, carrying bags, etc.—are also hoping for tips. A dollar or two is usually sufficient. You do not need to tip taxi drivers.

SPECIAL NEEDS TRAVELERS

Costa Rica requires that all hotels and businesses be wheelchair accessible, and some businesses actually comply, or at least say they do. **Go With Wheelchairs** (506-2454-2810; www.gowithwheelchairs.com) is a great source of unbiased information, and arranges all sorts of special tours. **The Association of Costa Rican Special Taxis** (506-2296-6443) has wheelchair-accessible vans.

Telephones

Costa Rica's international access code is 506. Local numbers have eight digits: Landlines begin with a "2" (506-2123-4567), cell phone numbers an "8" (506-8123-4567). From within Costa Rica, only dial the last eight digits.

Making international calls from Costa Rica is usually inexpensive. Internet cafés offer inexpensive online calls, or purchase a phone card and follow the easy, English-language instructions. Avoid credit card-operated BBG phones, which are scams that charge up to $40 for a five-minute call to the United States. Some hotels also use BBG, so ask.

The state telecommunication monopoly (ICE) restricts cell phones to residents and citizens, and many international plans don't cover Costa Rica. Your only other option, when this book went to press, was to rent a cell phone for $8 per day, not including calls. This will hopefully change with the passage of CAFTA, which may open ICE to competition.

Weddings and Honeymoons

Recently ranked one of *Modern Bride*'s "Top Five Wedding and Honeymoon Destinations" (and the only one of those among their "Affordable Destinations"), Costa Rica is an increasingly popular spot to tie the knot. And it's easy.

There are no certifications or minimum stay. If the bride was previously married, she cannot wed in Costa Rica until 300 days after her divorce is finalized (an archaic law designed to protect the paternity of unborn children). Normally, it takes three months for the Costa Rican Civil Registry to process the marriage license, but for an extra fee, they'll send it in 12 business days.

If you'd like help coordinating the happiest day of your life, these businesses can arrange flowers, photographers, hotels, airline tickets, cakes, canopy tours, and more.

Costa Rica Exotic Weddings (www.weddingincostarica.com) Based in Guanacaste, offers great package deals.

Costa Rica Paradise Wedding (506-2215-1490; www.costaricaparadisewedding.com) Tico outfit offers a selection of "Suggested Locations."

Costa Rica Wedding & Travel Planners (www.costaricaparadisewedding.com) Will customize your wedding.

Elopements in Costa Rica (www.elopementsincostarica.com) Keeps it simple for couples and small groups.

Pura Vida Weddings (506-2653-0744; www.weddingsincostarica) Plans weddings in and around Tamarindo.

Tropical Occasions (www.tropicaloccasions.com) Established company coordinates weddings in the Central Valley, Northern Zone, and Pacific Coast.

Weddings Costa Rica (www.weddingscostarica.net) Very elegant weddings.

Language

The official language of Costa Rica is Spanish, but English is widely spoken. Regardless, I highly recommend bringing a Spanish phrasebook, just in case; Amazon.com lists several. These schools can teach you the basics in a week, and have you chatting with the locals in a month. Here are just a few of the many Spanish schools operating in Costa Rica.

Adventure Education Center (www.adventurespanishschool.com) An accredited school with campuses in La Fortuna, Turrialba, and Dominical, plus classes for doctors, children, and more.

Cactus Language (www.cactuslanguage.com) This Jacó school offers deluxe amenities, including yoga classes and snorkel trips.

★ **Centro Panamerica de Idiomas** (506-2265-6306; 877-373-3116 USA; www.cpi-edu) Accredited school with campuses in Heredia, Monteverde, and Flamingo Beach.

Cultural Center of Languages Costa Rica (506-2256-8981; www.spanish-in-action.com) Intensive, one-month immersion courses in San José, Alajuela, and Heredia.

Instituto de Español (506-2283-4733; www.professionalspanish.com) Specialized courses for doctors, lawyers, businesspeople, and missionaries.

★ **Montaña Linda** (506-2533-3640; www.montanalinda.com; Orosí) Picturesque town has Costa Rica's best deal on Spanish classes.

Universal de Idiomas (506-2223-9662; www.universal-edu.com; San José) Offers a three-day, 18-hour "Survival Spanish" course, plus regular classes.

Events

January
New Year's Day (January 1)

March/April
Semana Santa (dates vary) Holy Week, the week before Easter, is Costa Rica's biggest party. Inland businesses shut down, beach businesses charge double, buses stop running Thursday and Friday, and beer is not sold from Thursday through Sunday. Plan ahead!

Juan Santamaría Day (April 11) Some businesses close, particularly in Alajuela.

May
Labor Day (May 1) President gives the State of the Union Address.

June
Father's Day (June 11)

Annexation Day (June 25) Parties all over Guanacaste, particularly Liberia, may mean crowds and high prices.

August
Mother's Day (August 15) Many businesses close.

National Parks Day (August 24)

September
Arrival of the Independence Torch (September 14) Runners carry a torch from Antigua, Guatemala, to Cartago, Costa Rica, celebrating Central America's independence from Spain. Schoolchildren parade with paper lanterns that evening.

Independence Day (September 15) Businesses close so folks can enjoy parades, fireworks, and barbecues.

October

Día de la Raza / Columbus Day (October 12) Parades and festivals all over the country, the best in Puerto Limón.

December

Christmas (December 25) Not a huge production compared to the United States, but businesses may close on both Christmas Eve and the day of Christmas.

3

SAN JOSÉ

Tropical Metropolis

San José, Costa Rica's capital and largest city, is the commercial, political, and geographic heart of this famously eco-friendly paradise. Surrounded by vivid green volcanoes cloaked in coffee fields and mist, this is a city of bracing weather, fine cultural attractions, festive nightlife, and bustling development.

But if you're looking for wild, unsullied nature, you are in exactly the wrong place. And indeed, despite their love for the capital they fondly call Chepe (a nickname for anyone named "José"), even Costa Ricans seem a bit embarrassed about its failure to live up to the whole "harmony with nature" thing. With more than 1.3 million people in San José proper, 2.5 million in the urban Central Valley, this is a big city, with big-city problems: pollution, traffic, overbuilding, and crime.

If you're interested in learning more about the remarkable history of this peaceful democracy, however, there is no better place to wander the plazas and museums. Or (more likely), if you're just spending the night between jaunts around the country, it's a great spot for a wonderful meal or night on the town.

The city center, with the most to offer by way of attractions and hotels, is built around parks, plazas, and pedestrian malls, making it easy to explore. To the east are the upscale embassy neighborhoods of Los Yoses, with fine dining and boutique hotels, and San Pedro, home to two major universities and all the associated bars, bookstores, and cheap eats.

West of downtown is La Sabana, a huge city park, surrounded by several hotels and restaurants. To the northwest, Pavas is home to San José's second airport, Tobias Bolaño (the Nature Air hub). Just beyond are the undulating hills of Escazú and Santa Ana, some-

---

Online Resources

Costa Rica Tourism (www.tourism.co.cr) Information and listings for all of Costa Rica, but focused on San José.

Escazú News (www.escazunews.com) Great bilingual reviews of Escazú restaurants, hotels, and other services.

San José Costa Rica Maps (www.sanjosecostaricamaps.com) Interactive Google maps help pinpoint hotels, restaurants, and other businesses.

Where in Costa Rica (www.whereincostarica.com) Online events listings for San José and elsewhere.

The National Theater is considered San José's most beautiful building.

times called "Little America" for their large expatriate populations and upscale services, including golf courses, posh shopping malls, chic restaurants and bars (as well as Hooters and T.G.I. Fridays), Rolex, Ferrari, and more. Also known as the "City of Witches," for countless centuries, this was once where both Spanish and indigenous peoples came for herbal medicines and magical potions. Today, the old Colonial adobes are filled with excellent clinics, dentists, medical spas, and plastic surgeons, still selling promises of eternal youth and true love.

GETTING AROUND

San José is oriented east-west along the InterAmericana, and divided into different neighborhoods, or *barrios*, useful when giving directions to your cabby. The city has implemented a logical, numbered grid of east-west *avenidas*, crossed by north-south running *calles*, which some locals actually use (though many stick stubbornly to the traditional directional system). The main drag is the InterAmericana, called Paseo Colón west of the city center, Avenida Central to the east; avenidas are even-numbered south of Av Central (Av 2, Av 4, etc), and odd-numbered to the north. It crosses Calle Central (from which calles are numbered, even to the west, odd to the east) in the pedestrian shopping district downtown, close to Plaza de la Cultura, where you can pick up a free city map at the ICT office, next to the Gold Museum. Most tourist sites are within walking distance of the city center, though pedestrians should be alert for thieves, gaping holes in the sidewalk, and impatient drivers.

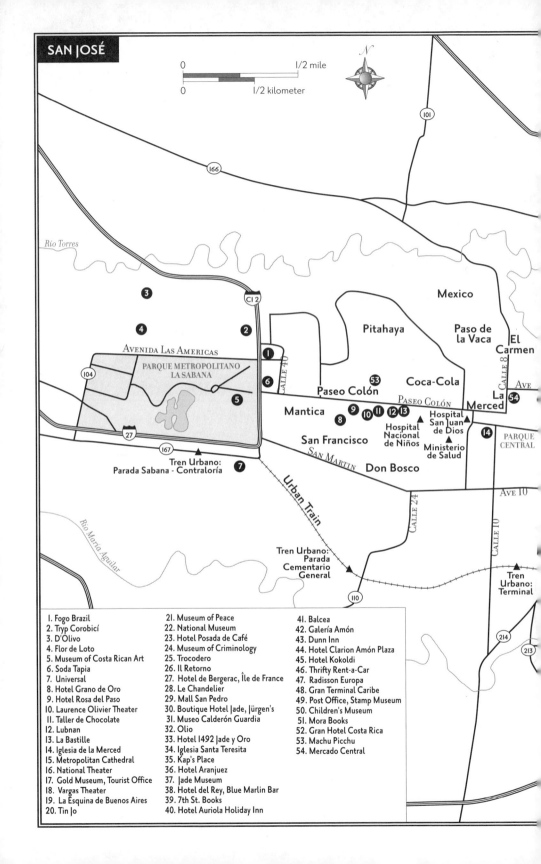

SAN JOSÉ

0 ——————— 1/2 mile
0 ——————— 1/2 kilometer

N

101

166

Río Torres

CI 2

3

4

2

AVENIDA LAS AMERICAS

1

PARQUE METROPOLITANO
LA SABANA

104

6

CALLE 40

53

Mexico

Pitahaya

Paso de
la Vaca

El
Carmen

CALLE 8

Paseo Colón

Coca-Cola

AVE

La
Merced

54

5

27

167

Mantica

Paseo Colón

9 10 11 12 13

8

Hospital
San Juan
de Dios

Hospital
Nacional
de Niños

14

PARQUE
CENTRAL

San Francisco

SAN MARTIN

Ministerio
de Salud

7

Tren Urbano:
Parada Sabana - Contraloría

Don Bosco

AVE 10

Urban Train

CALLE 24

CALLE 10

Río María Aguilar

Tren Urbano:
Parada
Cementario
General

110

Tren
Urbano:
Terminal

214

213

1. Fogo Brazil	21. Museum of Peace	41. Balcea
2. Tryp Corobicí	22. National Museum	42. Galería Amón
3. D'Olivo	23. Hotel Posada de Café	43. Dunn Inn
4. Flor de Loto	24. Museum of Criminology	44. Hotel Clarion Amón Plaza
5. Museum of Costa Rican Art	25. Trocodero	45. Hotel Kokoldi
6. Soda Tapia	26. Il Retorno	46. Thrifty Rent-a-Car
7. Universal	27. Hotel de Bergerac, Île de France	47. Radisson Europa
8. Hotel Grano de Oro	28. Le Chandelier	48. Gran Terminal Caribe
9. Hotel Rosa del Paso	29. Mall San Pedro	49. Post Office, Stamp Museum
10. Laurence Olivier Theater	30. Boutique Hotel Jade, Jürgen's	50. Children's Museum
11. Taller de Chocolate	31. Museo Calderón Guardia	51. Mora Books
12. Lubnan	32. Olio	52. Gran Hotel Costa Rica
13. La Bastille	33. Hotel 1492 Jade y Oro	53. Machu Picchu
14. Iglesia de la Merced	34. Iglesia Santa Teresita	54. Mercado Central
15. Metropolitan Cathedral	35. Kap's Place	
16. National Theater	36. Hotel Aranjuez	
17. Gold Museum, Tourist Office	37. Jade Museum	
18. Vargas Theater	38. Hotel del Rey, Blue Marlin Bar	
19. La Esquina de Buenos Aires	39. 7th St. Books	
20. Tin Jo	40. Hotel Auriola Holiday Inn	

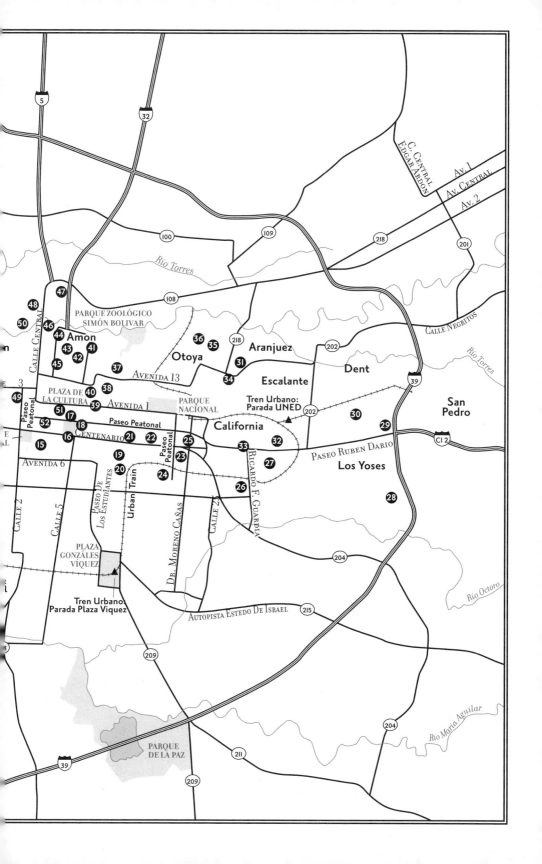

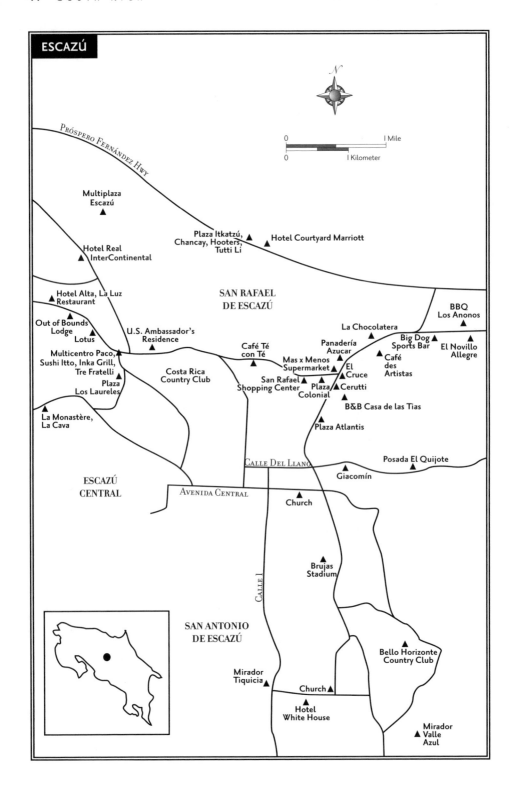

ESCAZÚ

N

0   I Mile
0   I Kilometer

Próspero Fernández Hwy

Multiplaza
Escazú ▲

Plaza Itkatzú,
Chancay, Hooters,
Tutti Li ▲   ▲ Hotel Courtyard Marriott

Hotel Real
▲ InterContinental

SAN RAFAEL
DE ESCAZÚ

Hotel Alta, La Luz
▲ Restaurant   BBQ
                                      Los Anonos
Out of Bounds ▲   La Chocolatera   ▲
Lodge   U.S. Ambassador's   Big Dog ▲
▲ Lotus   Residence   Panadería   Sports Bar   ▲ El Novillo
Multicentro Paco,   ▲   Café Té   Azucar ▲   Allegre
Sushi Itto, Inka Grill,   con Té   Mas x Menos   ▲ Café
Tre Fratelli ▲   ▲   Supermarket   El   des
Plaza   Costa Rica   San Rafael ▲ Cruce   Artistas
Los Laureles   Country Club   Shopping Center   ▲ Plaza
                                  Colonial ▲ Cerutti
▲ La Monastère,   B&B Casa de las Tias
La Cava   ▲ Plaza Atlantis

                                  Posada El Quijote
Calle Del Llano   ▲
ESCAZÚ   Giacomín
CENTRAL   Avenida Central
                   ▲ Church

                   ▲ Brujas
                   Stadium

Calle 1

SAN ANTONIO
DE ESCAZÚ

                        ▲ Bello Horizonte
                       Country Club
Mirador
Tiquicia ▲   Church ▲

           ▲ Hotel
         White House   Mirador
                             ▲ Valle
                             Azul

Crime

San José has a crime problem, though it's not nearly as bad as all those razor wire-topped fences would imply. Regardless, muggers, purse-snatchers, and pickpockets target tourists, so stay aware of your surroundings, and keep tight grip on your cameras, purses, and backpacks, even during the day. Leave your jewelry, credit cards, and passport (carry a photocopy) at the hotel whenever possible. Always use guarded parking, and take official taxis (making sure the meter is on), especially at night.

A network of clean, safe, inexpensive city buses connects the city, and route maps are also available from the ICT. Most tourists use cabs, which are safer, faster, and inexpensive; you can go anywhere in the city for under $5. Always use official red cabs, and make sure the meter is running. Urban Train San José (506-2221-0777) runs between San Pedro and Pavas during the morning and evening rush hours.

LODGING

Most accommodation options are located downtown, which is convenient, noisy, smoggy, and a tad sleazy in the evenings (see the Sex Tourism sidebar). Historic Barrio Amón, a few blocks north of the city center, has beautiful hotels, some inhabiting old colonial mansions. To the east, Barrio Los Yoses has a few quieter boutique properties. Just west of downtown, La Sabana and Rohrmoser have some of the city's best hotels, and many business-class options.

To the southwest, the upscale suburbs of Escazú and Santa Ana offer an excellent selection of upscale hotels and bed-and-breakfasts. For really fine hotels and resorts, look at the Central Valley chapter, which includes delightful options in Alajuela, five minutes from the international airport.

Lodging Price Code

Cost of lodging is based on an average per-room, double-occupancy rate at peak season (December through April). Costa Rica's 16.39 percent tax and gratuities are not included. Rates are often reduced during Green Season (May through November). An asterisk denotes that a full breakfast is included with the room price.

Inexpensive ($)	Up to $50
Moderate ($$)	$50 to $100
Expensive ($$$)	$100 to $200
Very Expensive ($$$$)	Over $200

Hotels

★ THE ALTA HOTEL

Manager: Deykel Luna
506-2282-4160
www.thealtahotel.com
dluna@thealtahotel.com
Old Carretera to Santa Ana, 2.5 km west of Centro Comercial Paco
Price: Very Expensive*
Credit Cards: Yes
Handicap Access: Yes

With a knockout view over San José from the windswept hills of Santa Ana, this cascading Spanish Colonial hotel is one of the finest in the region. Descend the arched adobe hallways, themselves a work of art, to your refined and stylish room, with private balconies or patios, fluffy bathrobes, and beautiful bathrooms. It's worth upgrading to a far more spacious junior suite, with pleasant sitting areas and a bathtub.

U.S.-Style Hotels

Looking for somewhere familiar in a foreign land? You've got it.

Aurola Holiday Inn (506-2222-2424; 800-465-4329 USA and Canada; www.aurolahotels.com; Av 5 & Calle 5, on Parque Morazán; $$$–$$$$) San José's only high-rise hotel has recently been remodeled to five star excellence.

Clarion Amón Plaza (506-2257-0191; 800-575-1253 USA and Canada; www.hotelamonplaza.com; Av 11 & Calle 3; $$$–$$$$) Offers every amenity from air-conditioning and WiFi to a small gym and business center.

Radisson Europa Hotel (506-2257-3257; 800-333-3333 USA and Canada; www.radisson.com; Calle Blancos behind La República; $$$–$$$$) The best chain hotel in San José proper has spacious rooms with big windows overlooking downtown.

★ **Real InterContinental San José** (506-2208-0101; www.ichotelsgroup.com; Escazú, Don Prospero Fernández Hwy; $$$$) The pinnacle of luxury in the region, every amenity—multiple pools, spa, shops, gym, tennis courts, fabulous rooms—is offered at this elite option, perfectly located in central Escazú.

A tour desk, small gymnasium, and spectacular pool and Jacuzzi are among The Alta's finer amenities. But the real gem is their outstanding, glass-enclosed, fine dining restaurant, **La Luz** (open 6:30 AM–10 PM, daily; $$$$). Reservations are recommended for this top-ranked restaurant, where attentive waiters in black bow ties exhibit the excellent wine list before recommending specialties such as the beautifully presented strawberry sirloin, served over champagne risotto topped with a white truffle pesto.

BOUTIQUE HOTEL JADE

Owner: Jürgen F. Mormels
506-2224-2455
www.hotelboutiquejade.com
info@hotelboutiquejade.com
Los Yoses, Av Central, 250m north of Autos Subarú
Price: Expensive
Credit Cards: Yes
Handicap Access: Yes

With all the little luxuries of a U.S.-owned chain, this boutique hotel in quiet Los Yoses also offers a taste of Costa Rica. The lobby, a jungle-chic patina of tropical greens, yellows, and burnt oranges, is accented with dark rattan furniture, subdued lighting, Persian rugs, and murals. Creatively decorated doubles come with fresh flowers, new mattresses, WiFi, and air-conditioning, while larger junior suites offer sitting rooms and enormous marble baths.

Your complimentary breakfast buffet can be taken in the garden, or cross the little bridge over the pool and fountain to dine in their excellent upscale restaurant, **Jürgen's** (506-2283-2239; L, D; $$$–$$$$). Power brokers both Tico and foreign lunch amidst the impressive architecture, making deals over prime cuts of beef or *corvina tropical*, sea bass curried with tropical fruits and mushrooms. The ambiance turns romantic after dark. The impressive wine list, featuring five pages of international vintages, offers bottles topping $400 (though there are several in the $10–$30 range).

HÔTEL DE BERGERAC

Manager: Lilian Vega
506-2234-7850
www.bergerachotel.com
bergerac@racsa.co.cr
Los Yoses, Calle 35 between Av Central and Av 8

Price: Moderate to Expensive
Credit Cards: Yes
Handicap Access: Yes

Elegant architecture and baroque furnishings are accented with indigenous sculptures and impressionist artwork in this perfectly executed boutique hotel. Set in a sprawling neocolonial mansion on a quiet but convenient side street, it's surrounded by gardens, just slightly overgrown and always in flower. Stay in one of the "superior" rooms, opening onto semi-private patios abuzz with hummingbirds, or ascend the spiral staircase lit with stained glass to a deluxe room, with cheerful floral coverlets, refrigerator, and other amenities, including a balcony with excellent city views.

The Grand Room is worth the extra cost for spectacular views of Poás Volcano rising above the city lights. Breakfast is served in the oh-so-French dining room, or enjoy room service—also available at dinner from the excellent adjacent restaurant, **Île de France** (506-2283-5812; D; $$$$), serving some of the city's finest French cuisine in either the stately dining room or courtyard gardens.

HOTEL CASA ROLAND
Owner: Don Robert Roland Bogdanovich
506-2231-6571
casa-roland.com

reservations@casa-roland.com
Pavas, 100m south of the end of Boulevard Rohrmoser
Price: Expensive
Credit Cards: Yes
Handicap Access: Yes
Special: Pets OK

With a cozy, dark, old-boys-club elegance, this comfortable and convenient boutique hotel is just five minutes from Tobias Bolaño Airport. Walls are thickly hung with original art and exotic plants, while richly upholstered furniture, oriental carpets, sculptural lighting, and leather couches add to the just slightly stuffy, over-the-top ambiance.

Ritzy regular rooms, with ornate furniture, wicker accents, fine bathrooms, and amenities including air-conditioning and DVD players, are fabulous. Suites are much more spacious, with limestone walls, sitting areas, and surround-sound entertainment systems. The apartment has three bedrooms, private garden, and a full kitchen. A business center, gym, terrace Jacuzzi, and plush little bar with a jazz soundtrack are all on-site.

★ HOTEL GRANO DE ORO
Manager: Gabriela Monge
506-2255-3322; 506-2221-2782
www.hotelgranodeoro.com

Sex Tourism in San José
Prostitution is legal in Costa Rica, and you really can't miss it in San José. An estimated 10 percent of Costa Rica's tourists are here to indulge, and you'll see them, too, concentrated in an area around Parque Morazán known as the "Gringo Gulch."

Action centers on the (in)famous **Blue Marlin Bar**, inside massive, pastel pink **Hotel Del Rey** (506-2257-7800; www.hoteldelrey.com; Av I & Calle 9; $$–$$$). There are also dozens of "massage parlors," "cigar bars," and hotels subtly advertised as "private clubs" with "attractive and service-oriented staff," where the world's oldest profession is also practiced.

Although most women are working of their own free will, and enjoy legal and police protection (I recently watched one young lady loudly threaten an elderly American with a lawsuit for failing to keep a scheduled "date"), Costa Rica is a recognized human trafficking destination. Please remember that the government does not test sex workers for HIV, despite what other guidebooks say.

Historic Hotels

Hotel Santo Tomás (506-2255-0448; www.hotelsantotomas.com; Av 7, Calles 3 & 5; $$*) Beautifully restored, century-old plantation mansion, appointed in hardwoods, handmade tiles, antiques, and original art, seems a world away from the scruff and bustle outside.

Hotel Don Carlos (506-2221-6707; www.doncarloshotel.com; Calle 9, Avs 7 & 9; $$*) Rambling, three-story mansion has housed two presidential families, their demanding tastes satisfied by beautiful ironwork, hand-painted Spanish tiles, and parquet wood floors in rooms of various shapes and sizes, some with adorable interior balconies overlooking soothing gardens with fountains and orchids.

Gran Hotel Costa Rica (506-2221-4000; 800-949-0592; www.granhotelcostarica.com; Av 2 at the National Theater; $$; three CST Leaves) Neoclassical Historic Landmark has presided over the Plaza de la Cultura since 1930, hosting VIPs from JFK to Pelé. Though the extravagant and remarkably tiled lobby is aging gracefully, rooms could use an update and soundproofing.

Hotel Milvia (506-2225-4543; www.novanet.co.cr/milvia; San Pedro, Barrio Lourdes; $$*) Huge wooden 1930s plantation mansion, built for engineer Ricardo Fernández Peralta, has been elegantly and eclectically refurbished with original art, lovely antiques, and modern amenities including WiFi, making it the most comfortable hotel in San Pedro.

Hotel Rosa del Paseo (506-2257-3213; www.rosadelpaseo.com; Paseo del Colón, calles 28 & 30; $$; one CST Leaf) Built by the Montealegre family, among the original exporters of coffee to Europe, this ornate 1897 bed-and-breakfast displays classic Caribbean Victorian styling, decorated with fine period pieces. Second floor rooms are nicer.

White House Costa Rica Hotel (506-2288-6362; Escazú; www.whitehousecostarica.com; $$$$) Originally built by the Shah of Iran, this deliciously decadent option offers opulent rooms that just ooze *film noir* glamour, with imposing antiques, richly embroidered fabrics, Persian rugs (of course), and huge stone fireplaces. Among the testosterone-laden amenities are a steakhouse, cigar bar, Harley and Hummer rentals, private helicopter transportation, and a casino boasting the "highest odds and limits in Costa Rica." Views over Escazú are fit for a president, shah, or king.

granoro@racsa.co.cr
Calle 30 between Av 2 and 4
Price: $$$–$$$$
Credit cards: Yes
Handicap Access: Challenging

At the "Grain of Gold," as coffee was called when it first funded the construction of such gracious Victorian estates, soft light glitters on trickling fountains, and dances across a warm collection of antiques, old photos, and art that ornament a labyrinth of exquisitely crafted hallways, lounges, terraces, and gardens flowing through the hotel.

Standard rooms are attractively appointed with comfy wrought iron beds and period furnishings, as well as modern amenities such as mini bars, safes, and hair dryers (but no air-conditioning). Larger and more luxurious suites include the elegantly appointed Garden Suite, with a private patio for lounging. Or ascend a private staircase to the richly appointed Vista de Oro suite, with views from your Jacuzzi across the Central Valley.

The rooftop terrace offers the same amazing views. There's also romantic ★**Grano de Oro Restaurant** (B, L, D; $$–$$$$), consistently ranked among Costa Rica's best, serving French-accented international cuisine either overlooking or amidst an interior courtyard garden.

Choices range from the classics—eggs Benedict, rack of lamb, duck confit with orange sauce—to more creative options, such as the leek-and-seafood crêpes, chicken breast stuffed with caramelized tropical fruits, and a dozen delectable desserts. Service at both the hotel and restaurant are world class.

PARQUE DEL LAGO

Manager: Raúl Hidalgo
506-2257-8787
www.parquedellago.com
info@parquedellago.com
La Sabana, Av 2 between Calles 40 and 42
Price: Expensive*
Credit Cards: Yes
Handicap Access: Yes
Special: Four CST Leaves

Convenient and comfortable business-class hotel close to Parque La Sabana offers excellent, modern rooms with business-people in mind, furnished with handmade Sarchí furniture for real Tico flavor. Rooms come complete with direct-dial phones, a minibar, air-conditioning, and WiFi. For a bit more space, book a junior suite, with wet bar, microwave, and sitting area, and wonderful volcano views (try to get a room ending in "07"). The penthouse has a Jacuzzi and full kitchen.

Bed-and-Breakfasts

HOTEL 1492 JADE Y ORO

Owner: Sabrina Vargas
506-2225-3752
www.hotel1492.com
info@cr-hotels.com
Los Yoses; Ave 1, Calles 31 and 33; 300m east of Cine Magaly
Price: Moderate
Credit Cards: Yes
Handicapped Access: Limited

A glass of wine greets you upon arrival to this immaculate, family-run inn, perfect for those who prefer the authentic, eclectic, and artistic. The colorful artwork, which graces every surface, was created by the Spanish-style mansion's original owner, Amalia Jiménez Volio. Murals of tropical flowers and pre-Columbian sculptures, colorful tile work, and other unusual accents make this place unique.

Rooms are furnished with comfortable but offbeat, somewhat dated furniture—think classic 1960s—and modern amenities including cable TV, telephone, WiFi, hair dryers, and fine bathrooms. There are several breakfast options, but be sure to enjoy yours in the tropical gardens out back.

CASA BELLA RITA BOUTIQUE BED & BREAKFAST

Owners: Steve and Rita DeVore
506-2249-3722
www.casabellarita.com
info@casabellarita.com
Brasil de Santa Ana, outside Escazú
Price: Expensive
Credit Cards: Yes

Overlooking a forested canyon in the hills between Escazú and the international airport (transfers are included), this charming country inn offers quiet communion with nature just minutes from San José. Gem-toned rooms with polished teak accents and fine mosaic tiles are restfully decorated with Balinese-influenced furniture, flowing fabrics, and top notch bedding, as well as modern amenities including WiFi, mini-bars, and iPod-ready radios. Flawless.

The pool and breakfast nook both offer wonderful views over the canyon, its wildlife, and rushing river, with a 100-meter (300-foot) waterfall close by.

★ POSADA EL QUIJOTE

Managers: Dick and Claudia Furlong
506-2289-8401
www.quijote.co.cr
quijote@quijote.co.cr

Tell your *taxista*: *De la fábrica Toycos 1km este, 25m sur, 50m este*
Price: Moderate to Expensive*
Credit Cards: Yes
Handicap Access: No

Tucked away in a corner of Escazú, with great views over San José, this spacious, Spanish-style bed-and-breakfast spreads across wonderful gardens, unfolding into cool, tiled, elegantly furnished yet still homey rooms with huge windows or private balconies. Airport transfers are included, as is full breakfast, cooked to order. Enjoy yours in one of the stylish and comfortable common areas, either inside, surrounded by glowing hardwoods, or *al fresco* on the terrace. Studio apartments come with full kitchens and can be rented weekly or monthly.

RESTAURANTS AND FOOD PURVEYORS

With the widest range of international and fine dining restaurants in the country, you can make the most of your stay in San José with a wonderful meal. Some of the best restaurants are located in the hotels listed above.

Restaurant and Food Purveyor Price Code

The following prices are based on the cost of a dinner entrée with a non-alcoholic drink, not including the 13 percent taxes and 10 percent gratuity added to the cost of almost all restaurant meals (except for the very cheapest *sodas*). Menus note whether or not their listed prices include this hefty 23 percent total surcharge, some listing two sets of prices.

Inexpensive ($)	Up to $5
Moderate ($$)	$5 to $10
Expensive ($$$)	$10 to $20
Very Expensive ($$$$)	$20 or more

Restaurants

SAN JOSÉ

★ BAKEA

506-2221-1051
www.restaurantebakea.com
Barrio Amón, Calle 7 and Av 11
Closed: Sun.
Price: Moderate to Very Expensive
Cuisine: International
Serving: L, D
Credit Cards: Yes
Reservations: Yes

Choose your ambiance in this restored 1934 Barrio Amón mansion, dining outdoors in the secluded garden, relaxing in the cozy lounge area, or enjoying the beautifully tiled main room. Though the home is a classic, the décor is modern, with art to match. Service is attentive and excellent. And all of this takes a back seat to Chef Camille Ratton's cuisine.

Using French techniques, Costa Rican ingredients, and inspiration from the Mediterranean, Asia, and Latin America, she has built a small, seasonal menu that might include Camembert *aux mûres* (soft cheese in a port and blackberry sauce), or the *paquetitos espartanos* (phyllo pastry laced with ricotta cheese, almonds, and honey mustard). Main dishes might include the New Zealand rack of lamb, or sesame-encrusted chicken breast stuffed with sautéed vegetables in tamarind sauce. The dessert and wine lists are outstanding.

NUESTRA TIERRA

506-2258-6500
Calle 15 and Av 2, across from Plaza de la Democracia
Price: Moderate
Children's Menu: Yes
Cuisine: Costa Rican
Liquor: Full
Serving: B, L, D
Credit Cards: No
Reservations: No

Businesspeople rush to work in San José's federal district.

The over-the-top rustic charm—Sarchí mandalas, *campesino*-style uniforms—at first made me wary of this ticky-tacky spot. But after glowing recommendations from Ticos and tourist alike, I gave it a try. Fabulous. Be sure to order coffee, brewed at your table using a traditional *chorreador*. Food is self-consciously typical and extremely well done; this may be the most beautiful *casado*, *arroz con pollo*, or *gallo pinto* you'll ever eat. Prices are at a premium for this sort of *soda* cuisine, but top-notch preparation, presentation, and service (fully bilingual) make it worth every colón.

TIN JO
506-2221-7605
www.tinjo.com

Av 8 and Calle 11
Price: Moderate to Expensive
Cuisine: Pan-Asian
Serving L, D
Credit Cards: Yes
Reservations: No

Beautifully decorated San José stalwart is not just the best Asian restaurant in the country, it's one of San José's premier dining experiences. The menu is eclectic, with pan-Asian classics such as pad Thai, Vietnamese-style chicken steamed with shitake mushrooms and ginger, Chinese mu shu, and even a very good Indian *palak paneer*. Attentive service and a classy ambiance make this a favorite for date nights.

Next door, **Don Wang** (506-2223-5925; www.donwangrestaurant.com; Calle 11, Avs

The plaza fronting Costa Rica's federal courthouse and judicial buildings combines Egyptian and Chorotega stylistic elements.

6 & 8; B, L, D; $$) isn't quite as famous, but dishes from its smaller menu are just as good.

ESCAZÚ AND SANTA ANA
BACCHUS
506-2282-5441
Santa Ana, Casa Quitirrisí, 300m east of Musmanni
Price: Moderate to Expensive
Cuisine: Italian
Serving: L, D
Credit Cards: Yes
Reservations: Recommended

Popular spot for Central Valley scenesters is also an excellent deal on splendid Italian cuisine. The delightfully remodeled century-old adobe, snuggled into the upscale community of Santa Ana, offers attractive outdoor seating on the wraparound patio, or inside, with beautiful red brick floors and period furnishings.

Handmade pastas are served with a selection of slow-simmered sauces ranging from a spicy marinera to a sinful Gorgonzola. Pizzas, calzones, and focaccias are baked in a wood-fired oven, or enjoy excellent seafood, steak, and poultry dishes. But please save room for the apple-stuffed fried ravioli, served with a toffee sauce and vanilla ice cream.

CERRUTTI RESTAURANT
506-2228-9954
www.cerruttirestaurant.com
San Rafael de Escazú, across from Centro

Comercial Escazú
Price: Very Expensive
Cuisine: Italian
Serving: L, D
Credit Cards: Yes
Reservations: Yes

This charming blue-and-white striped colonial-style adobe may be modest, but it houses one of Escazú's best restaurants. Chef Francesco Mansani changes the menu regularly, but you can count on Italian-accented seafood dishes, homemade pasta, and the specialty of the house, wild game, all paired with some excellent vintage from the serious wine list. Service is five star, as it should be at these prices. Budget gourmets can save with the Chef's Plate for Two: two appetizers, two mains, and one dessert for $45.

LA CASCADA

506-2228-0906
Behind Shell next to Saretto Supermarket, 600m west and 50m north of Los Anonos Bridge
Price: Expensive
Cuisine: Costa Rican, Steakhouse
Serving: L, D
Credit Cards: Yes
Reservations: Recommended

An Escazú favorite for 40 years, La Cascada is a classic spot for Ticos celebrating something special. Service is dependable and formal, the ambiance classic, and the menu simple but outstanding. Start with the avocado and shrimp appetizer, then carefully consider the signature dish, *rollizo*, heart of the tenderloin. Steak, fish dishes, lobster,

and simple sides have been the recipe for Costa Rica's most successful restaurant for decades.

★ MONASTÈRE RESTAURANT & BAR

506-2289-4404
www.monastere-restaurant.com
On the road from Escazú to Santa Ana, turn left at Multicentro Paco and follow the green crosses
Price: Very Expensive
Cuisine: European Gourmet
Serving: D
Credit Cards: Yes
Reservations: Recommended

Atop Escazú, this unusually beautiful restaurant is a rambling remnant of the region's religious past, a former monastery with incredible 270-degree views. It's now a point of pilgrimage for foodies from all over the country, who come to enjoy the five-star service (by waiters wearing the gold-and-crimson robes of 19th-century monks) and impeccable French-influenced menu.

Showy dishes, such as the great flambé, crêpes suzettes, and made-at-the-table Caesar salads, just add to the old world elegance of the place, perfect for business or pleasure. Try the venison tenderloin port flambé or wild boar chops with essence of truffle, paired with one of the wines stored in the monks' old cellar, which has been converted into an intimate (and less expensive) bar and grill, **La Cava**, offering the same great views with less expensive grilled meat dishes. The restaurant has also renovated an exquisite little chapel emblazoned with murals from Michelangelo's Sistine Chapel.

Food Purveyors

Bakeries

Trigo y Miel (506-2221-8995; Downtown, Calle 3, Av Central & 1; B, L, D; $) This chain has pastries, light meals, and bottomless cups of coffee.

★ **Giacomín** (506-2234-2551; www.chocolatesdelmundo.com; Los Yoses, Av Central &

Calle 41, next to Automercado; $) These Italian-style bakeries have beautiful cakes, wonderful chocolates, and stores in Escazú, Santa Ana, and Heredia.

Spoon (www.spoon.co.cr) Pastries, coffee, sandwiches, and light meals, available at outlets all over town.

Cafés

SAN JOSÉ

Café la Boemia (506-2258-8465; Av 2 & Calle Central; B, L, D) Next to the Melico Salazar Theater, offers attentive service and upscale ambiance.

Café de Artistas (506-2288-5082; Escazú, 100m south of Plaza Rolex; B, L; $$) Big breakfasts, light meals, and a champagne brunch with live music.

Café Teatro Nacional (506-2221-1329; Av 2 & Calle 3; B, L; closed Sun.) A fine excuse to linger inside the fabulous Teatro Nacional lobby.

La Esquina del Café (506-2228-7927; Escazú; Plaza Mundo, 900m north of BAC) Roasts gourmet coffee, sells it by the bag or cappuccino alongside pastries and sandwiches.

News Café (506-2222-3022; Av Central, Calles 7 & 9) Five-star people watching in the Gringo Gulch.

Café Moro (506-2223-3116; Calle 3, Avs 11 & 13; L, D; closed Sun.) Wraps, kebabs, and salads served in a "Moorish palace."

International Cuisine

Whether you're craving curry or colcannon, you'll find it here in San José.

Bohemia (Peruvian; 506-2253-6348; Barrio Escalante, 525m east of Santa Teresita Church; L, D; $$$$) Elegantly restored mansion offers top-notch Peruvian cuisine, with creative presentation and excellent service.

★ **Le Chandelier** (French; 506-2225-3980; www.restaurantlechandelier.com; San Pedro, 100m east and 100m south of ICE; L, D, closed Sun.; $$$$) If you're planning to propose, this is San José's most elegant eatery. Fine French cuisine fused with Tico ingredients includes divine dishes like jumbo shrimp in passion fruit and papaya, or sea bass au gratin with avocado. Go for the six-course *degustación*, paired with their wine and champagne list. Presentation is perfect, service superior, and desserts delectable.

Chancay (Peruvian, Chinese; 506-2234-3252; Curridibat, 200m south of Pop's) Elegantly appointed option specializes in *chifa*, or Chinese-Peruvian fusion cuisine.

★ **Little Israel Pita Rica** (506-2228-9775; pitarica@hotmail.com; Plaza Laureles, Carretera Vieja a Santa Ana; open 10 AM–7 PM Mon.–Sat.) Fabulous Middle Eastern deli offers all things kosher and *halal*, including falafel sandwiches, hummus, and a wonderful smoked trout spread.

Lubnan (Lebanese; 506-2257-6071l; Paseo Colón, Calle 22 & 24, across from Mercedes Benz; L, D; closed Sun. and Mon.; $$–$$$) Go all out with the huge meze platter, then return Thursday at 9 PM for belly dancing.

Stan's Irish Cuisine (Irish; 506-2253-4360; Zapote, 150m west of Presidential House; L, D; $$) Irish and international dishes in a cozy pub with the best selection of beer (55 varieties) in Costa Rica.

Taj Mahal (Indian; 506-2228-0980; Escazú, 1 km west of Centro Comercial Paco, Old Road to Santa Ana; L, D, closed Mon.; $$$–$$$$) Costa Rica's best Indian cuisine is served spicy on request.

Styles may change, but young Costa Ricans still woo one another in shady Parque Nacional.

Pizza

★ **Il Pomodoro** (506-2224-0966; 100m north of San Pedro Church; L, D; $$) Popular pizza place is packed with UCR students, who give thin-crust pizzas and pastas high marks.

Sale y Pepa (506-2289-5750; Escazú, El Cruce de San Rafael, Centro Comercial Del Valle; L, D; $$$; reservations recommended) Arguably Escazú's best pizza, served up in an elegant little dining room.

★ **La Piazzetta** (506-2222-7896; Paseo Colón, across from the BCR; L, D; $$$) Classic Italian cuisine, old world ambiance, excellent service, and wonderful pizza and Italian dishes earned this San José stalwart a coveted Five Fork rating.

Sodas

La Gauchada (506-2232-6916; Sabana Oeste, 175m south of Canal 7; L, D; $$) Revered Argentine *empanada* (fried turnover) outlet also serves good pastas.

Manolo's Restaurante y Churrería (506-2221-2041; Av Central, Calles Central & 2; open 24 hours; $–$$) Landmark downtown *soda* serves great Tico típico, including fresh ceviche, all night long.

Soda Tapia (506-2222-6734; La Sabana, Av 2 & Calle 42, open till 2 AM, 24 hours Fri. and
Sat; $) Huge, crowded, iconic *soda* overlooking La Sabana park and lots of traffic is a
nationally revered landmark and subject of many a story that begins, "We were so
drunk. . . ." Fill out an order form and enjoy the scene.

Steakhouses

★ **Fogo Brasil** (506-2248-2233; Sabana Norte, 100m east of Nissan; L, D; $$$) Brazilian-
style steakhouse has 16 different cuts of perfectly grilled meats accompanied by the
biggest salad bar in town.

★ **La Esquina de Buenos Aires** (506-2223-1909; www.laesquinabuenosaires.com; Calle
11 & Av 4; L, D; $$$) Downtown steakhouse offers rustic ambiance, incredible steaks,
and a full bar with imported liquors and wines from Argentina, Chile, and Italy.

Lukas (506-2233-8145; El Pueblo; L, D; $$) Best restaurant in the El Pueblo nightlife dis-
trict is conveniently open until 2 AM.

Parrillada Argentina el Novillo Alegre (506-2288-4995; San Rafael de Escazú, 200m west
of Los Anonos Bridge; L, D; $$–$$$$) Argentine chain has great steaks, empanadas,
Argentine wines, and sinful South American desserts.

Texas BBQ Company (506-2231-0025; www.crbbq.com; Sabana Sur, 150m south of the
controlaloria; L, D; $–$$) Texas-style barbecue and sides like mashed potatoes,
coleslaw, or barbecued beans, can be delivered. Nice.

Sushi

Fuji (506-2232-8122; Sabana Norte, Hotel Tryp Corobicí; L, D; $$$$) More expensive
because it's worth it.

★ **Matsuri Sushi** (506-2280-5522; Curridibat, Centro Comercial Plaza Cristal; L, D; $$$)
Good prices on spectacular sushi at this simple mall eatery.

Tanaka (506-2296-2255; Rhormoser, 1 km west of Plaza Mayor; L, D; $$$) A 60-item sushi
menu, great chicken yakatori, and warmed saki.

Vegetarian

Comida Para Sentir (506-2224-1163; 150m north of San Pedro Church; L, D; $$) Budget
vegetarian cuisine beloved by university students.

★ **Restaurant Vishnu** (506-2207-2130; Downtown, Av 1, Calles 1 & 3; B, L, D; $–$$)
Unassuming *soda*-style vegetarian joint has awesome green salads, vegetarian Tico typi-
cal food, and huge fruit salads swimming in ice cream that bring in even committed car-
nivores.

Shakti (506-2257-8914; Calle 13 & Av 8) Healthy, organic cuisine, including a few poultry
dishes.

CULTURE

San José is a young city; though the Spaniards colonized it early on, it was for centuries a
simple agricultural village on the outskirts of the glorious capital, Cartago. Incorporated in
1737 as Villanueva de la Boca del Monte, these simple farmers struck gold, or rather coffee,
in the early 1800s. When news arrived of Costa Rica's 1821 independence from Spain, the
newly wealthy, republic-minded populace fought Cartago's entrenched Spanish elite for the
right to build a democracy. They won the battle, and made San José their new capital.

Today, it is the seat of government, its striking buildings surrounded by parks, plazas, museums, and public art, most dedicated to the pursuit of peace, democracy, and freedom.

Architectural Walking Tour

Tico Walks (506-2283-8281; www.ticowalks.com; $10) offers guided tours of the city's most important sites and buildings; meet in front of the Teatro Nacional at 10 AM (no reservations required) Tuesday, Thursday, Saturday, or Sunday for a stroll through history. Or do it yourself.

Begin at the **Central Park** (Calle Central, Avs 2 & 4), centered on a pavilion donated by Nicaraguan dictator Anastasio Somoza. Presiding over the Plaza is 1871 **Metropolitan Cathedral** (Calle Central, Avs 2 & 4), built after the original was destroyed in an earthquake, and bedecked with wood columns and beautifully painted leaves. On the north side of the park is 1828 **Teatro Melico Salazar**.

Walk three blocks north on Calle 2 to the French-Baroque style **National Post Office** (Calle 2, Avs 1 & 3), home to the small **Postal Museum**. You could continue north to historic **Barrio Amón**, where century-old mansions have been transformed into wonderful restaurants and hotels. Or, backtrack to the pedestrian walk and make a left, to the **Plaza de la Cultura** (Av Central, Calles 3 & 5). Home to the 1897 **Teatro Nacional**, and the 1930 **Gran Costa Rica**, it's a great spot to relax over coffee before descending to the ★**Gold Museum**, next to the **ICT (Ministry of Tourism) office**, where you can pick up a free city map.

Continue east on the pedestrian walk and make a left on Calle 7 to **Parque Morazán** (Calle 7 & Av 3), home to the **Temple of Music**, patterned after the Trianon in Paris. Continue north another block on Av 7; on your left is the 1892 **Edificio Metálico**, designed by Victor Baltard, who also built Les Halles in Paris; it was cast in Belgium before being shipped here piece by piece. The skyscraper just east is home to the ★**Jade Museum** (Av 7

Free Museums

Get your daily dose of culture, on the house.

Museum of Contemporary Art & Design (506-2257-7202; www.madc.ac.cr; Av 3 & Calle 15; open 10 AM–5 PM Tue.–Sat.) More than 500 cutting-edge pieces, plus rotating exhibitions of sculpture, painting, photography, video, and a performance art space.

Museum of Criminology (506-2223-0666; Calle 21 & Av 8, Supreme Court Building; open 1 PM–4 PM Mon., Wed., and Fri.) Creepy collection of weapons and other crime tools, confiscated drug paraphernalia, and a brief history of crime and criminals in Costa Rica.

Museum of Peace (506-2223-4664; www.arias.or.cr; Av 2 & Calle 13; open 8 AM–noon and 1 PM–4 PM Mon.–Fri.) Ring the bell to see this tiny museum detailing the wars that consumed Central America during the 1980s, and the Esquipulas Peace Accords, championed by President Oscar Arías, that ended them.

Postal Museum (506-2223-9766; Calle 2, Avs 1 & 3; open 8 AM–4 PM Mon.–Fri.; you must buy a $0.40 phone card to enter) In the National Post Office, houses an impressive stamp collection and early communications technology.

Dr. Rafael Ángel Calderón Guardia Museum (506-2255-1218; Av 11 & Calle 25; open 9 AM–5 PM Mon.–Sat.) Beautiful 1912 French-style adobe building pays homage to the doctor and president who implemented the minimum wage, social security, and nationalized health care.

Monument to Juan Santamaría honors Costa Rica's favorite son.

& Calle 11); across the street is shady **Parque España**, featuring a controversial statue of a Spanish conquistador.

Continuing east on Av 7, you'll pass beautiful **Casa Amarilla** (Av 7 & Calle 11), home to the Foreign Ministry; the ceiba tree in front was planted by U.S. President John F. Kennedy. A half-block east is the imposing **National Cultural Center**, founded in 1856 by as the National Liquor Factory, now home to the **Contemporary Art Museum** (Av 7, Calles 11 & 15).

Make a left onto Calle 9 to visit **Parque Zoologico Simón Bolívar** (Calle 13 & Av 11), or continue on the tour, making a right onto Calle 15 to enjoy the lovely **National Park** (Calles 15 & 19, Avs 1 & 3), centered around the 1856 Battle of Santa Rosa Monument, depicting hero Juan Santamaría. The **National Library** is just north, or head two blocks east to see the **1907 Atlantic Railway Station**, (Calle 21 & Av 3).

From the park, continue south on pedestrian-only Calle 17, passing the **National Museum**. It overlooks the **Plaza de la Demócracia**, built in 1989. On the other side of the plaza are the ★**Artisan's Market** and the **Museum of Peace**. Continue south on the pedestrian walk to finish up at an Egyptian-style plaza, complete with a pyramid, fronting the **Supreme Court**.

Museums

INSECT MUSEUM
506-2225-5555
www.miucr.ac.cr
San Pedro, University of Costa Rica, in Ares Musicales
Open: 1 PM–5 PM, Mon.–Sat.
Admission: $2

Boasting more than a million specimens of insects collected from around the world, Museo de Insectos may be Latin America's most extensive entomological collection.

★ PRE-COLUMBIAN GOLD MUSEUM
506-2243-4202
www.museosdelbancocentral.org
Av Central and Calle 5
Open: 9:30 AM–5 PM, Tue.–Sun.
Admission: $7 per adult; $3 per student

Underneath the Plaza de la Cultura, this glittering collection of more than 2,600 pre-Columbian pieces can overwhelm. Most date from about 300–1500 A.D., with quality reaching its peak around 700 A.D. The museum offers guided tours in English, French, and Spanish to groups of 15 or more, as well as the Night of Gold tour, which includes dinner; call 506-2243-4219 for arrangements. Temporary exhibitions change every four months.

In the same underground complex, the **Numismatic Museum** (admission $3) has a collection of more than 5,000 coins, bills, and other objects dating to as early as 1502.

★ NATIONAL MUSEUM
506-2257-1433
www.museocostarica.go.cr
Calle 15 and Av 2
Open: 8:30 AM–4 PM, Mon.–Sat.; 9 AM–4 PM, Sun.
Admission: $4 per adult; $2 per student

San José's most striking building is the 1887 Bellavista Fortress, complete with massive Castilian turrets, that was once the headquarters of the Costa Rican military. The bullet holes that pepper its yellow walls remain from the 1948 civil war led by Don José "Pepe" Figueres, whose statue overlooks the neighboring Plaza of Democracy. After taking power, Figueres famously abolished the Costa Rican military, leaving this building to become one of San José's more interesting museums.

In addition to the classic colonial architecture and beautiful view (*bella vista*) over the city, permanent exhibitions include an amazing collection of pre-Columbian pieces, including gold, jade, and some of the most ornate and delicately carved stone *metates* (corn grinders) imaginable. Other rooms cover Spanish colonial history, including oxcarts and other old tools, and natural history.

MUSEUM OF COSTA RICAN ART
506-2222-7155
www.musarco.go.cr
Eastern edge of La Sabana Park
Open: 10 AM–4 PM, Tue.–Sun.
Admission: $7 per adult; $3 per student; free Sun.

In the Art-Deco-meets-Santa-Barbara-style terminal of San José's old airport, now La Sabana Park, more than 3,200 pieces of original Costa Rican artwork are on display. The Golden Hall, on the second floor of the building, features a bronze-painted relief mural depicting the history of Costa Rica on all four walls, painted by French artist Luis Ferrón. There's a groovy sculpture garden in the back.

At the southwest corner of La Sabana Park, you could also visit **La Salle Museum of Natural Science** (506-2232-1306; www.lasalle.edu.co/museo; open 8 AM–5 PM Mon.–Fri.; admission $1), with more than 20,000 specimens, including stuffed wildlife, skeletons, pinned butterflies, and a model leatherback turtle.

★ JADE MUSEUM
506-2287-6034
portal.ins-cr.com/social/museojade
Av 7 and 9, Calle 9 and 11
Open: 8:30 AM–3:30 PM, Mon.–Fri.; 9 AM–1 PM, Sat.
Admission: $2

The cult of jade, "gem of the gods," began in Costa Rica around 500 B.C.E., though the origins of the translucent stones remain something of a mystery; no significant jade deposits exist in Costa Rica. Regardless, the National Insurance Institute displays the largest collection in the Americas. Sadly, the museum has moved from the 11th floor of the building (which offered fine views), but you call still enjoy this amazing spectacle on the ground, as well as a good collection of pre-Columbian pottery and other artifacts.

Kid's Stuff
★ **National Children's Museum** (506-2223-7003; www.museocr.com; Calle 4 & Av 9; open 8 AM–4 PM, Tue.–Fri., 10 AM–5 PM, Sat.–Sun.; admission $2 per adult/$1.50 per child) This 1909 Spanish castle-style edifice was once a federal prison, but now houses a colorful collection of educational exhibits about Costa Rican history, geology, and wildlife, as well as interactive exhibits that teach life skills. The animatronic Franklin Chang-Diaz, Costa Rica's famed first astronaut, is cool in a very Westworld way.

Parque Zoologico Simón Bolívar (506-2256-0012; www.fundazoo.org; Calle 9 & Av 11; open 8 AM–3:30 PM, Mon.–Fri., 9 AM–4:30 PM, Sat. and Sun.; admission $3) Small but well-kept zoo has many of the rain forest animals you didn't see on your guided hikes.

★ **Pueblo Antiguo** (506-2231-2001; www.parquediversiones.com; 3 km west of Uruca; open 9 AM–5 PM, Mon.–Thu., 9 AM–7 PM, Fri.–Sun.; admission free) Half theme park, half living museum, all hokey, educational fun, "Old Town" reconstructs Costa Rica circa 1900, the boom years when the world discovered coffee. Roller coasters and other rides cost around $1 each. Friday and Saturday evenings are Costa Rican dance nights; Expediciones Tropicales (506-2257-4171; www.costaricainfo.com; $40) offers tours.

Spirogyra Butterfly Garden (506-2222-2937; www.butterflygardencr.com; 50m east, 150m south of El Pueblo; open 8 AM–4 PM, daily; admission $6 per adult, $5 per student). Escape the smog and traffic at this tropical oasis, featuring more than 50 species of butterfly.

Nightlife

The nation's best nightlife is covered by local magazines like *San José Volando* (www.sanjose volando.com) and *En Tarima* (www.periodicoentarima.com). **Filtro Rock** (www.filtrorock .com) covers rock shows, while **Reggae Source** (www.reggaesourcecr.com) lists reggae events.

The city's two top party spots are **Calle Amargura** (www.calleamargura.com) in San Pedro, a strip of bars catering to the college crowd that rage from noon till dawn; and **El Pueblo**, the city's official nightlife district in Barrio Tournon, with discos that get started around 11:30 PM. Both attract a young, wild crowd, and neither area is particularly safe. But there are other options.

Club Vertigo (www.vertigocr.com; Central Colón) Top dance club, with international DJs and VIP balcony seating, gets started around 10 PM.

El Cuartel de la Boca del Monte (506-2221-0327; Av 1, Calles 21 & 23, 50m west of Cine Magaly) Dress to impress at this hip Los Yoses restaurant and bar.

Grappa (506-2203-7543; www.grappalive.com; Santa Ana, Boulevard Lindora) Elegant, low-lit Mediterranean restaurant hosts excellent bands.

★ **Jazz Café** (506-2253-8933; www.jazzcafecostarica.com; San Pedro, Av Central, next to Banco Popular) Sophisticated club just blocks from Calle Amagura offers live music nightly, usually jazz, world music, or acoustic rock.

Mac's American Bar (506-2231-3145; Sabana Sur, 100m east of the Contraloría) Watch NFL, listen to the Blues Devils Band, or enjoy some serious nachos.

Gay and Lesbian Costa Rica

Despite resistance from the Catholic Church, Costa Rica stepped out of the closet in 1971, legalizing homosexuality, and is now a top destination for gays and lesbians. Find out the latest at **Don Pato's Gay Costa Rica** (www.donscostarica.com), **Gay Costa Rica** (www.gaycostarica.com), and **OrgulloGayCR** (www.orgullogaycr.com), all with links, singles sites, and more.

If you're staying in San José, check out **Colours Oasis Resort** (506-2296-1880, 866-517-4390; www.coloursoasis.com; Rohrmoser Boulevard; $$–$$$*), with soothingly painted rooms surrounding lush gardens and a small pool; and ★**Kekoldi Hotel** (506-2248-0804, 786-221-9011 USA; www.kekoldi.com; Barrio Amón, Av 9, Calles 5 & 7; $–$$*), in an airy old Barrio Amón mansion. Both offer information and organize tours (Kekoldi operates in Nicaragua as well).

There are several nightlife options in San José, including **La Avispa** (506-2223-5343; Calle 1 between Avs 8 & 10; open Tue.–Sun.) with three dance floors, pool tables, and a lady's crowd; and **Déjà Vu** (506-2223-3758; Calle 2, Avs 14 & 16) with two dance floors where gentlemen gather, sometimes for drag shows.

San José's Plaza de la Cultura is a favorite of pigeons and the children who love them.

Motorpsycho Bar & Grill (506-2203-8361; Santa Ana, 1.8 km west of the Red Cross) Live music and the Sunday Rock & Blues Jam and BBQ, as well as Harley repair.

Cinemas

There are at least a dozen modern movie theaters in and around San José; *La Nación* has listings. Cartoons are usually dubbed into Spanish, while other movies (mostly Hollywood blockbusters) are subtitled.

A more interesting option is the **Laurence Olivier Theater** (506-2223-1960; Av 2 & Calle 28), with European and independent American films, as well as live performances by the Little Theater Group (see below). **Centro de Cine** (506-2223-2127; behind the Jade Museum) shows independent and Latin films.

Theater

Costa Ricans love live performances, with one popular joke explaining that they'll never go to war because it might harm graceful **Teatro Nacional** (506-2221-5341; www.teatronacional .go.cr; Av 2 & Calle 3; admission $5). Completed in 1897 by coffee barons eager to impress visiting Europeans, the classical Renaissance masterpiece is a symphony in marble and gold, emblazoned with fine art including *Una Alegoría* by Aleardo Villa, inspiration for the five colón note depicting the harvest of coffee and bananas, now out of circulation but available in the gift shop. It still hosts the best local and international performers, or visit on a guided tour; there's also a wonderful café. There are many other theaters in the city, including:

National Auditorium (506-2249-1208; www.museocr.com; Children's Museum) Not just for kids, this stage hosts great grownup performances, too.

Little Theater Group (506-2289-3910; www.littletheatregroup.org; Los Yoses, Eugene O'Neill Theater, North American Cultural Center) The oldest English-language performance group in Central America has performances all over town.

Teatro Giratables (506-2253-6001; www.teatrogiratablas.com; Barrio La California, Calle 31 & Central Av) Alternative, cutting edge theater.

Teatro Melico Salazar (506-2221-4952; www.teatromelico.go.cr; Av 2 & Calle Central) Restored 1928 theater hosts international acts as well as the National Youth Symphony, National Choir, National Dance Company, and National Lyric Company.

RECREATION

Parks

In addition to the **National Park** and **Parque Morazán**, covered in the Architectural Walking Tour, San José has several good green spaces. The best is **Parque La Sabana**, on the west end of town. Once the international airport, today it holds the **Museum of Costa Rican Art**, as well as the **National Stadium**, an Olympic-sized public pool ($3), the **Costa Rica Tennis Club** (506-2232-1266; www.costaricatennisclub.com; $10), and even a canopy tour.

Canopy Tours and More

Aventuras La Carpintera (506-2278-3355; www.aventuraslacarpintera.com; Trés Ríos) Just east of San José, 13-platform canopy tour has hanging bridges, rappelling, and horseback rides.

Fossil Land (506-2276-6060; www.fossillandcr.com; Quebrada Honda de Patarrá, Desamparados; open by reservation only; admission varies, $65 for most half-day activities) Challenging attraction offers guided hikes, rappelling, caving, and an obstacle course involving cliffs and rivers.

Urban Canopy (506-2223-2544; La Sabana Park; $20) Smallish seven-cable canopy tour crosses a little lake.

Day Trips

Though there's not much to do in San José proper, it makes a comfortable base for day trips and longer tours. These are just a few of the many, many offerings; your hotel can recommend several more.

★ **Costa Rica Expeditions** (www.costaricaexpeditions.com) Excellent operator runs top-notch lodges and tours in Monteverde, Tortuguero, and beyond.

CODECE (www.codece.org) Rural tourism operator offers day trips to small communities east of San José.

Costa Rica One Day Tours (506-2282-2792; 800-329-8687; costaricaonedaytours.com) More than 20 day and half-day trips from San José.

Ecole Travel (506-2223-2240; www.ecoletravel.com) Multi-day trips to the Oso Peninsula.

Expediciones Tropicales (506-2257-4171; www.costaricainfo.com) Trips to Arenal, the Central Valley, and more.

Jungle Tom Safaris (506-2221-7878; www.jungletomsafaris.com; day trip $82, one night $89–$164, two nights $119–$240) Overnights to Tortuguero.

Lava Tours (506-2281-2458; 888-862-2424 USA and Canada; www.lava-tours.com) Serious bike treks around the countryside, with active add-ons including rafting and hiking.

Learning Trips (506-2258-7840; 800-723-2674 USA and Canada; www.costa-rica.us) Education-oriented, all-inclusive tours throughout the country.

Marbella Travel & Tours (506-2227-0101; 866-251-4461 USA; www.marbellatours.com) Great day trips through the Central Valley.

Tico Train Tour (506-2233-3300; www.americatravelcr.com) Runs day trips on an old narrow-gauge train every Sunday to the port of Caldera, on the Pacific Coast.

Wild Rider (506-2258-4604; 506-2844-6568; www.wild-rider.com) Guided motorcycle tours.

Spas

Aloa Skin Care & Medical Spa (506-2588-1790; Centro Comercial Atlantis Plaza, 200m south of the San Rafael crossroads) High-tech spot offers microdermabrasion, chemical peels, Botox, and more.

Amaral (506-2228-1176; Del BAC San José, 25m norte Guachepelin de Escazú; treatments $40 and up) Top-notch medical spa does facials, massages, and non-invasive cellulite and vein treatments.

San José's sense of humor comes through in its public art, such as this cow enjoying a canopy tour.

La Barbería (506-2282-0242; Centro Comercio Via Lindora, Santa Ana; $7–$50) Men only at this classic spot, with massages, haircuts, fresh-fruit masks, and more.

Costagenics (506-2288-6362, Escazú, White House Hotel) Medical spa and "youth maintenance center" offers standard spa services and non-surgical anti-aging treatments.

Harmony Centers (506-2288-4658; www.harmonycenters.com; San Rafael de Escazú) Acupuncture, aromatherapy, and holistic medicine in addition to standard spa treatments.

Mio Derma (800-627-2537; Los Yoses, 300m south of Spoon, next to Fatima Church) Variety of massages and treatments, some geared to post-op patients; makes house calls.

SHOPPING

With an array of consumer goods filling dozens of malls and shopping centers (*centros comerciales*), San José and Escazú are where Costa Rica comes to shop. **Try Costa Rica** (www.try costarica.com/f/shopping) has a comprehensive list of San José stores.

Malls and Markets

★ **Artisans Market** (Calle 13, Av Central & 2, Plaza del la Democracia; open 8 AM–8 PM, daily) Wide selection of reasonably priced souvenirs and handicrafts makes this open-air market a fine last stop before flying away.

★ **Central Market** (Av Central, Calles 6 & 8; open 6 AM–8 PM, Mon.–Sat.) Since 1880, this building has housed more than 200 merchants selling absolutely everything. If you've visited markets in less developed Latin American countries, you may be surprised by its orderliness; meats are displayed in modern refrigeration cases, and wonderful ★ *sodas* run very clean kitchens.

Downtown Shopping District (Av Central, between Calles 6 & 9) Eight-block pedestrian mall centered on the Plaza de la Cultura is lined with stores.

Mall San Pedro (506-2283-7540; San Pedro roundabout, Fuente de la Hispanidad; open 10 AM–8 PM, daily) Most convenient mall to downtown offers four stories of movie theaters, fast food, shopping, beauty salons, and tattoo parlors.

Multiplaza Escazú (506-2289-5350; www.multiplazamall.com; Guachipelín de Escazú; open 10 AM–8 PM, daily) Costa Rica's most opulent shopping destination offers everything you'd expect to find in, say, San Jose, California.

Books

There are dozens of mostly Spanish-language bookstores in town, including popular chains like **Librería Internacional** (506-2253-9553; www.libreriainternacional.com) and **Librería Universal**, with a location in the downtown pedestrian shopping center. **Libros Nueva Década** (506-2225-8540; San Pedro, Calle Amargura) offers a great selection of academia, fiction, and poetry.

Mora Books (506-2255-4136; Av 1 & Calle 3) Stacks of used English-language paperbacks, magazines, comics, guidebooks, CDs, DVDs.

Papyrus News & Gifts (800-738-4782; Alajuela, Cartago, Heredia, San José) Chain offers English-language magazines and newspapers; one outlet is across from the Gold Museum, downtown.

★ **Seventh Street Books** (506-2256-8251; Calle 7, Av Central & Av 1) The best English-language bookstore in the country stocks almost every book about Costa Rica in existence, scores of guidebooks, and a wide selection of thoughtfully chosen fiction, history, science, and political tomes.

Clothing

ReciclArte (www.terranostra-cr.org; 300m south of Multiplaza Escazú) Women's collective makes clothing and jewelry from soda pull-tabs and other recyclables.

Diamantes & Esmeraldas S.A. (506-2232-6795; South Sabana, 100m east, 50m south) Deals on Colombian emeralds and other jewelry.

The Leather Outlet Factory (506-2237-6574; Heredia) Call for free transportation to tour this Del Río leather factory, then stop to shop.

Galleries

The art scene has exploded in recent years, and you can visit a variety of galleries and studios on the **Costa Rica Art Tour** (506-2359-5571; www.costaricaarttour.com).

Arte Latino (506-2258-3306; Av 1, Calle 5) National and Latino artists.

Beisanz Woodworks (506-2228-6747; www.biesanz.com; San Miguel de Escazú) Truly fine hardwood bowls and boxes.

TEOR/éTica (506-2233-4881; www.teoretica.org; Barrio Amón; 400m north of Kiosco Morazán) Interesting installation pieces and wild original art.

★ **Galería Namu** (506-2256-3412; www.galerianamu.com; Av 7, Calles 5 & 7) Original art, Boruca masks, and other high quality offerings with an emphasis on women's and indigenous art.

Galería-Restaurante Brujas de Mercurio (506-2253-5342; San Pedro, Calle Amargura) Cool café and gallery offers Mediterranean food, art, and live music.

EVENTS

March

National Orchid Show (second weekend in March; 506-2223-6517; www.ticorquideas .com) Thousands of orchids on display.

Boyeros Day (Second Sunday in March, Escazú) Oxcart drivers parade their *carretas* to San Antonio Church.

June

San José Music Festival (506-2224-6266) Concerts all over town.

September

International Festival of the Arts (506-2223-6361) Showcases actors, artists, and other performers from all over the world.

November

National Dance Festival (first two weeks in November; www.teatromelicosalazar.go.cr) Dance troupes show their stuff.

December

Zapote Fiestas (Zapote; last week of December and first week of February) One of the country's most famous *topes*, or horse parades, as well as rodeos, fireworks, live music, carnival rides, and beer.

Costa Rican Military Abolition Day (December 1) The National Museum celebrates Costa Rica's brave commitment to peace.

The Central Valley's rich volcanic soil is carpeted with the world's finest coffee.

CENTRAL VALLEY

Misty Green Soul of the Nation

Costa Rica's cultural heart has always been the Central Valley, with a mild climate and rich volcanic soil that invited the region's first inhabitants to settle here some 3,000 years ago. The Spaniards, too, chose these fertile slopes as the site of their four great cities: Alajuela, today home to the international airport; Cartago, the original Spanish seat of government; Heredia, the "City of Flowers," now a high-tech hub; and San José, the current capital (with its own chapter, earlier). Together, they form the nation's urban nucleus, home to a combined 2.5 million people, more than half of Costa Rica's total population.

These cities are surrounded by beautiful, high-altitude natural areas, connecting each city, via the nation's best road system, to sites such as simmering Poás and Irazú Volcano National Parks, easily visited, or more challenging peaks like Cerro Chirripó, Costa Rica's tallest mountain. The steep and well-watered highlands are marbled with rivers and waterfalls, which pour from the peaks into some of the world's best white-water rafting runs. The cloud forests here offer excellent hiking and better birding than Monteverde, with just a fraction of the tourists.

Scattered through the primary forests and endless coffee plantations are several Colonial towns centered on graceful old churches, where you could enroll in Spanish classes or polish up your woodworking skills. Beautiful boutique hotels will massage every care away, while rustic nature lodges offer opportunities to enjoy the outdoors.

This chapter is divided into different sections, reflecting each area's position relative to San José, at the center of it all. Alajuela, "Costa Rica's Second City," offers a Colonial center rapidly modernizing as its importance as a travel hub grows. North of San José includes Heredia, home to Britt Coffee, Costa Rica's answer to Starbucks; as well as the cloud-forested Poás region, with family-friendly attractions.

West of San José are cute Colonial villages including Grecia, Sarchí, and Zarcero, heirs to recipes and craftsmanship handed down for generations. East of San José is a wilder region, including cultured Cartago and its massive basilica; but also tiny towns like Orosí, a quaint coffee-growing village with the country's oldest church; San Gerardo de Dota, with great lodges, better coffee, and the promise of quetzals; and Turrialba, with white-water rafting and archaeological parks.

This relatively rainy, high-altitude region gets chilly, so be sure to dress appropriately, packing a jacket and long pants despite the tropical latitudes.

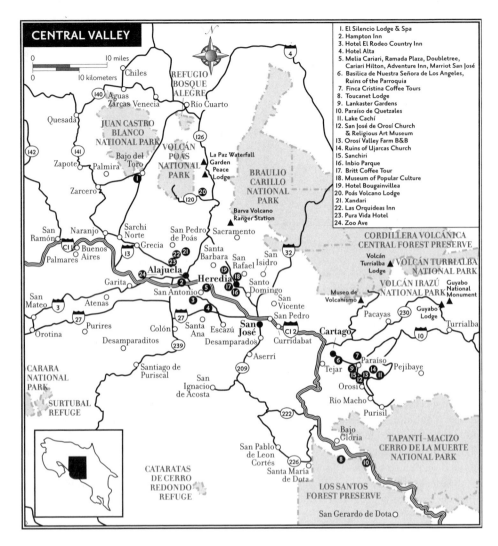

CENTRAL VALLEY

1. El Silencio Lodge & Spa
2. Hampton Inn
3. Hotel El Rodeo Country Inn
4. Hotel Alta
5. Melia Cariari, Ramada Plaza, Doubletree, Cariari Hilton, Adventure Inn, Marriot San José
6. Basilica de Nuestra Señora de Los Angeles, Ruins of the Parroquia
7. Finca Cristina Coffee Tours
8. Toucanet Lodge
9. Lankaster Gardens
10. Paraíso de Quetzales
11. Lake Cachí
12. San José de Orosí Church & Religious Art Museum
13. Orosí Valley Farm B&B
14. Ruins of Ujarcas Church
15. Sanchiri
16. Inbio Parque
17. Britt Coffee Tour
18. Museum of Popular Culture
19. Hotel Bougainvillea
20. Poás Volcano Lodge
21. Xandari
22. Las Orquideas Inn
23. Pura Vida Hotel
24. Zoo Ave

GETTING AROUND

Air

Juan Santamaría International Airport (SJO; 506-2437-2400, 506-2437-2626 information), the country's most important airport, is located in Alajuela, 16 kilometers (10 miles) from San José. The recently expanded terminal is easy to navigate and has several restaurants and souvenir shops. You must pay your $26 exit tax at the bank before checking in. This is a major Latin American hub, with direct flights to cities throughout the Americas, as well as several European cities.

Airport Transportation

Official airport taxis (506-2221-6865) are orange and charge $5 to Alajuela, $20 to San José. You can also make reservations with **Interbus** (506-2283-5573; www.interbusonline .com), which offers $6 transfers to area hotels. Many hotels in Alajuela and San José include or arrange airport transfers. Rental car companies send representatives to pick you up outside the terminal.

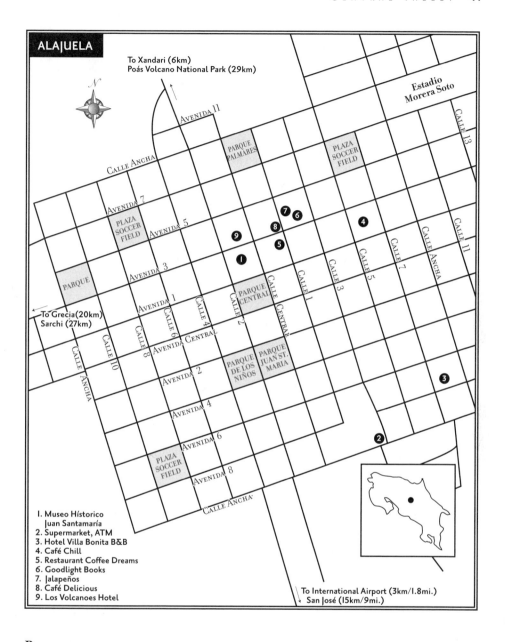

ALAJUELA

To Xandari (6km)
Poás Volcano National Park (29km)

Estadio
Morera Soto

AVENIDA 11

CALLE ANCHA

PARQUE
PALMARES

PLAZA
SOCCER
FIELD

CALLE 13

AVENIDA 7

PLAZA
SOCCER
FIELD

AVENIDA 5

❼ ❻
❽
❾
❺
❶

❹

CALLE 11

CALLE ANCHA

AVENIDA 3

PARQUE

CALLE 9

CALLE 7

CALLE 5

To Grecia (20km)
Sarchi (27km)

AVENIDA 1

CALLE 6

CALLE 8

CALLE 4

AVENIDA CENTRAL

CALLE 2

PARQUE
CENTRAL

CALLE CENTRAL

CALLE 1

CALLE 3

CALLE 10

CALLE ANCHA

AVENIDA 2

PARQUE
DE LOS
NIÑOS

PARQUE
JUAN ST.
MARÍA

AVENIDA 4

❸

AVENIDA 6

❷

PLAZA
SOCCER
FIELD

AVENIDA 8

CALLE ANCHA

1. Museo Histórico
   Juan Santamaría
2. Supermarket, ATM
3. Hotel Villa Bonita B&B
4. Café Chill
5. Restaurant Coffee Dreams
6. Goodlight Books
7. Jalapeños
8. Café Delicious
9. Los Volcanoes Hotel

To International Airport (3km/1.8mi.)
San José (15km/9mi.)

Bus

The Central Valley is connected by the best road system in the country, and public buses run between major cities and towns regularly. Private shuttle companies do not serve most of the Central Valley, although all of them can arrange transportation to the beaches and Northern Zone from either Alajuela or San José.

From Alajuela, you can catch public buses to Guanacaste and the Pacific Coast (tell the taxi driver to drop you at "La Parada de Radial"), or to the Northern Zone from the Alajuela Bus Terminal; either trip is a $5-cab-ride from the airport. For other destinations, you'll need to go to San José. Any hotel or tour desk can help you with schedules and bus terminals,

Online Resources

I Costa Rica Link (I-costaricalink.com) The Central Valley lacks good English-language Web sites, but this sprawling site covering the entire country offers excellent regional information. Also check out **Go Visit Costa Rica** (www.govisitcostarica.com).

Cartago Virtual (www.cartagovirtual.com) Spanish-language guide to Cartago.

Orosí Valley (www.orosivalley.com) Spanish-language site offers prices, pictures, and links to Orosí-area hotels and attractions.

San Ramón Guide (www.sanramon-costarica.com) A realty company put together this nifty English-language guide to San Ramón.

Zarcero Turismo (www.zarcero.co.cr) Spanish-language site has events listings, articles, and photo galleries.

or check the **Bus Schedule** (www.thebusschedule.com) and **Avenida Central** (www.avenidacentral.com) online.

Rental Car

This is an excellent region to explore on your own, as many roads are paved (if potholed) and well signed. Make sure to get a good map; I like the outdated but still excellent *National Geographic Costa Rica Map* ($10).

Roads in this mountainous region can be narrow, winding, slick, and cloudy, which when combined with slow-moving trucks and kamikaze Costa Rican drivers, spells trouble. The stretch of the InterAmericana southeast of San José that climbs Cerro Muerte ("Mountain of Death," *ahem*) is particularly dangerous, with fog, jackknifed trucks, and multiple-car pileups. Please drive defensively and be patient; trust me, there's another slow-moving caravan of trucks right in front of the one you're trying to pass.

LODGING

Though the Central Valley is home to the majority of Costa Rica's population, including large expatriate communities, it has a relatively limited range of accommodations. Alajuela and Heredia have dozens of hotels, but Cartago offers only one that can be recommended. Sarchí, a major shopping destination, also lacks hotels geared to international travelers. However, there are wonderful lodges and beautiful bed-and-breakfasts in destination towns such as Orosí, San Gerardo de Dota, and Turrialba, as well as stunning options surrounding the national parks and protected areas.

If you're in a pinch, most tiny towns offer basic *cabinas*, with thin mattresses and hopefully hot showers, which are more comfortable than sleeping in the car.

Lodging Price Code

Cost of lodging is based on an average per-room, double-occupancy rate at peak season (December through April). Costa Rica's 16.39 percent tax and gratuities are not included. Rates are often reduced during the Green Season (May through November). An asterisk denotes that a full breakfast is included with the room price.

Inexpensive ($)	Up to $50
Moderate ($$)	$50 to $100
Expensive ($$$)	$100 to $200
Very Expensive ($$$$)	Over $200

Hotels

ALAJUELA AND THE SURROUNDING AREA

★ MARRIOTT SAN JOSÉ

Manager: Christian Bocam
506-2298-0844; 800-228-9290 USA and
Canada
www.marriott.com
San Antonio de Belén, 700m west of the
Firestone
Price: Very Expensive
Credit Cards: Yes
Handicap Access: Yes

Rising from the immaculately landscaped
gardens covering what was formerly a 12-
hectare (30-acre) coffee hacienda, this is
one of Latin America's finest hotels. The
theme is Spanish Colonial, and as you enter
the sweeping lobby of arch-framed vistas,
thick rugs, and elegant furnishings, you'll
be treated to museum-quality artifacts such
as Peruvian *santos* (religious sculptures),
Mexican ceramics, and Guatemalan
antiques.

The lavish property offers a fitness center, spa, two pools (one heated), three tennis courts, Jacuzzi, driving range, a full
business center with translation services,
and several lovely shops, including one that
will plan your wedding at their gorgeous little California mission-style chapel. Rooms
are flawless, with tiny balconies offering
stunning views, 300-count Egyptian cotton
sheets, mp3/iPod-ready stereo system, and
enormous plasma TVs that work with your
computer. Of four restaurants on-site, the
best is top-rated **La Isabella Tapas & Wine
Bar** (506-2298-0145; open 6 PM—10 PM,
daily; $$$–$$$$), designed to resemble a
Colonial-era wine cellar, with a menu of
elegant Spanish cuisine.

ORQUIDEAS INN

Owner: Gary Stubbs
506-2433-9346
www.orquideasinn.com
info@orquideasinn.com

About 7 km north of Alajuela; Web site has
map
Price: Moderate to Expensive
Credit Cards: Yes
Handicap Access: Challenging

Just 10 minutes from the airport, this oasis
of tropical Costa Rica offers great value on
clean, colorful rooms scattered through the
gardens and groves. Avoid the inexpensive
roadside rooms, which can be noisy, and go
for a "superior room", with soothing views
of the gardens and mountains from a porch
furnished with Sarchí rocking chairs.
Rooms are all air-conditioned and cheer-
fully decorated with Guatemalan fabrics and
painted in rich tropical hues. The on-site
restaurant ($$), serves good international
and vegetarian cuisine, while "world
famous" Marilyn Monroe Bar overlooks the
lovely pool, with fish fountains. Airport
transfer is not included.

★ PURA VIDA HOTEL

Owners: Nhi Chu and Berni Jubb
506-2430-2929
www.puravidahotel.com
info@puravidahotel.com
Tuetal, 1.5 km north of Alajuela toward
Poás; make the signed left at the Punto
Rojo "Y"
Price: Moderate to Expensive*
Credit Cards: Yes
Handicap Access: Yes

Above the tiny coffee town of Tuetal, just
past Alajuela, this hotel may not look like
much from the outside. But step past the
lobby, stocked with board games and guide
books, and look out over fruit trees, flowers, and private villas in the gardens, to
Poás Volcano and the Río Itikis Valley
beyond.

Each cabin is unique, with different
sizes and prices, featuring stone terraces
and big windows designed with both views
and privacy in mind. Airy and spacious,
they have light colored tiles and walls, great

lighting, and handmade furnishings. Artistic touches—nature-themed murals throughout the property, cute ceramic frogs in the bathrooms—blend well with modern amenities including ceiling fans, coffeemakers, and one with a full kitchen. None has air-conditioning or television (you can watch TV in the common area). In addition to your excellent breakfast, you can make reservations to dine ($25) on the premises, a gourmet three-course prix fixe.

LOS VOLCANES HOTEL

Owner: Jose A. Quesada C
506-2441-0525
www.montezumaexpeditions.com/hotel
losvolcanes@racsa.co.cr
Downtown Alajuela, Av 3 between Calles Central and 2
Price: Inexpensive to Moderate*
Credit Cards: Yes
Handicap Access: Yes

Downtown Alajuela's best hotel, this well-maintained, tastefully remodeled 1920s mansion has high ceilings, gorgeous tile work, dark-polished wood, wrought iron curls, fresh flowers, free WiFi, and flawless gardens, including a friendly little fountain, breakfast nook, and hammocks. Service is excellent, and includes a tour desk and free airport shuttle. This is a budget hotel, and cheaper rooms share a bath. But the owners' commitment to high quality accommodations and great service make this a fine spot for almost anyone.

★ XANDARI HOTEL AND SPA

Owners: Sherrill and Charlene Broudy
506-2443-2020
www.xandari.com
paradise@xandari.com
4 km north of Alajuela on road to Poás; directions on the Web site
Price: Very Expensive*
Credit Cards: Yes
Handicap Access: Yes

Xandari is more than just a flawlessly executed, top-of-the-line property with inspiring views over the valley's twinkling lights. It is a work of art. The creative couple, an artist and architect, who designed the flowing main lodge and exquisite villas, have created uniquely sculptural modern bungalows, with colorful fabrics, hand-laid mosaic tiles, exquisite artwork, and beautiful hand-carved furniture. Spacious bathrooms, with glass doors opening onto the private, walled garden, make every shower divine. Spend some time outside on your freeform, flagstone patio as the sun sets over the cities.

The 16-hectare (40-acre) property, surrounded by coffee plantations, is threaded by 3 kilometers (1.8 miles) of trails that pass five pretty waterfalls in the jungle. Pretty pools, a full spa, and comfortable areas to relax and lounge make this a restful place to explore. Even if you aren't a guest, consider making reservations at their excellent fine-dining **Xandari Restaurant** ($$$$), with several healthy and vegetarian options, made with organic ingredients whenever possible.

NORTH OF SAN JOSÉ
★ FINCA ROSA BLANCA

Owner: Glen and Teri Jampol
506-2269-9392
www.fincarosablanca.com
info@fincarosablanca.com
Heredia
Price: Very Expensive*
Credit Cards: Yes
Special: Five CST Leaves

Designed by adventurous architect Francisco Rojas, this flowing white stucco edifice rises to 12-meter (40-foot) ceilings, strewn with slices of natural light that soar above a swirl of lounge-friendly built-ins, exotic gardens, eclectic art, and wonderful murals, all centered on a cozy fireplace radiating warmth across the polished wood floors.

Guests are invited to meet and greet over a gourmet meal, with much of the organic produce harvested right here. Views are outstanding and rooms are unique, all fluid art and architecture in cool white walls, tropical hardwoods, and glass windows overlooking paradise, furnished with amenities enough to satisfy even the pickiest resort aficionado. The delicious pool, with a wonderful waterfall, is wrapped in tropical gardens. An on-site spa offers massages, wraps, and other treatments. The honeymoon suite's glass enclosed tower offers incredible views. The desk can arrange all the usual area tours, as well as visits to their community-aid projects, a great way to get to know the real Costa Rica.

★ PEACE LODGE

Managers: Roy Torres, Luis Campos
506-2225-0643; 954-727-3997 USA
www.waterfallgardens.com
6 km (4 mi.) north of the signed turnoff at Vara Blanca gas station
Price: Very Expensive*
Credit Cards: Yes
Handicap Access: No

With a wholehearted embrace of the natural world, this unusual entry takes its architectural cues from forms found in the lush rain forests surrounding it. Every five-star amenity is hidden in this fairyland escape, including iPod-ready DVD players, full minibars, and more. But it is the polished tree trunks that support each hardwood-

Airport Hotels

There are wonderful lodges and bed-and-breakfasts within an hour of SJO that offer a very special first, or last, night in Costa Rica. But if you just want a comfortable bed right next to the airport, you can do that, too.

★ **Doubletree Cariari Hilton** (506-2239-0022; doubletree1.hilton.com; San Antonio de Belén, InterAmericana; $$$$*) Recently acquired by Hilton, this architectural marvel is constructed with river-rock walls beneath arcing *palapa*-style ceilings, and offers excellent service and all possible amenities: golf, tennis, three swimming pools, gym, sauna, horses, restaurants, bars, and a casino. It's hosted prime ministers, presidents, and celebrities too numerous to list.

Garden Court Hotel & Casino (506-2443-0043; www.gardencourtairporthotel.com; InterAmericana between Alajuela and San José; $$$*) Good security, a decent pool, and immaculate U.S.-style rooms chase the homesickness away. Enjoy your complimentary breakfast at Denny's, next door.

Hampton Inn & Suites (506-2436-0000; www.hamptoninn.com; $$$) Recently purchased by Hilton, expect this solid business-class hotel, with clean, spacious rooms, equipped with WiFi and other amenities, to be spruced up.

Ramada Plaza Herradura (506-2209-9841; www.ramadaherradura.com; Herradura; $$$$*) Ramada's top-of-the-line plaza property delivers, with excellent service, corporate rooms with all expected amenities (including computers in the suites), five excellent restaurants, four truly fabulous pools, and access to Cariari Golf Club.

★ **El Rodeo Hotel** (506-2293-3909; www.elrodeohotel.com; San Antonio de Belén; $$$–$$$$*; three CST Leaves) Tucked away in a quiet spot off the soulless suburban business strip that is Carretera Belén, which connects the airport to Escazú, this gem offers excellent service, recently renovated rooms with handmade furnishings, and amenities that include telephone, WiFi, air-conditioning, and cable TV. Don't miss the nationally revered **Rodeo Steakhouse** ($$), next door.

accented suite; the river rocks used to construct the oversized gas fireplaces; and the stained glass and wrought-iron sculptures depicting details from the rain forest, that make your wilderness abode something special.

The bathrooms deserve a special mention, crafted to resemble softly lit caverns, walls hung with real tropical plants and cascading waterfalls. Each has its own Jacuzzi where you can enjoy the ambiance, while better rooms have a hot tub overlooking the rain forest. There's a good on-site restaurant, hiking trails, and free access to **La Paz Waterfall Gardens** (See Parks and Preserves), next door, both before and after opening hours.

EL SILENCIO LODGE & SPA

Manager: Adriana Castro
506-2291-3044
www.elsilenciolodge.com
info@elsilenciolodge.com
Bajos del Toro, 18 km (11 mi.) north of Sarchí
Price: Very expensive
Credit Cards: Yes
Handicap Access: Yes

Secreted away in a 300-hectare (741-acre) cloud forest preserve near Bajos del Toro, this impressive new property is focused on wellness, relaxation, and getting in touch with nature. Your personal eco-concierge arranges complimentary guided hikes daily, or try white-water rafting, mountain biking, or shopping excursions to Sarchí. The hotel is non-smoking, and three daily meals (included in the price) are gourmet Costa Rican cuisine, all made with fresh, organic ingredients.

Private cabins have been designed to blend in with the area's climate and local architecture. Each is outfitted with gas fireplaces, covered porches, and personal hot tubs, as well as spacious, elegant, and almost minimalist interiors. Only one

amenity is missing: TV. Enormous windows onto the cloud forest may make up for that. A natural spa (using pyramid power) offers massages and other treatments, and there's also a meditation garden and yoga platform, next to a sparkling stream.

VILLABLANCA HOTEL

General Manager: Jim Damalas
506-2461-0300
www.villablanca-costarica.com
North of San Ramón
Price: Expensive to Very Expensive*
Credit Cards: Yes
Handicap Access: No
Special: Five CST Leaves

Originally founded by Rodrigo Carazo Odio, president of Costa Rica from 1978 to 1982, this luxury eco-lodge has changed owners (Green Hotels, also responsible for Si Como No in Manuel Antonio) and received a luxuriously sustainable face-lift. The real reason to visit is still 840-hectare (2,000-acre) Los Angeles Cloud Forest Reserve, with more than 300 bird species amidst primary rain forest and farmland, all threaded by well-maintained trails.

Emphasis is on sustainability, yet you sacrifice nothing; there's even an on-site movie theater and spa, as well as a restaurant that gets rave reviews. Less expensive cabins resemble traditional blue-and-white campesino cottages, but inside are spacious and luxurious, with cane roofs, leather furniture, and fireplaces; the bathrooms have glass windows with views to Arenal. This is a popular spot for weddings, which can be arranged at the adorable on-site Mariana Wedding Chapel.

EAST OF SAN JOSÉ
HOTEL CASA TURIRE

Managers: Daniel and Bernadette Allemann
506-2531-2244
www.hotelcasaturire.com
turire@racsa.co.cr

La Suiza, Turialba
Price: Expensive to Very Expensive*
Credit Cards: Yes
Handicap Access: Yes
Special: Two CST Leaves

Rising from the rolling hills of rural Turri-alba like something out of *Gone with the Wind*, this plantation-style manor is the region's best hotel. Enter the ornately tiled lobby, opening onto an interior, Cuban-style courtyard, where the helpful, bilingual staff can arrange spa treatments and high-quality tours.

Common areas are rendered luxurious with lots of marble, overstuffed leather couches in the gaming room, a fabulous pool, and fresh flowers. Rooms are individually decorated, with rich wooden floors, sweeping arches supporting high ceilings, and large glass doors opening onto balconies. Nicer rooms have Jacuzzis, mini-fridges, spacious living areas, and two floors (including two balconies). The hotel's delightful French **restaurant** ($$–$$$$) offers gourmet takes on Costa Rican and international cuisine.

OROSÍ LODGE

Owners: Andy and Connie
506-2533-3578
www.orosilodge.com
info@orosilodge.com
Central Orosí, 50m east of the balneario
Price: Inexpensive to Moderate*
Credit Cards: Yes
Handicap Access: No

Perfectly situated between the thermal springs and recommended Montaña Linda Spanish School, this solid, Colonial-style midrange lodge has attractive, immaculate and airy rooms with volcano views, great bamboo furniture, minibar, coffeemaker, and hot-water showers. Some have small verandas. The **café** (open 7 AM–7 PM, daily; $–$$) serves pastries, snacks, light meals, and coffee.

★ HOTEL Y RESTAURANTE SANCHIRI

Manager: Leonel Mata Sanchez
506-2574-3870, 506-2574-5454
www.sanchiri.com
sanchiri@racsa.co.cr
Orosí, 3 km south of Paraiso Park on Orosí Hwy (224)
Price: Inexpensive
Credit Cards: Yes
Special: Three CST Leaves

This family-run, unpretentiously eco-conscious lodge is simply an outstanding value on excellent accommodations with sweeping views over the Orosí Valley. There are two types of rooms, the first hewn from polished wood, offering a more rustic ambiance and all the amenities. Second are newer, more modern rooms, with a white-washed, airy and cleanly tiled space, plus sliding-glass doors that open onto a tiny balcony and enormous views. There's a small *mariposario* (butterfly garden) and a few short trails, as well as a great typical restaurant ($$).

Bed-and-Breakfasts

AMBROSIA EN LA MONTAÑA

Jainie Murray-McKenzie
506-2533-2336
ambrosiaenlamontana.com
ambrosi@hotmail.com
2.5 km above Orosí
Price: Moderate*
Credit Cards: Yes

Ascend the coffee fields on a narrow, unpaved, winding drive (a $5 cab ride from downtown Orosí) to this cute bed-and-breakfast in the clouds. There are only two immaculate wooden cabins, with simple furnishings and polished porches where you can take in the sights from chairs or hammocks slung beneath the eaves. Bathrooms are particularly well done, with hand-painted sinks imported from Mexico, along with much of the other décor. The

Zarcero is known for its homemade snack foods, including queso palmito *(string cheese) and yummy* toronjas rellenas *(candied grapefruit).*

restaurant serves Italian-accented organic cuisine, with a good wine list.

⍟ DANTICA LODGE & GALLERY

Owners: Joost Wilms and María Luísa Castro
506-2740-1067
www.dantica.com
info@dantica.com
San Gerardo de Dota; 4 km after well-signed turnoff at Km 89 Hwy 2 (InterAmericana)
Price: Expensive to Very Expensive*
Credit Cards: Yes
Handicap Access: Limited

Could you use a break from the whole "rustic" theme? Welcome to Dantica, an outpost of European cool in the cloud forest. Each bungalow is an ultra-modern space of gleaming chrome and black leather, with big-screen plasma television, and colorful feather bedspreads, black flagstone, and whitewashed walls with black ribbed ceilings. Glass walls bring the primary cloud forest to you. One of the bungalows offers two bedrooms and a full kitchen, perfect for families (and the owners can lend you toys). Be sure to stop by their fabulous gift shop, and hike the 2.5 kilometers (1.5 miles) of trails through 9-hectare (22-acre) private Reserva Forestal Los Santos, which begins just steps away from the bungalows.

OROSÍ VALLEY FARM

Owner: Ray Reynolds
506-2533-3001; 866-369-7871 USA and Canada
Orosí, 1 km north of town
www.orosivalleyfarm
Price: Inexpensive*
Credit Cards: Not yet, but plans to accept them
Handicap Access: No

About halfway into your descent from Paraíso into the Orosí Valley, this simple but sweet bed-and-breakfast is surrounded by gorgeous gardens, including an orchid collection, with wonderful views. Three comfortable if not luxurious rooms are cheerfully painted and eclectically decorated by the Kentucky-born host, with jewel-toned bedspreads, creative lighting, hammocks, and Sarchí furniture. The largest family room sleeps five, with a full kitchen. In the evening, you can sit out on your private porch and watch the sun set over one of the prettiest little places in Costa Rica.

Nature Lodges

POÁS VOLCANO LODGE

Owner: Michael Cannon
506-2482-2194
www.poasvolcanolodge.com
info@poasvolcanolodge.com
Vara Blanca, road to Poás Volcano
Price: Moderate to Expensive*
Credit Card: Yes
Handicap Access: No
Special: Two CST Leaves

A fern-strewn stone path leads to the entrance of this cozy stone and wood lodge, surrounded by dairy farms on the chilly cloud-forested skirts of Volcán Poás. An enormous sunken fireplace, a wall of natural rock, and comfortable sofas and chairs invite you to enjoy all sorts of games (pool, Ping-Pong, and board games), or perhaps a good book and WiFi access. Trails range into the garden, farm, and surrounding forest; you could see a quetzal on the hotel grounds. Perfect.

They offer a range of rooms; the two cheapest are tiny but tastefully decorated, and share a bathroom. Go for one of the spacious, rustic junior suites, with natural rock wall, bathtub, teakettle, and nicer views. The master suite is even nicer, with a Jacuzzi.

★ QUETZAL PARAISO

Owner: Jorge Serrano
506-2200-5915

www.exploringcostarica.com/mirador /quetzales.html
selvamar@ice.co.cr
Km 70, Hwy 2 (InterAmericana)
Price: Inexpensive to Moderate*
Credit Cards: Yes
Handicap Access: No

This modest, family-run ecolodge next to Quetzales National Park offers a clutch of tidy, tiny A-frame chalets overlooking a 2,600-meter (8,530-foot) altitude protected primary-forest *paraiso* (paradise), and the pretty village of Santa Marta. The simple pine cabins have decent beds, hot-water showers, and small bird paintings throughout, plus a few hand-hewn pieces of furniture packed in where possible.

You can also enjoy the vista from the cozy lodge, with a TV, sitting area, and porch, where you can watch hummingbirds so numerous that they sound like helicopters. Or descend into the cloud forest along their 4 kilometers (2.5 miles) of trails; there's a free, guided quetzal hike at 6 AM daily. Breakfast and dinner, cooked on a wood stove, are included and served family style. Day-trippers are welcome to use the trails ($6).

EL TOUCANET LODGE

Owners: Edna and Gary
506-2541-3045
www.eltoucanet.com
reserve@etoucanet.com
Copey de Dota, 8.5 km from Santa María de Dota
Price: Moderate to Expensive*
Credit Cards: Yes
Handicap Access: No

Devoted birders, or anyone in search of a beautiful spot in the bucolic Costa Rican countryside should consider making the ear-popping drop into this peaceful valley below Los Santos Forest Reserve and Los Quetzales National Park. Quetzals, most common December through April, are the big draw, and El Toucanet offers a free "quetzal hunt" on their private network of nature trails every morning year round. With more than 200 other bird species spotted in the area, you're sure to find something worth photographing.

Sweet and simple private cabins offer pleasant furnishings, soothing lighting, plus your own private porch for appreciating the view. Two junior suites come complete with fireplace, Jacuzzi, coffeemaker, and mini-fridge. They also have a wood-fired Jacuzzi outdoors, but a minimum of four people must make the request in advance.

Other Hotels

CARTAGO

Hotel Las Brumas (506-2553-3535; www .hotellasbrumas.com; 2 km east of Puente Beily on the road to Volcán Irazú; $–$$*) Cartago's downtown hotels are downright scary, but just above the city, this clean, new hotel offers ordinary, but very comfortable rooms with WiFi, phones, cable TV, and even small balconies boasting great city views.

SARCHÍ

Unfortunately, Sarchí doesn't have any hotels geared to foreign tourists, but comfortable, basic *cabinas* abound, including **Cabinas de Montaña Mananatial** (506-2364-8673; 300m toward Naranjo from Sarchí Norte gas station; $) or **Cabinas Mandy** (506-28140-1555; 400m north of the gas station, Calle al Estadio).

CIUDAD QUESADA

Hotel Loma Verde (506-2460-1976; emilie mendez@gmail.com; $*; MC, V) There's little reason to stay in Ciudad Quesada, but this clean, brightly decorated hotel with hot water, cable TV, and a small pool table in the outdoor common area is your best bet. It's well signed from La Fortuna, about 1 kilometer (0.6 mile) before town. Or try Ter-

males del Bosque (see Hot Springs, later in this chapter), just 12 kilometers (7 miles) from town.

RESTAURANTS AND FOOD PURVEYORS

Though there are a few excellent eateries in Alajuela and Heredia, the Central Valley is not known for its elegant international cuisine. The best gourmet restaurants are found at upscale hotels and lodges; otherwise, you'll be enjoying Costa Rican cuisine at *sodas* scattered throughout the region. Do yourself a favor and pull over at one of the *mirador* (viewpoint) restaurants perched atop the dramatic forested valleys, at least for a cup of coffee.

Restaurant and Food Purveyor Price Code

The following prices are based on the cost of a dinner entrée with a non-alcoholic drink, not including the 13 percent taxes and 10 percent gratuity added to the cost of almost all restaurant meals (except for the very cheapest *sodas*). Menus note whether or not their listed prices include this hefty 23 percent total surcharge, some listing two sets of prices.

Inexpensive ($)	Up to $5
Moderate ($$)	$5 to $10
Expensive ($$$)	$10 to $20
Very Expensive ($$$$)	$20 or more

Restaurants

ALAJUELA

It's only 20 minutes to San José and Escazú, with many more fine dining options. You could also grab a cab up to **Xandari Hotel** for fine dining with a view, or the **Marriott**, with several good restaurants.

ANTONIO RISTORANTE

506-2293-0622
Between Hotel Herradura and the Meliá

Enjoy the clouds, not the crowds, at Quetzal Paraiso's cute cabinas.

Cariari on the InterAmericana
Price: Expensive
Cuisine: Italian
Serving: L, D, weekdays; D, Sat. and Sun.
Credit Cards: Yes
Reservations: Yes

Conveniently located on the strip of high-end hotels east of town, this fine dining restaurant offers excellent Italian cuisine in upscale environs. Antonio, a veteran of several upscale Italian joints in New York City, now serves good pizzas and pastas, though the specialty is grilled meats and seafood dishes; try the calamari. There's a good wine list, live piano music, and a cigar bar.

CAFÉ CHILL PURA CRÊPE

506-2432-5767
Alajuela, 100m east, 25m north of Red Cross
Price: Moderate
Cuisine: Crêpes
Serving: L, D
Credit Cards: No
Reservations: No

Thin, delicious crêpes are internationally themed, such as the *Norwega*, which is Spanish for "Norwegian," (with salmon, lemon, and sour cream sauce), México (guacamole, onion, jalapeño, and cheese), and many more. If you can still handle the religious music blasting through the dining room, don't skip one of their dessert crêpes—the Tica, with chantilly cream, chocolate, and banana, is out of this world.

★ JALAPEÑOS CENTRAL

506-2430-4027
Downtown, 50m south of the post office
Closed: Sun.
Price: Inexpensive to Moderate
Cuisine: Tex-Mex
Serving: L, D
Handicap Access: No
Reservation: No

Oddly enough, one of the best Mexican restaurants in Costa Rica is run by a friendly Colombian New Yorker, who offers excellent takes on Tex-Mex classics such as chimichangas, enchiladas, and "supernachos," using serious spices, unlike most Costa Rican cuisine. Prices are good and the dining area relaxed, with views onto Alajuela's street scene.

RANCHO SAN MIGUEL

506-2438-0849
4 km (2.5 mi.) north of La Guácima
Price: Very Expensive
Cuisine: Costa Rican
Serving: D, Fri. and Sat. only
Credit cards: Yes
Reservations: Yes

This working horse ranch, which also arranges lessons and horseback riding treks on their Andalusian steeds, offers a festive dinner show on weekend nights. A big buffet featuring barbecue and Tico cuisine is served, while you enjoy the spectacle of these beautiful horses showing their mastery of Quadrilles dressage and other skills. There's a brief introduction to Costa Rican culture as well, and live music. Costs include transportation from your hotel.

NORTH OF SAN JOSÉ
LA LLUNA DE VALENCIA

506-2269-6665
www.lallunadevalencia.com
San Pedro de Barva de Heredia
Price: Expensive to Very Expensive
Cuisine: Spanish
Serving: D, Mon.–Sat.; L, Fri.–Sun.
Credit Cards: Yes
Reservations: Yes

Excellent restaurant is usually considered Heredia's best, in a fine old wood-framed house where you can sample the best paella in the country. Many people come to sample something off the outstanding wine list, with most vintages from Spain, then pick a few plates from the tapas menu. But there are also seafood dishes, best enjoyed with plenty of sangria, and other Iberian specialties.

JAULARES

506-482-2155
Fraijanes, on the road to Poás
Price: Moderate
Cuisine: Costa Rican
Serving: L, D
Credit Cards: Yes
Reservations: No

The tiny towns toward the top of Poás Volcano have several *sodas* and basic *cabinas*, many offering trout fishing, geared toward Ticos escaping the city. This is one of the best, with a rustic dining room bedecked in cloud-forest greenery, serving great typical cuisine, including *casados*, *gallos*, steak, and trout dishes, all perfectly prepared. They also rent basic cabins.

As long as you're up here, keep an eye open for roadside produce stands, often offering the region's famed strawberries.

REFUGIO DEL CHEF JACQUES

506-2237-9115
Heredia, 3.5 km north of Plaza de Barva
Price: Expensive
Cuisine: French
Serving: L, D
Credit Cards: Yes
Reservations: Yes

Within a romantic wooden cottage in the bucolic countryside, this out-of-the-way restaurant serves Heredia's finest French cuisine, with a view. Service is good, the ambiance cozy, and the wine list very good.

WEST OF SAN JOSÉ
Zarcero is well known for its amazing snack foods, sold at stands along the roads into town. Try *queso palmito*, balls of string mozzarella cheese or *cajetas*, homemade sweets. Adventurous eaters might enjoy a *toronja rellena*, hollowed-out, candied grapefruit rind stuffed with a rich, sweet, cheesy *cajeta*-style filling.

LA FIESTA DEL MAÍZ
506-2487-5757
Garita de Alajuela, between Alajuela and Orotina
Price: Inexpensive
Cuisine: Costa Rican
Serving: L, D
Credit Cards: No
Reservations: No

This landmark place packs 'em in on weekends, when families come to partake in the "Festival of Corn." Most items on the menu—served steam-table buffet style, just point and they'll serve—involve corn, including the very typical *chorreadas*, a thick, sweet tortilla made with fresh corn, to *pozole*, a stew with hominy, vegetables, and pork.

If the Fiesta is just too crowded, continue down the road to **Las Delicias del Maíz** (506-2433-4646; L, D, daily, B, L, D weekends; $$), which offers many of the same exciting incarnations of corn, but in a mellower environment.

EAST OF SAN JOSÉ
CASA VIEJA
506-2591-1165
Cartago, at Lankaster Garden entrance
Price: Expensive
Cuisine: Costa Rican
Serving: L, D, Tue.–Sun.
Credit Cards: Yes
Reservations: No

Worth a stop when visiting Lankaster Gardens, or heading south to Orosí, this elegantly restored old mansion offers gourmet Costa Rican cuisine in style, along with excellent coffee.

CASONA DE CAFETAL
506-2533-3280
Orosí, at Cachí Lake
Price: Moderate

Orosí's 1561 Convento San Francisco San José, most recently remodeled in 1743, is probably Costa Rica's oldest church.

The wonderful topiary of Zarcero's Francisco Alvarado Park was created by Evangelisto Blanco.

Cuisine: Costa Rican
Serving: L, D
Credit Cards: Yes
Reservations: No

You can't miss this landmark restaurant as you make the scenic drive from Orosí around Lake Cachí. The wonderfully rustic open-air dining serves local specialties such as trout from the surrounding streams, as well as high-quality typical dishes and a fabulous Sunday brunch buffet. Work up an appetite (or work off their coffee, which is grown all around here) on their short trails, with wonderful lake views.

POLLO A LA LEÑA EL CLON

506-2532-1228
South of Turrialba, on the road to Cartago
Price: Inexpensive to moderate
Cuisine: Costa Rican
Serving: B, L, D
Credit Cards: Yes
Reservations: No

This family-owned restaurant, with a wonderfully rustic dining room and views to the surrounding hills and volcanoes, specializes in *pollo a la leña* (wood-fired chicken) and other typical cuisine. And while you wait for your food, check out their fascinating displays (developing into a museum) that pay homage to the once mighty railway system. Photos dating to the 1860s document the challenges that faced those who laid the tracks to Limón. The gardens out back have sections of track, railroad signs, and a small room of railway artifacts and more photos. Proprietors can even arrange a five-hour guided hike to see abandoned trains and old stretches of railway.

RESTAURANT 1910

506-2536-7717
Cartago, 300m north of Cot-Pacayas intersection, toward Irazú Volcano
Price: Moderate
Cuisine: Costa Rican

Serving: L, D
Reservations: No

History buffs can make a pit stop here, in conjunction with a trip to Irazú National Park. The walls of the rustic dining room, where you'll enjoy above-average típico including excellent *chorreadas*, are covered with photos, newspaper clippings, and other artifacts of the 1910 earthquake that leveled colonial Cartago.

Food Purveyors

Bakeries

Le Mirage (506-2443-1706; Alajuela, diagonal from Centro Commercial La Estación, 400m west of Catholic church) Fabulous cakes and fine pastries.

Pastelería Merayo (506-2556-6060; 200m from Central Park) Turrialba's favorite bakery does cakes, breads, and pastries without preservatives or chemicals.

Repostería and Panadería El Gran Pan (Orosí south side of plaza) Basic bakery in Orosí.

Cafés

Coffee Dreams (506-2430-3970; Alajuela; Av 3 & Calle 1; 8 AM–8 PM, Mon.–Sat., 11 AM–7 PM, Sun.; $) Cozy and homey, decked out in souvenir plates, dolls, and other frills, perfect for coffee, pastries, quiches, tamales, and more.

Cafeteria (506-2454-1497; Sarchí, across from ICE) In addition to espresso beverages, enjoy typical Costa Rican food or a *pupusa* (a Salvadorian specialty, basically a thick corn tortilla stuffed with meat, cheese, or beans, then grilled), perhaps at their lunch buffet.

Gran Oporto Café (506-2263-2059; Heredía, behind Hipermás) Light meals, sandwiches, and other café fare.

Mirador del Cafetal (506-2446-7361; www.cafetal.com; 5 km north of Atenas; B, L; $) Attached to a cute bed-and-breakfast ($$*) in the coffee fields, offers coffee and light meals with a view.

Sodas

Chubascos (506-2444-2280; 16 km from Alajuela on the road to Poás Volcano; $$) Grab a hillside table and enjoy the views over a casado and smoothie made with fresh local strawberries.

Soda Gimbel (Downtown Heredia, 425m north of the Catholic Church, across from the high school; $) Serving what some folks swear are the best *casados* in Costa Rica, this basic little *soda* offers excellent value.

Restaurant/Bar Coto (Orosí; Central Park) Right on the plaza, looks great.

Restaurant Los Helechos (506-2454-4560; Sarchí Sur, Plaza de la Artesania; $$) Tico classics and decent Mexican food are served in a cute courtyard underneath umbrellas.

Soda La Garza (Downtown Turrialba, Central Park; $–$$) Cozy restaurant and bar serves the best *casados* in town next to big windows with a view on the bustle.

Soda El Rancho (Orosí; $$) Right on the town square, this self-consciously rustic *soda* does great typical food in an open-air dining room next to the church and museum.

Mi Tierra (506-2553-3535; Cartago, 2 km east of Puente Beily, Carretera to Volcán Irazú; $–$$) Enjoy excellent comida tipíca, including great *chorreadas* at this cozy *soda* overlooking Cartago, Costa Rica's original capital, on the road to Irazú Volcano.

Grocery Stores

Megasuper (Alajuela; across from the central park; open 8 AM—9 PM daily) The biggest grocery store in town has a Cirrus/ Plus ATM.

Super Market (Orosí; 300m south of central park) The valley's biggest grocer is fairly
small; neighboring fruit stands and a Musmanni bakery help. Paraíso has several huge
grocery stores.

Supermercado Selection (Sarchí; 100m east of central park) is larger, but **Pequeño Super**
(506-2454-4136) delivers.

Pizza

Cafeluna (506-2352-0080; Downtown Cartago, 100m south and 50m east of the court-
house; L, D, Mon.–Sat.; $$$) With a warm and pleasant dining room quite popular with
locals at lunch, this is a fine place for a pie, some pasta, or a few Mexican-themed dishes
after visiting the church and ruins.

Charlie's (506-2557-6565; Downtown Turrialba) This pizza place delivers.

Las Fresas (506-2482-2620; www.lasfresas.com; 5 km south of Fraijanes; L, D; $$–$$$)
This well-signed Italian eatery toward the top of Poás Volcano offers wood-fired pizzas,
pastas, steaks, and other dishes.

CULTURE

The Central Valley is home to Costa Rica's finest collection of churches and plazas, most
built in the late 1500s and leveled by earthquakes and volcanoes several times since.

Museums

★ CONVENTO SAN FRANCISCO SAN JOSÉ DE OROSÍ

506-2533-3051
Dowtown Orosí
Open: 9 AM—noon, 1 PM—5 PM, Tue.–Sun
Admission: $.75 per adult; $.50 per student

Considered Costa Rica's oldest church, this classic Spanish Colonial beauty was originally
built in 1561 and remodeled in 1699 and 1743. The squat, *tejas* (tile)-topped, mission-style
structure, surrounding a pretty courtyard, was declared a national monument in 1920. The
hand-hewn hardwood ceiling gracing the simple interior sets off the beautifully carved
altar.

Attached is a surprisingly good museum of religious art, with a small collection of richly
toned religious paintings from Mexico, silver pieces brought from Spain, unnecessarily
elaborate antique furniture, and several *santos* (carved wooden saints), including a very
nice Virgin from Guatemala. Most signage is in Spanish.

MUSEO DE CULTURA INDÍGENA KURIETÍ

506-2573-7113
West of Cartago, 4 km from the El Quijongo exit on the road to Tobosí del Guarco
Open: 9 AM—5 PM, Wed.–Mon.
Admission: $2

This tiny museum is one man's attempt to preserve what little remains of the Kurietí culture, including cooking utensils and other tools, medicinal plants, burial rituals, and illustrated legends. Admission includes a guided tour (Spanish only) by owner Angel Ramirez.

MUSEO DE CULTURA POPULAR

506-2260-1619
www.ilam.org/cr/museoculturapopular
Heredia, Santa Lucía de Barva
Open: 9 AM–4 PM, daily
Admission: $2

Great little museum is a real boon for architecture buffs, who will enjoy seeing a real Colonial plantation mansion restored to its former glory, complete with period furnishings and docents decked out in the outfits of the age. Displays show how the *bahareque*-style adobe home was refurbished using century-old tools and techniques. There's a small *soda* on-site, selling wood-fired typical cuisine.

MUSEO OMAR SALAZAR OBANDO REGIONAL MUSEUM

506-2558-3615
Turrialba, at the University of Costa Rica
Open: 9 AM–noon, 1 PM–4 PM, Tue.–Sat.
Admission: $2

Before taking in the ruins at Guayabo, stop at this small university museum that preserves many indigenous artifacts, many salvaged from archaeological sites that were flooded by the 2000 damming of Lake Angosura. Signage is mostly in Spanish.

★ NOCHEBUENA MUSEUM OF VULCANICITY

volcanirazu@mac.com
Outside Irazú Volcano National Park
Open: 9 AM–3:30 PM, daily
Admission: Museum $4 per adult; $2 per child; trail access $3

Geared toward kids with brightly colored displays explaining how volcanoes and plate tectonics work, this museum is worth visiting just for the movie (with English subtitles) about Irazú's 1963 eruption. Harrowing footage of people fleeing huge clouds of ash, and later working round the clock to manage the deadly threat of floods and mudslides, offer insight into the serious business of volcano management. There's a beautiful, glass-enclosed restaurant on site (B, L; $$) and 2 kilometers (1.2 miles) of trails through the almost Alpine environs (10,000 feet).

JUAN SANTAMARÍA MUSEUM

506-2441-4775
Alajuela, Calle 2 and Av 6
Open: 10 AM–6 PM, Tue.–Sun.
Admission: $2
Special: Temporarily closed for renovation at press time; prices and hours may change.

This museum, in a gorgeous old Colonial home, is dedicated to Alajuela's favorite son, hero Juan Santamaría, and his role in the 1856 defeat of U.S. mercenary William Walker (see Santa Rosa National Park, in the Guanacaste and Nicoya chapter). The museum contains artifacts from the battle and interesting displays on Alajuela history, but was closed at press time for renovations.

Spanish Churches and Ruins

This was once the center of Spanish settlement, and boasts Costa Rica's finest *iglesias* (churches). Some have crumbled as volcanoes rumbled, but their photogenic facades remain.

Though most people come for the handicrafts, Sarchí's church is a beauty.

Basílica de Nuestra Señora de Los Ángeles (Cartago) Stately Byzantine basilica is home to Costa Rica's patron saint, La Virgen de Los Angeles, better known as La Negrita, the Black Madonna. She chose the site of this church herself, appearing here to a young indigenous girl in 1635. Despite attempts to move her, the Virgin always mysteriously returned, so they built a chapel on the spot.

After Cartago lost the 1823 Civil War, and the capital moved to San José, the victors once again tried to remove the Virgin. La Negrita would have none of it, however, and stubbornly reappeared right here. And by Her mandate, Cartago remains the spiritual capital of the country, a point of pilgrimage every August 2, when folks from around Costa Rica come to pay their respects.

Catedral de la Mercedes (Grecia) After their first two churches were destroyed by earthquake and fire, Grecians commissioned this unusual 1897 Gothic cathedral to be cast entirely of metal in Belgium. After perusing the interior, head across the plaza to tiny **Elías Leiva Ethnographic Museum** (506-551-0895; Colegio San Luis Gonsaga; open 7 AM–2 PM, Mon.–Fri.), with a collection of antiques, including Spanish-era religious art and furniture.

Iglesia de San Rafael (Central Zarcero) This 1895 gilded beauty, crafted mostly of painted metal despite appearances, plays second fiddle to the famed topiary of **Parque Francisco Alvarado**, in front. Sculpted by Evagelisto Blanco into animals, landscapes, and archways of cypress, this is the most impressive central park in the country.

Iglesia Santiago Apóstal (Cartago) The Cartago Ruins, as these spectacular stone ruins are known, are all that's left of a church destroyed in the massive 1910 earthquake.

La Inmaculada Concepción (Heredia) Pale Gothic masterpiece dates to 1796, with bells imported from Cuzco, Peru, and stained glass that is among the oldest in the country. Other historic buildings are close by, including **El Fortin**, designed by the same architect as Alajuela's cathedral.

Nuestra Señora de la Limpía Concepción (Valle de Ujarrás, Lake Chachi, well signed from Orosí) The Ujarrás Mission, as these ruins are known, was first founded in 1560, then rebuilt in 1693 of limestone to the ornate façade that still stands. It once housed another miraculous Virgin Mary statue, pulled from the water by a local Huetar Indian, which was later responsible for saving the small town from flooding and pirates. But when the Río Reventazón rose in 1833, even she couldn't stop the church from being destroyed. The Virgin now resides at the Paraíso Church, also home to the **Museum of Religious History of Our Lady of Ujarrás** (506-2574-7376; www.parroquiaparaiso.4t.com; open 8 AM–noon, 2 PM–5 PM, Mon.–Fri.; donations appreciated), with religious artifacts, old photos, and the tale of two churches.

Music and Nightlife

Most nightlife options are in Alajuela and Heredia; smaller towns offer more basic bars.

Green Dragon (506-2267-6222; Heredia, Hotel Chalet Tirol, Monte de la Cruz; L, D; $$$) Scottish-style bar has a fireplace, great pub grub, and sometimes, live music.

Palenque de Ojo de Agua (506-2441-1309; Belén, across from Balneario Ojo de Agua) Popular dance and hangout spot also serves food; there's live music on weekends.

La Puerta de Alcalá (506-2267-7277; Monte de la Cruz, Heredia, 300m east El Castillo entrance; D, $$) Cozy bar has good food and live music on weekends.

Recreation

Parks and Preserves

The Central Valley has several other national parks and preserves as yet undeveloped for tourism; **Costa Rica National Parks** (www.costarica-nationalparks.com) has complete listings.

Alajuela and North of San José

BRAULIO CARRILLO NATIONAL PARK (BARVA SECTOR)

506-2261-2619, 506-233-4533 general information
www.costarica-nationalparks.com/brauliocarrillonationalpark.html
Sacramento, Heredia
Open: 8 AM–4 PM, Tue.–Sun.
Admission: $7–$15

Though this park is more easily accessible elsewhere, to climb Barva Volcano, you begin at Puesto Barva. The four-wheel-drive road begins in Sacramento, 20 kilometers (12 miles) from San José, passing simple *sodas* and cheap *cabinas* as the road begins to deteriorate, usually 3–4 kilometers (1.8–2.4 miles) before the entrance to the park. Once you've arrived, sign in and start the steep and scenic 2-kilometer (1.2-mile) hike to the ancient crater, filled with a chilly lake surrounded by luxuriant growth. Serious hikers can walk from here to La Selva Biological Station in Sarapiquí; rangers can arrange guides.

★ INBIOPARQUE

506-22507-810
www.inbioparque.com
Santo Domingo, Heredia; 500m south and 250m east of the Red Cross
Open: 8 AM–6 PM, daily
Admission: $23 per adult; $13 per child

InBio, the National Biodiversity Institute, offers this outstanding environmental showcase including examples of several different Costa Rican biomes, such as tropical dry forest, rain forest, and cloud forest, complete with native wildlife wandering through. There's also a butterfly garden, aquarium, organic farm, and more.

LA PAZ WATERFALL GARDENS

506-2225-0643; 954-727-3997 USA
www.waterfallgardens.com
Open: 8 AM–5 PM, daily
Admission: Entrance only $32 per adult; $20 per child. Package: $65 per adult; $55 per child

One of Costa Rica's most popular destinations, this top-notch roadside attraction is perfect for families and folks with limited mobility (but not wheelchairs) who still want to experience the rain forest. Principally built around a 3.5-kilometer (2-mile) trail past five photogenic waterfalls, it's now home to several wildlife displays, a trout lake, spa services, fabulous buffet restaurant, swimming pool, and even a reproduction Costa Rican farm, built with tools from the 1800s, where you can help milk cows.

Grecia's 1897 Catedral de la Mercedes was cast entirely of metal in Belgium.

POÁS VOLCANO NATIONAL PARK

506-2442-7041
www.costarica-nationalparks.com/poasvolcanonationalpark.html
30 km (19 mi.) northwest of San José
Open: 8 AM–3:30 PM, daily
Admission: $10

The world's largest volcanic crater and Costa Rica's top tourist attraction, 5,319-hectare (13,138-acre) Poás Volcano National Park makes a great early morning excursion from San José or Alajuela. Bring a jacket, as the average temperature is 12°C (54°F). Get there as early as possible and head straight for the main crater; cloud cover almost always obscures the view by 10 AM. Afterward, explore the informative visitor's center, beautiful Botas Lagoon, with a picnic area, and almost 3 kilometers (1.8 miles) of paved, wheelchair-accessible trails.

The volcano is still very active, and in 1989 destroyed 75 percent of Grecia's coffee crops. There's no camping in the park, but **Lagunillas Lodge** (506-2448-4958; $$), 2.5 kilometers (1.5 miles) from the entrance, has very basic bungalows, horseback rides, and trout fishing.

WEST OF SAN JOSÉ
BAJOS DEL TORO AMARILLO

24 km from Sarchí (turnoff 100m east of the Río Trojas); 14 km from Zarcero (turn at the Catholic Church)
Open: 24/7
Admission: varies

A popular summer escape for Ticos, at altitudes ranging from 1,400 to 2,450 meters (4,200 to 7,350 feet), this red-roofed mountain village is surrounded by rain forest, with public gardens, rustic hotels, picnic areas, and pretty little lakes. Between Poás and Juan Castro Blanco National Parks, this lush and rainy region is threaded by rivers including Río Toro, which cascades more than 100 meters (300 feet) as the **Catarata del Toro** (506-2399-7476; www.catarata-del-toro.com; 7 km north of Bajos). You can visit the *catarata* (waterfall) on a day trip ($10), or stay over night at the rustic lodge ($$*).

Nearby, **Bosque de Paz Rain/Cloud Forest and Lodge** (506-2234-6676; www.bosquede paz.com; 2km from Bajos on road to Zarcero; tours $35 with guide, $65 including transport from San José; $100 with lodging and meals) offers even nicer accommodations overlooking a private preserve protecting some 1,000 hectares (2,471 acres) of almost Alpine wilderness. Stay overnight or visit on a day trip and explore 22 kilometers (13 miles) of hiking trails, waterfalls, and hummingbird gardens.

EAST OF SAN JOSÉ
CHIRRIPÓ NATIONAL PARK

506-2771-5116; 506-2233-4070
www.costarica-nationalparks.com/chirriponationalpark.html
San Isidro de El General
Open: 5 AM–noon, daily
Admission $15

This glacier-carved, high-altitude *páramo* park protects 3,819-meter (12,530-foot) Cerro Chirripó, Costa Rica's highest peak, once held sacred by indigenous tribes. Today, Los Cre-

Sarchí's rocking chairs are almost as famous as its oxcarts.

stones, naked upheavals of ancient rock atop the mountain, remain a pilgrimage-worthy destination, usually planned as a two-day, non-technical trek from San Isidro, with an overnight in the dorm-style base camp (make reservations). Most folks start before dawn, taking the 5 AM bus from San Isidro to the trailhead at San Gerardo de Rivas. Area hotels can arrange guides. It can get cold at the top, -9°C (12°F), so dress accordingly. **Costa Rica Trekking** (www.chirripo.com) offers guided trips.

GUAYABO NATIONAL ARCHAEOLOGICAL MONUMENT
506-2559-1220
www.costarica-nationalparks.com/guayabonationalmonument.html
19 km (12 mi.) northeast of Turrialba
Open: 8 AM–4 PM, daily
Admission: $4

This park preserves Costa Rica's most important archaeological site, the remains of an indigenous city that once held perhaps 10,000 people, from 1,000 B.C. until 1,400 A.D., when it was mysteriously abandoned. Perhaps a ceremonial site, it features cobbled roads, bridges, still-functioning aqueducts, tombs, and the circular foundations of South American-style *palenque* houses. There are also several petroglyphs that probably date much earlier. It can't compare with, say, Machu Picchu or Chichen Itza, but a guided tour through the ruins is still a fascinating way to spend the day. Or camp overnight, next to the ranger station ($).

IRAZÚ VOLCANO NATIONAL PARK
506-2551-9398
www.costarica-nationalparks.com/irazuvolcanonationalpark.html
Admission: $7; parking $1.50
Open: 8 AM–3:30 PM, daily

Costa Rica's tallest (3,432 meters/11,257 feet) and most feared volcano, looms above the city of Cartago. Eruptions and earthquakes destroyed the city in 1723, 1841, and 1910; a 1963 eruption coincided with a visit from John F. Kennedy, causing Ticos to joke that even their volcanoes were hailing the popular U.S. president. But as tons of ash continued to rain down, stained clothes and collapsed roofs were only the beginning. Crops were lost and animals starved as the ash became too thick to clear.

More of a concern was the buildup of ash on the steep-sloped sides of the volcano. Beginning in 1964, scientists and engineers built a series of barriers to divert a potential mudslide, and instituted a mandatory evacuation of heavily populated Cartago as the rainy season began. The city and countless lives were saved.

You can drive to the top and walk around the massive craters, from which you can see both the Caribbean and Pacific on a clear day. There's a café at the park, but no camping, though cheap *cabinas* line the road to the top.

LOS QUETZALES NATIONAL PARK
506-2416-7068
Km 76 Hwy 2 (The InterAmericana)
Open: 8 AM–4 PM, daily
Admission: $6

Costa Rica's newest national park opened in July 2005, a 5,000-hectare (12,350-acre), steeply pitched swath of primary rain forest that gives birth to the Río Savegre, and is home to 14 distinct ecosystems, glacier lakes, and at least 25 endemic animal species. It's still a work in progress, and at press time, only 2 trails (of 11 planned) were open to the public, an

Main crater at Irazú Volcano National Park

easy 3-kilometer (1.8-mile) trail, and a steep and muddy 11-kilometer trek that usually takes two days. Park rangers can find guides.

TAPANTÍ-MACIZO CERRO DE LA MUERTE NATIONAL PARK

506-2771-3297
www.costarica-nationalparks.com/tapantinationalpark.html
Orosí, 10 km (6 mi.) after signed turnoff from road to Paraiso
Open: 5 AM–5 PM, daily
Admission: $7

Climb into the cloud forest just an hour from San José, at this 58,343-hectare (144,058-acre) national park in the northern Talamanaca Mountains, which protects Cerro de la Muerte (2,553 meters/8,397 feet). This is one of the rainiest spots in the country, receiving up to 711 centimeters (280 inches) of rainfall annually, but that doesn't stop birders in search of some 300 local species.

Three short trails begin at the main entrance; bring a picnic lunch to enjoy by the swimming area. Trout fishing is allowed May 1 to January 31. There's no camping, but if you go to the second park entrance, just past the turnoff to Copey de Dota, you can reserve dorm-style lodging at InBio's **La Esperanza de El Guarce Biological Station** (506-2233-4160; $), with cold showers, electricity, and access to a hike up Cerro de la Muerte.

Adjacent to the park on the road from Orosí, **Monte Sky** (506-2231-3536; www.intnet .co.cr/montsky; open by reservation only; admission $10) is a private reserve with hiking trails, camping ($), fishing, trails, and a rustic *soda* nearby.

TURRIALBA VOLCANO NATIONAL PARK

506-2232-5324
www.costarica-nationalparks.com/turrialbavolcanonationalpark.html
From Santa Cruz (13 km/8 mi. from Turrialba), 18 km (11 mi.) on signed, 4WD-only road
Open: 7 AM–5 PM, daily
Admission: Free

Costa Rica's second-tallest volcano (3,340 meters/11,000 feet) is often called Irazú's twin, but unlike its popular sister, this less accessible mountain remains one of the country's least visited national parks. The trail begins near **Volcán Turrialba Lodge** (506-2273-4335; www.volcanturrialbalodge.com; $$*), offering cozy, rustic, wooden rooms with private hot-water showers and typical meals, right in the saddle between Irazú and Turrialba; they'll let you park here as well. The 5-kilometer (3-mile) climbs rises through the cloud forest to the active volcanic crater, with fumaroles and mud pits to explore.

Botanical Gardens

Botanical Orchid Garden (506-2487-8095; www.orchidgardencr.com; La Garita de Alajuela, 800m southeast of Fiesta del Maíz; open 8:30 AM–4:30 PM, Tue.–Sun.; admission $12 per adult, $6 per student) Ten minutes from the airport, orchid nursery offers tours of their greenhouses; on-site **Vanilla Café** ($$) displays vanilla orchids.

★ **CATIE** (506-2556-2700; www.catie.ac.cr; Turrialba, 4 km from town on the road to La Suiza; open 7 AM–3 PM, daily; admission $10–$25, depending on tour) The Agricultural Center for Tropical Studies and Learning is geared to researchers helping Latin American farmers develop ecologically friendly, economically successful crops. Guided tours of their incredible gardens are amazing, and you can do it on mountain bikes.

Else Kientzler Botanical Garden (506-2454-2070; www.elsegarden.com; Sarchí Norte, 800m north of the stadium; open 7 AM–4 PM, daily; admission $12 per adult, $6 per student) These 7-hectare (17-acre) gardens have 2,000 species of tropical plants from all over the world. Much of it is wheelchair accessible, and there's a garden for the blind.

★ **Lankester Botanical Gardens** (506-2552-3247; www.jardinbotanicolankester.org; Km 4, Road to Cartago from Paraíso; open 8:30 AM–4:30 PM, daily; admission $6) World-famous gardens, operated by the University of Costa Rica, display some 10,000 orchids from more than 1,000 species, as well as 3,000 other plant species, in their 11 hectares (27 acres) of gardens. There are also 2.5 kilometers (1.5 miles) of wheelchair-accessible trails.

Canopy Tours and More

Colinas de Poás (506-2430-4575; www.colinasdelpoas.com; Fraijanes, 22 km north of Alajuela on the road to Volcán Poás; open 8 AM–4 PM, daily; admission $50, package $80) Extensive 14-cables canopy tour also has hiking trails, trout fishing, and an add-on tour to Poás National Park.

Recreo Verde (506-2472-1020; www.recreoverde.com; Marsella de Venezia, San Ramón) Adventure lodge offers guided hikes, a canopy tour, hot springs, rustic lodging ($), and the "Cave of Death," an infinitely deep hole belching carbon monoxide.

Tropical Bungee (506-2248-1212; www.bungee.co.cr; Heredia; $65) Take an 80-meter (265-foot) plunge off the Old Colorado Bridge, near Heredia, then indulge in the climbing wall or canopy tour.

Turu Ba Ri Tropical Park (506-2250-0705; www.turubari.com; Santiago de Puriscal, 75 km (47 mi.) west of San José; canopy $55, two tours $89) Adventure park offers canopies, botanical gardens, hiking trails, horseback rides, an aerial tram, and a 75-meter (246-foot) rappelling and climbing wall.

Agricultural Tours

Britt Coffee Tour (506-2277-1600; www.cafebritt.com; Heredia, signed 500m north and 400m west of Automercado; open 9 AM–3 PM, daily; admission $19 per adult, $14 per child) Kid-friendly coffee tour uses a hokey skit and silly jokes to explain how coffee is grown, harvested, and processed. The fabulous gift shop offers all things Britt, while the on-site restaurant, **Don Próspero** (open 8 AM–5 PM, daily; $$–$$$) has great typical food.

Doka Estate (506-2449-5152; www.dokaestate.com; 9 km from Central Alajuela, signed from road to Poás; open 8 AM–5 PM, daily; admission $16) The other major-label coffee tour (they sell coffee to Starbucks) convenient to San José, this is a bit more serious than Britt, and just as informative. They have several restaurants and pleasant **Siempre Viva B&B** ($$).

Café Cristina (506-2574-6426; 800-355-8826; www.cafecristina.com; Orosí; $10 per person) Small, family-run organic coffee farm offers tours of their sustainable, shade-grown operation, between Cartago and Orosí.

Golden Bean Coffee Tour (506-2531-2008; www.goldenbean.net; Turrialba, Atirro; admission $27) Hacienda Real offers tours of their coffee plantations and processing facility.

Panaca: Natural Park of Farming Culture (506-22428-9857; panaca.com.co; 1 km from

The world's largest oxcart, built by Chaverri Oxcart Factory, is in Sarchí Norte's central park.

San Mateo de Alajuela; open 8:30 AM–6:30 PM, daily; admission $20 per adult, $17 per teen, children free) Part of a Colombian chain of agriculture parks, this model ranch has 200 species of animals, green spaces, restaurants, cowboy shows, and rides.

Los Trapiches (506-2444-6656; Grecia, well signed from road to Santa Gertrudis Sur; open 8 AM–5 PM, Tue.–Sun.) Sugarcane processing facility offers educational tours plus swimming holes, a lake for boating and fishing, and sometimes live music.

El Tronco (506-2245-1340; www.eltroncoadventures.com; open Tue.–Thu. and Sat.; admission $69, including lunch and transport) Guided hikes and horseback rides in the cloud-forested skirts of Irazú volcano include a cultural tour of Coronado village's neo-Gothic cathedral and dairy farms.

Golf

Though Guanacaste gets all the ink, the Central Valley has more mature options.

Cariari Country Club (506-2293-3211; www.clubcariari.com; Alajuela) Guests at Ramada Plaza Herradura can use this George Fazio-designed, par-71 course.

Los Reyes (506-2438-0858; www.losreyescr.com; Alajuela) Nine-hole, par-70 course is conveniently close to the airport.

Parque Valle del Sol (506-2282-9222; www.vallesol.com; Pozos de Santa Ana, 1700m west of HSBC) This 7,000-yard, 18-hole, par-72 professional course has been certified ecologically sound.

Hot Springs

Orosí offers two developed hot springs, basically plain cement pools, surrounded by chairs and umbrellas, that hover around 10°C (50°F): **Balneario Orosí** (506-2533-2156; open 7:30 AM–5 PM, daily; admission $2), in central Orosí, with a simple *soda* and several pools, including one for lap swimmers; and **Balneario Los Patios** (506-2533-3009; open 8 AM–4 PM, Tue.–Sun.; admission $2), 1.5 kilometers from town, with much better views.

★ **Termales del Bosque** (506-2460-4740; www.termalesdelbosque.com; Ciudad Quesada, 7 km on road toward Aguas Zarcas; $$*) Wonderful hotel has stunning, natural hot springs, most warm and one very, very hot, overlooking a river rushing through the deep forest, patrolled by bright blue morpho butterflies. Rooms are standard, but clean and spacious, and there's hiking, horseback riding, and other activities on-site. The restaurant is great.

Other Tours

Railbike Tours (www.railbike.com; 506-2303-3300; $75 per adult, $70 per student) A cool company based in Alajuela has adapted bicycles to use abandoned railroad tracks for a 15-kilometer (9-mile) trek from Ciruelas and Atenas, crossing the tallest bridge in Costa Rica, and through farmland ranches. Prices include lunch and hotel pickup.

Real Places, Real People (www.realplaces.net) Arranges three-day cultural tours of the valley.

Redatour (www.costaricaruraltourism.org) Association of more than 100 Central Valley families offers homestays, guided hikes, cooking courses, Spanish lessons, and more.

White-Water Rafting

Aventuras Naturales (506-2225-3939; www.toenjoynature.com) Offers overnight trips at their Pacuare Jungle Lodge.

Costa Sol Rafting (506-2431-1183; www.costasolrafting.com) Offers day trips and overnights on the Pacuare and other rivers.

Loco's Tropical Tours (506-2556-6035; www.whiteh2o.com) Recommended Turrialba-based operation.

Ríos Tropicales (506-2233-6455; www.riostropicales.com) The country's biggest white-water operator also offers area tours, with overnights in their own Pacuare Lodge.

Tico's River Adventure (506-2556-1231; www.ticoriver.com) All the river runs, plus multi-day trips.

Wildlife Displays and Rescue Centers

The Butterfly Farm (506-2438-0400; www.butterflyfarm.co.cr; La Guácima de Alajuela, 14 km south of Alajuelá) Tours of one of the country's most extensive butterfly gardens are included on package day trips.

Flor de Mayo (506-2441-2658; www.hatchedtoflyfree.org; 3 km southeast of Alajuela; admission $20 donation) You must make an appointment for a two-hour tour of this breeding facility for green and scarlet macaws, surrounded by marvelous botanical gardens.

Parque Viborana (506-2538-1510; Pavones, 8 km from Turrialba; open 9 AM–5 PM, daily, admission $5) Venom specialist Minor Camacho offers an educational look at Costa Rica's snakes.

World of Snakes (506-2494-3700; www.snakes-costarica.com; 1.5 km (1 mi.) southeast of Grecia, on road to Alajuela; admission $12 per adult, $7 per child; open 8 AM–4 PM,

Sarchí: Cradle of Costa Rican Crafts

Craft lovers, recreational shoppers, and above all, anyone who loves working with wood, really must visit the winsome and flower-filled town of Sarchí, where even the waste bins and telephone poles are decorated with the swirling, psychedelic mandala patterns that have become so symbolic of Costa Rican culture.

Most famous for its colorful oxcarts, or *carretas*, proclaimed by UNESCO part of the Intangible Patrimony of Mankind, this adorable town is part of every package tour in the region. If you stick to the souvenir megastores, where your tour bus will drop you off, you'll find fine souvenirs such as kitchen utensils, toys, and tiny wooden oxcarts with coffee beans glued inside. Cute. You can also watch oxcarts being made the old-fashioned way, with century-old tools and perhaps even water wheels.

Or explore the smaller storefronts all over Sarchí, where more than 200 mostly family-run operations sell truly beautiful handmade furniture, perhaps only a few pieces at a time, and may let you watch them work the wood, probably with modern equipment. It's fascinating, and if you're considering buying a home down here, this is the very best place to furnish it. No matter what, be sure to visit the central park in Sarchí Norte, where the World's Largest Oxcart, built of bitter and laurel, stands 5 meters (16.5 feet) tall, 6 meters (19.5 feet) long, and 3 meters (9.8 feet) wide. It was donated to the city by **Chaverri Oxcart Factory** (506-2454-4940; Sarchí Sur), one of the region's oldest and largest. Other *mueblerías* (furniture stores) include:

Eloy-Alfaro Fábrica de Carretas (506-2454-3500; www.maosoft.net/mueblerialosalfaro; Sarchí Norte, 250m north of Plaza de la Artesanía) The most famous factory in the region, this family business has been turning out oxcarts since 1923, and still uses old-school technology.

Muebleria San Judas (506-2454-2401; Sarchí Norte, 300m east of the park) Fluid lines, modern styles, and top-notch construction; they also do stonework.

Muebles Campos (506-2454-3455; Sarchí Sur; across from the Plaza del Mueble) Almost '60s-style sensibilities.

Rocking Chair Factory (506-2454-4586; www.simesacr.com; between Sarchí and Naranjo) Second only to oxcarts in national prominence, Sarchi's comfortable rocking chairs, featuring leather pieces stamped with pictures of, well, oxcarts, are easy to collapse and ship home.

Brenes Furniture Factory (506-2454-3020; Sarchí Norte, across from gas station) Boxy pieces made of dry tropical hardwoods, including cenizaro and guanacaste.

daily) Price includes a guided tour of more than 40 species of snakes from around the world, some involved in breeding programs.

★ **Zoo Ave Wildlife Conservation Park** (506-2433-8989; www.zooave.org; 15 min. west of Alajuela; open 9 AM–5 PM, daily; admission $9 per adult, $1 per child) Unique "zoo" is Costa Rica's finest, a rescue operation and genetic ark (most animals are former pets, injured wildlife, or captured contraband), breeding and releasing more native species than any other zoo in Latin America.

Spas

Grupo de Giras (506-2410-0029; grugiras@racsa.co.cr; San Ignacio) Operated by a local women's collective, this health center offers massage, herbal teas, natural foods, and health counseling.

Xandari (506-2443-2020; www.xandari.com; 4 km north of Alajuela on road to Poás) This colorful resort has an equally creative take on spa architecture, with wide-open views over the Central Valley.

SHOPPING

Malls and markets abound in the urbanized center of the valley, but head into the mountains to witness the country's most important crafts traditions.

Books

★ **Goodlight Books** (506-2430-4083; www.goodlightbooks.com; Alajuela, 100m north, 300m west of La Agonía Curch) A wide selection of new and used books, most in English, includes guidebooks, Latin American studies, and much more; there's also a small café and WiFi.

The Literate Cat (506-2262-5206; Heredia, Plaza Heredia) Stocks books in several languages, including English.

Galleries

Casa del Soñador (The Dreamer's House; 506-2533-3297; Orosí) On the shores of Lake Cachí, Miguel and Hermes Quesada are carrying on the primitive sculpture tradition of their father, Macedenio Quesada, a self-taught artist who became a UCR art professor. Eco-friendly sculptures are often figurative, using scrap coffee roots and fallen wood but no varnishes or sealants.

Dantica Gallery (506-2740-1067; www.dantica.com; San Gerardo de Dota; open 7 AM–6 PM, daily) Stylish selection of modern and traditional handicrafts, sculptures, and jewelry from all over Latin America.

Mystica Rustica (506-2828-2261; Orosí, next to Coto Restaurant) Artsy ceramics, picture frames, wooden boxes, and unusual jewelry; also astrological readings from 9 AM–noon, daily.

EVENTS

January

Fiestas Palmares (fiestaspalmares.com) Just west of San José, this tiny town throws Costa Rica's biggest blowout at the end of January, with concerts, carnival rides, horse parades, rodeos, and a whole lot of drinking.

May

Orosí Valley Adventure Race (506-2280-8054; www.adventureracingcostarica.com/ctoc .html) Ten-day race involves hiking, running, biking, rafting, and otherwise testing your mettle.

July

Sarchí Craftwork and Industry Fair (506-2454-3870; Sarchí) Live music, traditional dancing, and delightful handicrafts—including beautifully painted carretas, fully operational and on parade.

August

Nuestra Señora La Virgen de Los Angeles Day (Cartago) On August 2, pilgrims walk, sometimes on their knees, from around the country to the Cartago Basilica.

October

Pejibaye Fair (506-2535-0094; third week in October; Cartago) In honor of Costa Rica's most unusual fruit, the starchy "peach palm," offers food, beer, and fun.

December

Chicharrón Fair (506-2416-7886; second week of December; Puriscal) Celebrate bite-sized bits of fried pork, served with limes, tortillas, and beer.

Waiting for sunset and watching for lava at Arenal Volcano

5

THE NORTHERN ZONE

Elemental Costa Rica: Erupting Volcanoes, Untamed Rivers, and Cloud Forests

The fiery heart of *La Zona Norte*, stretching north from the Central Valley to the Nicaraguan border, is famed Arenal Volcano, reliably belching lava and ash since 1968. This oft-photographed attraction has also erupted into a gleeful tourist claptrap of shops, hotels, restaurants, hot springs, waterfalls, and endless opportunities for eco-fun, all centered on the tiny town of La Fortuna, just 6 kilometers (3.5 miles) away from the rumbling cinder cone.

Note that Arenal is usually veiled in cloud cover; there's a very real chance that you won't even catch a glimpse of the 1,633-meter (5,436-foot) volcano behind a seemingly flat and featureless gray sky. Moreover, Arenal has, in recent years, taken to pouring its molten heart down its northwestern side, out of sight of La Fortuna and the string of fabulous resorts enfolded into the mountain's thickly forested skirts. Instead, ringside seats for the show can be found in the once forgotten backwater village of El Castillo, now building restaurants and hotels at a furious clip. Geological time is faster than you think, so check the flows online before making your reservations.

Follow the road around the mountain, and continue across the country's most important hydroelectric dam to the silvery blue expanse of Lake Arenal, fringed with an eclectic collection of unique and lovely lodges, as well as the totally Tico towns of Nuevo Arenal (built after the original Arenal was flooded by the lake in 1973) and the hard-working ranching center of Tilarán, topped with Latin America's largest wind farm. Known for excellent *guapote* (rainbow bass) fishing, the lake also boasts some of the best sailboarding and kiteboarding in Central America.

The vast plains extending northeast of the lake to the Caribbean lowlands, called the Llanura de San Carlos, are home to a handful of attractions usually arranged as day trips from La Fortuna, including Caño Negro, a wetlands reserve that reels in the birders and sportfishers, and San Rafael de los Guatusos, home of the Malekú Indians. At the border town of Los Chiles, begin the scenic river border crossing to San Carlos, Nicaragua, with access to the Solentiname Archipelago and Río San Juan.

To the east of La Fortuna are the humid tropical lowlands of Sarapiquí, famed for almost untamed Braulio Carrillo National Park, the white-water rafting center of La Virgen, and the river port village of Puerto Viejo de Sarapiquí (not to be confused with the Caribbean beach town of Puerto Viejo de Talamanca). With beautifully eco-conscious lodges, some luxurious and some remote, this less-touristed region is well worth an overnight exploration

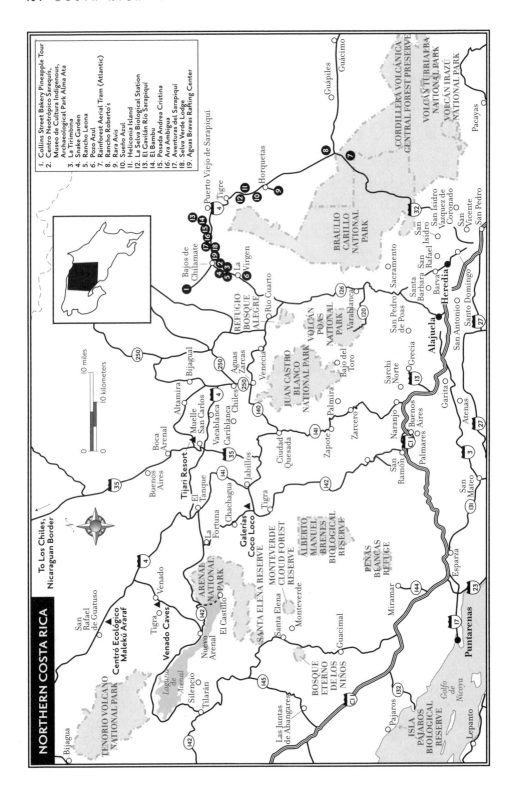

NORTHERN COSTA RICA

1. Collins Street Bakery Pineapple Tour
2. Centro Neotrópico Sarapiquís,
   Museo de Cultura Indigenous,
   Archaeological Park Alma Ata
3. La Tirimbina
4. Snake Garden
5. Rancho Leona
6. Pozo Azul
7. Rainforest Aerial Tram (Atlantic)
8. Rancho Roberto's
9. Rara Avis
10. Sueño Azul
11. Heliconia Island
12. La Selva Biological Station
13. El Gavilán Río Sarapiquí
14. El Bambu
15. Posada Andrea Cristina
16. Ara Ambigua
17. Aventuras del Sarapiquí
18. Selva Verde Lodge
19. Aguas Bravas Rafting Center

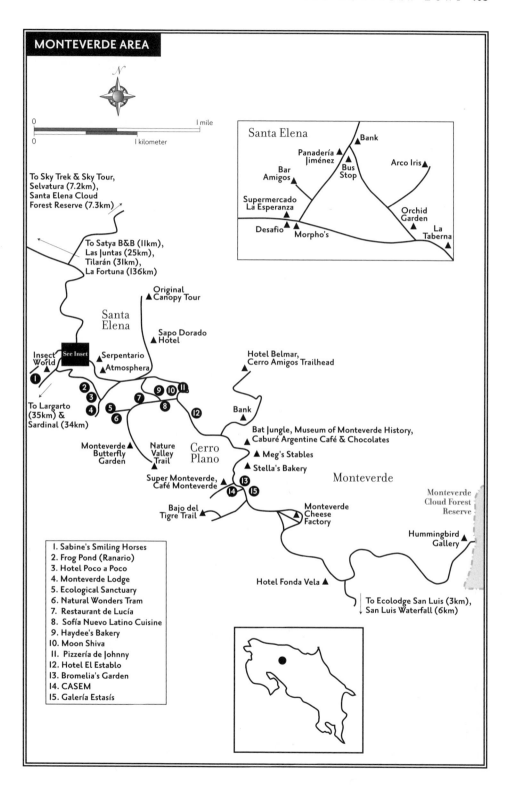

MONTEVERDE AREA

N

0   1 mile
0   1 kilometer

To Sky Trek & Sky Tour,
Selvatura (7.2km),
Santa Elena Cloud
Forest Reserve (7.3km)

To Satya B&B (11km),
Las Juntas (25km),
Tilarán (31km),
La Fortuna (136km)

Santa
Elena

Original
Canopy Tour

Sapo Dorado
Hotel

Insect
World

Serpentario

See Inset

Atmosphera

Hotel Belmar,
Cerro Amigos Trailhead

To Largarto
(35km) &
Sardinal (34km)

Bank

Bat Jungle, Museum of Monteverde History,
Caburé Argentine Café & Chocolates

Monteverde
Butterfly
Garden

Nature
Valley
Trail

Cerro
Plano

Meg's Stables

Stella's Bakery

Monteverde

Super Monteverde,
Café Monteverde

Bajo del
Tigre Trail

Monteverde
Cheese
Factory

Monteverde
Cloud Forest
Reserve

Hummingbird
Gallery

Hotel Fonda Vela

To Ecolodge San Luis (3km),
San Luis Waterfall (6km)

Santa Elena

Panadería
Jiménez

Bank

Bar
Amigos

Bus
Stop

Arco Iris

Supermercado
La Esperanza

Orchid
Garden

Desafio

Morpho's

La
Taberna

1. Sabine's Smiling Horses
2. Frog Pond (Ranario)
3. Hotel Poco a Poco
4. Monteverde Lodge
5. Ecological Sanctuary
6. Natural Wonders Tram
7. Restaurant de Lucía
8. Sofía Nuevo Latino Cuisine
9. Haydee's Bakery
10. Moon Shiva
11. Pizzería de Johnny
12. Hotel El Establo
13. Bromelia's Garden
14. CASEM
15. Galería Estasís

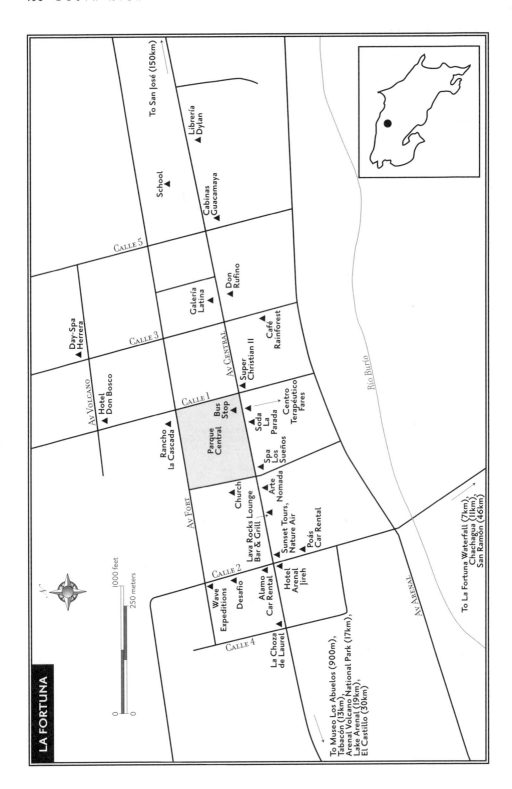

LA FORTUNA

To San José (150km)

Librería
Dylan ▲

School ▲

Cabinas
Guacamaya ▲

CALLE 5

Don
Rufino ▲

Galería
Latina ▲

Day-Spa
Herrera ▲

CALLE 3

Café
Rainforest ▲

AV VOLCANO

Hotel
Don Bosco ▲

Super
Christian II ▲

AV CENTRAL

CALLE 1

Rancho
la Cascada ▲

Parque
Central

Bus
Stop ▲

Soda
La
Parada ▲

Centro
Terapéutico
Fares ▲

Spa
Los
Sueños ▲

Church ▲

Arte
Nomada ▲

AV FORT

Lava Rocks Lounge
Bar & Grill ▲

Sunset Tours,
Nature Air ▲

Poás
Car Rental ▲

CALLE 2

Wave
Expeditions ▲

Desafío ▲

Alamo
Car Rental ▲

Hotel
Arenal
Jireh ▲

CALLE 4

La Choza
de Laurel ▲

AV ARENAL

RÍO BURÍO

To La Fortuna Waterfall (7km),
Chachagua (11km),
San Ramón (46km)

To Museo Los Abuelos (900m),
Tabacón (13km),
Arenal Volcano National Park (17km),
Lake Arenal (19km),
El Castillo (30km)

1000 feet
250 meters
0

at the very least, perhaps as part of an alternate route between La Fortuna and the Caribbean Coast.

To the west of La Fortuna is Costa Rica's other ecotourism superstar, the cloud forests of Monteverde (Green Mountain). Not exactly a town, Monteverde is more a cluster of tiny farming communities strung together by a winding road that connects three private cloud forest preserves. The most developed town is Santa Elena, a bustling backpacker-friendly hodgepodge of hotels, restaurants, and tour operators, while Cerro Plano, originally settled by a group of Alabama Quakers in the 1950s, offers more upscale options. Most visitors come to hike the Monteverde Cloud Forest, but if the fog is too thick to spot much wildlife, you can enjoy a huge variety of family-friendly attractions displaying frogs, butterflies, bats, giant hissing water cockroaches, and more. Or, if you're up for it, take an 80-kilometer-per-hour (48-mile-per-hour) high-altitude ride on what may well be the world's finest collection of zip-line canopy tours.

GETTING AROUND

Car

While most roads in this region are paved and well-signed, a four-wheel-drive vehicle is recommended for the unpaved roads leading to Monteverde, El Castillo, and some remote lodges. The road around Lake Arenal is paved, but can wash out for days during rainy season.

From San José to La Fortuna, it's a smooth, paved, and scenic drive on Highway 35 through the heart of the Central Valley; follow the erupting volcano signs. The confusing city of Ciudad Quesada connects La Fortuna to Sarapiquí's main artery, beautifully paved Highway 4, from which all resorts and hotels are clearly signed. Sarapiquí and Highway 4 are also accessible from Highway 126 from Alajuela and La Paz Waterfall Gardens. The loop makes a scenic alternate route between San José and the Caribbean.

Monteverde is only accessible by 3 four-wheel-drive-only unpaved roads; allow two hours to negotiate any of the well-signed, 35-kilometer (21-mile) roads from the Inter-Americana (at Sardinal and Las Juntas de Abangares) or Tilarán. Although Monteverde looks tantalizingly close to La Fortuna on the map, it takes at least three hours by car to skirt that erupting volcano and sizeable lake, before reaching the Tilarán entrance. If you've foregone the rental car, the jeep-boat-jeep option (see below) is faster and more fun.

La Fortuna has two rental car offices, Alamo (506-2479-9090; www.alamocostarica.com), one block west of the church; and Poás (506-2479-8418; www.poasrentacar.com), about half a block farther west.

Private Shuttle

Almost all private shuttle companies serve La Fortuna, but **Interbus** (506-2283-5573; www.interbusonline.com) is the only private shuttle with regular service to Sarapiquí.

Several shuttle companies also serve Monteverde, or try homegrown operators **Turiverde** (506-2645-5855; www.turiverdetransfer.com), with connections to major Costa Rican cities; and **Quality Transfers** (506-2645-6263; www.qualitytransfers.com), also serving Liberia and the Nicoya beaches.

Jeep-Boat-Jeep

La Fortuna and Monteverde are linked by three-hour "jeep-boat-jeep" services, arranged at any hotel or tour desk. Travel by jeep to Lake Arenal, boat across, then by jeep directly up to Monteverde.

Several companies, including ★**Desafío** (www.desafiocostarica.com), offer part of the trip on horseback. Beginners can ride the trail from El Castillo around the lake, then use a jeep for the final climb, while experienced riders can go the entire 13-kilometer (8-mile), five-hour trail to Monteverde, which is steep and difficult, and dangerous in rainy season.

Boat

The northern plains and Caribbean lowlands are connected by a system of navigable canals and rivers connecting Puerto Viejo de Sarapiquí, Caño Negro, and Los Chiles; as well as the Caribbean ports of Puerto Limón, Tortuguero, and Barra del Colorado; and the Nicaraguan port of San Carlos, with public boats to the Río San Juan, Solentiname Archipelago, and Granada.

Public boats are inexpensive but sometimes inconvenient; it's often easier to arrange private transport or tours. Several tours run from Puerto Viejo de Sarapiquí to Tortuguero and Nicaragua; Caño Negro and Los Chiles are connected by regular boat taxis.

LODGING

Scores of hotels for every budget are arranged in a loose crescent around Arenal Volcano, concentrated in La Fortuna, with nicer resorts lining the road to and around Lake Arenal. Check online for dozens of other options.

Sarapiquí is much less developed for tourism, but offers a handful of nature lodges ranging from relatively luxurious to truly remote. Budget options are clustered around the tiny rafting center of La Virgen, and Puerto Viejo de Sarapiquí.

Monteverde, like Arenal, has dozens of hotels. Santa Elena has the highest concentrations of services, but finer lodging can be found on the road connecting Monteverde and Santa Elena preserves.

Relatively untouristed northern towns such as Tilarán, Upala, and Los Chiles (the border crossing to Nicaragua), all offer basic but acceptable lodging, listed under Other Hotels.

Lodging Price Code

Cost of lodging is based on an average per-room, double-occupancy rate at peak season (December through April). Costa Rica's 16.39 percent hotel tax is not included. Rates are often reduced during Green Season (May through November). An asterisk denotes that a full breakfast is included with the room price.

Inexpensive ($)	Up to $50
Moderate ($$)	$50 to $100
Expensive ($$$)	$100 to $200
Very Expensive ($$$$)	Over $200

Hotels

ARENAL AREA
HOTEL KIORO
Owner: Don Ricardo Araya
506-2461-1700
www.hotelarenalkioro.com
info@hotelarenalkioro.com
11 km (6 mi.) west of La Fortuna, toward Arenal Volcano
Price: Very Expensive*
Credit Cards: Yes
Handicap Access: Yes

I will always remember my first sight of erupting Arenal, from what our guide explained was the best viewpoint in the entire region: "Mirador Kioro," with one modest, open-air restaurant so close to the crater that you could hear the molten rock tumble.

Flash forward a few years, and that steep ascent to this beloved viewpoint is landscaped in tropical plants, a kaleidoscope of color from which rises the region's most luxurious resort. Lounge beneath those remarkable volcano views behind the enormous picture windows in each of the 53 splendid suites, or perhaps from your private Jacuzzi. You can enjoy the view from the magnificent lounge area (with WiFi) or excellent on-site restaurant, open to everyone. Airy accommodations include every possible amenity, including marble bathrooms with deluxe showerheads, fully stocked minibar, DSL access, lovely sitting rooms, a small gym, hiking trails, and more. All Kioro lacks is hot springs, an absence for which they've tried to compensate with a heated pool and free transport to diminutive Titokú Hot Springs, right next to Baldi.

★ LA MANSIÓN INN
Owner: Godfried Ponteur
506-2692-8018
www.lamansionarenal.com
info@lamansionarenal.com
Lake Arenal, 8 km (5 mi.) east of Nuevo Arenal
Price: Very Expensive*
Credit Cards: Yes
Handicap Access: Yes

The most intimate and opulent property on Lake Arenal, La Mansión's sublime selection of distinctly decorated and artfully accommodating almond-wood villas seems designed with a romantic honeymoon in mind. This is not the best choice for those who want the full resort experience; pampering is personalized, and amenities individual rather than institutional, just like each of the unique lakefront cabins. Each lavishly decorated room, with ornate tiles and exotic furnishings, is imbued with a sumptuous Italian elegance complemented with modern amenities including private Jacuzzis. All offer private porches and enormous picture windows perfect for enjoying spectacular sunsets over the lake and volcano, or relish the view from the heated, spring-fed pool.

The open-air restaurant, famed for its friendly, boat-shaped bar, serves three-course gourmet dinners ($20–$25) with reservations. Note that there's not much within walking distance; this is a much better option for those with a rental car.

HOTEL SAN BOSCO
Manager: Vladamir S. Villegas
506-2479-9050
www.arenal-volcano.com
hotelsanbosco@ice.co.ct
Downtown La Fortuna, 200m north of Gasolinera Fortuna
Price: Moderate*
Credit Cards: Yes
Handicap Access: Yes

If you enjoy La Fortuna's cheerful tourist-town atmosphere, or simply appreciate the convenience, San Bosco is the city's best hotel. Service is excellent, if not always bilingual, and there's a nice pool and guarded parking. Well-lit rooms are clean and comfortable, if unremarkable, with WiFi, cable TV, air-conditioning, and excellent beds; rates include a five-star buffet breakfast. If you don't mind the exercise, ask for an upstairs room with better views, but either way be sure to climb to their third-floor *mirador* (lookout), where you can relax in a plastic chair and, if you're lucky, watch Arenal fuming above the city.

Another great in-town option is **Hotel Arenal Jireh** (506-2479-9004; www.hotel arenaljireh.com; 100m north of the Central Park; $$–$$$*), with excellently appointed rooms and great views from the third floor.

HOTEL EL SILENCIO DEL CAMPO

Owners: Luis Diego Zuñiga and Kattya Hidalgo
506-2479-7055
www.hotelsilenciodelcampo.com
info@hotelsilenciodelcampo.com
4 km (2.3 mi.) west of La Fortuna
Price: Expensive*
Credit Cards: Yes
Handicap Access: Yes

This family-run collection of 12 quiet, architecturally interesting cabins scattered throughout attractive, well-kept gardens is among the best of the cookie-cutter "resort" options lining the road between La Fortuna and Arenal National Park. Paved paths connect simple but spacious cabins containing two queen-sized beds, simple but quality furniture, mini-fridge, and coffeemaker, with the understated but excellent restaurant and nicely landscaped pools, one for children, poured into a nice wooden deck.

Filmy curtains cover big windows offering great volcano views from the cabins, but the best amenity of all is El Silencio's proximity to your choice of two hot springs: It's a 10-minute walk to either bodacious Baldi or understated Eco Thermales.

TABACÓN GRAND SPA AND THERMAL RESORT

Manager: Uwe Wagner
506-2265-1500; 877-277-8291 USA and Canada
www.tabacon.com
sales@tabacon.com
13 km (8 mi.) west of La Fortuna, toward Arenal Volcano
Price: Very Expensive*
Credit Cards: Yes
Handicap Access: Yes
Special: Five CST Leaves

Costa Rica's most famous resort is an enclave of over-the-top elegance with one of the most fabulous amenities anywhere, absolutely incredible hot springs elaborately sculpted from a steaming 39°C (104°F) river pouring from the mountain. Waterfalls, pools, wet bars, lounge areas, and the fabulous spa are all hidden in the outrageous gardens, as is the restaurant revered for its legendary buffet.

Rooms are perfect if not particularly original, each spacious, climate-controlled, option accented in earth tones and tasteful, handcrafted furnishings, soothing art, and all the extras you expect in this price range. Be sure to reserve a room with volcano views. Note that the springs are in a "danger zone," and have been evacuated in the past; the hotel is better protected.

SARAPIQUÍ
CENTRO NEOTRÓPICO SARAPIQUÍS

Manager: Emiliano Naranjo
506-2761-1004
www.sarapiquis.org
magistra@racsa.co.cr
La Virgen
Price: Moderate*
Credit Cards: Yes

Handicap Access: Yes
Special: Three CST Leaves

The ancient and overgrown orchard at the entrance, home to the region's best-preserved archaeology site, is being returned to the jungle slowly and serenely, a process expected to take one human generation. This Belgian-run nonprofit center is also home to one of the country's best museums and a great hotel, and is also walking distance from one of the region's finest nature preserves, Tirimbina.

Rooms, surrounded by native plants beloved by butterflies and hummingbirds, resemble *palenques*, circular Malekú Indian buildings with peaked, thatched roofs, designed to keep rooms cool using fans rather than air-conditioning (Tirimbina offers unremarkable but air-conditioned rooms for similar prices). Dark flagstones and high ceilings, arcing up to 6 meters (18 feet) at the pinnacle, open onto eight rooms per *palenque*, where freshly cut flowers, heavy carved wood furniture, and indigenous artwork contrast with surprisingly modern touches, such as glass sinks and steel sculptures that serve as clothes hangers. The shared wraparound patio offers fine wildlife watching, including 350 bird species and, when I was there, a troupe of howler monkeys. Breakfast is included and other meals ($10) are served buffet style, served overlooking the unchlorinated infinity pool and hectares of primary and secondary rain forest.

★ LA SELVA VERDE

Manager: Don Gabriel Gonzalez
506-2766-6800, 352-377-7111 USA

La Mansión Inn on Lake Arenal offers some of the loveliest rooms in Costa Rica.

www.selvaverde.com
odalis@selvaverde.com
La Virgen
Price: Expensive*
Credit Cards: Yes
Handicap Access: No
Special: Three CST Leaves

One of the first ecolodges in Costa Rica, lovely Selva Verde welcomes you into its polished tropical oasis beneath a delicate, hardwood ceiling that arches high over the lobby, open on all sides to a murmuring jungle whose flowers and fruit attract all sorts of colorful feathered guests. The effect is that of relaxing beneath the rain forest canopy, dry and pampered, while still able to hold out your hand to touch the rain.

Take the covered walkways to your room, past a sparkling pool snuggled into the heliconias and vines, or grab a pair of complimentary rubber boots and take the hanging bridge across the river into the primary rain forest. Spacious, simple, fan-cooled rooms are elevated above the jungle floor on polished hardwood platforms furnished with hammocks and rocking chairs, while luxurious bungalows have more privacy, nicer bathrooms, a coffeemaker, screened-in-porch, and air-conditioning. Though you can spend days exploring the expansive property—200 hectare (500 acres) at last count—reception offers several tours, including white-water rafting, horseback riding, wildlife river floats, even cooking classes. Packages including buffet meals can be arranged, or enjoy the gourmet Italian restaurant that they were putting the finishing touches on when I was there.

MONTERVERDE AREA
HOTEL EL ESTABLO
Owner: Arnoldo Beeche
506-2645-5110
www.hotelelestablo.com
establo@racsa.co.cr
Cerro Plano, 3 km (1.8 mi.) west of Santa Elena

Price: Very Expensive*
Credit Cards: Yes
Handicap Access: No
Special: Three ICT Leaves

Amenity for amenity, this enormous property is probably the most luxurious option in Monteverde. It's not for everyone: With 155 rooms, two pools, three restaurants, and an 18-platform canopy tour at the very top of its steeply sprawling, 45-hectare (112-acre) property (on-site shuttle service included), this family-owned hotel is not exactly intimate.

Not a problem? Forego the older, poorly located standard rooms for a deluxe in one of the cavernous hilltop buildings, each with two floors, lovely (if somewhat open) bathrooms, cable TV, coffeemakers, telephones, hair dryers, and best of all, truly incredible views from the Sarchí rocking chairs on your private balcony, over the rain forest and all the way to the Nicoya Gulf. Suites are even larger. The 500 block has the nicer of the two pools, partially enclosed and heated to 28°C (84°F), attached to a small gymnasium. There's also an exquisite spa, tennis courts, and a brand-new fine dining restaurant, **Lagos**, which was almost ready to open at press time.

★ HOTEL FONDA VELA
Owners: Paul and Steven Smith
506-2645-5550
www.fondavela.com
reservations@fondavela.com
5 km west of Santa Elena
Price: $$$
Credit Cards: Yes
Handicap Access: Yes

This intimate option sits on 15 hectares (35 acres) of reforested former farmland originally settled by the owners' father, Paul Warren Smith, who also painted the impressionist artwork that adorns the generously sized wooden rooms. The ambiance is that of a log cabin, all gleaming hardwoods illuminated by large windows that frame the cloud forest in frilly curtains. Amenities are all there: minibar, telephone, coffeemaker, cable TV, and DSL; WiFi is available in the lobby. Furniture is basic but functional, in keeping with the rustic theme, and bathrooms are on the small side.

Breakfast ($9) is served buffet style, while other meals ($$$) are offered in either of their two restaurants, the expansive **Galería**, with a wall of large windows, or the cozier **Fireside Room**. If the weather's nice, opt for the airy outdoor seating area, overlooking the rain forest and Gulf of Nicoya. The location is great if you love both wildlife watching and long walks, as it's about 2 kilometers (1.2 miles) to either Monterverde Preserve or central Cerro Plano.

MONTEVERDE LODGE
Manager: Havale Amsbury
506-2257-0766
www.costaricaexpeditions.com
costaric@expeditions.co.cr
1 km (.6 mi.) southwest of Santa Elena
Price: Expensive
Credit Cards: Yes
Handicap Access: Yes

Often cited as the apex of luxury in Monteverde, this extremely comfortable and architecturally interesting ecolodge offers polished pastoral ambiance, upscale rustic furnishings, the recommended **Garden Restaurant** (open 6 AM–9:30 AM and noon–9 PM, daily; $$–$$$), in-room WiFi, and other amenities that use solar power, which supplies more than half of the lodge's electricity. Sure, this eco-consciousness means you'll be foregoing a few extras luxury lovers might desire (televisions and hair dryers, for example), but they make up for it with an attentive staff, in-room bathtubs, and a fine solar-powered Jacuzzi, enclosed in an atrium for garden views.

And what a garden, among the loveliest in Monteverde, with some 2 kilometers (1.2 miles) of trails winding through subtly sculpted cloud forest and over a singing brook all the to the Ecological Sanctuary (see Guided Hikes). Or, just enjoy the view from your wicker table and chairs, occupying one glass-enclosed corner of your flawless, if not extravagant, room. Best of all, despite the seemingly secluded sylvan environs, Santa Elena is just a 10-minute walk away.

HOTEL POCO A POCO
506-2645-6000
www.hotelpocoapoco.com
info@hotelpocoapoco.com
Santa Elena, 100m east of the Frog Pond
Price: Moderate*
Credit Cards: Yes
Handicap Access: Yes

With a great location close to the Ranario, this whimsically decorated spot offers great service and a very good **restaurant** (open 6:30 AM–9:30 AM and noon–9 PM, daily; $$) serving typical food and international cuisine that's worth sampling even if you're not a guest. Rooms are colorful, clean, and comfortable, with WiFi, cable TV, DVD players, laptop rental, and room service that could include a massage; upstairs rooms have a view. The heated pool and Jacuzzi area is nicely done, with a wet bar, wheelchair ramps, and kids' area. The property isn't exactly luxurious, but it's an excellent deal on fine midrange accommodations that are perfect for families or anyone with impaired mobility.

Bed-and-Breakfasts

ARENAL AREA
★ LA CEIBA TREE LODGE
Owner: Malte von Schlippenbach
506-2692-8050
www.ceibatree-lodge.com
ceibaldg@racsa.co.cr

Quakers of Monteverde

The tangle of townships collectively known as Monteverde was settled in 1918 by a handful of Costa Rican dairy farmers, who founded Santa Elena and San Luis. They were joined in 1951 by some very unusual new neighbors, a group of 40 Quakers from Alabama, who called their new home Monteverde, or "Green Mountain."

The Quakers, part of a religious sect committed to the Christian ideal of nonviolence, had left the United States after four members were jailed for refusing to fight in the Korean War. They chose Costa Rica, which had abolished its own military in 1948, and founded the Monteverde Cheese Factory here in the cloud forest.

The dairy farmers left much of the primary rain forest above their land intact, hoping to protect their settlement's watershed, but could not dissuade encroaching poachers and loggers. When a young biology student named George Powell visited in the early 1970s, his amazement at the region's beauty and biodiversity was tainted with the fear that it would eventually be destroyed. Together, he and Quaker activist Wilford Guindon convinced the Guacimal Company (which owned the land) to donate 328 hecatares (820 acres) for perpetual preservation.

Management of the cloud forest preserve was assumed by the Tropical Science Center (CCT; www.cct.or.cr), which evicted the squatters and began working with organizations worldwide to purchase and protect the surrounding land. Their efforts did not go unnoticed: After a 1977 BBC documentary about Monteverde's bird life, the first wave of tourists flooded the region, which hosted some 2,000 visitors in 1978. Surprised, both Quakers and Ticos began opening hotels and restaurants to care for the crowds.

These early efforts to protect the undeveloped cloud forest have grown into one of the world's most audacious experiments in ecotourism, by almost any measure a success. The region's three major preserves protect more than 36,510 hectares (90,180 acres), attracting some 200,000 tourists annually, providing wildlife with the world's largest preserved cloud forests, and locals with one of the highest standards of living in Latin America.

6 km west of Nuevo Arenal
Price: Moderate*
Credit cards: No
Handicap access: No

This unusually beautiful property, about 40 kilometers (25 miles) west of La Fortuna on Lake Arenal, is presided over by a majestic 500-year-old tree recently awarded the "Most Beautiful Ceiba in Costa Rica" by the federal government. Indigenous Americans believe that each ceiba, or kapok, tree is actually a fountain of energy, which perhaps inspires some outstanding artistry as well. La Ceiba's five rooms (plus one tiny second-floor single) are uniquely handcrafted, with carefully chosen furniture, attractive lighting, original art, and fresh flowers placed around raised wooden floors and slate tiles; the honeymoon suite has one of the finest views around.

You'll probably spend most of your time on the expansive front porch, contemplating the view: The country's largest lake, most impressive volcano, most important dam, and even Tilarán's wind farm—and, of course, the regal ceiba within whose protective shade you'll sleep. Rates include a huge German breakfast.

VILLA DECARY

Owners: Jeff Crandall and Bill Hemmer
506-2383-3012
http://villadecary.com
villadecary@yahoo.com
2 km east of Nuevo Arenal

Price: Expensive*
Credit Cards: Yes
Handicap Access: Limited

This beautiful property overlooking Lake
Arenal is perhaps best loved for its gener-
ous and congenial hosts, who have turned
this bright spot into a bird-watcher's paradise. Their rooms are a delight, spacious
and spiced up with Guatemalan bedspreads
and indigenous artwork, as well as very
comfortable beds and lots of light, courtesy
of picture windows that open onto semi-
private porches. There's even a casita with a
full kitchen. Breakfast is legendary, served
while you watch some of the region's 350
species of birds frolic out front, perhaps
trying to identify them with one of the
hotel's many birding guides.

LUCKY BUG B&B

Owner: Monica Krauskopf
506-2694-4515
www.luckybugcr.com
info@luckybugcr.com
3 km west of Nuevo Arenal
Price: Moderate to Expensive*
Credit Cards: Yes
Handicap access: No

The Lucky Bug is home to one of the country's best art galleries, so it's no wonder that
these five magical rooms are decorated (or
handcrafted) according to bright natural
themes with eclectic art and furnishings.
The "Bug Room," for example, features
insect art including sculptural furniture,
mosaics, murals, and other quirky elements
that come together with glee. Another offers
a gecko-themed bathroom, with a hand-
painted sink and cheerful lizard tiles that
makes every shower fun. All the rooms are
cozy and clean, some spacious and others
snug (as a bug in a rug?), with refrigerator,
coffeemaker, and a porch offering views
over both Arenal and their own pretty little
lake, stocked with rainbow bass. The on-
site restaurant, **Caballo Negro**, is excellent.

HUMMINGBIRD NEST I

Owner: Ellen Neely
506-2875-8711
www.hummingbirdnestbb.
nidocolibri@hotmail.com
El Castillo, 14 km west of Arenal Dam
Price: Moderate*
Credit Cards: Yes
Handicap Access: No

A fine spot to sleep in El Castillo, with wonderful volcano views, this beautiful if basic
bed-and-breakfast is accessible only via a
steep climb through the hummingbird gardens to the hilltop overlook. Each of the
three rooms' enormous windows, or the
relaxing wraparound porch, offer views of
lava streaking down the mountain. Or, better yet, enjoy those eruptions from the
Jacuzzi outside. Rooms are large, simple,
and soothingly decorated in blues and
greens, with smallish hot-water bathrooms,
mini fridges, and fans. And even if the
clouds aren't cooperating, you'll still be able
to enjoy the gardens, with dozens of hummingbird species vying for a taste of the
bouquet that surrounds you on all sides.

   If it's full, my second choice in El
Castillo is **Hotel Linda Vista del Norte**
(506-2692-2090, 866-546-4239 USA and
Canada; www.hotellindavista.com; $$–
$$$*) with pretty, well-appointed bunga-
lows but rather poor service.

SARAPIQUÍ
★ POSADA ANDREA CRISTINA

Owners: Alex and Floribell Martinez
506-7266-6265
www.andreacristina.com
alex6265@hotmail.com
1 km (.5 mi.) west of dock
Price: Inexpensive*
Credit Cards: No
Handicap access: No

If you're feeling cynical about ecotourism,
visit this truly charming bed-and-breakfast, run by caring naturalists, activists, and
multilingual guides who have long champi-

. real rural tourism. Enter the grounds .rough a tunnel of greenery; the *rancho* (gazebo) on your right is where you'll enjoy a huge, homemade Tico breakfast. Older rooms in the main house are fine, but go for one of the bungalows, crafted from 90 percent recycled, untreated wood that's been cleverly manipulated into wonderful built-in furniture, all decorated with bright tropical colors by Floribell, whose penchant for flowers extends from the festively painted furnishings and colorful mosquito netting to the translucent, handmade papier-mâché lamps.

This is real sustainable tourism, so don't expect air-conditioning or hot water showers, though you'll almost certainly see plenty of monkeys, sloths, and birds; the father-son team of Alex and Kevin recently spotted two nesting red macaws (long absent from the area) nearby. They organize all manner of excellent, eco-friendly tours.

MONTEVERDE
★ ARCO IRIS
Owner: Susanna Stoiber
506-2645-5067; 506-2645-5022 fax

www.arcoirislodge.com
arcoiris@racsa.co.cr
Price: Inexpensive to Very Expensive
Credit Cards: Yes
Handicap Access: No

Although the Arco Iris (meaning "Rainbow") is conveniently located in downtown Santa Elena, it seems a world away, tucked into a little valley with cloud-forest views and private trails, as though you were on a country getaway to the quiet place that Monteverde once was.

Each cabin, from the standard rooms to the refined honeymoon suite, furnished with a Jacuzzi, four-poster bed, complimentary champagne, and private garden, is individually fashioned from tropical hardwoods and local stone, with simple, sturdy, and finely balanced Sarchí furniture. The largest bungalow sleeps six, with two separate bedrooms and sofa bed in the living area, attached to a full kitchen. Though the inn still has that personalized bed-and-breakfast feel, the highly recommended German-style breakfast is no longer included with the price; it's $6.50 per person.

Leafcutter ants on parade through Lucky Bug Gallery on Lake Arenal

SATYA B&B

Owners: Iñaki and Satya Tablado
506-2373-6952
www.satyabb.com
info@satyabb.com
San Rafael de Abangares, 11 km from Santa
Elena on road to Las Juntas
Price: Moderate*
Credit Cards: No, but will accept them in
the future
Handicap access: No

This exquisite two-room bed-and-breakfast ensconced in 2.4 hectares (6 acres) of
organic coffee (which you'll sample with
your full breakfast) offers views from the
porch and hammocks over their caffeinated
crops and secondary rain forest all the way
to the Nicoya Gulf. Built by hand by your
Spanish hosts (Satya, who speaks fluent
English, is also a carpenter), details include
lamps carved from native jícaro gourds,
unusually crafted furniture, and polished-
wood sliding doors, as well as modern com-
forts including refrigerator, microwave, and
hot water showers. There's also a solar-
powered Jacuzzi and big-screen TV in the
"screening room," though you'll be more
entertained by the Tablados' animated tour
of their burgeoning coffee business. Taxis
from Monteverde cost about $15, and buses
run twice daily.

Nature Lodges

★ ARENAL OBSERVATORY LODGE

Manager: William Aspinal
506-2290-7011 reservations; 506-2692-
2070 lodge
www.arenalobservatorylodge.com
info@arenalobservatorylodge.com
El Castillo, 15 km from turnoff to Arenal
National Park
Price: Moderate to Expensive*
Credit Cards: Yes
Handicap Access: Yes

Originally constructed in 1987 as a research
station, this excellent option is off the

beaten track, an hour by car (and $30 in a
taxi) from La Fortuna—but just 3 kilometers
(1.8 miles) from the active volcano. Unlike
other area lodges, it's well protected from
itinerant eruptions by a natural ravine,
though hiking trails extend all the way to
lava still steaming from a 1992 eruption.
There are several types of rooms, from basic
bungalows with shared bath to expansive
junior suites boasting enormous picture
windows, private porches, beautiful
ceramic-tile art, coffeemakers, mini
fridges, small living rooms, and more. I
prefer the midrange, spacious, wheelchair-
accessible Smithsonian rooms, reached via
suspension bridge; be sure to request one
with a balcony.

Rates include a buffet breakfast and one
free guided hike daily through the 350-
hectare (870-acre) grounds, which include
2 kilometers (1.2 miles) of wheelchair-
accessible trails, 4.5 kilometers (2.7 miles)
of biking trails, and scores of other trails,
including one climbing Cerro Chato. Afterward, you could visit the tiny, on-site
Museum of Vulcanology, or just relax in the
spring-fed infinity pool and Jacuzzi. The
on-site restaurant serves excellent international cuisine ($10–$25 per meal), and the
front desk offers good rates on tours.

NATURAL LODGE CAÑO NEGRO
WILDLIFE REFUGE

Manager: Marina Zanirato
506-2471-1426
www.canonegrolodge.com
Caño Negro
Price: Moderate to Expensive*
Credit Cards: Yes
Handicap Access: Yes
Special: Three CST Leaves

This Italian-designed clutch of comfortable
bungalows set amidst a swirl of fruit trees
and flowers is the nicest overnight around
Caño Negro Wildlife Refuge. Air-conditioned casitas are simple but attractively
finished in hardwoods and muted colors,

with amenities including satellite television and hair dryers. **Restaurant Jabiru** ($$–$$$) is recommended. The big draw is sportfishing, and the lodge rents fully equipped boats, including guides who'll find tarpon, snook, *guapote* (rainbow bass) and garfish. They also organize guided boat trips for birders and wildlife watchers.

If they're full, another good option is **Hotel del Campo Caño Negro** (506-2471-1012; www.hoteldecampo.com; $$*), also geared to sportfishers and birders.

RARA AVIS

Owner: Amos Bien
506-2764-1111
www.rara-avis.com
raraavis@racsa.co.cr
Sarapiquí, 15 km (9 mi.) west of Horquetas
Price: Expensive*
Credit Cards: Yes
Handicap Access: No
Special: Reservations are required

Despite the price, this wonderful, rainy, and remote lodge is not for luxury lovers, though it's well worth roughing it for some. Set amidst a 1,280-hectare (3,163-acre) private reserve abutting untamed Braulio Carrillo National Park, Rara Avis was founded in 1979 by biologist Amos Bien as an experiment in sustainable use of the rain forest. Today a success, his reserve protects some 362 species of birds, including the rare green macaw, as well as jaguars, ocelots, dantas (tapirs), sloths, and three species of monkeys. Tempted?

Begin your adventure in the village of Horquetas with a scenic (read: wet, bumpy, and uncomfortable) three-hour trip up the mountain in a modified tractor. The best rooms are in the simple, wooden Waterfall Lodge, with hot showers, porches overlooking the rain forest, and mosquito nets over the fairly good beds. The on-site double waterfall is "only" 25 meters (70 feet) tall, so consider taking your daily guided hike

(included, along with three basic meals, in the price) to the 75 meter (245 foot) La Plantanilla instead. Sarapiquí's sweetest spot isn't for everyone, but if you're willing, the real Costa Rica is waiting.

★ SAN LUIS ECOLODGE

Manager: Fabricio Camacho Céspedes
506-2645-8049
www.uga.edu/costarica
fabricio@uga.edu
Monteverde area; 6 km south of Cerro Plano, 11 km from Santa Elena
Price: Expensive*
Credit cards: Yes
Handicap Access: Yes
Special: Three CST Leaves

If you're eager to spend some time in the clouds without fighting the crowds, consider heading "down the hill" to the tiny community of San Luis, home to Monteverde's most famous waterfall and most comfortable research station. Run by the University of Georgia, this is the real thing, a magnet for biology and tropical agriculture students, some of whom lead your daily guided hikes, birding treks, and other trips.

In addition to the inexpensive bunkhouse for students and volunteers, they offer large, wooden bungalow rooms located close to the main buildings, perfect for families and folks with limited mobility; or (better) more comfortable wooden *cabinas*, with balconies over the San Luis River Gorge. All meals are included, hearty Tico classics, including lots of rice and beans.

Other Hotels

TILARÁN
La Carreta (506-2695-6593; $$*; MC, V) Tilarán's best hotel has clean, tiled, air-conditioned rooms with TV, private bath, and decent décor, plus a great restaurant.

MUELLE
★ **Tijari Resort** (506-2469-9091, fax 506-

2469-9095; www.tilajari.com; 1 km east of Cruce de Muelle; $$$*) Sprawling, comfortable, popular resort offers scores of tours, six sets of tennis courts (one of them covered), and lovely rooms accented in gleaming dark cedar—spring for the wonderful river views. Great for kids.

UPALA

Cabinas Maleku (506-2470-0142; $) Upala's most comfortable hotel, with Sarchí furnishings, hot water, and air-conditioning, is popular with Tico businesspeople but can arrange Caño Negro excursions.

LOS CHILES

Rancho Tulípan (506-2471-1414; http://ranchotulipan.com; $–$$*) Wait for your boat across the border at Los Chiles' best hotel, with spacious, air-conditioned rooms, hot water, cable TV, and tour desk, just a block from the docks. **Cabinas Jibarú** (506-2471-1055; $) is a much more basic second choice.

RESTAURANTS AND FOOD PURVEYORS

As two of Costa Rica's biggest draws, both Monteverde and La Fortuna have a range of international restaurants, including several fine-dining options. Sarapiquí and other small towns in the Northern Plains have much more limited selections, primarily typical Costa Rican cuisine.

Restaurant and Food Purveyor Price Code

The following prices are based on the cost of a dinner entrée with a non-alcoholic drink, not including the 13 percent taxes and 10 percent gratuity added to the cost of almost all restaurant meals (except for the very cheapest *sodas*). Menus note whether or not their listed prices include this hefty 23 percent total surcharge, some listing two sets of prices.

Inexpensive ($)	Up to $5
Moderate ($$)	$5 to $10
Expensive ($$$)	$10 to $20
Very Expensive ($$$$)	$20 or more

Restaurants

LA FORTUNA/ARENAL

★ RESTAURANT CABALLO NEGRO

www.luckybugcr.com
506-2694-4757
Lake Arenal, 3 km west of Nuevo Arenal
Price: Inexpensive to Moderate
Credit Cards: Yes
Cuisine: German, Healthy International
Serving: B, L, D
Handicap Access: Yes
Reservations: No

Part of the **Lucky Bug Gallery** (see Shopping) on Lake Arenal, wonderful Caballo Negro has a playfully decorated dining room, with mosaic-tiled tables, sculptural lamps, and other artwork, all overlooking two lovely lakes and some very pretty gardens. Stop in for a coffee and sweet treat, or stay for unusual offerings that range from hearty Central European fare such as homemade spaetzel, bratwurst, and different schnitzels, to a wide variety of vegetarian options, including the recommended veggie lasagna. Almost everything is made with fresh, mostly organic ingredients. Locals, however, love the burgers, made with USDA beef, with more fat (and taste) than their leaner Tico cousins.

LA CHOZA DE LAUREL

506-2479-7063
www.lachozadelaurel.com
400m west of the church
Price: Moderate to Expensive
Credit Cards: Yes
Cuisine: Costa Rican
Liquor: Beer and wine
Serving: B, L, D
Handicap Access: Yes
Reservations: For large groups

Hotel Las Colinas, one of the first structures built by Alabama Quakers upon arriving at Monteverde

Once a tiny but tasty *soda* known for its *a la leña* (wood-fired) chicken, this classic La Fortuna eatery has grown, quite literally, with the town, and now caters to large groups, complete with a tour desk and souvenir stand. Regardless, it still serves some of the best typical food in town, with excellent roasted chicken and truly beautiful *casados*. They've also added more upscale offerings, including buffalo steak, seafood dishes, and a few vegetarian options, all served in their faux-rustic, open-air dining room complete with volcano views.

★ DON RUFINO

506-2479-9997
www.donrufino.com
100m east of the Central Park
Price: Moderate to Very Expensive

Credit Cards: Yes
Cuisine: International; Steakhouse
Serving: L, D
Handicap Access: Yes
Reservations: Recommended
Special: Bar open until 2:30 AM

The classiest night out in La Fortuna, Don Rufino's gleaming wooden interior extends to a softly glowing bar that wraps around to the sidewalk, where much coveted outdoor seating attracts Ticos and tourists alike to enjoy innovative entrées and a popular full bar. The vibe is casual, but service is five-star.

The specialty here is meats, choice cuts raised without antibiotics or hormones, and expertly prepared by a chef trained at the Four Seasons. Reliance on locally grown, often organic ingredients means that there are several excellent vegetarian options, such as the exquisite roasted hearts of palm and delicious cream of *pejibaye* soup, a delicacy made from the starchy, orange palm fruits and served with homemade croutons. Other dishes have an international flair.

RONDORAMA ARENAL

506-2692-8012
www.pequenahelvecia.com
Lake Arenal; 7 km (4 mi.) east of Nuevo Arenal
Price: Expensive
Credit Cards: No
Cuisine: Swiss, Costa Rican, International
Serving: B, L, D
Handicap Access: Challenging
Reservations: Required at least one day in advance, with five-person minimum
Special: A $10 entrance fee includes round-trip transport by miniature train

The crowning achievement of wacky, wonderful, kid-friendly **Hotel Los Heroés** ($$), a cute Swiss-style chalet on Lake Arenal, is Costa Rica's first rotating restaurant, with 360-degree views of the volcano, lake, and rain forest. After stopping to appreciate the grounds (be sure to admire the adorable chapel's interior), you'll make a 3.5-kilometer (2-mile) trip on a small Swiss Tren, chuffing through tunnels, across tropical green pastures, and over aqueducts to Rondorama Arenal, where you'll enjoy each 45-minute rotation overlooking the lake, volcano, and rain forest while dining on authentic Swiss cuisine. Try the *zürcher geschnetzeltes* (veal and mushrooms in a white sherry sauce) or *bundnerteller* (thinly sliced dried beef, ham, and cheese), just be sure to get their famed *röesti* (Swiss hash browns) on the side. Or, go for one of the fondues. Costa Rican and other international options are also on offer, but as long as you're in the Switzerland of Central America, go for the Swiss cuisine.

Monteverde
RESTAURANT DE LUCÍA

506-2645-5976
www.costa-rica-monteverde.com
Cerro Plano
Price: Moderate to Expensive
Credit Cards: Yes
Cuisine: Italian, Latin
Serving: L, D
Handicap Access: Yes
Reservations: Yes

Emphasis is on presentation in this soft-lit, hardwood dining room, with enough elegant extras to enrich the rustic appeal. It's popular with vacationing Ticos, who come for the Peruvian ceviche, while vegetarians go for the recommended baked eggplant lasagna, perfect after a chilly day in the rain forest. Lucía's caters to carnivores, however. Choose your cut of beef and have it made-to-order; the local favorite comes wrapped in bacon, topped with mushroom sauce.

No matter what you have, start with the fresh-made tortillas that come to your table with four toppings (guacamole, jalapeño peppers, *pico de gallo*, and refried beans), and finish off with one of their Italian-accented desserts, such as the *pannacota* flan.

PIZZERÍA DE JOHNNY

506-2645-5066
www.pizzeriadejohnny.com
2 km (1 mi.) east of Santa Elena
Price: Moderate
Credit Cards: Yes
Cuisine: Italian
Serving: L, D
Handicap Access: Challenging
Reservations: Recommended

Delicious, thin-crust, wood-fired pizzas are served piping hot in elegant environs, with muted paint schemes and arched windows that welcome cloud-forest views. This cozy, congenial spot has been Monteverde's favorite evening out for years, and it's not just pizza, either: Affordable sandwiches and pastas, and more upscale fish dishes and lamb, are all complemented by a variety of fresh, organic salads, made with herbs from the garden and mozzarella made right here. The candlelit indoor dining area is great when the mist rolls in, but try to grab a seat on the lovely outdoor terrace when the sun shines. Service is excellent, the bruschetta appetizer delish, and there's a small bar in the corner for just enjoying the evening.

★ SOFIA NUEVO LATINO CUISINE
506-2645-7017
Cerro Plano, 100m after turnoff at Hotel Heliconia
Price: $$$
Credit Cards: Yes
Cuisine: Latin Fusion
Serving: L, D
Handicap Access: Yes
Reservations: Recommended

Monteverde's finest dining is served with real panache beneath Spanish-Colonial style candelabras and elegantly arched windows that open onto a deep green forest. Take a seat and peruse the short menu, starting, perhaps, with a Sofia colada, just one of their great cocktails involving maracuyá juice, coconut milk, and two kinds of rum. The menu changes regularly, but always features a creative combination of Costa Rican, Caribbean, and other Latin cuisines.

Our appetizer, the *yuca encebollada* (stuffed manioc) could come filled with Monteverde cheese, beef, or both; we chose both, and were pleased with rich flavors wed within a crunchy exterior, perfectly accented with spicy chipotle cream sauce and caramelized purple onions. My dining companion enjoyed his shrimp in mango curry, served over coconut rice, but I was more impressed with the vegetarian chile relleno, filled with black bean sauce, a delicious picadillo, and Monteverde cheese.

Food Purveyors

Bakeries

ARENAL AREA
★ **Tom's Pan** (506-2694-4547; Nuevo Arenal; open 7 AM–5 PM, Mon.–Sat.; $–$$) A Lake Arenal institution, the "German Bakery" offers hefty homemade breads and exquisite European pastries, as well as sandwiches, sausages, and light meals.

MONTEVERDE
Panadería Jiménez (Santa Elena; open 5 AM–6:30 PM, daily; $) The earliest cup of coffee in town, served with sweet or savory pastries, is across from the bus station.
★ **Stella's Bakery** (506-2642-5560; Cerro Plano; $) I will design my entire day around lunch here, with savory delectables such as feta-and-veggie phyllo pastries, quiches, and empanadas; and sweet treats including rich brownies or delicate fruit-stuffed pastries. Or, fill out an order form for a custom sandwich, with your choice of bread, fillings, and condiments, then help yourself to a bottomless cup of coffee.

Cafés
Caburé Argentine Café and Chocolates (506-2645-6566; Cerro Plano; open 10 AM–6 PM; $–$$$) Enjoy sunset from the balcony of this chocolate shop and Argentinian café, also surving *canalones*, quiches, organic salads, and amazing chocolate desserts.

Café Monteverde (Cerro Plano; open 8 AM–6 PM; $–$$) Sample several types of Monteverde organic coffee before deciding on a cup or a pastry.

Café Rainforest (506-2479-7239; open 8 AM–8 PM; downtown La Fortuna; $): Popular, central spot to meet and greet does gourmet coffee beverages, light breakfasts, and snacks.

★ **Toad Hall** (506-2692-8020; Lake Arenal, 8 km/5 mi. east of Nuevo Arenal; open 8:30 AM–4 PM; $–$$$) Walk through the whimsical gallery to enjoy delicious sweets, sandwiches, and light meals with lots of vegetarian options, such as the excellent marinated eggplant with basil on macadamia bread.

Sodas

La Casona (506-2766-7101; www.hotelaraambigua.com; Sarapiquí, Ara Ambigua Lodge, 3 km from Puerto Viejo; $–$$) Sarapiquí's best restaurant, just outside town, is at this rustic all-wood lodge paved in dark gray flagstones and serving well prepared typical dishes, steaks, and seafood, plus a few mildly spiced Mexican offerings.

★ **Morpho's** (506-2645-5607; Santa Elena; open 11 AM–10 PM, daily; $$–$$$) Gourmet *soda* brings in the crowds with excellent fruit drinks (some blended with yogurt) and gourmet-ish typical cuisine; try the sea bass in avocado sauce.

Soda La Parada (506-2479-9547; La Fortuna, across from Central Park; open 24 hours; $) Right across from the bus stop, this basic but tasty *soda* offers Tico classics around the clock.

Grocery Stores

Super Christian II (La Fortuna, across from the Central Park) On the main road, has the best selection in town.

Supermercado Esperanza (Santa Elena, downtown) The best-stocked grocery store in Monteverde.

Super Monteverde (Cerro Plano, next to CASEM) Smaller selection, but more convenient to Cerro Plano.

CULTURE

The fertile lowlands of the *Zona Norte* have long lent themselves to logging, ranching, and farming, with large-scale agribusiness the region's economic backbone since the early 1900s. It is also among the most biologically diverse regions on Earth, a fact finally noticed in 1968, when that rich volcanic soil yielded up one of the world's most photogenic attractions, erupting Arenal Volcano.

Overnight, the tiny town of La Fortuna was hosting an international mix of scientists, thrill seekers, and photographers—and their hard currency. Soon after, Sarapiquí's La Selva Biological Station began hosting a similar mix of scientists, birders, and tourists, around the same time that the Quakers founded what would become Monteverde Cloud Forest Preserve.

And here begins the tale of history's first and grandest experiment in ecotourism. Throughout the 1980s, Monteverde and La Fortuna's impressive eco-attractions were drawing in a whole new type of tourists, here to enjoy the wild nature their forebears had tamed back home. This tourism meant development, and both regions thrived in what the world called Central America's success story.

Sarapiquí suffered a different fate. During Nicaragua's Contra War of the 1980s, rumors of spillover violence discouraged tourism in the region. Big agribusiness was less worried about war than ecotourists, however, and Sarapiquí's forests fell like pickup sticks to accommodate mostly U.S.-owned banana, sugarcane, and pineapple plantations that still carpet the region. Though the Contra War is long over, the disparities in development compared to Arenal and Monteverde are still obvious. Lower incomes, literacy rates, and life spans characterize Sarapiquí's hard-working population.

Today, ecotourism may be one of the travel industry's big buzzwords, and it's easy to be cynical about "sustainable" travel. But here in Costa Rica's Northern Zone, you can see the difference that your eco-dollar really makes. To learn more, check out the **Centro Científico Tropical** (506-2253-3267, 800-2230-4926; Monteverde; www.cct.or.cr; www.cloud forestalive.org); **Monteverde Institute** (506-2645-5053; Monteverde; www.mvinstitute .org); **Organization for Tropical Studies** (506-2524-5774; 919-684-5774 USA; Sarapiquí www.ots.ac.cr); and **San Luis Research Station** (506-2645-8049; Monteverde; www.uga .edu/costarica); all of which offer classes, seminars, and more.

Museums

MUSEO DE CULTURA INDIGENOUS DR. MARÍA EUGENIA BOZZOLI & ARCHAEOLOGICAL PARK ALMA ATA

506-2761-1004
www.sarapiquis.org
Centro Neotrópico Sarapiquís, La Virgen de Sarapiquí
Admission: $12 museum; $5 Alma Ata
Open: 9 AM–5 PM, daily

Named for Costa Rica's first female anthropologist, this museum is the best of its kind in the country. Housed in a handsome *palenque*-style building, sleek, modern exhibits focus on indigenous culture, with Spanish and English signage covering subjects such as shamanic healing, musical instruments, masks, and more. They also show a documentary about the area's indigenous history.

Afterward, walk over to Alma Ata Archaeological Park, being excavated in conjunction with the National Museum, which displays the remains of a 600-year-old village; some artifacts date back to 800 B.C. Paths lead around the remains of several tombs, petroglyphs, and a reconstructed town typical of 15th-century Costa Rica. Also on-site is a free interpretive trail through the Chester Field Biological Gardens.

MUSEO LOS ABUELOS

506-2479-7306
www.museolosabuelos.com
La Fortuna, 900m east of Central Park on the road to Arenal
Open: 8:30 AM–6 PM, daily
Admission: $8 with guide; $6 without guide

If you're going to spring for the "Museum of Grandparents," you might as well get a guide to help you sift through two rooms of rummaged antiques, including a 200-year-old drill, 1884 gun carriage, 1910 tractor, and a collection of 1970s Costa Rican disco albums. There's also a solid international currency collection, which includes a coin featuring Roman

The Northern Zone is marbled with tiny rivers and streams.

Emperor Marco Aurelio, dating to 187 A.D. More pertinent, and interesting, are several newspaper clippings from the 1968 eruption.

MUSEUM OF MONTEVERDE HISTORY

506-2645-6566
paseodestella.googlepages.com/home
Monteverde; Cerro Plano, 150m east of CASEM
Open: 9 AM–6 PM, daily
Admission: $8

A work in progress at press time, this much-needed museum tells the story of Monteverde, beginning with the region's natural history, including disconcerting graphs that chart Monteverde's rising temperatures against dropping amphibian populations. Still bare-bones exhibits also touch on tales of the Tico dairy ranchers who first settled the wild region, the Quakers' exodus from Alabama and arrival on Green Mountain, and the rise of ecotourism. One of the Quaker community's founders, Marvin Rockwell, sometimes gives talks here. Packages include visits to the neighboring Bat Jungle.

Music and Nightlife

ARENAL AREA

Lava Rocks Lounge Bar & Grill (506-2479-8039; La Fortuna, south side of Central Park; $$–$$$) Popular restaurant and nightspot offers upscale Tico cuisine, great live music (usually jazz), and a festive ambiance.

Volcán Look (506-2961-4691; open 7 pm–close, Wed.–Sat.) A $5 cab ride from La Fortuna toward Arenal is "Costa Rica's largest disco," which gets packed on weekends.

Equus Bar-Restaurant (open 11 AM–midnight; 13 km west of Nuevo Arenal) Rustic lake-front watering hole has a full bar and good restaurant.

MONTEVERDE

Several spots show evening slide shows, including **Hotel Fonda Vela** (6 PM, nightly; admission $5), covering Quaker history; and wildlife photos at the **Monteverde Lodge** and **Hummingbird Gallery**.

Bar Amigos (Downtown Santa Elena) Boasting the best bar food in Monteverde, Amigos also has pool tables and live music on Friday.

La Taberna (100m east of Santa Elena, toward Serpentario) Tourists and Ticos alike start showing up at 10 PM to groove to the Latin beats.

Moon Shiva (506-2645-6270; www.moonshiva.com; Cerro Plano; open at 11 AM) Hipster hot spot offers movie nights and live music; schedules are posted on the door. The restaurant ($$–$$$) does great Middle Eastern food.

Bromelia's Music Garden (506-2645-6272; www.bromeliasmusicgarden.com; across from CASEM, Cerro Plano) Offers two performing arts venues: An indoor music hall that's usually free; and the outdoor Monteverde Amphitheater that hosts big-name artists and events for around $10–$15.

Wildlife Displays and Rescue Centers

ARENAL AREA

Butterfly Conservatory (506-2306-7390; www.arenalbutterfly.com; El Castillo; open 8 AM–8 PM, daily; admission $15 with guide, $12 without guide) El Castillo's *mariposario* claims to be the largest in Costa Rica, and offers amphibian exhibits, impressive gardens, and the opportunity to see butterflies emerge from their chrysalises most mornings.

Jardín Ecologico Serpientes de Arenal (506-2399-5272; El Castillo; open 8 AM–9 PM, daily; admission $10, including guide) Next door, this awesome "Snake Garden" shows off 32 of Costa Rica's slithering species, as well as frogs, turtles, spiders, and butterflies.

SARAPIQUÍ

Santuario Mariposas Aguas Silvestres (506-2761-1095; www.pozoazul.com; Hacienda Pozo Azul, La Virgen; open 8 AM–5 PM, daily; admission $8 with guide, $5 without guide) More than 20 butterfly species on 30 hectares (74 acres) of secondary rain forest with trails, botanical gardens, poison dart frogs, and a swimming hole on the Río Bajigual.

Serpentario Snake Garden (506-2761-1059; La Virgen, 200m from Centro Neotrópico; open 9 AM–5 PM, daily; admission $6 for adults, $4 for children) Classic roadside attraction displays some 70 species of snakes, and several other reptiles as well.

MONTEVERDE

★ **Bat Jungle** (506-2645-6566; paseodestela.googlepages.com/home; Cerro Plano; open 9 AM–8:30 PM, daily; admission $10 for adults, $8 for students) Scores of bats flitting about are on a reverse schedule, and like to hang out and eat fruit (or, in the case of the hummingbats, sip nectar) during the day, when you'll also get an informative and interesting tour. Author of *Bats of Costa Rica*, Richard LaVal, sometimes gives lectures here.

★ **Frog Pond** (506-2645-6320; www.ranario.com; 500m south of Santa Elena; open 9 AM—8:30 PM, daily; admission $10 for adults, $8 for students, including a guide) The wonderful Ranario displays more than 30 species of adorable amphibians in attractive aquariums connected by a faux forest trail. Admission includes a repeat visit that evening, when many of these kissable critters are more active. At press time, a butterfly garden was in the works as well.

Monteverde Butterfly Garden (506-2645-5512; www.monteverdebutterflygarden.com; Cerro Plano; open 9:30 AM—4 PM; admission $10 for adults, $7 for students) After an educational tour (with views into a leafcutter ant burrow), see more than 50 butterfly species from four different ecosystems. Tarantulas, scorpions, and other creepy crawlies are also on display.

Mundo de Insectos (506-2645-6859; 400m from Santa Elena; open 9 AM—7 PM; admission $8 for adults, $6 for students) Small but potent collection of insects includes the most venomous spider in Costa Rica and largest bug in the world. There's also a butterfly enclosure.

Serpentarium (5062-645-6320; www.skytrek.com; downtown Santa Elena; open 8:30 AM—8 PM; admission $8 for adults, $6 for students) This collection brings in the Harry Potter fans with 40 snake species (including the deadly fer-de-lance), plus other reptiles and amphibians.

RECREATION

Parks and Preserves

ARENAL AREA
ARENAL NATIONAL PARK
506-2461-8499
www.costarica-nationalparks.com/arenalnationalpark.html
Open: 8 AM—4 PM, daily
Admission: $10 at ranger station; $7 at Arenal Observatory Lodge; La Fortuna trail to Cerro Chato free

The original eruption on July 19, 1968, which first blasted through the Earth's crust where famed Tabacón Hot Springs now steams, killed 87 people; several have died since, including a few tourists foolish enough to climb the mountain. Today, the reliably erupting volcano is one of Costa Rica's most popular attractions, a fearsomely symmetrical cone echoed to the south by dormant, and climbable, Cerro Chato (1,100 meters; 3,608 feet), topped with a crater lake, all part of a 12,124-hectare (29,946-acre) national park.

There are three main ways to enter the park. First is at the ranger station, 3.5 kilometers (2 miles) from the well-signed turnoff before Arenal Dam. There are almost 5 kilometers (3 miles) of trails, which pass a still-steaming lava flow from 1992 and a *mirador* (viewpoint), where you can watch fresh lava roll down the mountain. Arenal Observatory Lodge offers another 6 kilometers (3.7 miles) of trails to guests and day-trippers. Budget hikers take the free, grueling four- to five-hour hike to Cerro Chato and its cool crater lake from the La Fortuna Waterfall parking lot. Any tour agency can arrange an assortment of guided hikes, including transportation.

Photographing wildlife at Heliconia Island in Sarapiquí

CAÑO NEGRO WILDLIFE REFUGE
506-2471-1309
www.costarica-nationalparks.com/canonegrowildliferefuge.html
25 km (16 mi.) west of Los Chiles
Open: 8 AM–4 PM, daily
Admission: Free, but you must hire a boat to explore the reserve

Usually arranged as a day trip from La Fortuna, bird-watchers and sportfishers alike make their way to this 9,969-hectare (25,100-acre) protected tropical marshland, which provides shelter for migratory birds and waterfowl, and most famously the roseate spoonbill. Naturalist guides leading boat tours can also point out caimans, turtles, and bull sharks. Most visitors, however, are sportfishers interested in tarpon, snook, *mojarra*, and *guapote*. Fishing licenses ($30; available July–March) can be purchased at the ranger station. Waterways expand and contract with the seasons, opening up a few hiking trails by mid-March. You can camp next to the ranger station for $6 per person.

LA FORTUNA WATERFALL
7 km southwest of La Fortuna
Open 8 AM–5 PM, daily
Admission $6

Just outside La Fortuna is this beautiful 70-meter (230-foot) waterfall, pouring down a rain-forested cliff into a narrow, verdant valley that's home to some of the most scenic swimming holes anywhere—but please don't swim under the waterfall, as that's very dangerous. From the parking lot (a steep 7 kilometers/4 miles from La Fortuna, $3 in a taxi) with small food stands and souvenir shacks, it's a very steep and sometimes slippery 20-minute walk to the bottom of the waterfall.

SARAPIQUÍ
BRAULIO CARRILLO NATIONAL PARK
www.costarica-nationalparks.com/brauliocarrillonationalpark.html
Province of Heredia
Open: 8 AM–4 PM, daily
Admission: $7–$15

The most important protected area in the region is this massive, almost undeveloped 45,899-hectare (113,370-acre) park. There are three ranger stations in the park, all accessed from the Central Valley; from this side of the protected area, the easiest entries are through La Selva Biological Station and Rara Avis Lodge. Excursions farther into the park are best undertaken with a trained guide. With 6,000 species of plants, 333 species of birds, nine dormant volcanoes, and untold numbers of hot springs, this difficult-to-visit attraction is worth the effort for healthy adventurers.

HELICONIA ISLAND
506-2766-6247
www.heliconiaisland.nl
Bijajua de Upala, 8 km (5 mi.) south of Puerto Viejo de Sarapiquí
Open: 8 AM–4 PM, daily
Admission: $15 with guide; $10 without guide; $35 for a night tour

The belle of the tropical bouquet and perhaps the most beautiful blossom to grace the jungle's understory, some 80 varieties of the pendulant and polychromatic heliconia have long been the star of these bewitchingly beautiful 2.3-hectare (5.6-acre) gardens, cradled within two branches of the Río Puerto Viejo. You'll also see scores of orchids, ferns, palms, and other tropical plants. Area lodges arrange tours to this exquisitely arranged Eden, or you could spend the night in one of their appealing, tastefully decorated rooms ($$, all inclusive) with enormous windows and outstanding cane furniture.

The lovely Dutch owners offer guided and self-guided tours throughout their property, as well as hikes to a swimming hole, butterfly farm, sugar mill, or the Bijajua Waterfall. An on-site restaurant offers a limited menu of international cuisine.

LA SELVA BIOLOGICAL STATION
506-2524-5774; 919-684-5774 USA
www.threepaths.co.cr; www.ots.ac.cr
3 km (1.8 mi.) south of Puerto Viejo de Sarapiquí
Open: By reservation only
Admission: Guided hikes $28–$40 per person

You must have reservations to visit this 1,480-hectare (3,656-acre) preserve bordering Braulio Carrillo National Park, which offers guided birding tours and night walks, boat tours on the Sarapiquí River, and workshops that range from tropical photography to scientific exploration. Serious hikers can walk from here south to Braulio Carrillo's Barva Volcano ranger station in the Central Valley, but much shorter and no less scenic jaunts abound. La Selva also offers very basic, fan-cooled rooms, most with bunk beds and shared cold-water bathrooms ($$), including cafeteria-style meals.

TIRIMBINA BIOLOGICAL RESERVE

506-2761-1579; 414-272-2702 USA
www.tirimbina.org
La Virgen
Open: Tours available by reservation; self-guided tours 8 AM–5:30 PM, daily
Admission: Self-guided tours $15; guided tours $20–$30

The 405-hectare (1000-acre) reserve of mostly primary rain forest protects one of the last remaining stands of mid-elevation rain forest, with a fine trail system that includes Costa Rica's longest suspension bridge and 9 kilometers (5.4 miles) of trails, including a 1-kilometer (.6-mile) wheelchair-accessible route. Allow at least two hours for the self-guided hike, longer if you plan to enjoy the swimming hole on the south side of Tirimbina Island. Reservations are required for guided tours, which include night walks where you may see bats captured in the station's mist nets; birding expeditions in search of the reserve's 420 species; and the Chocolate Tour, operated in conjunction with a local indigenous women's association. The reserve also offers simple but well-appointed rooms ($$$*), as well as dorm beds and camping at their research station.

MONTEVERDE

Appreciating Monteverde properly is a chilly (18°C/64°F average), misty, muddy business. You'll need warm clothes, rain gear, and for serious hikes, rubber boots, rented all over town.

BOSQUE ETERNO DE LOS NIÑOS

506-2645-5003
www.mclus.org
Admission: Bajo del Tigre Trail $7 per adult; $4 per student; guided hikes $15
Open: 6:30 AM–4 PM; night hike 8:15 PM

Beginning in 1987, a small army of children from 41 countries set out to save the cloud forest by purchasing it at $250 per hectare, with spare change collected door-to-door; perhaps you helped. If so, this is what you bought: 21,870 hectares (54,000 acres) of tropical rain forest, the largest private preserve in Costa Rica, only partially opened to tourism and 100 percent protected for the animals who live here. Re-inspired? They're still taking donations, and buying more rain forest.

Most people visit on Bajo del Tigre trail, located just past CASEM, which offers guided hikes on 3.5 kilometers (2 miles) of trails. With advance reservations, sturdy hikers can spend the night in very basic dorms ($$$, including all meals) at either San Gerardo Field Station (506-2645-5200; 7 km/4 mi. from Santa Elena), with 5 kilometers (3 miles) of trails, two waterfalls, and guided birding hikes; or the Pocosol Field Station (506-2468-0148; 13 km/8 mi. from Tigra de San Carlos), with 10 kilometers (6 miles) of trails accessing bubbling volcanic mud pots.

MONTEVERDE CLOUD FOREST BIOLOGICAL PRESERVE

506-2253-3267; 506-2645-5112 to reserve guided hikes
www.cct.or.cr
7 km east of Santa Elena
Open: 7 AM–4 PM, daily; night walks 7:15 PM
Admission: $15, plus $15 per guide; night walks $17

This is it, the Holy Grail for nature lovers, a 3,500-hectare (8,645-acre) swath of cloud forest straddling the continental divide, with at least four different ecosystems home to 101 species of reptiles, 121 species of mammals (including all six Costa Rican cats), 425 species of birds, 755 species of trees, and 500 species of orchids. It's popular (some call it the "crowd forest"), so get here early, as only 120 people are allowed to access the 13 kilometers (8 miles) of developed trails at any one time. Guides are highly recommended.

While you wait near the entrance, you can visit the cafeteria (open 7 AM–4 PM, daily; $) or the fairly fabulous gift shop. Serious trekkers can make reservations to hike on unimproved (think chilly, thigh-deep mud) trails and spend the night in one of three simple shelters ($) with dorm beds and cooking equipment.

Santa Elena Cloud Forest Reserve

506-2645-5390
www.reservasantaelena.org
5 km northeast of Santa Elena
Open: 7 AM–4 PM, daily; guided hikes at 7:30 AM and 11:30 AM
Admission: $9 for adults; $5 for students; $15 for guided hikes

Monteverde's *other* cloud forest reserve is much smaller (310 hectares or 765 acres), with a bit less biodiversity because it only covers one side of the continental divide. It's also less crowded than Monteverde. The preserve, administered by the Santa Elena High School, offers 12 kilometers (7 miles) of trails, including a 1.4-kilometer (1-mile), 45 minute "Youth Challenge," and 15-meter (45-foot) observation tower, with views of Arenal Volcano if it's clear.

Jurassic foliage at Monteverde Cloud Forest Biological Reserve

Tourist in the mist at Monteverde Cloud Forest Biological Reserve

Agriculture Tours

SARAPIQUÍ

Dole Banana Tour (506-2383-4596; www.bananatourcostarica.com, 5 km from Puerto Viejo) Dole shows how bananas are grown, picked, processed, and shipped.

Chiquita Banana Show (506-2766-6010; www.chiquitabananashow.com; Tue. at 1:30 PM; $12–$15) Next door to Dole, Chiquita offers a "Banana Show," with singing and dancing.

Finca Corsicana Pineapple Tour (506-2820-6489; pineappletour@fincacorsicana; 2 km past La Quinta in Puerto Viejo) Visit an operating organic pineapple farm, where you'll learn the history of pineapple, see people working, and drink fresh pineapple juice.

MONTEVERDE

Don Juan Coffee Tour (506-2645-7100; www.donjuancoffeetour.com; admission $25 per adult, $20 per student) Tico-owned coffee plantation now offers tours.

Jardín de Orquídeas San Bosco (506-2645-6410; jardinorquideas@costarricencense.cr; Santa Elena; open 7 AM–4 PM, daily; admission $7 per adult, $5 per student) A guided tour of more than 500 species of orchids, including the largest and smallest (a magnifying glass is included) orchids in the world, as well as trails and a bromeliad garden.

★ **Monteverde Cheese Factory Tour** (506-2645-7090; www.crstudytours.com; Cerro Plano; tours at 9 AM and 2 PM; admission $8 per adult, $6 per student) Monteverde's *Lechería*, founded half a century ago with 50 dairy cattle and one product (gouda cheese), now produces 14 of Central America's best cheeses and ice creams, and yes, there are free samples.

Monteverde Coffee Tour (506-2645-5901; www.monteverde-coffee.com; tours at 8 AM and 1:30 PM, daily; admission $30 per adult, $26 per student, $12 per child) Make reservations for Monteverde's original coffee tour, which takes you to small organic farms.

El Trapiche Tour (506-2645-5834; www.eltrapichetour.com; tours at 10 AM and 3PM, Mon.–Sat. and 3 PM, Sun.; admission $25 per adult, $20 per student, $10 per child) Take an oxcart through coffee, plantain, and pineapple fields to a trapiche, where you'll see sugarcane juice squeezed the old-fashioned way. Sweet.

Boat Tours

Arenal Area

Lake Arenal offers excellent *guapote* (rainbow bass) fishing; your hotel can arrange a fully equipped boat and guide for around $150 per half day/$250 per full day for four people.

Aventuras Arenal (506-2479-9133; www.arenaladvenures.com) Offers Caño Negro tours, white-water rafting, and Lake Arenal trips.

★ **Canoa Aventura** (506-2479-8200; www.canoa-aventura.com; 1.5 km/.9mi. west of La Fortuna) Offers canoe, kayak, and pontoon boat tours on Lake Arenal, Caño Negro, and area rivers, plus a remote lodge on Río Tres Amigos for serious paddlers.

Lake Arenal Boat Tours (506-2694-4547; arenalboattours@yahoo.de; Nuevo Arenal) The German Bakery in Nuevo Arenal offers waterskiing and overnight camping trips on a lake island.

Sarapiquí

Oasis Nature Tours (506-2766-6108; www.oasisnaturetours.com) Guided trips on the Río Sarapiqui, or longer trips to Tortuguero, the Río San Juan and beyond.

Travesía Sarapiquí (506-2766-5625; www.travesiasarapiqui.com) Boat tours along the Río Sarapiquí, Río San Juan, and Río Colorado, including trips to Tortuguero and San Carlos, Nicaragua.

Solentiname Tours (505-2270-9981; info@solentinametours.com) Arranges multi-day trips to Nicaragua.

Canopy Tours and More

Arenal Area

This is just a sample of the many, many canopy-type tours in the area.

Arenal Bungee (506-2479-7440; arenalbungee.com; $39) In addition to regular bungees, try night jumps, water touchdowns, and rocket launchers.

★ **Puentes Colgantes de Arenal** (506-2479-9686; www.puentescolgantes.com; next to Arenal Dam; open 7:30 AM–4:30 PM; admission $22 per adult, $12 per student) "Hanging Bridges" and raised trails meander through 250 hectares (600 acres) of tropical rain forest canopy, crossing two tiny rivers and one lovely waterfall. Make reservations for guided hikes, which include hotel pickup and one return visit.

Pure Trek Canyoning (506-2479-9940; www.puretrek.com; 2 km west of La Fortuna; $90) Rappel down four waterfalls and one dry canyon wall; prices include transport.

★ **Sky Trek Arenal Rain Forest** (506-2645-6003; www.skytram.net; canopy open 7:30–3:30, daily, night hikes 6 PM, birding hikes 6 AM; admission $60 per adult, $38 per child) Begin with a 1 kilometer (.6 mile) ride on the "sky tram," soaring 40 meters (120 feet) above the treetops, followed by 2.8-kilometer (1.5-mile) of zip lines. They also offer night treks and guided hikes.

SARAPIQUÍ

Rainforest Arial Tram Atlantic (506-2257-5961; www.rfat.com; Highway 32, east of Braulio Carrillo National Park; admission $60) The world's first rain forest aerial tram glides 40 meters (120 feet) above the ground. Snake, butterfly, and frog exhibits, trails, and a smallish seven-cable canopy tour cost extra, or can be part of packages that include transport from San José.

Sarapiquí Canopy Tour (506-2290-6015; www.crfunadventures.com) With 13 platforms, this respectable canopy also offers horseback and boat tours, plus a frog exhibit.

MONTEVERDE

Like La Fortuna, there are simply too many canopy eco-attractions to list here.

Monteverde Extremo Canopy (506-2645-6058; www.monteverdeextremo.com; 4.5 km/3 mi. from Santa Elena; tours $37 per adult, $27 per student) "Extreme" canopy tour offers 14 cables, including one 364-meter (2,250-foot) breathtaker, plus rappelling and a Tarzan swing.

Natural Wonders Tram (506-2645-5960; naturalwonders@racsa.co.cr; Cerro Plano; $15) Basically a ski lift into the cloud forest canopy, this handicap-accessible ride is a relaxing way to see the wilderness.

★ **Selvatura** (506-2645-5929; www.selvatura.com; entrance of Santa Elena Reserve; admission to bridges is $20 per adult, $15 per student; to canopy $40 per adult, $30 per student; other attractions, $5–$10 each) Classy attraction takes you into the canopy along 3 kilometers (1.5 miles) of elevated walkways. Or, spring for a package deal including guided hikes; a 19-platform, 15-cable canopy tour; butterfly, frog, snake, and hummingbird exhibits; and the truly awesome Jewels of the Rainforest, the world's third largest insect collection, hallucinogenically and informatively displayed.

★ **SkyWalk & SkyTrek** (506-2645-6003; www.skytrek.com; 5 km north of Santa Elena; open 7 AM–4 PM, daily; admission $60 per adult, $38 per children) Sure, this eco-attraction offers guided hikes on raised walkways, but you're really here for some of the highest towers, longest cables, and fastest zip lines in the country.

Guided Hikes

LA FORTUNA

Reserva Privada El Silencio (506-2388-3821; www.miradorelsilencio.com; 16 km (10mi.) west of La Fortuna; open 7 AM–9 PM, daily; admission: $5) This 225-hectare (556-acre) private reserve has seen attendance on its four trails skyrocket since the lava shifted to this side of the volcano; it gets crowded at sunset.

SARAPIQUÍ

★ **Grassroots Expeditions** (506-2766-6265; www.tierrahermosa.com; Puerto Viejo) Alex Martinez arranges a variety of day hikes and multi-day treks with an emphasis on sustainable and community-based tourism.

Hacienda Sueño Azul (506-2764-4244; www.suenoazulresort.com; Horquetas; $79) Luxury lodge's One Day Tour offers guided hikes, horseback tours, a canopy tour, tubing, hanging bridges, waterfalls, and swimming holes. They also offer excellent rooms ($$$*).

MONTEVERDE

Monteverde's options for guided hikes are endless, or take Sendero Los Amigos (5 kilometers/3 miles, 3 hours) to the top of Cerro Los Amigos (1,840 meters/6,000 feet) for free; the signed trail begins at Hotel Belmar in Cerro Plano.

Association of Naturalist Guides of Monteverde (506-2645-6282; aguinamon@yahoo .com.mx) This organization of accredited, multilingual guides arranges all sorts of specialty hikes.

Ecological Sanctuary (506-2645-5869; santuarioecologico@yahoo.com; open 6:30 AM–5 PM, daily, night tour 5:30 PM; admission $7 per adult, $5 per student) Family-owned, 4-hectare (119-acre) swath of secondary rain forest offers trail access by day, guided hikes at dusk.

Hidden Valley Trail (506-2645-6601; infovalleescondidio@yahoo.com; self-guided hikes 7 AM–4 PM, daily, guided hikes 7 AM, 9:30 AM, 2 PM, 5:30 PM; admission $5; guided hikes $15 per adult, $10 per student) I chose Sendero Valle Escondido for a night hike with my parents, and we were not disappointed, as guides with walkie-talkies radioed one another about the locations of sloths, monkeys, porcupines, and other animals, explaining in English how each contributed to Monteverde's mystical biome.

Sendero Tranquilo (506-2645-7711; www.sapitotoursmonteverde.com; admission $20) Hotel El Sapo Dorado offers guided hikes and night tours of their private reserve for small groups only. (Reservations recommended.)

Horseback Riding Tours

Any hotel can arrange horseback riding tours, but inexperienced riders are often better off with established companies. ★**Desafio Tours** (www.desafiocostarica.com) has locations in La Fortuna (506-2479-9464; next to the Catholic Church); and Santa Elena (506-2645-5874; across from Supermercado Esperanza).

ARENAL AREA

Rancho Arenal Paraiso (506-2460-5333; www.arenalparaiso.com) Offers horseback riding tours at their ranch on the flanks of Arenal Volcano.

MONTEVERDE

Sabine's Smiling Horses (506-2645-6894; www.smilinghorses.com; $35 for 2.5 hours) Offers trips to hot springs and waterfalls, as well as sunset and moonlight tours.

Meg's Stables (506-2357-3855; Cerro Plano, next to Stella's Bakery) Offers similar tours at similar prices.

Hot Springs

All of these springs are in the Arenal area. For the famous and fabulous **Tabacón Hot Springs** (www.tabacon.com; $55–$70), see Accommodations. Both Tabacón and Baldi are often offered as part of multi-destination day trips from La Fortuna or San José, which are usually much better deals.

Baldi Hot Springs (506-2479-9651; www.baldihotsprings.com; admission $28) With Las Vegas-style extravagance, glitzy gardens are festooned with wet bars selling pricey drinks, strategically placed waterfalls, and glamorously tiled lounging areas offering better volcano views (and much louder music) than Tabacón. At press time they were building a huge waterslide and hotel.

Eco-Termales (506-2479-8484; ecoterfo@racsa.co.cr; across from Baldi; $14) Reservations are required for a specific four-hour time slot to enjoy these quieter, jungle-enshrouded springs lined with river rocks, but no volcano views. Their "gourmet typical food" ($$) gets raves.

Las Fuentes Termales (506-2460-2020; $10) One block downhill from Tabacón, these simple springs cater to Tico tourists with five sandy-bottomed pools and a simple *soda*.

Other Activities

Bike Arenal (506-2479-9454; 866-465-4114 USA; www.bikearenal.com; La Fortuna) Offers a variety of bicycle tours, some in conjunction with white-water rafting and other activities.

Centro Ecológico Malekú Araraf (506-2839-0540; San Rafael de Guatuso; open by reservation only; admission $35) The Malekú Indians, who live in small subsistence farming communities around San Rafael de Guatuso, are still trying to organize real tourist infrastructure, but trips usually organized from La Fortuna often include a guided tour, meal, and traditional dance. They also offer several craft shops selling colorful and elaborately carved masks, as well as a small museum.

Raid Arenal (506-2479-7259; www.raidarenal.com; El Castillo) This French-owned operation offers quasi-military training and jungle survival skills on multi-day treks.

Venado Caves (506-2478-8071; 4 km south of Venado; open 7 AM–4 PM daily; admission $10) This 3-kilometer (1.8-mile), eight-chamber limestone labyrinth of stalagmites and stalactites features formations like the "hugging papaya," plus lots of bats, spiders, and mud (bring a change of clothing). Make reservations if you'll be visiting on your own.

White-Water Rafting and Kayaking

Although La Virgen de Sarapiquí is closest to the white-water action, tours can be arranged from La Fortuna and Puerto Viejo.

LA FORTUNA

Exploradores Outdoors (506-2479-7500; www.exploradoresoutdoors.com) Rafts the Picuare, Reventezón, and more.

Wave Expeditions (506-2479-7262; www.waveexpeditions.com) Offers Class I, II, and III trips on the Río Toro, Río Balsa, and Río Sarapiquí in rafts or inflatable kayaks.

SARAPIQUÍ

Aguas Bravas (506-2292-2072, www.aguasbravas.com; 1 km from La Selva Verde) Specializes in rafting, but also offers hiking, horseback rides, and mountain bike tours.

Aventuras de Sarapiquí (506-2766-6768; www.sarapiqui.com) Near Selva Verde, offers white-water rafting, canoe trips, canopy tours, mountain bikes, and more.

★ **Rancho Leona** (506-2761-1019; www.rancholeona.com; La Virgen) Excellent kayak tours can include lodging at this wonderful but basic hostel ($).

Windsurfing and Kitesurfing

Perhaps you noticed the windmills—Lake Arenal's consistent wind speed of 25 to 50 kilometers (15 to 30 miles) per hour make this one of Central America's best windsurfing and kitesurfing regions. November through January is prime time, June and October a bit wet.

Enjoy a tipple while you soak at one of Baldi Hot Springs' swim-up bars.

Tico Wind (506-2695-5387; 800-433-2423 USA and Canada; www.ticowind.com) Australian-run operation opens from December through April on western shore of Lake Arenal.

Tilawa Viento Surf Center (506-2695-5050; windsurfcostarica.com) Open year-round at breezy, Roman-themed **Hotel Tilawa** (www.hotel-tilawa.com; $$–$$$*) on Lake Arenal, offers windsurfing and kitesurfing, with classes and packages, as well as a skateboard park, tennis courts, and a pool.

Spas

ARENAL AREA

Several of Arenal's resorts have truly fabulous spas, including **Tabacón** (506-2265-1500; 877-277-8291 USA and Canada; www.tabacon.com), **En Gadi Spa at Montaña del Fuego** (506-2460-1220; www.montanadefuego.com); and **Neidín Spa at Hotel Kioro** (506-2461-1700, 888-886-5027 USA and Canada; www.hotelarenalkioro.com). Or, pay half the price at a simple day spa in La Fortuna.

Centro Terapéutico Fares (506-2872-5876; 506-2819-6443; second floor of Galaxia, across from the Central Park) In addition to offering wraps, masks, facials, massages, and reflexology, they'll come to any (spa-free) hotel in the region.

Day-Spa Herrera (506-2479-9016; 30m east of the Clinica Publica) The most established La Fortuna Spa.

Spa Los Sueños (506-2479-8261; lorenaserenity@yahoo.es; 200m east of the Central Park) La Fortuna's newest spa offers excellent rates on massages, wraps, facials, and other treatments.

MONTEVERDE

As in La Fortuna, many hotels offer spa treatments, including El Establo's gleaming **Green**

(506-2645-5110; www.hotelestablo.com) with scores of treatments, including
e wraps and milk baths, perfect for Monteverde.

Atmosphera (506-2645-6555; complejoatmosphera.com; downtown Santa Elena) Offers
spa treatments, tours, and real estate information.

Shopping

Books

Librería Dylan (506-2479-7130; La Fortuna, frente ICA) Mostly Spanish-language books,
but also a few English-language travel and nature guides.

★ **Chunches** (506-2645-5147; ranariomv@racsa.co.cr; downtown Santa Elena; 8 AM–6 PM,
Mon.–Sat.) The region's premier English-language bookstore offers travel guides and
other Costa Rica-themed books, as well as newspapers, magazines, coffee, snacks, laundry service, and tourist information.

Galleries

Arenal Area

Arte Nomada (506-2479-7346; sancezdeosrius@yahoo.com; La Fortuna, next to the Central Park) Beautiful and unusual jewelry made by local artisans, some inexpensive and
some quite fine.

★ **Galeria Artstudio Lago Arenal** (506-2695-8624; www.artstudio-lakearenal.com; from
Tilaran, 800m after Hotel Tilawa) Leona's dreamy wildlife-inspired canvases and silk
scarves are even lovelier than the view.

Galería Latina (506-2479-9151; 150m south of the church, second floor) Original paintings and wood sculpture by artists from Costa Rica, Nicaragua, Peru, Ecuador, and elsewhere in Latin America.

Galerías Coco Loco (506-2468-0990; kwetonal@racsa.co.cr; San Isidro de Peñas Blancas,
17 km from La Fortuna on road to San Ramón) Eye-catching art gallery offers top-of-
the-line original work, from the owners' paintings to Boruca masks, contemporary
Chorotega pottery, and gorgeous marble and wood carvings from Central America. Pur-
chases of more than $250 are shipped free.

Sarapiquí

Rancho Leona (506-2761-1019; www.rancholeona.com; La Virgen) Rancho Leona's
unusual line of stained glass, jewelry, and clothing provides the perfect gift for that colorful hippie in your life.

Monteverde

Galería Extasis (506-2645-5548; open 9 AM–6 PM, daily) Off the road between Santa Elena
and Cerro Plano, this gallery features the fine woodwork and sculpture of the Brenes
family and other local artists. **Alquimia Gallery** is next door.

★ **The Hummingbird Gallery** (506-2645-5030; hummingbird_gallery@hotmail.com;
open 6 AM–5 PM, daily) At the entrance of Monteverde Preserve, this gallery offers original art including the owners' amazing hummingbird photos. Or take a few snaps of your
own in their beloved hummingbird garden.

Masks both Boruca and modern are displayed at Galerías Coco Loco in San Isidro de Peñas Blancas.

EVENTS

January

Fiestas Cívicas La Fortuna (La Fortuna; last week of January through mid-February) La Fortuna erupts with festivities honoring patron San Bosco with fireworks, oxcart parades, Masses, all-night discos, and carnival rides set up near the bull ring.

February

Fiestas Cívicas Tilarán (Tilarán) Tilarán takes over hosting the party during the last week of February.

Vuelta al Arenal (Lake Arenal; www.vueltaallago.net) Annual 137-kilometer (85-mile) bike ride is "100 percent noncompetitive."

Monteverde Music Festival (www.mvinstitute.org; admission $12) From February through April, the Monteverde Institute hosts Costa Rica's finest musicians, playing everything from marimba to classical to reggaeton.

April

Expo San Carlos (Platanar) Part state fair, part cattle roundup.

October

Fiestas Cívicas Los Chiles (Los Chiles) This scruffy little border town gets gussied up in honor of the Patron Saint San Francisco de Asís.

6

Guanacaste and the Nicoya Peninsula

Everything Under the Sun

Welcome to warm and wonderful Guanacaste (pronounced "wan-a-KAS-tay"), Costa Rica's wild west, a vast province of broad sandy beaches, rustling grassland savannahs, and simmering volcanoes. For centuries, *sabaneros*, white-hatted cowboys, have roamed these rocky ranges on fine horses, watching over big Brahma cattle beneath the spreading guanacaste trees. Until very recently, this was one of the nation's poorest provinces.

Beginning in the late 1990s, however, North American developers realized that Costa Rica's driest, sunniest spot resembled the white-hot real estate of Southern California. Even the region's annual transformation, from rainy season's fertile greens to the honey blonde of the hot, dry summer, appealed. The name "Gold Coast" was coined, beachfront developments began breaking ground, and the rush was on.

As you race from San José up the smoothly paved InterAmericana, with a row of cloud forest-topped volcanoes on your right and the Gulf of Nicoya on your left, the landscape begins to change; you'll know you're in Guanacaste when the savannah opens up on all sides. The culture, too, is different; until July 25, 1824, Guanacaste was a province of Nicaragua, which had become embroiled in a seemingly pointless civil war. Thus Guanacaste rose up one of the world's genuine democratic revolutions, demanding (nicely) to become part of peaceful Costa Rica. Annexation Day is still one of the biggest parties in the country, celebrated with two weeks of debauchery and *topes* (horse parades) in the provincial capital of Liberia.

Liberia was originally built at this important crossroads by wealthy Nicaraguan ranchers, and still boasts Costa Rica's finest Spanish colonial architecture. Though it is Guanacaste's cultural, political, and economic center, the city has little to offer the casual tourists, other than convenience: Close to the Nicaraguan border and Nicoya's beaches, and home to the hemisphere's fastest growing international airport (10 kilometers/6 miles from downtown), Liberia is an important travel hub. Its malls, hotels, restaurants, and easy access to several national parks might keep visitors here for a few days longer. But most tourists head straight to the beaches.

Guanacaste's older urban centers are all well inland, however, quiet agricultural centers with fine plazas, good hospitals, and friendly residents, but little for tourists. On the Inter-Americana, the old gold mining town of Las Juntas de Abangares is now home to a great

The Nicoya Peninsula is scalloped with pretty bays and beaches.

museum and handful of hot springs. Friendly Cañas is the first real *sabanero* town you'll come to, worth visiting for its outstanding mosaic-tiled church (and matching plaza) as well as access to nearby Tenorio Volcano National Park, fringed with nature lodges; and misty Miravalles Volcano, with low-key hot springs resorts geared to Tico tourists. North of Liberia, Salinas Bay offers some of Central America's best kitesurfing.

West of Liberia, the Nicoya Peninsula has two major inland cities: Santa Cruz, the "Cradle of Costa Rican Folklore," known for its marimba (a type of wooden xylophone) music, and Nicoya, whose 1644 San Blas church is one of the oldest in the country. These *sabanero* centers are now also service towns for rapidly developing beach communities at the epicenter of Costa Rica's real estate boom.

Until recently havens for surfers and backpackers, beaches like Playas del Coco, Playa Flamingo, Tamarindo, and to a lesser extent Sámara and Montezuma, are raising 10-plus stories of upscale hotels and condos, with more construction underway. In 2004, Guanacaste's outstanding Four Seasons upped the ante even further, and is now the flagship property of the most exclusive luxury development in Latin America, the Papagayo Project.

Playas del Coco was home to the first hotel on the Nicoya Peninsula, and remains the service hub for several beautiful beach towns surrounding the broad bay. Playa Hermosa, 12 kilometers (7 miles) north of Playas del Coco, is a "Pretty Beach" flying the blue flag, flanked by residential and retirement communities. Just north, Playa Panamá is a calm, quiet cove where families come to swim and enjoy several lodging and dining options. To the south of Playas del Coco are the original resort towns of Ocotal and Pez Vela, with salt-and-pepper beaches presided over by the stately grand dame of luxury lodging, Ocotal Resort, with access to some of Costa Rica's best snorkeling and diving.

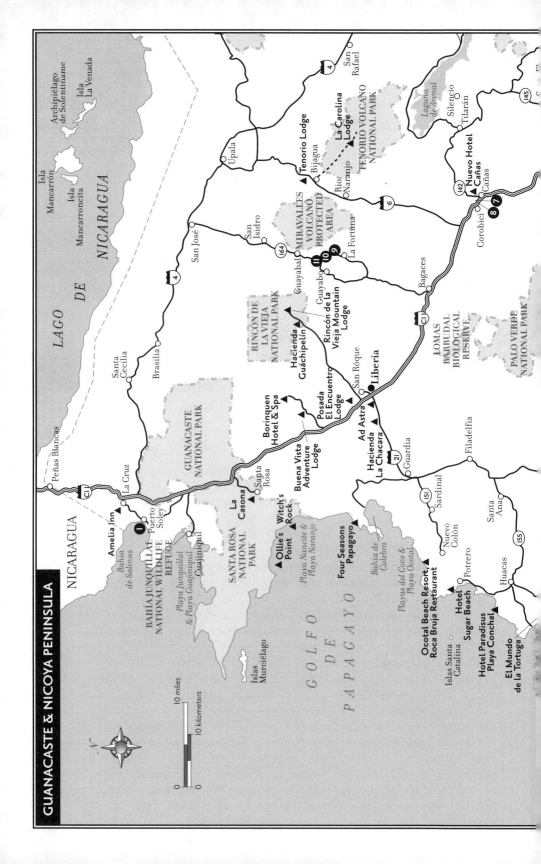

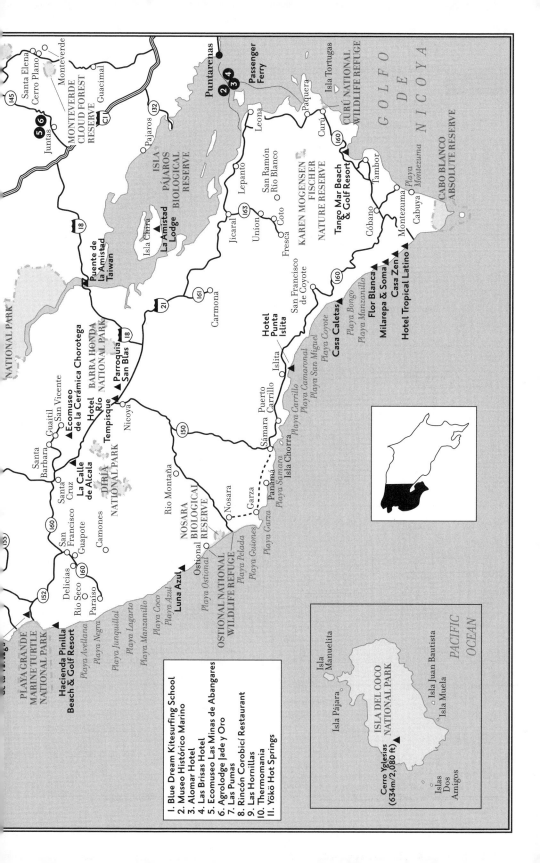

PLAYA GRANDE
MARINE TURTLE
NATIONAL PARK

Hacienda Pinilla
Beach & Golf Resort

Playa Avellana
Playa Negra
Playa Junquillal
Playa Lagarto
Playa Manzanillo
Playa Coco
Playa Azul

Luna Azul ▲

OSTIONAL NATIONAL
WILDLIFE REFUGE

Playa Ostional

Playa Pelada
Playa Guiones

Playa Garza

NOSARA
BIOLOGICAL
RESERVE

Nosara

Rio Montaña

Garza

Camones

Guapote

Rio Seco
Paraíso

Delicias

Santa
Cruz

Santa
Francisco

San
Francisco

Santa
Barbara

Guaitil

San Vicente

Ecomuseo
de la Cerámica Chorotega

La Calle
de Alcala

DIRIÁ
NATIONAL PARK

Río
Tempisque

Hotel
Río

Parroquia
San Blas ▲

BARRA HONDA
NATIONAL PARK

Nicoya

Puente de
la Amistad
Taiwan

Santa Elena
Cerro Plano
Monteverde

MONTEVERDE
CLOUD FOREST
RESERVE

Juntas

Guacimal

Pajaros

Pájaros

ISLA
PÁJAROS
BIOLOGICAL
RESERVE

Isla China

La Amistad
Lodge

Jicaral

Lepanto

San Ramón
Río Blanco

Union

Coto

Fresca

Carmona

Islita

Hotel
Punta
Islita

Puerto
Carrillo

Sámara

Panamá

Playa Sámara
Isla Chorra

Playa Camaronal
Playa Carrillo

San Francisco
de Coyote

Playa San Miguel
Playa Coyote

Playa Bongo
Playa Manzanillo

Casa Caletas ▲

Flor Blanca ▲
Milarepa & Soma ▲
Casa Zen ▲
Hotel Tropical Latino ▲

Tango Mar Beach
& Golf Resort ▲

KAREN MOGENSEN
FISCHER
NATURE RESERVE

Curú

CURÚ NATIONAL
WILDLIFE REFUGE

Cóbano

Tambor

Playa
Montezuma

Montezuma

Cabuya

CABO BLANCO
ABSOLUTE RESERVE

Paquera

Passenger
Ferry

Puntarenas

Isla Tortugas

G O L F O
D E
N I C O Y A

Leona

PACIFIC
OCEAN

Isla
Pájara

Isla
Manuelita

Isla Juan Bautista

ISLA DEL COCO
NATIONAL PARK

Isla Muela

Islas
Dos
Amigos

Cerro Yglesias
(634m/2,080 ft) ▲

1. Blue Dream Kitesurfing School
2. Museo Histórico Marino
3. Alomar Hotel
4. Las Brisas Hotel
5. Ecomuseo Las Minas de Abangares
6. Agrolodge Jade y Oro
7. Las Pumas
8. Rincón Corobicí Restaurant
9. Las Hornillas
10. Thermomania
11. Yökö Hot Springs

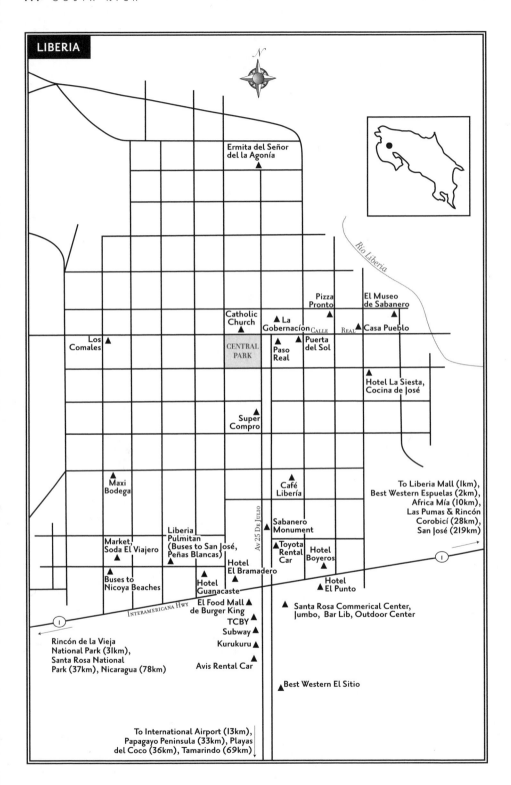

LIBERIA

N

Ermita del Señor del la Agonía ▲

Río Liberia

Pizza Pronto ▲

El Museo de Sabanero ▲

Catholic Church ▲

▲ La Gobernación CALLE

REAL ▲ Casa Pueblo

Los Comales ▲

CENTRAL PARK

Paso Real ▲

▲ Puerta del Sol

▲ Hotel La Siesta, Cocina de José

Super Compro ▲

Maxi Bodega ▲

Café Liberia ▲

To Liberia Mall (1km), Best Western Espuelas (2km), Africa Mía (10km), Las Pumas & Rincón Corobicí (28km), San José (219km)

Liberia Pulmitan (Buses to San José, Peñas Blancas) ▲

Market, Soda El Viajero ▲

Av 25 DE JULIO

Sabanero Monument ▲

▲ Toyota Rental Car

Hotel Boyeros ▲

Hotel El Bramadero ▲

Buses to Nicoya Beaches ▲

Hotel Guanacaste ▲

Hotel El Punto ▲

INTERAMERICANA HWY

El Food Mall ▲ de Burger King

TCBY ▲

▲ Santa Rosa Commerical Center, Jumbo, Bar Lib, Outdoor Center

Rincón de la Vieja National Park (31km), Santa Rosa National Park (37km), Nicaragua (78km)

Subway ▲

Kurukuru ▲ ▲

Avis Rental Car ▲

▲ Best Western El Sitio

To International Airport (13km), Papagayo Peninsula (33km), Playas del Coco (36km), Tamarindo (69km)

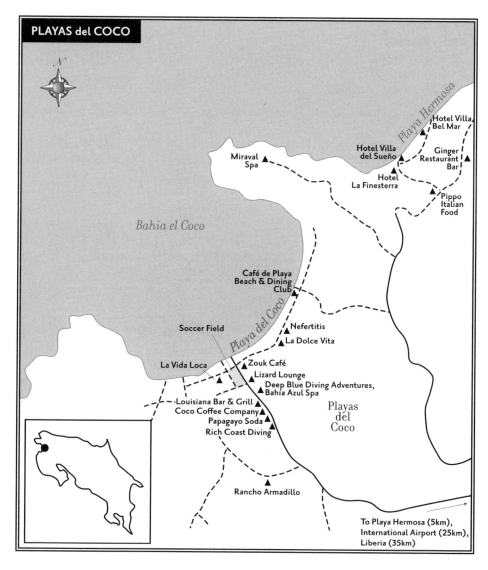

PLAYAS del COCO

Bahia el Coco

Playa Hermosa

Miraval Spa

Hotel Villa del Sueño

Hotel Villa Bel Mar

Ginger Restaurant Bar

Hotel La Finesterra

Pippo Italian Food

Café de Playa Beach & Dining Club

Playa del Coco

Soccer Field

Nefertitis

La Dolce Vita

La Vida Loca

Zouk Café

Lizard Lounge

Deep Blue Diving Adventures, Bahía Azul Spa

Louisiana Bar & Grill

Coco Coffee Company

Papagayo Soda

Rich Coast Diving

Playas del Coco

Rancho Armadillo

To Playa Hermosa (5km), International Airport (25km), Liberia (35km)

Farther south is Tamarindo, with the best PR machine on the peninsula, selling surf, sand, and plenty of real estate to eager expatriates anticipating an endless summer. Originally planned for a maximum of 1,000 families, the current boom has overtaxed Tamarindo's modest infrastructure, while a skyline pierced with unstoppable cranes has made this more the endless construction site. The goal—a glittering, ecologically sound resort town—will one day be realized, but at press time the legendary surf spot was in that awkward "tween" stage, caught between an idyllic beach-bum past and its inevitably upscale future.

But you can forget those early morning jackhammers with a jaunt north to Playa Grande, preserved as Las Baulas Marine National Park, with turtle nesting sites and a few relatively modest hotels and restaurants. Or head south, past posh Playa Langosta (now almost a suburb of Tamarindo), to a string of beaches that still cater to the surfing set: Playa Avellana

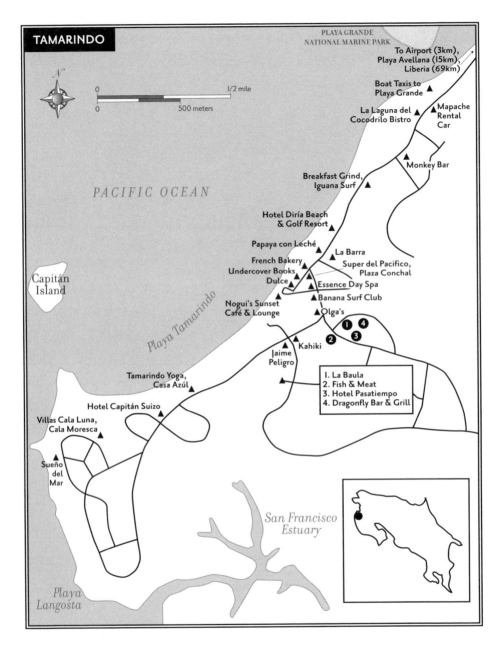

TAMARINDO

PLAYA GRANDE
NATIONAL MARINE PARK

To Airport (3km),
Playa Avellana (15km),
Liberia (69km)

Boat Taxis to
Playa Grande

La Laguna del
Cocodrilo Bistro

Mapache
Rental
Car

Monkey Bar

Breakfast Grind,
Iguana Surf

Hotel Diría Beach
& Golf Resort

Papaya con Leché

La Barra

French Bakery
Undercover Books
Dulce

Super del Pacifico,
Plaza Conchal

Essence Day Spa

Banana Surf Club

Nogui's Sunset
Café & Lounge

Olga's

Kahiki

Jaime
Peligro

Tamarindo Yoga,
Casa Azúl

1. La Baula
2. Fish & Meat
3. Hotel Pasatiempo
4. Dragonfly Bar & Grill

Hotel Capitán Suizo

Villas Cala Luna,
Cala Moresca

Sueño
del
Mar

PACIFIC OCEAN

*Capitán
Island*

Playa Tamarindo

*San Francisco
Estuary*

*Playa
Langosta*

N

0 ———— 1/2 mile
0 ———— 500 meters

and Playa Negra, with mostly basic restaurants and accommodations; then the isolated Edens of Playa Junquillal, Playa Manzanillo, and Playa Azul.

The final clutch of developed beaches on the easily accessed Northern Nicoya is centered on safe and friendly Sámara, still that cute little beach town of your dreams. Just north is serene and beautiful Nosara, not really a town at all, but a community connected by dirt roads criss-crossing the hills in paradise, with access to the turtle-nesting beaches of Ostional National Wildlife Refuge.

The Southern Nicoya has always been separate; it's not technically part of Guanacaste

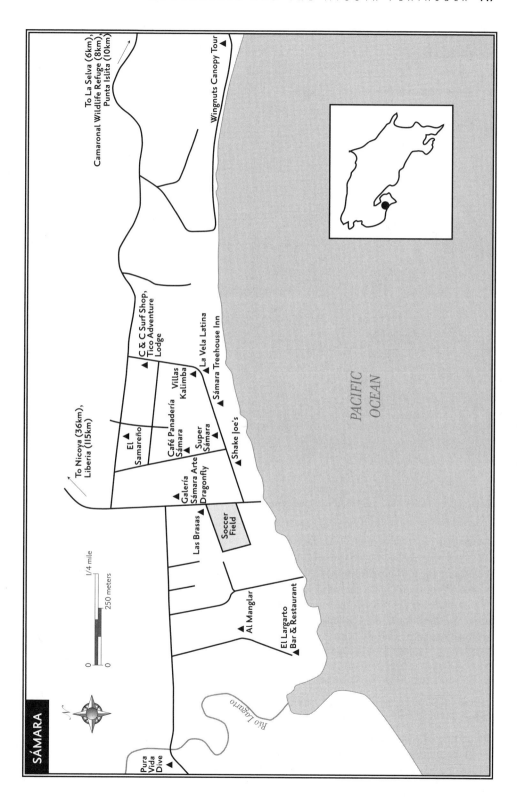

SÁMARA

To La Selva (6km),
Camaronal Wildlife Refuge (8km),
Punta Islita (10km)

Wingnuts Canopy Tour

To Nicoya (36km),
Liberia (115km)

C & C Surf Shop,
Tico Adventure
Lodge

La Vela Latina

Villas
Kalimba

Sámara Treehouse Inn

El
Samareño

Café Panadería
Sámara

Super
Sámara

Shake Joe's

Galería
Sámara Arte
Dragonfly

Soccer
Field

Las Brasas

1/4 mile

250 meters

0

0

Al Manglar

El Largarto
Bar & Restaurant

Río Lagarto

Pura
Vida
Dive

PACIFIC
OCEAN

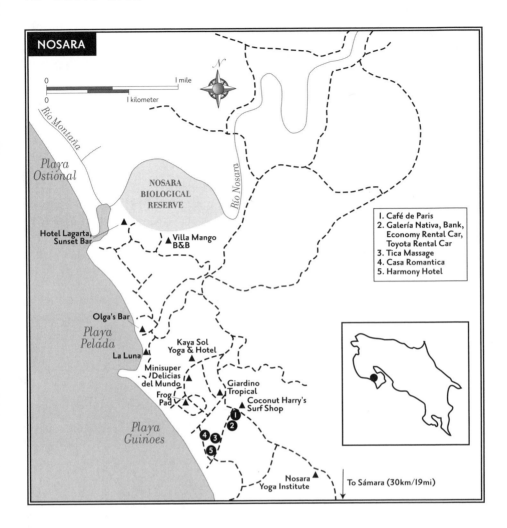

(it's actually in the Province of Puntarenas), nor was it ever administrated from Nicaragua. Though a dirt road connects this region to the rest of Nicoya, the easiest access is still by car ferry from the town of Puntarenas, just two hours from San José. Here, the festive beach towns of Montezuma, Malpaís, and Santa Teresa have become Costa Rica's hippest destinations, attracting celebrities and supermodels to its photogenic white-sand beaches, while still catering to the budget backpackers and surfers who started the trend. With vegetarian restaurants, yoga studios, and other groovy business (but no high-rise retirement condos—yet) strung along several kilometers of blue-flag beaches, this is one of the country's most desirable destinations.

SAFETY

Major tourist destinations—in particular Tamarindo and Playas del Coco, and to a lesser extent Montezuma and Sámara—have problems with tourist-related crimes, such as car break-ins, muggings, and swiping anything at all off the beach. Big city rules apply: Don't

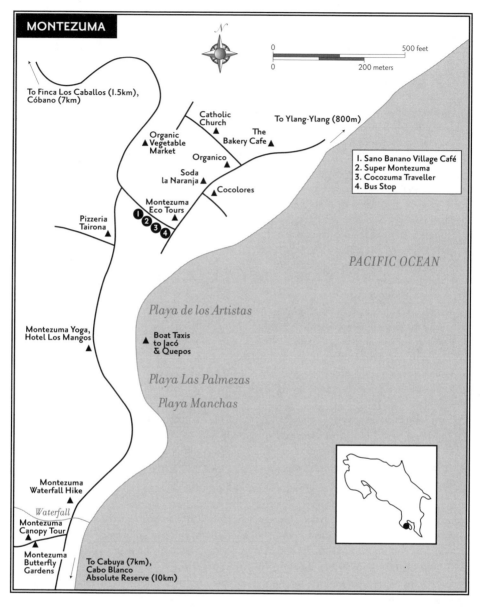

MONTEZUMA

To Finca Los Caballos (1.5km),
Cóbano (7km)

Catholic
Church

To Ylang-Ylang (800m)

Organic
Vegetable
Market

The
Bakery Cafe

Organico

Soda
la Naranja

Cocolores

Montezuma
Eco Tours

Pizzeria
Tairona

1. Sano Banano Village Café
2. Super Montezuma
3. Cocozuma Traveller
4. Bus Stop

PACIFIC OCEAN

Playa de los Artistas

Montezuma Yoga,
Hotel Los Mangos

Boat Taxis
to Jacó
& Quepos

Playa Las Palmezas

Playa Manchas

Montezuma
Waterfall Hike

Waterfall

Montezuma
Canopy Tour

Montezuma
Butterfly
Gardens

To Cabuya (7km),
Cabo Blanco
Absolute Reserve (10km)

leave anything in the car, use guarded parking, be alert when walking around at night, and
please stay away from the drugs you may be offered.

GETTING AROUND

Liberia is the region's transportation hub, at the crossroads of the InterAmericana and
Highway 21, and home to the Daniel Oduber Quirós International Airport (LIR), more often
referred to as the "Liberia Airport." A thatch-roofed regional airstrip until its major over-
haul to international status in 2002, this is now the fastest growing airport in the hemi-

Online Resources

The Beach Times (www.thebeachtimes.com) English-language weekly focuses on business, news, and entertainment.

Costa Rica Travel Magazine (www.online-costarica.com) Free tourist magazine covers Papagayo Gulf and Gold Coast.

InfoSamaraBeach (www.infosamarabeach.com) Information about hotels, tour operators, and more in Sámara.

The Howler (tamarindobeach.net/thehowler/index.html) Tamarindo's monthly glossy has great articles.

Liberia Costa Rica Info (www.liberiacostaricainfo.com) Huge site offers information and links for hotels, transportation, and airport.

★ **Nicoya Peninsula** (www.nicoyapeninsula.com) Excellent online guide covers the entire peninsula with maps, links, and more.

Nosara.com (www.nosara.com) Pithy Web site offers information about hotels, restaurants, businesses, and more; also try **Nosara Travel** (www.nosaratravel.com).

Playa Carmen (www.playacarmen.net) Hotels, vacation rentals, car rentals, ferry tickets, and tour companies in Santa Teresa and Malpaís.

Playa Montezuma (www.playamontezuma.net) Attractions, businesses, and vacation rentals in the southern Nicoya.

Montezumahotels.com (www.montezuma-hotels.com) Information and links to Montezuma, Malpaís, and Santa Teresa services.

Redes de la Península (www.redesdelapeninsula.com) Spanish-language magazine geared to tourists, with events listings, businesses, and attractions.

Samara Beach (samarabeach.com) Sprawling Web site has lots of links and useful information.

Tamarindo (www.tamarindo.com) Listings and links for Tamarindo area hotels, B&Bs, restaurants, and activities.

Tamarindo Beach (tamarindobeach.net) Cutesy Web site has good map and information.

Tamarindo News (www.tamarindonews.com) Bilingual news and business monthly.

Utopia Magazine (www.utopiacostarica.com) Travel guide and 'zine serves Guanacaste.

Zoom Nicoya Peninsula (www.zoomcostarica.com) Covers the Southern Nicoya Peninsula.

sphere, jetting from 56,000 passengers in 2002 to more than 400,000 in 2007. The small terminal, with a bank, ATM, and a couple of snack bars, will probably be remodeled while this book is still on the shelves. Note that your $26 exit tax must be paid in cash (colones or U.S. dollars) at the bank *before* checking in with your airline.

Schedules change frequently, but here were some airlines and flights available at the time of research:

Air Canada (www.aircanada.com) Weekly Toronto flight.

American Airlines (506-2668-9010, 506-668-1181; www.aa.com) Flights from Miami and Dallas several times per week.

Continental (800-044-0005, 506-2668-1186; www.continental.com) Houston daily, and Newark twice weekly.

Delta (506-2668-1050, 506-2668-1052; www.delta-air.com) Daily service to Atlanta.

First Choice (www.firstchoice.co.uk) One flight weekly to London.

Sky Service (419-679-5700 Canada; www.skyserviceairlines.com) Weekly to Calgary and Toronto.

United Airlines (www.ual.com) Once weekly to Chicago.

US Airways (506-2668-1141, 506-2669-1137; www.usairways.com) Several flights weekly from Charlotte.

Xtra Airways (www.xtraairways.com) Once weekly to Orlando.

Taxis from the airport to Liberia cost around $10, to Playas del Coco $30, and to either Tamarindo or the Nicaraguan border $70. There are several rental car companies (see sidebar), which will pick you up at the airport.

Regional Air Service

Guanacaste and the Southern Nicoya Peninsula have several small regional airports. **Sansa** (506-2290-4400, 506-2290-4100; www.flysansa.com) offers direct flights from Liberia to Arenal, Islita, Quepos, San José, Tamarindo, and Tambor; and from San José to Islita, Liberia, Nosara, Tamarindo, and Tambor.

Nature Air (506-2299-6000; www.natureair.com) offers flights from Liberia to Arenal, Bocas del Toro, Islita, Limón, Nosara, Palmar Sur, Puerto Jiménez, Quepos, San José, Tamarindo, and Tambor. From San José, there are direct flights to Islita, Liberia, Nosara, Tamarindo, and Tambor. Tamarindo is another NatureAir hub, with direct flights to Arenal, Bocas del Toro (Panama), Quepos, and Puerto Jiménez.

Driving

Guanacaste and the Nicoya Peninsula are known for their terrible roads. The good news is that major highways, including the InterAmericana, Highway 21 (Liberia to the Nicoya Beaches), and Highway 6 (Cañas to Upala) have been smoothly paved. Papagayo Peninsula south to Playa Ocotal, as well as the access roads to Tamarindo and Samará, are also paved. But if you plan to go anywhere else, or simply do some exploring, rent a four-wheel-drive.

Nicoya's incredibly scenic but sometimes stressful coastal road, sometimes called the Congo Trail or Monkey Trail, is mostly unpaved, but usually passable in the dry season for normal four-wheel-drive cars south to Sámara. The segment between Sámara and Southern Nicoya can only be used between February and May, when water levels in the half dozen rivers you'll need to ford drop below the level of your windshield. Even during droughts, ask locally about road conditions, and test river levels before crossing. Your rental car agreement probably does not cover damages incurred by driving into a river. You can almost always arrange special transportation to spots like Ostional Wildlife Refuge and the beaches of Santa Rosa National Park, with access roads that are impassable to normal four-wheel-drive cars in rainy season.

The major road connecting the Northern and Southern Nicoya Peninsula, via the cities of Nicoya and Playa Naranjo, is also unpaved, but it is maintained well and passable most of the year; ask locals during the rainy season. Afterward, you'll understand why most people take the ferry from Puntarenas.

International Buses

Comfortable international buses, with toilets, air-conditioning, and really loud action movies, leave Liberia for Nicaragua daily. Get tickets at least one day in advance.

Central Line (506-2257-7214) and **Nica Express** (506-2256-3139) Get tickets and buses at

Hotel Guanacaste (506-2666-0085; www.higuanacaste.com; 25m west of Liberia Pulmitan) in Liberia.

Tica Bus (506-2666-0371; www.ticabus.com) Tickets at the Liberia-Pulmitan bus station; buses stop in front of Hotel El Bramadero.

Private Shuttle

Grayline Fantasy Bus (506-2232-3681; www.graylinecostarica.com) Hotel-to-hotel service between Flamingo, Hermosa, Jacó, Liberia, Papagayo, San José, Sámara, Tamarindo, and more; plus international service to Granada and Managua, Nicaragua.

Interbus (506-2283-5573; www.interbusonline.com) Service to Liberia, Montezuma, Nicoya, Nosara, Playas del Coco, Puntarenas, Sámara, Tamarindo, Tambor, and more.

Tamarindo Shuttle (506-2653-2626; www.tamarindoshuttle.com; Tamarindo) Service from Tamarindo to Liberia Airport ($15) and other destinations.

Tour Bus Shuttle Service (506-2440-8078 Tambor, 506-2642-0919 Montezuma; www.montezumaexpeditions.com) Serves Tambor Airport, Montezuma, Malpais, Santa Teresa, Sámara, and Tamarindo, as well as boats to Jacó.

Boat

Puntarenas to the Southern Nicoya

Ferries for the Southern Nicoya leave from Puntarenas, 1.5 hours from San José, daily; docks are at the end of the peninsula, about 2 kilometers (1.2 miles) from the bus station, on Av Central. Ferries serve Paquera (**Naviera Tambor** 506-2661-2084; **Ferry Peninsular** 506-2641-0515; $4 for first class/$2 second class; $10 per car and driver) eight times daily; and **Naranjo** (506-2661-1069; admission $2, $12 for cars). Schedules change frequently, and are much shorter on Sunday, so check ahead. Ferries do sell out, so get there early and don't count on making a quick connection. Foot passengers can also take the smaller **Lancha de Paquera**, which leaves twice daily from behind the Puntarenas fish market, about three blocks from the main dock.

Taxis and buses meet all ferries at the terminal, from which it's a 24-kilometer (15-mile) drive to Montezuma or a 48-kilometer (30-mile) trek to Malpaís.

Tamrindo to Playa Grande

A boat taxi (for $1.50) makes the 5-minute trip across the Río Matapalo between Tamarindo and Playa Grande National Park from 8 AM–4 PM, daily. If you miss the return boat, Hotel Bula Bula, 10 minutes east of the beach, can arrange private transport for a few dollars.

Montezuma to Jacó

Several private tour companies run passenger boats between Montezuma and Jacó for about $30 each way; most arrange continuing service to San José, Quepos, and other destinations. If they don't offer you a life preserver when you board, ask for one. Operators include:

Cocozuma Traveler (506-2642-0911; www.cocozumacr.com) Besides tours they also offer horseback riding, ATV tours, sportfishing trips, and Tortuga Island tours.

Montezuma Eco Tours (506-2642-0467; www.montezumaecotours.com) Full service tour operator arranges anything on the Southern Peninsula.

Sunset & Waves Tropical Tours (506-2640-1900; www.caboblancopark.com/tropical/tours) Also arranges shuttles around the peninsula.

LODGING

Until recently, Guanacaste's lodging options were plentiful and comfortable, but pretty basic; only a handful of stately resorts sat atop the region's most wonderful coastlines. Then, in the late 1990s, Costa Rica's "Gold Coast" was discovered; some 15 resorts have opened here in the past two years alone.

The beach communities closest to the airport, from the Papagayo Peninsula south to Playa Ocotal, are the best developed in the country, boasting many of Costa Rica's best resorts as well as excellent options in the midrange and high end categories; budget travelers may feel priced out of the region. Other popular resort towns, such as Tamarindo, Sámara, Nosara, and Montezuma, also offer upscale accommodations, including private boutique hotels on quieter beaches nearby. More isolated beaches may only have simple *cabinas*, aimed at surfers and vacationing Ticos, with a few splendid exceptions. Expect all beachfront rooms to triple in price and fill weeks in advance for Semana Santa (Easter Week) and Christmas.

Lodging Price Code

Cost of lodging is based on an average per-room, double-occupancy rate at peak season (December through March). Costa Rica's 16.39 percent tax and gratuities are not included. Rates are often reduced during Green Season (May through November). An asterisk denotes that a full breakfast is included with the room price.

Inexpensive ($)	Up to $50
Moderate ($$)	$50 to $100
Expensive ($$$)	$100 to $200
Very Expensive ($$$$)	Over $200

Hotels

THE VOLCANIC HIGHLANDS
See Nature Lodges for more options.

BORINQUEN HOTEL

Manager: Mario Jimenez

506-2690-1900
www.borinquenhotel.com
reservations@borinquenhotel.com
23 km east of InterAmerica (intersection 13 km north of Liberia)
Price: Very Expensive*
Credit Cards: Yes
Handicap Access: Yes
Special: Three CST Leaves

Once you've made it up the rough rural road, you'll find this divine property, set into a scenic hollow in the skirts of Rincón de la Vieja volcano. Guanacaste's finest hot springs resort, Borinquen is spread over 200 hectares (500 acres) of tropical forest, centered on three developed springs set into a wooden deck above the singing Salitral River. Short hiking trails (including one to an ancient petroglyph), a small canopy tour, a gorgeous spa and natural "steam baths," which are basically wooden huts suspended above simmering volcanic fumaroles, accent the elegant grounds.

Even the least of Borinquen's ivy-covered cottages, the "villas," are spacious, handsomely crafted, and tastefully appointed in rich fabrics, ceramic tiles, heavy wooden furniture, and wrought iron details, plus amenities that include satellite TV, coffeemakers, and minibar. Bungalows are worth the upgrade, with more privacy and larger hammock-strewn porches. Much more modern junior suites perched atop the property offer great views to the Pacific plus well-equipped kitchenettes, plasma TVs, and in-suite hot tubs. Grounds are steep and isolated (golf carts are provided, but you will still get some exercise); consider picking up snacks in Liberia.

NORTHERN NICOYA PENINSULA
(PAPAGAYO PENINSULA TO PLAYA OCOTAL)

HOTEL BAHIA DEL SOL

Manager: Daniel Chavarría
506-2654-5182; 866-2223-2463
www.bahiadelsolhotel.com
reservations@potrerobay.com

Liberia Hotels

The pretty and pastoral provincial capital offers options aplenty for budget and midrange travelers, but still lacks a really good hotel. And, sadly, a new crop of deluxe chains, including Holiday Inn and Hilton, are breaking ground next to the airport, far from town. But there are a handful of comfortable options close to the shady city center, all just minutes from that early morning flight.

Best Western Hotel & Casino El Sitio (506-2666-1211, 800-780-7234; www.bestwestern.com; northwest of Liberia stoplight $$*) Reliably clean, modern rooms, a small casino, and a fabulous pool, make this a winner. A second **Best Western** (506-2666-2441; $$*), 2 kilometers (1.2 miles) south of Liberia on the InterAmericana, is almost as nice.

Hotel Boyeros (506-2666-0722; www.hotelboyeros.com; Liberia intersection with InterAmericana, $–$$) Adequate, air-conditioned rooms, guarded parking, two pools, and a 24-hour restaurant make this Liberia's second-best option.

★ **Posada El Encuentro Lodge** (506-2848-0616; www.posadaencu.com; info@posadaencu.com; $–$$*) This friendly and slightly frilly bed-and-breakfast is located just outside town, 4 kilometers (2.5 miles) from the InterAmericana, on the road to Rincón de la Vieja National Park, in the heart of the tropical dry forest. Large, immaculate rooms all have private hot baths and cutesy knick-knacks, while the partially covered pool terrace has hammocks and volcano views. The friendly English-speaking hosts, Luis and Sharon, make great breakfasts and arrange all tours and transportation.

El Punto Bed & Breakfast (506-2665-2986; www.liberiacostarica.com; just south of the stoplight on the InterAmericana; $$*) Brightly colored rooms with interesting architectural flourishes make this convenient bed-and-breakfast unique.

Hotel La Siesta (506-2666-2950; lasiestaliberia@hotmail.com; 200m west and 250m south of church; $$) This out-of-the-way spot offers immaculate, air-conditioned rooms, quite nice upstairs, surrounding a tiny pool and attached to the very best *soda* in town, ★**Cocina de José** ($–$$), serving lunch and dinner.

Playa Flamingo, Potrero Bay
Price: Expensive to Very Expensive*
Credit Cards: Yes
Handicap Access: Yes

This intimate oceanfront property, on a dramatic black-sand beach close to Playa Flamingo, offers affordable prices, excellent service, and an air of elegance you usually only get with a few more stars. Standard rooms are fine, with clean tile floors, large windows, colorful accent pieces, and WiFi. But consider upgrading to one of the much larger, cheerfully painted suites, with dining rooms, sitting areas, full kitchens, and original artwork including Chorotega pottery and edgy modern pieces. The beach is calm and protected, for families rather than surfers, and the pool is outstanding, with padded wooden lounge chairs and thatched umbrellas. The resort has upgraded its *palapa*-topped poolside dining area into one of the region's best gourmet restaurants ($$$), serving great international cuisine and haute seafood dishes beneath its spectacular cane roof.

FIESTA PREMIER RESORT & SPA
Manager: Danny Hughs
506-2664-4250 (reservations); 506-2672-0000 (hotel)
www.fiestapremier.com
Playa Panamá
Price: Very Expensive
Credit Cards: Yes
Handicap Access: Yes

Guanacaste's first all-inclusive resort overlooks a calm crescent of the perfect Pacific, Playa Panamá. Accommodations at this 410-room hotel are spacious and well designed, though it's hard to compete with newer properties. Many are in quiet duplex villas with marble floors, huge bathrooms, and private patios, all large enough so families can get some rest between enjoying the pools, tennis courts, restaurants, spa, children's programs, fitness room, and on-site casino.

All of this was in some disarray when I visited, however, as Hilton had just announced its purchase of the venerable resort. The new owners will hopefully lavish upon this five-star property the attention and investment it so richly deserves. Check more recent reviews to find out how things are going, and let us know what you think. If you don't think much of it, consider neighboring **Nakuti Resort** (506-2672-0121; www.nakutiresort.com; Playa Panamá; $$–$$$*), a more downscale, but fun, all-inclusive.

★ FOUR SEASONS
Manager: Luis Argote
506-2696-0000
www.fourseasons.com/costarica
Papagayo Peninsula
Price: Very Expensive
Credit Cards: Yes
Handicap Access: Yes

Enter atop the spine of the paradisiacal Papagayo Peninsula on "the longest hand-laid stone road in the Americas," lined with royal palms. This is one of the finest Four Seasons properties anywhere, with understated rooms laden with elegant examples of nature's best work: Brazilian cherry wood, dark lava stone, richly veined marbles, gold, jade, glass, and incomparable views.

The clubhouse would do any maharaja proud, a symphony of arches and light that seem some tropical homage to the Sydney Opera House. Costa Rican architect Ronald Zürcher said he wanted "to start our own

new architecture," and perhaps he has; the organic lines and natural materials of this masterpiece are inspiring a new generation of resorts. Service is personalized and impeccable, with 800 employees for 153 incredible rooms, ranging from $850 for a beachfront bungalow to $10,000 for the presidential suite with a wall of glass taking in the finest views in Costa Rica.

Even if you won't be staying at the Four Seasons' elegant digs, there are myriad reasons to visit: The fabulous golf course, free public beaches (really!), and several gourmet restaurants; reservations (506-2696-0006) are required. Favorites include **Di Mare** ($$$$; open 6 AM–10 PM; reservations required) with elegant, Italian-accented fine dining; relaxed **Caracol** ($$$–$$$$; open 11 AM–10 PM), convenient to the golf course; and **Papagayo** ($$$–$$$$; open 6 AM–11 AM, noon–3 PM, and 6 PM–10 PM), a more casual, poolside option, with creative Latin-Asian fusion cuisine.

OCOTAL BEACH RESORT
506-2670-0321
www.ocotalresort.com
reservations@ocotalresort.com
Playa Ocotal
Price: Expensive*
Credit Cards: Yes
Handicap Access: Yes
Special: Three CST Leaves

One of Costa Rica's long-standing luxury properties, Ocotal is renowned as a very comfortable base for world-class scuba diving and sportfishing, as well as wonderful views over pristine Playa Ocotal (but just minutes from convenient Playas del Coco). Though the picturesque property, with its wonderful grounds, service, and amenities, is still the sentimental favorite, compared to Guanacaste's new crop of sparkling super-resorts, Ocotal Beach could be spruced up. Some rooms are fabulous, perhaps a bit worn but boasting beautiful beach views from the private patios, as well as original art, brightly colored fabrics, parquet floors, and all the usual deluxe amenities. Other rooms are less well preserved; ask to see a couple if you're unimpressed.

The on-site **Roco Bruja Restaurant** ($$$) is known for good seafood and solid high-end international cuisine, but legendary for the stunning 270-degree views over the bay, the boats, and that black-sand beach.

HOTEL PARADISUS PLAYA CONCHAL

Manager: Paula Martinez

506-2654-4123

www.paradisusplayaconchal.travel
Playa Conchal
Price: Very Expensive*
Credit Cards: Yes
Handicap Access: Yes

Considered Costa Rica's finest resort until the Four Seasons opened its doors, this sprawling, glamorous, five-star Melia Sol property still delivers paradise on a platinum platter with 406 suites, six restaurants, several beautiful pools, an 18-hole Robert Trent Jones II golf course, boutiques, tennis courts, spa, disco, casino,

The Papagayo Peninsula Project

Snaking out into the deep blue Bahia Culebra, the picturesque Papagayo Peninsula, scalloped with some 20 beaches and serrated with dramatic cliffs, was once sacred to the Chorotega people. Today, it is at the center of Central America's most ambitious luxury tourism project, a collection of sustainable, world-class resorts designed to lie lightly upon the land.

The 930-hectare (2,300-acre) peninsula was set aside for tourism in the 1980s as the "Papagayo Project," originally slated for development by a Mexican corporation that pitched a Cancún-style, 16,000-room, high-rise jungle of cookie-cutter all-inclusives. Builders repeatedly ran afoul of Costa Rica's stringent environmental laws, however; construction was shut down after they dynamited a coral reef to "improve" the beach. Ahem.

Enter San José developer Alan Kelso, the Tico businessman who had just pulled off the stunningly successful Marriott Los Sueños. Impressed, the makers of Imperial beer, minority partners on the Papagayo Project, approached Kelso in 2001 about buying the Mexicans out.

The rest, as they say, is history. Plans for the mega-resorts were scrapped, and Kelso began working with the Four Seasons on low-density, high quality, eco-friendly accommodations. Kelso called in Ronald Zürcher (www.zurcherarquitectos.com), the Tico architect who had designed such eco-fabulous properties as Los Sueños, Si Como No, and Punta Islita. The dream team came through yet again, and in 2004 the Four Seasons opened to accolades.

Papagayo's hand-picked collection of resort properties will soon be joined by offerings from Mandarin and One and Only, as well as an exclusive $400 million "village" of deluxe vacation cottages (priced between $2 million and $12 million) designed for the global glitterati. Also in the works is Central America's largest and most luxurious marina; two more golf courses (one designed by Arnold Palmer); and Elerstina Costa Rica, a world-class polo field. Best of all, 70 percent of the peninsula will remain open space, so the howler monkeys will always have somewhere to hang.

All's not quite perfect in paradise. At press time, the Federal Environmental Commission had temporarily shut down one of Papagayo's top resorts, and was investigating another, for failure to treat wastewater properly (it was damaging the coral). By making an example of such prominent properties during peak tourist season, the world's most eco-friendly government sent a signal to all foreign developers; both resorts are cleaning up their acts. And that, more than any world-class golf course or $10,000-hotel room, is what makes Papagayo special.

plus that gorgeous white-sand beach. Elegant rooms (complete with Grecian columns) are decorated with classic furnishings in rich gem tones, polished wood, and soothing neutrals. Spacious and immaculate, they come standard with fine sitting rooms, large terraces, satellite TV, fully stocked minibar, IDD telephone, and more. Not enough for you? Consider upgrading to one of their specialty services.

The family concierge option offers huge guest rooms with separate living areas, stocked with child-sized bathrobes, beach kits, and minibar choices, plus walkie-talkies to keep in touch across the enormous resort grounds. Or go with Royal Service, including rooms in an exclusively adult complex, complete with a private pool, personal butler, and access to the **Gaby**, perhaps the best of several restaurants on site.

WESTERN NICOYA
(TAMARINDO, SÁMARA, NOSARA)

★ LOS ALTOS DE EROS

Owners: Calvin and Jacqueline Haskell
506-2850-4222; 786-866-7039 USA
www.losaltosdeeros.com
info@losaltosdeeros.com
20 min east of Tamarindo
Price: Very Expensive*
Credit Cards: Yes
Handicap Access: Yes

Climb into the Tamarindo hills to experience the Gold Coast's finest boutique hotel. This award-winning property only offers five spacious and serene deluxe suites surrounding the divine pool with ocean and forest views. Each is soothing, an earth-tone embrace of architecture and design, with pale white archways and curtains, glowing teak ceilings, organic sculpture, and large windows that welcome wonderful views. Of course each is air-conditioned with WiFi, free international calls, and stocked with all sorts of lovely organic toiletries.

This is a lovers' haven, offering sunset massages and intimate candlelit dinners worth experiencing even if you aren't a guest. If you are, breakfast and lunch are included, as is a personal driver, customized yoga classes, 5 kilometers (3 miles) of trails, and all the personalized attention Eros loves to lavish on its guests. Spectacular.

HOTEL BULA BULA

Owners: Wally and Todd
506-2653-0975
www.hotelbulabula.com
frontdesk@hotelbulabula.com
Playa Grande, on the estuary
Price: Moderate to Expensive*
Credit Cards: Yes
Handicap Access: Challenging

Just a few minutes by boat from Tamarindo on protected Playa Grande, are several inexpensive family-style hotels scattered through the forest. One of the best is Hotel Bula Bula (Fiji for "Happy Happy"), also home to the recommended **Great Waltini Restaurant**.

Enjoy some solitude in nature along the slow flowing river, perhaps wandering the gardens, or diving into the deep, cool pool. Ten rooms are painted in soothing colors, with tropical-themed art, large closets, and relaxed lighting that's just perfect after spending a day in the sun. Each is outfitted with a mini fridge, air-conditioning, satellite TV, DVD player, WiFi, and coffeemaker, though my favorite amenity is probably a shared porch overlooking the gardens, furnished with comfortable rattan rocking chairs. Polished.

If you're planning to stay in Playa Grande, also consider **Hotel Las Tortugas** (506-2653-0458; www.lastortugashotel .com; $–$$), a very attractive and sustainable beachfront hotel geared toward higher-end surfers.

Friendly young sabanero, *or Guanacasteco cowboy, saying "buenos dias"*

HOTEL CAPITÁN SUIZO

Owners: Ursula and Ruedi Schmid
506-2653-0075
www.hotelcapitansuizo.com
info@hotelcapitansuizo.com
1.5 km south of Tamarindo on road to Playa Langosta
Price: Expensive to Very Expensive
Credit Cards: Yes
Handicap Access: Yes

Quite simply the best beachfront hotel in the Tamarindo area, this secluded spot is elegant without being extravagant. Even the breezy, less expensive, fan-cooled rooms, on the second floor, are spacious and delightfully decorated, more like split-level apartments with sitting areas and private balconies overlooking lush landscaped grounds maintained without chemicals. Air-conditioned rooms downstairs are similarly superb, and even better are the bungalows hidden in the gardens, angled to offer privacy behind huge walls of glass where you can watch troupes of howler monkeys swing past.

The Swiss-German breakfast buffet is legendary, the pool is fabulous, the service outstanding, and the location is perfect, far enough from Tamarindo's fiestas and construction to relax, but close enough to walk into town for dinner. Though, foodies-in-the-know often make their way here, where the popular **restaurant** ($$$) delights diners with gourmet European-Latin fusion, made with mostly local and organic ingredients. Wednesday and Saturday are marimba nights; Friday is the barbecue (make reservations!).

HOTEL DIRIA TAMARINDO BEACH & GOLF RESORT

Manager: Oscar Sánchez
506-2653-0032; 866-2603-4742
www.tamarindodiria.com
reserves@tamarindodiria.com
Central Tamarindo, on the beach
Price: Expensive

Credit Cards: Yes
Handicap Access: Yes

If you want to stay right in downtown Tamarindo (probably a more appealing option by 2010 or so, once construction is finished), this quite civilized resort-style oasis of calm is just steps from the beach, as well as that dusty but fun conglomeration of surf shops, jewelry vendors, and bars just outside. The 183 rooms are perfectly acceptable, with large, modern bathrooms, tiled floors, new furnishings, WiFi, and U.S.-style amenities and layout, which may make families feel more at home. Standard rooms are a bit dark and cramped for the price; it's worth $50 to upgrade to larger accommodations with porches overlooking the landscaped gardens, enormous pool, and busy beach. A seven-story annex was under construction across the street.

FLYING CROCODILE

Owner: Anke and Guido Scheidt
506-2656-8048
www.flying-crocodile.com
flycroco@web.de
7 km north of Playa Sámara, on the road to Nosara
Price: Inexpensive to Moderate
Credit Cards: Yes
Handicap Access: Yes

On isolated Buena Vista beach, just north of Sámara, this is a unique hotel with remarkable amenities: An airstrip and ultralight aircraft, something like a cross between a motorcycle and hang glider. The owners offer rides, rentals, classes, and licensing (a 20-hour endeavor), and if you're even a bit tempted, you've got to at least check out the amazing videos on the Web site.

The hotel is geared toward visitors with their heads in the clouds, and makes no attempt at average, instead opting for flowing, brightly hued architecture inspired by Gaudi, intricate murals and groovy furnishings with an Ikea-style edge: bold colors, glass shelves, beds on platforms, weird windows. All are comfortable, with air-conditioning and hot showers, and include either kitchenettes or refrigerators. In addition to the pool, with waterslide and diving platform, Ping-Pong table, darts, and full bar with a great suspended grille, they also rent mountain bikes. Adrenaline, anyone?

HARMONY HOTEL

Manager: Fabien Palma
506-2682-4114
www.harmonynosara.com
info@harmonynosara.com
Nosara, Playa Guiones, 300m west of Café de Paris
Price: Expensive*
Credit Cards: Yes
Handicap Access: Yes

Imbued with the low-key glamour of a jungle hideaway, this clutch of luxury bungalows is operated by the green geniuses behind such fine properties as Lapa Rios and Morgan's Rock, but isn't quite as exclusive. The focus here is yoga, surfing, and healthy living, learning to treat your body and mind with the respect all natural environments deserve. As part of their "alternative development model," which includes a commitment to recycling, renewable energy, and community outreach, they also offer all-natural spa treatments—for example, ear candling and toxin-free pedicures. The gorgeous open-air restaurant ($$$) offers mostly organic, vegetarian cuisine, and some seafood; carnivores can find several meatier options within walking distance of the hotel.

Rooms are large, simple, and spotlessly clean, with lots of teak, ceramic tile, and unbleached cotton. WiFi, and a few laptops, are also available for use, but you'll probably be spending more time on your private patio or porch, perhaps in one of those comfortable hammocks.

HOTEL PUNTA ISLITA

Manager: Alonso Bermúdez Paniagua
506-2231-6122
www.hotelpuntaislita.com
info@hotelpuntaislita.com
Playa Camaronal, 9 km (5 mi.) southeast of
Sámara (4WD recommended)
Price: Very Expensive
Credit Cards: Yes
Handicap Access: yes

When this out-of-the-way, ultra-sustainable luxury hotel opened its doors in 1994 next an isolated blue-flag beach known mostly for its lousy roads and nesting sea turtles, most thought the remarkable venture quixotic. Today the resort is reliably ranked among Latin America's finest by *Conde Naste*, and remains a beacon of sincerely sustainable tourism, with educational tours, child care, and a very cool community-supported **Contemporary Art Museum**, all without compromising the plush promise of this place.

Some of the older concrete cabanas may look like traditional Tico houses, but inside feature fine hand-carved furniture, private plunge pools, shady porches, and modern amenities including minibars and coffeemakers. Standard rooms are almost as nice, and all have access to the spectacular grounds, free transport to the beach (and beach break), and infinity pool. The spa gets raves; the restaurant not so much, and only a continental breakfast is included in the price. They also arrange tours to nearby Cameronal Wildlife Refuge.

HOTEL SUGAR BEACH

Manager: Eric Barrantes
506-2654-4242
www.sugar-beach.com
sugarb@racsa.co.cr
Playa Pan de Azucar, 7 km north of Brasalito
Price: Expensive
Credit Cards: Yes
Handicap Access: Yes

One of my personal favorite escapes from Liberia, this lovely little two-star resort sits pretty above Playa Pan de Azucar, a perfect little beach bookended by tide pools, with safe swimming and solitude that seems a world away from the hubbub of Tamarindo or Coco. Standard rooms are very standard, older and plain, with air-conditioning, cable TV, and shared porches. Since you're already paying for the location, go ahead and upgrade to one of their more modern, brightly painted deluxe rooms, enormous suites or even the villa, with a full kitchen and laundry machine. The restaurant is very good but pricey (bring snacks from town) and the infinity pool gorgeous, with lots of resident iguanas who just love French fries with catsup.

PUNTARENAS AND THE SOUTHERN NICOYA PENINSULA

CASA CALETAS

Manager: Henry
506-2655-1271; 800-850-4592 USA and
Canada
www.casacaletas.com
info@ticoresort.com
Playa Coyote, 39 km northwest of Malpaís
(4WD only)
Price: Expensive to Very Expensive*
Credit Cards: Yes

Far from civilization, atop a promontory overlooking an untamed estuary of the Río Jabillo, with its attendant howler monkeys and crocodiles, is the resort's infinity pool. Part of a group of ecolodges built with loans from the World Bank, this rustic but very comfortable spot offers large, simple, air-conditioned rooms with handsome, high-end, hand-carved furnishings superbly crafted from polished branches, earth-toned original art, and awesome porches with great estuary views. Loft rooms have ladders leading to an upper mezzanine, with two twin beds.

Breakfast is included and other meals

Villas at the Peninsula's Tip

The newest trend in Southern Nicoya's luxury lodging are fabulously appointed villas offering every amenity (French chefs, private infinity pools, personal yoga instructors) and personalized service, all in absolute privacy.

Casa Chameleon (unlisted phone number; www.hotelcasachameleon.com; Malpaís; $$$$*) Booked months in advance, this exclusive and award-winning boutique hotel offers three ocean-view bungalows adorned in pale ceramics and tropical hardwoods.

Villas Hermosas (506-2640-0630; www.villashermosas.com; Montezuma; $$$$*) Airy, modern villas come fully equipped with full kitchens and upscale extras; some sleep six.

Latitude 10 (506-2640-0396; latitude10resort.com; Santa Teresa; $$$–$$$$*) Six sweet surfside bungalows are hewn with smart architectural flourishes from rich glowing teak, conjuring almost an imperial ambiance with chaise lounges, armoires, and antiques. Extras (organic toiletries, incense, pillow softness, minibar snacks) are customized in advance to your personal preference.

Milarepa (506-2640-0023; www.milarepahotel.com; Santa Teresa, 3 km north of Cabo Blanco National Park; $$$*) Named for the first Buddhist monk to achieve enlightenment in one life-time, these exquisite bamboo-and-teak abodes also offer some serenity on this graceful stretch of sugary white beach. Breezes perfumed by crashing waves wash through each open-air villa's gauzy curtains, elegant Indonesian furnishings, and al fresco showers. The Asian-Latin fusion restaurant, **Soma** ($$$–$$$$), is one of the region's best.

are served, or visit the tiny village of San Francisco de Coyote, with a gas station, grocery store, Internet café, and a few simple restaurants serving fresh seafood. The desk can arrange horseback rides, kayak excursions, and tours to see nesting turtles at neighboring beaches.

FLORBLANCA RESORT

Owners: Susan Money and Greg Mullins
506-2640-0232
www.florblanca.com
info@florblanca.com
Santa Teresa
Price: Very Expensive
Credit Cards: Yes
Handicap Access: Yes

The theme is Balinese and amenities first class at this classy boutique resort, arguably the best accommodations in Southern Nicoya. Ten splendid villas, with one or two rooms, are set into the jungle that surrounds the waterfall pool. Fine furnishings reveal quiet Asian accents, and simple but dramatic touches such as the pale sweeping curtains around fine beds and sunken bathtubs. Exquisite.

The focus is healthy relaxation, with an oceanfront yoga studio, small gymnasium, organic spa, and excellent restaurant, **Nectár** (open 7 AM–9 PM; $$$$; reservations recommended) serving healthy Asian-influenced entrées that always include vegetarian choices. They'll also prepare your catch, perhaps as sushi, should you indulge in one of their fishing tours. Your personal, bilingual naturalist-guide (included in the rates) can also arrange horseback riding trips, mountain bike tours, snorkeling, canopy tours, even surf lessons, using the complimentary surfboards.

HOTEL TROPICO LATINO

Manager: Marco D'Annuncio
506-2640-0062
www.hoteltropicolatino.com
tropico@centralamerica.com
Malpaís, Playa Carmen

Artist Otto Apuy decorated the Cañas church with fantastic mosaic tiles.

Price: Moderate to Expensive
Credit Cards: Yes
Handicap Access: Yes

This solid midrange option offers 10 spacious, comfortable bungalows scattered through its overgrown gardens, and centered around a big beachfront pool. The ambiance is hippie-upscale, with rooms constructed from local, low-impact materials, and furnished with renewable bamboo-framed beds, paper lamps, and other sustainable extras. Cavernous stone bathrooms come complete with organic amenities, but enthusiasts really need to check out the spa, offering all-natural facials, pedicures, massages, and packages that seem perfect for the conscientious girls' surfing safari.

There's a point break right in front of the hotel, which also arranges horseback rides, yoga classes, and all sorts of tours. The restaurant gets rave reviews.

YLANG YLANG
Manager: Moraya Iacono
506-2642-0636

www.ylangylang.com
reservations@ylangylangresort.com
Montezuma; walk south of town 10 minutes along the beach
Price: Expensive*
Credit Cards: Yes
Handicap Access: No

The calls of howler monkeys echo above the crashing waves, as all car noise is left behind. As you walk south of Montezuma along the shore—there is no road—each footstep sinking just slightly into the soft sand, you'll see it, hidden behind lush cascades of greenery and flowers: Your rainforest hideaway. And best of all, your bags are waiting in the room (brought by special vehicle from Sano Banano, downtown), which may detract a bit from the authenticity of your adventure, but whatever. Settle into one of those poolside hammocks or the beachfront bar.

Rooms, of which there are several shapes and sizes, are exceptionally creative and comfortable, some large enough for families, but overall a bit small and basic for what you're paying. But they're adorable and thoughtfully decorated, with Guatemalan tapestries, original art, nifty built-ins, and amenities including minifridges, hair dryers, safes, coffeemakers, and hot showers—but no air-conditioning. It's worth dropping by for a sunset cocktail or meal at their ★**restaurant** ($$–$$$), with an oceanfront happy hour and excellent international cuisine and seafood; try the shrimp bruschetta with white wine sauce, or sushi; there are always vegetarian selections as well.

Bed-and-Breakfasts

NORTHERN NICOYA PENINSULA
(PAPAGAYO PENINSULA TO PLAYA OCOTAL)

HOTEL VILLA BEL MAR
Owner: Pedro Belmar
506-2672-0276
www.hotelvillabelmar.com
info@hotelvillabelmar.com
Playa Hermosa, second entrance, on the beach
Price: $$*
Credit Cards: No
Handicap Access:

Simple and sweet, this modest hotel is my midrange choice on Playa Hermosa, a pretty crescent of sand separating the much busier towns of Playas del Coco and Flamingo. Settle into your airy, immaculate, whitewashed rooms, some with ocean views, and all with lots of light, hand-carved Sarchí furnishings, potted plants, appealing artwork, and cable television, air-conditioning, and hot showers. A full breakfast is served in the shady common area in front of the pool, just steps from the ocean. Another good oceanfront option nearby is **El Valero Hotel** (506-2672-0036; www.costaricahotel.com; $$), with more rooms and similar amenities.

RANCHO ARMADILLO
Owners: Rick and Debbie Vogel
506-2670-0108
www.ranchoarmadillo.com
info@ranchoarmadillo.com
Playas del Coco, 2 km west of Playa Hermosa turnoff
Price: Moderate to Expensive*
Credit Cards: Yes
Handicap Access: No

Ranked by *Bride* magazine as one of Central America's best honeymoon spots, this hilltop bed-and-breakfast overlooks Playas del Coco, with a perpetual view of the beaches, sunsets, and stars from the pretty pool, excellent rooms, or shady open-air lounge areas. The swish spot doesn't try to compete with those all-inclusives, however. Six simple suites are set into the gardens, with fabulous showers, better views, comfortable décor, handmade furniture carved into scenes from rural Guanacaste, rich indigenous fabrics, and minifriges; guests are welcome to use the hotel kitchen any time. The friendly owners can arrange any tour, recommend operators, restaurants, and cab drivers, organize airport transfers, or even plan your wedding down to the last detail. Rick, a retired chef, can prepare meals, and offers cooking classes upon request.

WESTERN NICOYA
(TAMARINDO, SÁMARA, NOSARA)

VILLA MANGO
Owner: Joe and Agnes Pinhiero
506-2682-0130
www.villamangocr.com
villamango@racsa.co.cr
Nosara, north end
Price: Moderate*
Credit Cards: Yes
Handicap Access: Yes

I love the way the sunset plays across this welcoming bed-and-breakfast's wraparound porch, from which all of Nosara rolls toward the sea in greens and golds. You'll watch the waning sun bathe every exposed inch of ground in reddish gold, from the glittering Pacific to the hammocks strung here. Rich woodwork is complemented with handmade furniture on this most amazing porch, and stocks of books and board games will let you while away your time while watching the butterflies and hummingbirds, or pizotes (white-nosed coatis) and monkeys, sharing the gardens and pool.

The artists' touch is obvious throughout the simple but beautiful rooms, three of which offer air-conditioning. All very elegantly furnished, with large, gorgeous bathrooms and plenty of light. Big breakfasts inspire repeat visits, as do the multilingual owners who will arrange a delicious gourmet dinner. Or ask about tours—they can send you out on horses, surfboards, or riverboat trips, then welcome you home with a drink from the full bar.

VILLAS KALIMBA

Manager: Roberto Carrer
506-2656-0929
www.villaskalimba.com
villaskalimba@racsa.co.cr
Sámara, 200m east of Guardia Rural
Price: Moderate to Expensive
Credit Cards: Yes

Encircling a colorful courtyard garden and fabulous pool inlaid with sandstone, these six delightfully constructed private villas are perfect for families, friends, or even a low-key honeymoon. The *tejas*-topped bungalows aren't on the beachfront; you'll have to walk two minutes across the street, but even that offers an extra level of safety and seclusion.

Each golden villa offers a shady front porch veiled in greenery for some privacy, complete with hammocks and graceful guanacaste-wood tables and chairs. Inside, each is ample and unique, with full kitchens and fine built-ins that swirl organically among the original art, well-placed lamps, exposed stone, and dreamy faded color schemes, all functional and fabulous at the same time. Most have two bedrooms, and

all include air-conditioning, wicker fans, cable TV, telephone, and security boxes. They also rent two private homes in town. Breakfast is included, but Roberto also cooks dinner several nights a week; it's always Italian (even the locally-renowned barbecues), and always includes imported wines.

SÁMARA TREEHOUSE INN

Manager: María Esther Díaz
506-2656-0733
www.samarabeach.com
samaratree@yahoo.com
Sámara, center of town, beachfront
Price: Expensive*
Credit Cards: Yes
Handicap Access: No

This is a great concept, perfectly executed: Six "tree houses" rise above the beachfront (on stilts, not trees, but that's a minor detail), with polished teak interiors, elegantly rustic furnishings, and wonderful views; make sure to reserve a beachfront room. Each is upscale, if compact, with amenities including WiFi, telephones, fans, full kitchens, and bathrooms (you'll love the creative tile work), high-quality bamboo furnishings, and just look out that seaward wall, almost entirely open to every bit of Sámara's salty crash, complete with knock-out views of Isla Chorra. Beneath each unit is a private patio, slung with hammocks, equipped with a shady seating area and barbecue grill; there's a nice pool nearby. The property is adult-only (the setup is a bit precarious for children anyway), and is not for folks with mobility issues. Romantics with a sense of adventure, however, have found their nest.

Puntarenas and Southern Nicoya Peninsula

HORIZON YOGA HOTEL

Manager: Yoav and Gali Geller
506-2640-0524
www.horizon-yogahotel.com

horizon.cr@gmail.com
Santa Teresa, .5 km (.2 mi.) past Frank's
Place, up the hill 100m
Price: Expensive
Credit Cards: Yes
Handicap Access: No

This peaceful wooden bed-and-breakfast, a steep five-minute climb from Santa Teresa, caters to yoga aficionados with its all-teak, ocean-view ashram at the highest point above the sea. There are wonderful views from all of the rooms, as well as the relaxing triangular pool that must meet some sort of feng shui criteria. All accommodations, with one or two bedrooms, are hewn from slender logs and simply furnished with soothingly arranged beds, paper lamps, full kitchens, air-conditioning, hot-water showers, TV, DVD, and lovely private porches; the villas have private pools. The main building has a great common area as well, with books and board games.

They provide healthy, mostly organic meals in their Tea House, but you're also a short walk from the region's best restaurants. Non-guests are welcome to daily yoga classes ($10) as well as the small spa, offering several types of massage.

MARIPOSARIO MONTEZUMA BUTTERFLY GARDENS

Manager: Joshua Bickle
506-2888-4200, 503-922-0769 USA
www.montezumagardens.com
info@montezumagardens.com
Montezuma, 350m south of the canopy tour
Price: Inexpensive to Moderate
Credit Cards: Yes
Handicap Access: Challenging

Atop the Montezuma Waterfalls (you can make the region's classic hike in reverse, down their rushing cascades to the beach, should you choose) is this delightful bed-and-breakfast featuring a very colorful amenity, and a wonderful *mariposario,* or butterfly garden. Brightly painted rooms,

with butterfly themes and all-natural art, are basic but very comfortable, offering air-conditioning, hot showers, WiFi, cable television, and private porches over all that wild nature.

Trails lead through the brilliant gardens, planted with fruits and flowers that attract all manner of wildlife. And it's all within arm's reach of a balcony splashed with cheerful Mexican *telas* (fabrics) where you'll enjoy your complimentary breakfast.

Nature Lodges

LIBERIA AND THE VOLCANIC HIGHLANDS (TENORIO, MIRAVALLES, RINCÓN DE LA VIEJA)

★ LA CAROLINA LODGE

506-2380-1656; 843-330-4178 USA
www.lacarolinalodge.com
info@lacarolinalodge.com
Bijagua, outside Tenorio National Park
Price: Moderate*
Credit Cards: No
Handicap Access: No

The four-wheel-drve-only ascent to La Carolina is fantastically beautiful, transforming from golden dry tropics to cool, humid cloud forest before your eyes. Behind you is Lake Nicaragua's shimmering expanse; in front, hidden in thickening jungle, volcanic-blue Río Celeste, where according to indigenous legend, "God washed his brush after painting the sky."

La Carolina is a special place, but rustic—not "upscale rustic," but actually rustic, with no hot water (except for the hot springs), no electricity (candles and kerosene lamps are provided), and not much English-speaking staff. Not for you? Try the very comfortable and modern **Tenorio Lodge** (506-2466-8282; www.tenoriolodge.com; $$$), offering gorgeous glass-enclosed cabins, at the foot of the mountain. But if you want to sleep just a short horseback ride (included) from the rushing rivers of this ancient volcano, these simple wooden rooms with

Montezuma is the quintessential beach town.

basic furnishings, and three typically Tico meals cooked on a wood-fired stove, may be just perfect.

RINCÓN DE LA VIEJA MOUNTAIN LODGE

506-2200-0238
www.rincondelaviejalodge.net
rincondelaviejalodge@gmail.com
1 km from Rincón de la Vieja Park, Paillas Sector
Price: Moderate
Credit Cards: Yes
Handicap Access: No

This clutch of quiet wooden cabins, on the site of a former 400-hectare (1,000-acre) hacienda slowly returning to forest, isn't luxurious, but each simple wooden room has a tiny balcony above the burbling Río Achuello, which also supplies the lodge's electricity. Furnished with homey hand-carved furnishings, comfortable beds, and hot showers, it's just a short walk to the Paillas Sector of Rincón de la Vieja National Park, close to cement-paved hot springs. You're rather far from the more popular Santa María sector, which accesses the main volcanic crater, bubbling mud pots, and waterfalls, but the hotels will arrange transport, or you can hike 7 kilometers (4 miles) through the forest. Typical Costa Rican meals served in the cozy restaurant are excellent.

NORTHERN AND WESTERN NOSARA (PAPAGAYO, PLAYAS DEL COCO, TAMARINDO, SÁMARA, NOSARA)

★ HOTEL LAGARTA LODGE

Managers: Regina and Amadeo Amacker
506-682-0035
www.lagarta.com
lagarta@racsa.co.cr
North Nosara
Price: Moderate
Credit Cards: Yes
Handicap Access: No

From its thickly wooded 40-meter (131-foot) perch above the nesting turtles of

Playa Ostional, and its own private 35-hectare (90-acre) wildlife refuge, this cozy nature lodge protects the wildlife-rich confluence of the Río Nosara and Río Montana. Fan-cooled rooms are clean and comfortable but by no means luxurious, with whitewashed walls, relaxed wooden furniture, and bright-colored accents. It's all about the view, however, from your private balcony or terraces just steps away from hiking trails through all that nature. Or, arrange a trek by horse or boat.

Stop by for the views from the breakfast buffet ($$–$$$) before hitting the trails. But make reservations for dinner; this popular restaurant is well known for its top-flight seafood and upscale Tico cuisine over the sea. Or make your way down to the rocky promontory reaching out into the bay. This is the **Sunset Bar**, open to everyone and offering fine wine, lovely cocktails, and tasty appetizers, served alongside "the best sunset in Nosara."

PUNTARENAS AND SOUTHERN NICOYA PENINSULA (MONTEZUMA, MALPAÍS, SANTA TERESA)

HOTEL LUNA AZUL

Managers: Rolf Lichtenstein and Andreas Baumann
506-2821-0075
www.hotellunaazul.com
info@hotellunaazul.com
1 km north of Ostional Wildlife Refuge
Price: Moderate to Expensive*
Credit Cards: Yes

Just north of Ostional Wildlife Refuge, Costa Rica's most important nesting ground for olive ridley turtles, this gem is more boutique bed-and-breakfast than nature lodge. But since you'll need to ford serious rivers (they'll pick you up in Nosara) to get here, I've listed it as a lodge. The trip, by the way, is worth it. Each of seven bungalows, with cane roofs, open showers, and private terraces, offers cool built-ins, tasteful furnishings,

and tropical accents. Upscale amenities, including minifridge, telephone, Internet access, and satellite TV, are also accounted for, as is one very nice infinity pool.

The Swiss owners specialize in alternative health treatments, and can arrange massages, acupuncture, homeopathic medicine, and even classes in Japanese Reiki. Or, just arrange a guided turtle tour. Breakfast is included, and though there are a few *sodas* in town, stay for at least one elegant dinner, enjoying sunset over gourmet Tico and Swiss specialties.

★ FINCA LOS CABALLOS

Owner: Christian Klein
506-2642-0124
www.naturelodge.com
naturelc@racsa.co.cr
4 km south of Cóbano
Price: Expensive
Credit Cards: Yes
Handicap Access: No

Just above the steep drop into Montezuma, this absolutely beautiful nature lodge is all about *los caballos*, "the horses," and is home to several remarkable steeds. Canadian champion Barbara McGregor originally built these stables, which current owner Christian Klein has since maintained. The lodge itself offers 12 jungle- or garden-view rooms, discerningly decorated with dark wood and rattan, flattering lighting, and flagstone bathrooms and porches. All include minifridges, CD players, coffeemakers, and fans, but no air-conditioning. The full buffet breakfast is served on the wooden porch, above a small pool with huge views to the Pacific. If you opt for dinner, you can choose to have it here or on your private patio.

This is the best option for high-quality riding tours, which are pricier than most ($18/hour) but worth it for the professional bilingual guides and healthy, well-trained horses.

Other Hotels

CAÑAS

Nuevo Hotel Cañas (506-2669-1294; 50m east of the InterAmericana; $$) The nicest hotel in this tidy agribusiness town has modern air-conditioned rooms, private hot showers, and a really nice pool.

LA CRUZ

Amalia Inn (506-2679-9618; 100m south of the plaza; $*) Scruffy La Cruz has incredible views over beautiful Bahía Salinas, the very best from this once relatively glamorous inn, today in some decline. Rooms are still clean and comfortable (but not air-conditioned), with mod '60s furnishings and amazing contemporary art by the owner's husband, who has since passed away but left a great mural by the pool.

LAS JUNTAS DE ABANGARES

Agrolodge Jade y Oro (506-2225-3752; www.hotel1492.com; 4 km from Las Juntas on road to Monteverde; $$*) If the handful of very basic $10–$20 *cabinas* in central Las Juntas fails to impress, try this "agricultural lodge," with large, nicely decorated wooden rooms—but no air-conditioning—inside Abangares Protected Area. There are hiking trails on the property, and they arrange gold mine and park tours.

NICOYA

Hotel Río Tempisque (506-2686-6650; hotelriotempisque.com; 800m north of Nicoya empalme (three-way intersection); $$–$$$) In the heart of the peninsula, this excellent midrange hotel offers clean, cool, tiled rooms in soothing blues and whites, outfitted with air-conditioning, cable TV, microwave ovens, and coffeemakers; a large pool and Jacuzzi are outside.

PLAYA NARANJO

El Ancla (506-2641-0815; www.hotelelancla.biz; $–$$) You're probably here because you already missed your ferry, so relax. Cute, clean, teak-topped rooms with plenty of character come with air-conditioning, hot-water showers, and a nice pool. The restaurant is top-notch.

SANTA CRUZ

La Calle de Alcalá (506-2680-1633; hotel alcala@hotmail.com; 100m south of Parque de los Mangos; $–$$) Lovely gardens with lots of ginger surround a pretty pool and good air-conditioned rooms decorated with indigenous art, wicker furniture, hand-carved doors and Chinese lamps; the suite even has a Jacuzzi.

Vacation Rentals

Bahia Pez Vela (506-2670-0129; www.bahiapezvela.com; Playa Ocotal; $$$–$$$$) Fully equipped beachfront condos sleep up to eight, just steps from an "ebony sand" beach.

Casas de Soleil (506-2640-0476; www.casasdesoleil.com) Beautiful beachfront cottages in Santa Teresa and Malpaís.

Coast to Coast (506-2670-0472; 877-589-0539 USA and Canada; www.rentalsincostarica.com) Weekly and monthly rentals around Playas del Coco.

Exclusive Escapes (506-2898-8640; www.exclusiveescapes.cr) Upscale vacation homes around Sámara.

Harbor Reef Costa Rica (506-2682-1000; www.harborreef.com; Nosara) Sprawling across Playa Guiones, this vacation community is geared toward families and surfers.

Journey Costa Rica (506-2640-0614; journeycostarica.com) Vacation rentals in Malpaís and Santa Teresa, plus tours, shuttles, and more.

Nosara House Rentals (506-2682-4109; www.nosarapropertymanagement.com) Rents wonderful properties all over Nosara.

Samara Rentals (506-2835-4067; www.samararentals.com) Property management and a wide range of rentals, from luxury condos to jungle escapes.

Puntarenas Hotels

It's easy to understand why optimists pitch this narrow sandbar stretching into the Gulf of Nicoya, with 9 kilometers (5 miles) of golden beaches all boasting incredible views, as a town with real tourist potential. But the reality, thus far, is that Puntarenas is a friendly, blue-collar fishing village, pleasant but polluted, with little to offer the casual tourist beyond a strip of souvenir shops close to the docks. That said, you may spend the night here before catching the ferry to the Southern Nicoya Peninsula.

Alamar Hotel (506-2661-4343; www.alamarcr.com; southwest tip of the point; $$*) The best hotel in town offers cheerfully painted, modern rooms, some with Jacuzzis, surrounding a pleasant courtyard and excellent pool.

Las Brisas Hotel (506-2661-4040; www. lasbrisashotelcr.com; next to Alamar; $$) Spotless and secure, this Greek-run hotel (complete with columns and a Mediterranean restaurant) offers modern, comfortable rooms with WiFi, air-conditioning, plus a great pool.

Doubletree Resort by Hilton Puntarenas (formerly Fiesta Resort and Casino; 506-2663-0808; www.hilton.com; 4 km south of Puntarenas turnoff, on road to Jacó; $$$$*) In another league altogether, this deluxe all-inclusive resort overlooking a striking black-sand beach, popular with vacationing Joséfinos, was just purchased by Hilton; expect its 300+ rooms and magnificent free-form pool to be upgraded to Doubletree standards.

RESTAURANTS AND FOOD PURVEYORS

Guanacaste's recent upswing in international visitors has inspired some of the finest dining in Central America, with fabulous gourmet restaurants from every culinary tradition opening at a furious clip in major beach towns. This is a young and volatile industry on the Nicoya Peninsula, and many eateries will open and close while this book is on the shelves; ask at your hotel for up-to-date recommendations.

And don't miss out on tradition Guanacasteco food. Similar to typical Tico fare, *sabaneros* use more beef, seafood, and corn than meals cultivated in the moist mountains of the Central Valley. Simple *sodas* and civic festivals are great places to find traditional dishes like *arroz de maiz*, something like corn grits, cooked with chicken and vegetables; *torta de elote*, a sweet corn pudding; and *chicha*, a sometimes alcoholic beverage made from corn. And keep your eyes open for Del Salto jams, made from local fruits, without preservatives. *¡Buen provecho!*

Restaurant and Food Purveyor Price Code

The following prices are based on the cost of a dinner entrée with a non-alcoholic drink, not including the 13 percent taxes and 10 percent gratuity added to the cost of almost all restaurant meals (except for the very cheapest *sodas*). Menus note whether or not their listed prices include this hefty 23 percent total surcharge, some listing two sets of prices.

Inexpensive ($)	Up to $5
Moderate ($$)	$5 to $10
Expensive ($$$)	$10 to $20
Very Expensive ($$$$)	$20 or more

Restaurants

LIBERIA AND THE VOLCANIC HIGHLANDS

Homesick? In Liberia, they actually give directions from "El Food Mall de Burger King," at the intersection of the InterAmerica and Highway 21; it also houses Papa John's Pizza and Church's Chicken. Pizza Hut, TCBY, and Subway are all close by.

EL BRAMADERO

506-2666-0371
www.hotelbramadero.com
InterAmericana, across from El Food Mall de Burger King
Price: Moderate to Expensive
Credit Cards: Yes
Cuisine: Steakhouse, Costa Rican
Serving: B, L, D
Handicap Access: Challenging
Reservations: No

This is cattle country, and El Bramadero has been serving Liberia's best steaks for almost a century in their open-air dining room. The atmosphere is casual, with yellow tablecloths and views of trucks trying to negotiate the confusing Liberia intersection, while service is formal and the steaks outstanding. Choose your cut of export-quality beef and enjoy it served alongside *gallo pinto*, plantains, and fries, but do consider starting with the ceviche. The attached hotel offers clean, basic, air-conditioned rooms ($–$$) that will do in a pinch.

★ PASO REAL

506-2666-3455
Liberia, south of central park
Price: Moderate
Credit Cards: Yes
Cuisine: Seafood
Serving: L, D
Handicap Access: No
Reservations: Yes

This second-story restaurant is one of my favorites in Costa Rica, and not just for the fabulous outdoor seating on the wrap-around porch, which you'll want to snag around sunset for a grackle's-eye-view over Liberia's central park. Start with one of the fantastic smoothies, made with fresh or frozen fruit, and relax.

Though there are a variety of international options, including a few uninspired vegetarian dishes, stick to the seafood; this spot has some of the best in the country. I like the catch of the day broiled with garlic; others enjoy it smothered in creamy mushroom sauce or a spicy marinara. Shrimp and other shellfish are always excellent as well. Finish your meal with a perfectly prepared espresso beverage as you linger over the view.

PIZZA PRONTO

506-2666-2098
200m south, 100m east of the Catholic Church
Price: Moderate
Credit Cards: Yes
Cuisine: Pizza
Serving: L, D
Handicap Access: No
Reservations: No

Considered the best pizza in Costa Rica (and with reason) this is also a great spot for architecture buffs eager to see the interior of an old Spanish-Colonial adobe, appealingly restored with warm yellow paint and glowing polished wood, with an authentic wood-fired oven where you can watch your thin-crust pie being cooked to perfection.

Service is great and the menu is simple, including good pastas, salads, and a full bar, but you're really here for the pizza. I like mine with seafood and vegetables, but they offer several spectacular combos worth trying.

★ PUERTA DEL SOL

506-2666-0161
100m south of the Catholic Church
Price: Inexpensive to Moderate
Credit Cards: No
Cuisine: Peruvian
Serving: L, D

Handicap Access: Yes
Reservations: No

Peruvian cuisine, considered Latin America's finest, has become quite popular throughout Costa Rica thanks to foreign chains. This outstanding exception, locally owned by Peruvian expats, specializes in Peruvian-style ceviche (fresher and more flavorful than the Tico or Mexican versions) as well as simple but flawlessly prepared Peruvian classics including *aji de gallo*, a mouthwatering dish involving shredded chicken simmered in an outstanding yellow sauce (*aji*), and *ocopa*, made with seasoned mashed potatoes and boiled eggs in a sauce made from cheese and nuts.

★ RINCÓN COROBICÍ

506-2669-6262
InterAmericana, 5 km (3 mi.) north of Cañas
Price: Moderate
Credit Cards: Yes

Cuisine: Costa Rican
Serving: B, L, D
Handicap Access: Yes
Reservations: For groups

The breezy wooden deck above a bubbling set of rapids on the Río Corobicí is situated so that you can see perhaps a kilometer upstream, where kingfishers dive and monkeys howl. This is also a rafting center, where you can arrange family-friendly Class I and II floats without reservations, or real white-water rafting trips for the next day. But take some time out for some reliably excellent Costa Rican cuisine, with great seafood, soups, salads, and well-done typical dishes, with a view.

NORTHERN NICOYA
(PAPAGAYO, PLAYAS DEL COCO)

CAFÉ DE PLAYA
BEACH AND DINING CLUB

506-2670-1621

Playa Sámara's hammocks offer outstanding views of Chora Island, just offshore.

www.cafedeplaya.com
Playas del Coco, 900m east of the entrance of Calle Chorrera
Price: Expensive
Credit Cards: Yes
Cuisine: International
Serving: B, L, D
Handicap Access: Yes
Reservations: Yes

Escape the dust and bustle of Playas del Coco at this Italian-style beach club, which offers, in addition to plush hotel rooms ($$$), spa services, boat tours, and equipment rental, fine dining at their beautiful beachfront bar and restaurant. The excellent wine and sushi menus are complemented with well-prepared and presented seafood and pasta prepared with Italian flair. There's often live music, too.

LA FINISTERRA

506-2670-0293
www.lafinisterra.com
Playa Hermosa, on the north ridge
Price: Expensive
Credit Cards: Yes
Cuisine: International
Serving: B, L, D
Reservations: Yes

This very pretty midrange hotel, a short but steep climb from Hermosa Beach, is renowned for its simple open-air dining room and wooden bar, plain but comfortable, all arranged on a cool patio overlooking the pretty crescent of sand below. This is one of the region's finest restaurants.

The menu, handwritten on a chalkboard, changes daily, but look for pan-Latin approaches to the finest seafood and pastas, such as the *calamaris rellenos* (squid stuffed with Spanish sausage), seafood lasagna, or Thai curried shrimp. The chefs who built this menu hailed from Barcelona, Paris, and Peru; the wines come from Argentina, Chile, and Europe. Salads are also out-

standing, and don't skip the passion fruit. At least come for drinks and a sunset.

★ GINGER RESTAURANT BAR

506-2670-0867
Playa Hermosa, 75m south of the Condovac entrance
Closed: Mon.
Price: Moderate to Expensive
Credit Cards: Yes
Cuisine: Asian Fusion
Serving: D
Handicap Access: Yes
Reservations: Recommended

This sleek and modern open-air restaurant, just above Playa Hermosa, attracts an upscale crowd of local scenesters with its creative cocktails and delectable tapas: Try the ginger rolls, with poached salmon, mango, cucumber, and pickled ginger; or perhaps the pepper-encrusted filet of seared ahi tuna, served in a crispy fried taco shell with gingered slaw and citrus sauce. The Asian vibe continues throughout the menu, which offers Balinese-style chicken satay and Mongolian ribs, plus well-prepared vegetarian cuisine. The nightly specials are often the best, and be sure to save room for dessert.

LOUISIANA BAR & GRILL

506-2670-0882
Playas del Coco, 200m from beach on main road
Price: Moderate to Expensive
Credit Cards: Yes
Cuisine: Seafood, Cajun
Serving: L, D
Handicap Access: No
Reservations: Yes

This pillar of Playas del Coco society has offered the day's catch to discriminating visitors for years. Grab a table on the outdoor deck, where you can watch the beach bunnies and babes cruise by. The specialty is Cajun cuisine, and the blackened red snapper (or whatever the catch of the day might be) is always outstanding. Jambalaya and other Louisiana specialties are also offered. But the menu also offers seafood prepared with Costa Rican, Asian, and other recipes, so enjoy.

⭐ MARIE'S RESTAURANT

www.mariesrestaurantincostarica.com
506-2654-4136
Playa Flamingo, at the Plaza Shopping Center
Price: Inexpensive
Credit Cards: No
Cuisine: Costa Rican, International
Serving: B, L, D
Reservations: No

This very basic restaurant has long been Playa Flamingo's favorite place to get its grub on, even claiming to be "the premier culinary experience in all Costa Rica." That's a bold statement, but when five-star chefs from area resorts come here for their hangover breakfasts, who am I to disagree? Marie's has recently relocated from its beachfront hole in the wall to new, almost elegant digs at Flamingo's posh Plaza, but still offers the same great food at fabulous prices, now with free WiFi. Big breakfasts, from Tico típico and papaya pancakes to French toast and bagels, are legendary, while lunchtime burgers, sandwiches, and fish platters go perfectly with a cold Imperial. Everything goes a bit more upscale at dinner, with serious steaks, fresh seafood, and cocktails. But you can still get away with wearing a bikini top.

MAR Y SOL

506-2654-5222
www.marysolflamingo.com
Playa Flamingo, North Ridge, 150m uphill from Banco Costa Rica
Price: Moderate to Very Expensive
Credit Cards: Yes

Cuisine: French, International
Serving: D
Handicap Access: Challenging
Reservations: Yes

Atop a ridge with panoramic views across Playa Flamingo, this quietly elegant eatery offers real French cuisine, as well as French takes on Continental, Costa Rican, and Asian classics. Sit indoors or out, but start with the gazpacho Andaluz, a cold soup recipe that has been in the Taulere family, originally from Perthus, France, for generations. Both the father, Alain, and son, Jean-Luc, have won awards in Europe and the United States, but finally settled here in paradise to serve such dishes as tuna tartar on avocado with white truffle oil, rack of lamb with rosemary bordelaise sauce, Japanese sushi with ginger sorbet, or a classic surf-and-turf that features the region's finest fresh lobster and wood-grilled Guanacaste steak. The spot is perfect for sunsets, and opens for wine and cocktails at 4 PM daily.

⭐ VILLA DEL SUEÑO RESTAURANT

506-2672-0026
www.villadelsueno.com
Playa Hermosa, 200m from the beach
Price: Very Expensive
Credit Cards: Yes
Cuisine: International
Serving: B, L, D
Reservations: Yes

This condominium-style resort property ($$–$$$), which resembles an Orange County gated community right down to the modern rooms, fabulous pools, and fresh *tejas* roofs, is also home to this highly recommended restaurant that brings in tourists from the Four Seasons.

The appealingly decorated, open-air dining room, with salto tiles, fine fabrics, and simple but elegant furnishings, is surrounded with glamorously lit gardens through which flagstone paths meander. Service is prompt and professional; they know their reputation as the best restaurant in the region, and aren't going to let you down. Try to come when there's live music, three times a week, from mariachis to jazz to blues, on the small stage. The menu changes daily, depending on what's available and the whim of the chef; when I was there, the filet mignon in a brandy and cream three-pepper sauce was highly recommended by the staff. The Quebecois owners add French flair to the whole proceedings.

WESTERN NICOYA
(TAMARINDO, SÁMARA, NOSARA)

LAS BRASAS
506-2656-0546
Sámara main street, next to soccer field
Price: Moderate to Expensive
Credit Cards: Yes
Cuisine: Spanish
Serving: L, D

Reservations: Yes

Sámara's classiest evening out, this cozy restaurant is guarded by massive stone statues filled with plants, and serves traditional Spanish dishes, including paellas, tortas, and seafood cooked *a la Gallega*, with olive oil and smoked paprika, served with potatoes. The beef is imported from the United States, while the wine list includes many vintages from Spain. Or enjoy one of their fruity cocktails, made with the freshest ingredients. There's not really an ocean view, but the upstairs balcony offers five-star people watching.

CALA MORESCA
506-2653-0214
www.calaluna.com
Playa Langosta, just south of Tamarindo, in Hotel Cala Luna
Price: Expensive
Credit Cards: Yes
Cuisine: Italian, International
Serving: B, L, D

Though Puntarenas isn't a top tourist draw, it offers incredible views over the Gulf of Nicoya.

Handicap Access: Yes
Reservations: Yes

At ★**Cala Luna**, a swish, Italian-owned luxury hotel ($$$$) just south of Tamarindo, this casual restaurant is getting rave reviews for fine Italian fusion cuisine. It's at its loveliest in the evening, when the courtyard garden sparkles around the romantically lit thatched ranchero. The specialty of the house is, of course, lobster (*Playa Langosta* means "Lobster Beach" in Spanish); try the lobster and asparagus crêpes, in season.

The short menu changes regularly, but there's always some spectacular seafood, perhaps presented in harmony with pro-sciutto de Parma in parsley, garlic, and white wine sauce; as well as rabbit, chicken, and vegetarian selections. Also making an appearance in the menu is a gourmet take on classic Costa Rican cuisine. The wine list includes vintages from Europe, California, Chile, Argentina, New Zealand, and South Africa.

DRAGONFLY BAR & GRILL

506-2653-1506
www.dragonflybarandgrill.com
Tamarindo, 100m after turnoff at Hotel Pasatiempo
Price: Moderate to Expensive
Credit Cards: Yes
Cuisine: Gourmet International
Serving: D
Handicap Access: No
Reservations: Recommended

On everyone's list of Tamarindo's best restaurants, this unassuming eatery tucked away in a quiet corner of downtown offers a very full bar with several festive cocktails, and huge servings of creative international cuisine. Some of the best items, such as the fresh red snapper served over spinach, leeks, and plantains seasoned with coconut milk, or the filet mignon with cilantro horseradish sauce, are cooked atop the wood-fired grill upon which the dining room is centered. Other dishes, such as the Nigiri-style spice shrimp rolls or Asian chicken salad, come cold and delicious, perfect on a hot Guanacaste evening.

CASA ROMANTICA

506-2682-0272
www.casa-romantica.net
Nosara, signed from road 200m past Café de Paris
Closed: Tue.
Price: Moderate to Expensive
Credit Cards: Yes
Cuisine: International
Serving: D
Handicap Access: No
Reservations: Yes

Truly romantic, this sweeping Spanish-Colonial-style bed-and-breakfast ($$) has lovely, well-appointed rooms just steps from the beach, but really shines after sunset. That's when candles are lit, calling diners-in-the-know from all over Nosara, who make their way through the sweet-scented gardens to this open-air patio. One of the best restaurants in the area, prices are very reasonable for gourmet international cuisine that might include a delicious fish curry, with hints of the Caribbean's sweet flavors, or Swiss specialties like *rösti* (fried potatoes), served alongside any number of Continental dishes. Dessert is divine, perhaps a mousse or flan, and there's a good wine list.

★ LA LAGUNA DEL COCODRILO BISTRO

506-2653-0255
www.lalagunadecocodrilo.com
North end of Tamarindo, on the beach
Closed: Sun.
Price: Expensive
Credit Cards: Yes
Cuisine: Mediterranean, Californian, International
Serving: D
Reservations: Recommended

Perhaps Tamarindo's most elegant restaurant, this small seaside eatery overflows into a beachfront garden of glittering lights and candlelit tables beneath the palms. Peruse the wine and cocktail list (Tamarindo's best) before choosing an appetizer from Chef Dylan Montaño's menu, which changes depending on the day's catch. Perhaps a coconut lemongrass soup, or duck confit with arugula, pistachio, dates, mint, and tamarindo vinaigrette?

With the freshest and finest ingredients on hand, the Cocodrilo uses French, Asian, and California methods for their spicy blackened tuna, Danish blue cheese soufflé, or Australian rack of lamb. Presentation is also important with each architecturally interesting dish sculpted into a creation so beautiful that one might be tempted, for just one moment, to resist eating it. The sensation won't last.

EL LAGARTO BAR & RESTAURANT
506-2656-0750
Sámara, 200m west of main beach entrance
Price: Expensive
Cuisine: International
Serving: L, D
Handicap Access: No
Reservations: Yes

For a memorable evening out, head to the beach in Sámara. On the west end of town, overlooking a fine stretch of sand, this basic *palapa*-style restaurant specializes in barbecue, grilled on the huge, open, wood-burning air grill that also provides the evening's entertainment. Top quality cuts of beef, pork, chicken, and seafood are served in the rambling wooden ranchero and, this being Costa Rica, there's even a grilled veggie platter. This is a prime sunset spot, with a full bar famed for festive cocktails, live music, and, depending on the crowd, dancing.

Next door, in another breezy beachside rancho 100m east through the slender palm trees, **Al Manglar** (506-2656-0096; open 6 PM—10 PM; $$$) serves authentic handmade pizzas and pastas, including a standout lasagna, and also has a very good wine list.

LOLA'S
506-2658-8097
Playa Avellanas, south of Tamarindo
Price: Inexpensive to Moderate
Credit Cards: No
Cuisine: International
Serving: L
Handicap Access: No
Reservations: No

Just south of Tamarindo, on the almost pristine surfing beach of Playa Avellanas, is this collection of big umbrellas and low-slung tables scattered in the sand. It's not fancy, but it's fabulous: Outstanding pizza and crisp fries, big salads, plenty of fresh seafood, and lots of creative vegetarian options prepared as organically and sustainably as possible. One thing you'll never find on the menu? Pork. For that, look under the palm trees, or perhaps frolicking in the surf, where Lola, the very large pet pig, is waiting for an ear scratching. Lola's might be closed during September and October, or may stay open for dinner—it all depends on the crowds, the surf, the owners, and probably the pig.

LA LUNA
506-2682-0122
Nosara, Playa Pelada 200m north of Olga's on the beach
Price: Moderate to Expensive
Credit Cards:
Cuisine: International
Serving: L, D
Handicap Access: Challenging
Reservations: Yes

On the beach below the bizarre and beautiful onion spires of Nosara Beach Hotel (which cannot be recommended to anyone until it gets a Joan Rivers–quality face-lift), this is one of the best locations in Nosara. They've done it justice with this romantic restaurant, just a few meters from the breaking waves. Watch the sunset while sipping a cocktail, as you examine the ever-changing menu. Perhaps you can start with the Thai coconut-lime chicken soup, or a shrimp and dorado ceviche; creative salads are always recommended. While the seafood is always fresh and excellent, often available in exotic curries or garlic sautés, there are always great pasta, chicken, and beef dishes available.

★ NOGUI'S SUNSET CAFÉ & LOUNGE
506-2653-0029
Tamarindo, circle on the south end
Closed: Wednesday
Price: Moderate
Credit Cards: Yes
Cuisine: Costa Rican
Serving: B, L, D
Reservations: Recommended for the Sunset Lounge

This is actually two recommended beachfront restaurants: The café, downstairs, offers surfer-sized portions of excellent, if basic, food, with great *gallo pintos*, omelets, and American breakfasts in the morning, moving on to huge fried-fish sandwiches, steak burgers, and the ever popular banana cream pie after noon. The upstairs lounge, open for dinner, takes things to a whole other level.

Recently voted the best sunset spot in Tamarindo, Nogui's Lounge is open for dinner only, with a full bar and short menu of tapas, appetizers, and international seafood dishes. The menu changes daily, but you can count on international cuisine such as eggplant caviar, peppered tuna medallions, or perhaps Thai-influenced spring rolls with mango and avocado.

★ HOTEL PASATIEMPO
506-2653-0096
www.hotelpasatiempo.com
Central Tamarindo, near crossroads to Playa Langosta

Price: Moderate to Expensive
Credit Cards: Yes
Cuisine: International
Serving: B, L, D
Handicap Access: Yes
Reservations: No way

This landmark Tamagringo institution has long been a friendly beacon to travelers in search of a beer, a hammock, a plate of nachos, or even a solid midrange hotel ($$–$$$*). English is spoken, advice is given, tours are arranged, NFL games are shown on the gigantic TV, and every Tuesday there's an open-mike night that brings in party people from up and down the coast.

The big *palapa*-style Yucca Bar, known for the "Best Bar Food in Town" (though Kahiki gives them a run for their colones), offers pizzas, Tex-Mex, seafood, *casados*, and awesome quesadillas, all highly recommended, as well as a wide range of cocktails.

GREAT WALTINI'S
506-2653-0975
www.hotelbulabula.com
Playa Grande, overlooking the estuary, at Hotel Bula Bula
Closed: Monday
Price: Moderate to Expensive
Credit Cards: Yes
Cuisine: Fusion of the Americas
Serving: B, L, D
Handicap Access: Yes
Reservations: Recommended

Located just across the Río Matapalo from Tamarindo, overlooking the wild estuary, this excellent restaurant offers great food all day long, perfect for day trippers who want to relax in the elegant outdoor dining room, with fine jungle views. Or make it memorable: Dinner reservations include a complimentary water taxi from Tamarindo, taking you into the mangrove forest just as its nocturnal denizens awake.

The cuisine is "Pan-American Fusion," offering regional dishes like Maryland blue crab with prawn cakes, Cajun-style shrimp,

St. Louis pork barbecue, Mexican seafood enchiladas, with a few Costa Rican dishes thrown in for good measure.

PUNTARENAS AND SOUTHERN NICOYA PENINSULA

Some of the region's finest dining can be found at hotels, including **Flor Blanca**, **Milrepa**, and **Ylang Ylang**.

CASA ZEN

506-2640-0523
Santa Teresa, 1.5 km (1 mi.) from El Cruce (Frank's Place)
Price: Inexpensive to Moderate
Credit Cards: Yes
Cuisine: Asian, Vegetarian
Serving: B, L, D
Handicap Access: Yes
Reservations: Yes

The hippie-fabulous little beachside hotel ($–$$) has a fine little rancho-style restaurant catering to a healthy, centered clientele with fresh, mostly local and organic ingredients (most from the local farmers market), including enormous pancakes and big egg breakfasts. In addition to lots of meat-free options such as creative sandwiches and salads, Thai-influenced noodle dishes and stir fries, and Hindu-style curries, you can get all-beef burgers or indulge in chicken, seafood, and meat versions of their more exotic fare.

COCOLORES

506-2642-0348
Montezuma, downtown
Price: Moderate to Expensive
Credit Cards: Yes
Cuisine: International
Serving: B, L, D
Reservations: Yes
Handicap Access: No

Beneath the trees, hung with colorful lanterns, right in the heart of Montezuma, this fun outdoor restaurant makes a great first date or special meal. Grab a candlelit wooden table a few meters from the waves, where the just slightly formal and very attentive servers will offer you a drink while you peruse a broad international menu. The specialty is ★banana curry, while the mixed seafood platter is enough for two.

ORGANICO

506-2359-4197
www.organicomontezuma.com
Montezuma, across from the church
Open: 8 AM–5 PM, Tue.–Sun.
Price: Moderate
Cuisine: Vegetarian
Serving B, L
Handicap Access:
Reservations: No

This excellent gourmet restaurant uses fresh, organic, vegetarian ingredients for its beautifully presented and absolutely delicious creations, with a focus on unusual and balanced salads, burgers, and sandwiches (I liked the nicely spiced eggplant), and light meals like the bowl o' love, with brown rice, lentils, veggies, and avocado in a spicy sauce, or muchacho nachos, a huge veggie delight. Kids and kids at heart will also enjoy the wonderful selection of homemade ice creams (some deliciously dairy free) and milk shakes.

★ PLAYA DE LOS ARTISTAS

506-2642-0920
playaarte@hotmail.com
Montezuma
Closed: Sun.
Price: Expensive to Very Expensive
Cuisine: Mediterranean
Serving: L, D
Handicap Access: No
Reservations: Recommended

Perhaps *the* romantic dining experience in Costa Rica, this world-famous restaurant seems little more than a collection of heavy wooden tables on one of the most beautiful beaches anywhere. Here, lovers glowing in the candlelight review a handwritten menu

Santa Cruz boasts one of Costa Rica's truly fabulous central parks.

that changes daily depending on what's fresh and delicious.

Fresh bread arrives as you choose your vintage. Then, perhaps, begin with the thinly sliced carpaccio, simply presented on a square ceramic dish with sliced onion. The specialty is seafood, often served whole in some delectable sauce, though steak and vegetarian dishes are also on offer. Light music plays above the ocean waves while your server attends with a dreamy sort of joy amidst all this good energy. Don't miss this place.

EL SANO BANANO VILLAGE CAFÉ
506-2642-0638
www.elbanano.com
Montezuma, downtown
Price: Moderate

Credit Cards: Yes
Cuisine: International
Serving: B, L, D
Handicap Access: Yes
Reservations: No

This no-nonsense health food restaurant has plastic chairs, a spacious fan-cooled dining room, and fine outdoor terrace. All sorts of fruit smoothies (some made with yogurt) are offered, as are vegetable curries, creative sandwiches, great chicken quesadillas, and a variety of coffee beverages, many of them icy cold, to keep you going all day. Get there early for a good seat at their Toucan Movie House, with free movies every night at 7:30 PM in the dining room. There's also free WiFi.

Food Purveyors

Bakeries

LIBERIA AND NORTHERN NICOYA (PAPAGAYO PENINSULA SOUTH TO PLAYA OCOTAL)

El Castillo Bakery (Playa Potrero, diagonal from Bahia del Sol Hotel) Open at 6 AM, daily, serves espresso beverages, pastries, breads, cakes, pizzas, and light meals.

★ **German Bakery/Café Europa** (506-2668-1081; www.panaleman.com; Liberia, just east of the airport; $) Be sure to stop here, between Liberia and the airport, for sandwiches, German breads and pastries, imported sausages, great coffee, and free WiFi. They also deliver to hotels around Playas del Coco, Tamarindo, and Jacó; check their Web site for schedules.

WESTERN AND SOUTHERN NICOYA

The Bakery Café (506-2642-0458; sanforest@hotmail.com; Montezuma, main road) Try the banana and coconut breads, or perhaps salads, sandwiches, and other light meals, on this popular bakery's outdoor porch.

Café Panadería Sámara (Sámara; closed Tues; $$) Also called the Czech Bakery, this cute sidewalk café does coffee beverages, sandwiches, salads, and crêpes.

★ **French Bakery** (Downtown Tamarindo; $) This sinful bakery has desserts (get there early for the chocolate croissants), savory pastries, lasagnas, pizzas, and more.

Cafés

LIBERIA

Café Liberia (506-2665-1660; Liberia downtown, 75m south of Banco Credito Agricola; closed Sun.; $) A welcome blast of air-conditioning makes perusing the desserts, quiches, sandwiches, and snacks at this classy sofa-strewn café even more enjoyable.

★ **TCBY** (506-2665-5353; Liberia, west of El Food Mall de Burger King; open 7 AM–11 PM) More than just frozen yogurt, this excellent gourmet coffee shop serves the best desserts in town, as well as sandwiches, salads, wraps, and other light meals on a shady, vine-covered wooden porch overlooking the beach-bound traffic.

NORTHERN NICOYA (PAPAGAYO PENINSULA SOUTH TO PLAYA OCOTAL)

Coco Coffee Company (Downtown Playas del Coco, across from Coco Verde Hotel; open 7 AM–4 PM, Mon.–Sat.; $) Excellent coffee, plus bagels, muffins, sandwiches, salads, and filled croissants. There's always a soup of the day.

Zouk Café (www.zouksantana.com; Playas del Coco, downtown at the Chorrera entrance, left side) Great music, fabulous coffee, free WiFi, and Coco's only cigar bar make this restaurant-by-day, groovy-lounge-by-night place very cool.

WESTERN NICOYA (TAMARINDO, NOSARA, SÁMARA)

★ **Breakfast Grind** (6 AM–11:30 AM, Tues.–Sun.; inside Iguana Surf on the road to Playa Langosta) Best breakfast in Tamarindo—huge portions, endless cups of coffee, great *gallo pinto*, and real biscuits and gravy—will keep you surfing all day long.

Café Playa Negra (506-2652-9351; www.playanegracafe.com; Playa Negra, south of Tamarindo; $–$$) Famed for its totally tubular beach break, this sandy beach town is also home to Café Playa Negra, a simple but sublime restaurant serving Peruvian cuisine, with great ceviche.

Café de Paris (506-2682-1036; Nosara; $–$$) Nosara landmark offers excellent pastries and light meals, and rents good rooms ($$$) and arranges surf lessons.

Olga's (Tamarindo; crossroads to Langosta) Fabulous organic coffee, snacks, and great people watching.

Shake Joe's (506-2656-0252; Sámara, 50m east of main beach entrance) Surf shack serves bottomless cups of joe and awesome breakfasts in a sandy "lounge," furnished with hammocks and sofas. Dude.

SOUTHERN NICOYA PENINSULA (MONTEZUMA, MALPAÍS, SANTA TERESA)

Café Artemis (506-2640-0579; Santa Teresa, Centro Comercial Playa Carmen) Free WiFi, fine coffee, and good food make this café, lounge, and bistro a winner.

Café Azucar (506–2642-0198; Cóbano; closed Sun.; $–$$) Behind the bank, this café serves coffee beverages, milk shakes, sandwiches, light meals, and tasty pastries in air-conditioned comfort.

Pizza

Il Basílico (506-2656-8035; Nosara, Playa Bahía Garza, on beach; $$–$$$) Enjoy pizza and international cuisine in this thatched-roof, open-air bar and restaurant.

★ **La Baula** (506-2653-1450; Tamarindo, 100m after turnoff before Hotel Pasatiempo; open 5:30 PM–9ish; $$–$$$) Great gourmet pizzas in a fabulous open-air dining room, with a little playground right in front. Voted best pizza in Tamarindo.

La Dolce Vita (Playas del Coco; well signed downtown) Cozy, popular little Italian joint has been baking great pizzas in their wood-fired ovens since before this place was paved.

El Jardin (506-2654-4397; Playa Brasilito, main road across from beach) Rather upscale steakhouse and pizzeria also delivers.

★ **Giardino Tropicale** (506-2682-4000; www.giardinotropicale.com; Nosara, Playa Pelada; $$–$$$) Nosara's favorite wood-fired pizza and pasta in gorgeous gardens or a cool slate-and-muraled interior. Seafood recommended as well; service is slow.

★ **Mary's** (506-2640-0153; north Malpaís; $$) Tiny, popular local joint offers thin-crust, wood-fired pizzas, plus pastas and seafood, including awesome fish tacos. It gets crowded.

Tato's (506-2642-0403; Cóbano; open 7 AM–11 PM; $$) Next to the Megasuper on the road to Montezuma, Tatós delivers pizza, Tico and international cuisine; there's a nice wine list if you're eating in.

Sodas

Bliss (Santa Teresa, near Hotel Point Break) Tiny *soda* with a view offers cheap *casados*, fish tacos, burritos, and smoothies.

Los Comales (Liberia; 400m north of Catholic Church) Traditional, hearty, Guanacasteco meals prepared by a grassroots women's collective.

★ **Doña Ana's Kitchen** (506-2656-8085; Playa Garza, between Sámara and Nosara; open 8 AM–7 PM, Tue.–Sun.) Tico típico and very fresh seafood with a fabulous view.

Papagayo Soda (Playas del Coco, across from Coco Verde Hotel) The best casado in Coco.

El Samareño (Sámara, 50m south of Belvedere Hotel and Escuela Pelicano) Great *casados* with Italian flair.

Soda El Viajero (Liberia Market, across from the bus station) Tidy Liberia Market offers several simple *sodas*, but this one is my favorite.

Soda La Naranja (506-2642-1001; Montezuma, across from Hotel El Pargo Feliz; $$) Bottomless cups of coffee, *casados*, and seafood.

The province is named for the mighty guanacaste, or "ear tree," named for its ear-shaped seed pods.

Soda Pedro Mar (506-2640-0069; Malpaís, on the beach) Cheap seafood and *casados*, plus the very best view in town. What's not to love?

Specialty Foods and Delis

Delicatessen Marino (506-2847-4730; Cóbano, across from Video Club) Imported wines, cheeses, meats, sweets, and more, most from Italy.

Don Fernando (506-2653-2264; across from Tamarindo Heights, next to Banco Cuscatlan) Costa Rica's finest organic beef and meats, plus traditional Tico deli salads.

Moe's Health Food (506-2640-0519; Malpaís, near el Cruce de Frank's) Organic meat and produce, fine cheeses, and local coconut products round out this cosmically conscious collection.

Organic Vegetable Market (Southern Nicoya) Fresh, organic produce at Montezuma Park, 10 AM–noon, daily; Playa Carmen in Santa Teresa at 3 PM.

Pippo Italian Food (Playa Hermosa, main entrance) Gourmet deli and grocer offers imported Italian pastas, olives, sauces, wines, and liquors, including several grappas.

Grocery Stores

Liberia has the best selection, including a tourist-oriented **SuperCompro** on the main drag, and **Jumbo**, with lots of North American brands, in the Santa Rosa Commercial Center.

Automercado (Tamarindo, Garden Plaza, leaving town toward Liberia) Huge new supermarket has great prices, organic options, and North American brands.

Megasuper (Cóbano, road to Montezuma) The last large supermarket before you hit the beach towns.

Minisuper Delicias del Mundo (506-2682-0291; Nosara, near the Gilded Iguana) Upscale grocer offers imported international goodies, deli items, and wine.

Super del Pacifico (Tamarindo, downtown behind Voodoo Lounge) Has a central location and solid deli.

Super Sámara (beachfront road, across from Sámara Treehouse Inn) Best selection in town.

CULTURE

Central America has long bridged the empires of North and South America, and Costa Rica was where they met: Though most of the country's indigenous dialects are distinctly South American, the Chorotega Indians of Guanacaste spoke Nahuatl, a language of the Aztec Empire, which was based in what's now Mexico.

Even the name *Guanacaste* comes from the Nahuatl word for "ear tree," a reference to the ear-shape seed pod of the massive (35-meter/115-foot) Costa Rican national tree, for which the province is named. The Chorotega also used distinctively Aztec ceramics, still made in Guaitíl; and fashioned polished granite spheres, which you'll see displayed throughout the region. Their diet was based on corn, a Mexican-style staple, as opposed to yuca, more popular among tribes originating in South America. Culturally, the Chorotegas, as Spanish chroniclers called them, were more connected with the indigenous people of what's now Nicaragua than the people of the Central Valley.

The Chorotegas were first "discovered" by the Spanish conquistador Gil Gonzalez Davila, who traveled through Guanacaste in 1522, claiming for Spain the indigenous cities now called Santa Cruz, Puntarenas, and Nicoya, the last named for a Chorotega chief. As part of the Spanish Empire, Guanacaste was administered from Granada, Nicaragua, among the first Spanish cities in the Americas.

Wealthy Granadino families operated vast ranches on the sweeping Guanacaste savannahs, and by the early 1700s had begun building country homes at the crossroads of the Calle Real, which ran from Taos, New Mexico, to Lima, Peru; and the road to Nicoya. Christened Guanacaste in 1769, after the massive tree that once shaded what's now Liberia's central park, the town was constructed in classic Spanish-Colonial style.

After Central America's 1821 independence from Spain, many of these wealthy landholders rushed back to Granada, where a civil war was brewing. Those who remained to work Guanacaste's agricultural holdings were a mostly blue-collar bunch, many of them indigenous and black, with few civil liberties under Nicaraguan law. As Nicaragua's vicious civil war dragged on, these Guanacastecos were actually taxed by one side, while their sons were drafted by the other. In 1824, Guanacaste's provincial government wrote San José, asking to be annexed to peaceful Costa Rica.

The Costa Ricans agreed, on one condition: the measure be put to a vote. What followed was a true democratic revolution, as Guanacastecos overwhelmingly chose annexation. Nicaragua protested, arguing that non-landowners had no voting rights in Nicaragua (though they did in Costa Rica), but were too busy with the civil war to do anything about it. The town of Guanacaste changed its name to Liberia, Costa Rica gave Nicaragua full rights to the Río San Juan, and for the next several decades sabers rattled at the border.

In 1856, a U.S.-backed private army, led by Tennessee native and Nicaraguan "President" William Walker, crossed that border, and was defeated by the Costa Rican military at

Hacienda Santa Rosa, today a national park (see below).

Despite Guanacaste's wealth of cultural and natural wonders—broad Pacific beaches, steaming hot springs, fantastic hiking—the region remained one of the nation's poorest and least developed until just a few years ago. In the 1990s, adventurous Americans and Canadians, many of them blue-collar workers seeking inexpensive retirement options, began buying beachfront property—often with no electricity, running water, or roads—on the Nicoya Peninsula. Today, as the real estate boom blossoms, many of those energetic oldsters have become millionaires.

Even as the beach towns have become "Americanized," however, real Guanacaste culture remains relatively untouched. Neither the Spanish nor Chorotega ever built cities on the coast (hmmm...), so *sabanero* centers are usually located well inland, where Ticos maintain their festivals, customs, and culture with little interference from these new arrivals.

And even upscale developments like the Papagayo Project aren't all condos and infinity pools: New neighbors also include primate researcher Jane Goodall's **University for a Sustainable Future** (www.celidon.org), offering environmental education to students from all over the world; and Costa Rican astronaut Franklin Chang-Diaz's **Ad Astra Rocket Lab** (www.adastrarocket.com), currently developing a plasma-based rocket in conjunction with NASA, that will one day propel human beings to Mars.

Architecture

Once called the "White City" for the pale volcanic tuff from which its buildings were originally constructed, Liberia is the finest example of Spanish-Colonial architecture in Costa Rica. Don't get too excited—it can't compare with the grandiosity of, say, Granada, Nicaragua, or Antigua, Guatemala. This was always a poor provincial capital, and its graceful old adobes are simple, with enormous windows and doors carved from dark guanacaste, colorful Spanish tiles, and old *tejas* roofs. Architecture buffs will appreciate the Spanish ingenuity, such as corner doors (*puertas del sol*) that can be adjusted for maximum breezes and minimal heat, but most visitors don't even notice Costa Rica's only historic city center.

At the southeast corner of the Central Park is La Gobernación (Government Building) a relatively ornate example of Colonial-style elegance, with a wide front walkway that's one of the best spots for watching Liberia's parades. This is the original Liberia crossroads: Here, the Calle Real, parallel to the InterAmericana, is crossed by the road to Nicoya.

Five blocks east, the Nicoya road ends at lovely little Ermita del Señor del la Agonía, an 1852 gem that will be home to the **Museum of Religious Art** (506-2666-0107), with examples of Colonial-era furniture, sculpture, and religious accouterments. Or walk the Calle Real, with old adobes including artist Karen Clacher's (www.karenclachar.com) grandparents' home, now her latest project, *Huellas de una Herencia* ("Footprints of a Heritage"). She has covered the house in black-and-white photos of old Liberia, and made cement footprints of local *sabaneros*, all of which will be donated to the long-promised Museum of Liberia, if and when it opens.

La Chacará Hacienda (506-2666-8238; www.haciendalachacara.com; 8km east of Liberia Airport) offers guided city tours, on a *sabanero*-style schoolbus that has cow horns on the grill.

La Ermita del Señor del la Agonía is one of Liberia's, and Costa Rica's, best examples of Spanish colonial architecture.

Museums

MUSEO HISTÓRICO MARINO

506-2661-5036

Puntarenas, Edificio de la Antigua Comandancia de Plaza

Open 9:45 AM–noon and 1 PM–5:15 PM, Tue.–Sun.

Admission: Free

If you're waiting for your ferry, or are just a big naval buff, this small museum inhabiting a recently restored fortress offers bilingual exhibits about the peninsula's natural history, as well as archaeological evidence that the port was used for centuries before the Spanish arrived. The bulk of the museum details Puntarenas' importance as a strategic naval base, fishing port, and tourist stopover ever since. There's also a good exhibit about Isla del Coco and its pirate treasures.

Also on the plaza is Puntarenas' striking Gothic church, originally constructed in 1902—with portholes, which perhaps helped sailors feel more at home during Mass.

ECOMUSEO DE LA CERÁMICA CHOROTEGA

506-2257-1433

San Vicente de Nicoya, 14 km northwest of Santa Cruz

Open: 8 AM–4 PM, daily

Admission: $1

Off the beaten path, this pretty little museum can be visited in conjunction with the ceramic center of Guiatíl. The museum studies the region's 4,000 years of settlement through artifacts, exhibits, and lots of pottery, including temporary exhibitions by modern artists. There are also pottery demonstrations by local artists and a top-notch gift shop.

ECOMUSEO LAS MINAS DE ABANGARES
506-2662-1349; 506-2662-0129
Las Juntas de Abangares, 2 km toward Monteverde
Open: Open 8 AM–4 PM, Tue.–Sun.
Admission: $2

A great place to stretch your legs before hitting the rough road to Monteverde, this excellent museum offers trails through the dry tropical forest and into Costa Rica's past. After gold was discovered here in 1884, U.S. railroad and banana magnate Minor C. Keith opened the Abangares Gold Fields of Costa Rica, which at their peak employed more than 4,000 workers. After the stock market crash of 1929, however, demand for gold dropped and the mines shuddered to a close. Machinery, tools, and tunnels that run 2 kilometers (1.2 miles) into the ground have been preserved, and you're welcome to wander through it all. The small museum has photographs and models.

EL MUNDO DE LA TORTUGA
506-2653-0471
200m from Playa Grande Headquarters
Open: 4 PM–6 PM daily, Oct.–May
Admission: $5, $25 for guided tour, including beach walk

Turtle World is a great way to kick off a nighttime trip to Playa Grande, with an informative audio tour in several languages that illuminates the mysterious world of turtle dating, mating, and of course, nesting. Displays are colorful and kid friendly, with fun turtle facts and interesting models. Others might give you pause: In the 1980s, 200 leatherbacks nested here per night, in season. In all of 2006, only 58 of the big beauties made the trip. This is apparently the end of an era, one that stretches back more than 30 million years.

EL MUSEO DE SABANERO
506-2666-1606
Liberia, 300m south, 75m east of Catholic Church
Open 8:30 AM–noon and 2 PM–4 PM, Mon.–Sat., usually
Admission: Donations appreciated

Inside this spiffily restored, century-old Spanish-Colonial mansion is a tourist information desk and Cowboy Museum. Old photos and other *sabanero* memorabilia include hacienda-era cooking utensils, leatherwork, and branding irons, as well as furniture expertly handcrafted more than a century ago from ancient guanacastes.

PARROQUIA SAN BLAS
506-2685-5109
Central Nicoya
Admission: $2
Open: 8 AM–4 PM Mon.–Fri.; 8 AM–noon Sat.

Arguably the oldest church in Costa Rica, San Blas was founded in 1644, though its graceful adobe façade, reminiscent of California mission-style architecture, was built in the 1840s. Today the elegant adobe houses a small museum with religious artifacts from the Colonial period, and a few much older archaeological finds. Fronting the shady central park and surrounded with other interesting buildings, this is a nice spot to relax in the heart of Nicoya.

Music and Nightlife

Liberia

The cowboy capital has several basic bars, most with twanging *norteños* on the jukebox. For a less *sabanero*-style evening, try **Casa Pueblo**, 300m south of La Gobernacíon on Calle Real, with sofas and a laid-back atmosphere. **Bar Lib**, in the Santa Rosa Commercial Center, is a sleek new upscale hangout.

Northern Nicoya (Papagayo to Playa Ocotal)

★ **Father Rooster** (506-2670-1246; www.fatherrooster.com; Playa Ocotal) Right on pearl gray sands of Playa Ocotal, this 1917 wooden farmhouse is a Gold Coast classic, with great seafood (and better nachos), Bob Benjamin on guitar, and a cold Tica Linda (a frozen cocktail involving orange juice, lime, grenadine, and *guaro*—distilled from sugar cane) in the sunset.

Happy Snapper (Brasilito, main street) Cane-roofed, open-air bar serves quality seafood and cold beer; there's live music on weekends.

Lizard Lounge (506-2670-0307; Playas del Coco, main street) Party palace has Reggae Night on Thursday, Latin Nights on weekends, and Ladies Night on Wednesday.

La Vida Loca (506-2670-0181; Playas del Coco, beachfront) Quality place for a beachside beer offering free WiFi and popcorn, tasty bar food (German cuisine on Sunday), live music, Ping-Pong, pool, and a dance floor.

Western Nicoya

Cigar Lounge & Factory (506-2351-7209; Tamarindo, on road to Langosta) Tamarindo's largest wine, cigar, and whiskey list; sometimes live entertainment in the lounge.

Olga's Bar (Nosara, Playa Guiones; open 6:30 AM–10 PM; $) Fishing boats pull up onto the beach at sunset, when Nosarans gather at this bar and *soda*.

★ **Kahiki Bar & Restaurant** (506-2653-0148; www.iguanasurf.net; Tamarindo, on road to Langosta) Recent polls voted this spot best bar hangout, best cocktail list, best martini, and for all you early risers, the best bloody Mary. Food is also great, with Hawaiian-style seafood, huge burgers, sushi, and more.

Monkey Bar (506-2653-0114; Tamarindo Best Western, across from Joe's) Absolutely packed on Friday nights (watch your wallet!).

La Vela Latina (506-2656-0418; Sámara, 400m east of the post office; closed Tue.) Right on the beach, cute little joint has good music outside, big-screen TVs inside, all tuned to NFL in season.

Southern Nicoya Peninsula

Day & Night Beach Club (506-2640-0353; 100m toward Santa Teresa from Frank's Place) Groovy spot serves light meals by day, cool cocktails, live DJs, and world music by night.

La Lora Amarilla (Montezuma, main road) International DJs on Tuesday with electronic music, Thursday with reggae and hip-hop, and Saturday for Noche Latina.

Relaxing at the Llanos de Cortez, just south of Liberia

RECREATION

Parks and Preserves

LIBERIA AND THE VOLCANIC HIGHLANDS

GUANACASTE NATIONAL PARK

506-2666-5051

www.costarica-nationalparks.com/guanacastenationalpark.html

Main Quebrada Grande entrance is 10 km (6 mi.) northeast of the InterAmericana; exit at Potrerillos

Open: 8 AM–4 PM, daily

Admission: $6

Not really developed for casual tourists, this huge (32,512 hectares/80,336 acres) and rugged park offers excellent opportunities for serious hikers, who usually arrange guides, dorm beds, and simple meals through one of three research stations. Cacao Biological Station is the base for the Cacao Volcano climb, with relatively easy access from the main Quebrada Grande entrance. Maritza Biological Station, farther north, is close to a vast petroglyph field. The much less developed Pitilla Sector ($), close to the town of Santa Cecelia, accesses the very difficult hike up Orosí Volcano.

   Next to the Quebrada Grande entrance and Cacao Biological Station, the **Curubanda Lodge** (506-2661-8177; bricha@racsa.co.cr; $*), offers simple rooms with private hot showers, and arranges several tours and hikes in the park.

LOMAS BARBUDAL BIOLOGICAL RESERVE AND LLANOS DE CORTÉZ

506-2686-4967

www.costarica-nationalparks.com/lomasdebarbudalbiologicalreserve.html

Bagaces; 7 km from InterAmerica (turnoff 12 km north of Bagaces)

Open: 8 AM–4 PM, daily
Admission: $6

This 2,279-hectare (5,629-acre) biological reserve is still being developed for tourism; road access is four-wheel drive only, even in dry season. The small Casa de Patrimonio museum at the reserve entrance, from which several trails begin, still lacks trail maps (you can pick those up in Bagaces from Friends of Lomas Barbudal; 510-526-4115 USA). You can camp, but there are no facilities. The park is really here to protect some 240 species of bees, which live in hives, as loners, and even underground, representing 25 percent of the world's bee-odiversity. Butterflies, moths, and beetles are similarly overrepresented in this flower-filled dry tropical wilderness.

More tourists visit via the Llanos de Cortéz, an absolutely stunning set of waterfalls with a small sandy beach just 15 kilometers (8 miles) south of Liberia on the InterAmericana; the sign faces south only. About 2 kilometers (1 mile) on an unpaved road west of the highway (look for the faded turn arrow, on a large rock, about 1 kilometer in), you'll find a parking lot just above the falls; entrance is free.

PALO VERDE NATIONAL PARK

506-2661-4717
www.costarica-nationalparks.com/paloverdenationalpark.html
Well signed, on unpaved 28 km road south of Bagaces
Open: 8 AM–dusk, daily
Admission: $7.25

The waters of the Río Tempisque fluctuate dramatically between the seasons, rising with the rain to a swampy expanse of exuberant life. The park is home to the largest concentration of crocodiles in Costa Rica, as well as monkeys, squirrels, bats, and more than 250 species of birds. The star of the show is the roseate spoonbill, which gathers on the Isla de Pájaros (Birds Island) in record-breaking numbers, along with all sorts of herons, egrets, ibis, anhinghas, and huge red macaws.

Wildlife is even easier to see in dry season, however, when all this life is concentrated into smaller pools, and the leaves fall from the trees, offering better views. Trails are usually flooded during rainy season, but boat tours can be arranged year-round. **Palo Verde Biological Station** (506-2524-5774, 919-684-5774 in the USA; www.threepaths.co.cr; $–$$$*) offers basic lodging in dorms or simple rooms, meals, and dozens of guided hikes, boat tours, and other treks, all of which must be arranged in advance.

★ RINCÓN DE LA VIEJA NATIONAL PARK

506-2661-8139
www.costarica-nationalparks.com/rincondelaviejanationalpark.html
27 km (17 mi.) northeast of Liberia
Open: 7 AM–3 PM, Tue.–Sun.
Admission: $6

Protecting the enormous volcanic massif of Rincón de la Vieja (1,895 meters; 6,215 feet), a 600,000-year-old volcano dubbed "a natural lighthouse" by Spanish sailors, this is my favorite national park. The lava stopped flowing in 1851, though the mountain still rumbles, last acting out in 1998, when it hurled plumes of ash 1,000 meters (3,280 feet) into the atmosphere.

A haven for amateur hikers, Rincón offers several well-marked and rewarding trails, including a relatively flat 4 kilometers (2.5 miles) loop past bubbling mud pots, steaming fumaroles, boiling lakes, popping vents, and a sweet little *volcanicito* (baby volcano) bubbling away. Active day trippers can also visit one of two waterfalls, another, steeper 4.5 kilometers (2.8 miles), or just spend the day hiking the strenuous 8-kilometer (5-mile) climb to the park's simmering crater lake. There are great, developed campsites by the main Santa María entrance, as well as the less visited Las Paillas Sector, close to some mediocre hot springs, and several other trails to explore.

SANTA ROSA NATIONAL PARK
506-2666-5051
www.costarica-nationalparks.com/santarosanationalpark.html
Santa Elena Peninsula
Open: 8 AM–4 PM, daily
Admission: $10; $15 for surfers; camping $2 per day

Encompassing the entire Santa Elena Peninsula, this 49,515-hectare (122,305-acre) pristine promontory into the Pacific contains a dozen different biomes, from dry tropical forest to muddy mangrove swamp, and scores of untouched beaches. Most of the park is difficult to access, except for Costa Rica's most-beloved historical site, Hacienda Santa Rosa. High school students visit "La Casona" to see where a hastily assembled Costa Rican militia took on Tennessee-born mercenary William Walker and his polished private army of experienced soldiers, well armed and well funded by pro-slavery members of the U.S. government. Walker had already conquered Nicaragua, and invaded Costa Rica in an effort to control Central America. On March 20, 1856, Costa Rican soldiers surrounded him here at Santa Rosa. After a battle that lasted only 14 minutes, the Americans fell into a flustered retreat.

The Ticos gave chase, and on April 11, the armies clashed again in the decisive Battle of Rivas. Walker's men had occupied an almost impenetrable position; there was only one option. After making sure his single mother would be cared for, a drummer boy named Juan Santamaría volunteered for the suicide mission, rushing through the gunfire with a lit torch, which he hurled into the *palapa*-topped outpost with his last breath. The building erupted in flames, and Walker's men were either killed or captured as they rushed from the smoking building. Walker himself escaped, but would later be executed by a Honduran firing squad. Santamaría remains Costa Rica's only national hero with his own public holiday, not to mention several statues, schools, and an international airport named in his honor.

Though the original Casona was itself a victim of arson in 2001, it has since been rebuilt, and houses a new museum that enthusiastically commemorates one of Costa Rica's least peaceful moments—which was, after all, in self-defense. Several trails begin at La Casona, including a 2-kilometer (1-mile) nature loop and the 13-kilometer (8-mile) jaunt to the beaches, famed for nesting olive ridley turtles, which arrive at Playa Nancite from September through December, and one of the best surf spots in Costa Rica, Witch's Rock. Surfers and nature lovers camp at Playa Naranjo, with few facilities and no potable water, usually arranging special transport from Liberia (the road is generally impassable to regular four-wheel-drive cars) or boats from Playas del Coco.

You can also visit the park's Murciélago Sector, via the tiny town of Cuajiniquil, where the perfectly acceptable, two-story teak **Santa Elena Lodge** (506-2697-1106; www.santa

elenalodge.com; next to Arrecife Restaurant; $$*) arranges guided hikes throughout the sector, as well as neighboring Junquillal Bay Wildlife Refuge. This area remains relatively undeveloped, having been militarized during the 1980s as a "secret" CIA training and supply camp for Nicaraguan Contras, part of the Iran-Contra Affair. History buffs will note that a nearby surf spot, Ollie's Point, is named for former Lieutenant Colonel Oliver North, who illegally ran arms to the Contras through the park.

Divers also visit the Islas Murciélagos (Bats Islands), with the country's best diving, usually offered as a three-tank, seven-hour boat tour from the Playas del Coco area.

★ TENORIO NATIONAL PARK

506-2200-0135
www.costarica-nationalparks.com/tenorionationalpark.html
Open: 8 AM–4 PM, daily
Admission $6

Allow at least an hour for the 31-kilometer (19-mile) unpaved climb (four-wheel-drive only), from Bijagua to the top of Tenorio Volcano. Two hikes begin at the basic ranger station, one a steep six hours to the dormant twin Montezuma craters, the other an easy 2.5-kilometer (1.5-mile) walk through primary cloud forest to one of Costa Rica's crown jewels: the Río Celeste. The vivid volcanic blue waterfall thunders into a series of swimming holes that are, in my opinion, more scenic than any in the world.

Or hike another few minutes to the source of this celestial blue river, where two crystal-clear streams come together, and suddenly become that vivid blue. It isn't exactly magic: The water crosses a vein of colloidal silica, acquiring microscopic shards of glass that somehow refract through the ripples in an azure illusion. But then, I suppose it all depends on how you define magic. If you continue another 3 kilometers (1.8 miles), you'll arrive at untamed hot springs and mud pots, some blistering hot.

NICOYA PENINSULA
BARRA HONDA NATIONAL PARK

506-2659-1551
www.costarica-nationalparks.com/barrahondanationalpark.html
62 km (38 mi.) from Liberia
Open: 7 AM–1 PM, daily
Admission: $35–$45, including equipment and guides

To visit this mostly underground attraction, you must make reservations through your hotel or the **Association of Naturalist Guides for Barra Honda** (506-2659-1716). You'll begin with a somewhat strenuous hike through the forest to a mesa above the Tempisque Valley, where you might see deer, pizotes, anteaters, or monkeys. Then, you'll don a rappelling harness and helmet before beginning the 17-meter (56-foot) descent on an aluminum ladder into the limestone interior of the peninsula.

Caverns filled with evocative calcium carbonate deposits are home to thousands of bats, whose nightly flight led to the caves' discovery. Only 19 of more than 40 caves have been explored, and 2 are open to the general public, Terciopelo (for visitors over 12) and family-friendly Cuevita. Serious spelunkers can make special arrangements to visit other caves. The caves are closed in rainy season, but you can camp ($2) year-round by the ranger station, and watch huge clouds of bats pour out of the caverns each evening.

Exploring the Nicoya Peninsula coast by boat—now that's living the dream.

CAMARONAL WILDLIFE REFUGE

www.costarica-nationalparks.com/wernersauterwildliferefuge.html
Playa Camaronal, 8 km (5 mi.) south of Sámara
Open: 24 hours
Admission: Free during the day, $4 at night

This mostly undeveloped wildlife refuge was created in 1994 to protect 3 kilometers (2 miles) of coastline used as a nesting ground by leatherback, hawksbill, and olive ridley turtles. Though numbers had been dwindling for decades, the conservationists were successful: In 2006, the first *arribada*, or mass arrival, of olive ridleys swarmed the beaches, and they're still coming. There are campsites at the Camaronal Quebrada estuary and Vuelta Beach, accessible only at low tide.

PLAYA GRANDE MARINE TURTLE NATIONAL PARK

506-2653-0470
www.costarica-nationalparks.com/lasbaulasnationalmarinepark.html
Playa Grande, just north of Tamarindo
Open: 24 hours
Admission: Free until 6 PM; $16 between 6 PM—6 AM

Just north of Tamarindo, a 5-minute, $2 water-taxi ride across the Río Matapalo (or dusty 45-minute drive, inland through Huacas), is this broad and protected beach, with a handful of hotels and restaurants tucked away in the tropical forest just inland. Surfers come for the one of the most consistent high-tide swells in the country, but may be barred when expectant sea turtles arrive, as they do year round. Green turtles nest here throughout the year, while endangered leatherback turtles, or *baulas*, arrive between November and April. Olive ridley turtles also nest here.

Most of the ladies arrive late at night, when you'll need reservations to enter the park: Get them at the **Playa Grande Headquarters** (506-2653-0470; 100m east of Hotel Las Tortugas) or arrange a tour from Tamarindo, which will handle everything, including transportation. Guides are required, flash photography is forbidden, and if you are lucky enough to see a nesting turtle, please try to accord her the space and dignity you'd expect in the same situation. Keep an eye out for adorable baby turtles pushing their tiny heads up out of the sand; they usually make their run for the ocean at dawn.

Contiguous with Playa Grande is the Tamarindo Estuary Wildlife Refuge, a tangled maze of mangrove wetlands with little tourist infrastructure. You can arrange tours from Tamarindo for about $20. **Hotel Las Tortugas** (506-2653-0423; www.lastortugashotel.com; 100m west of park headquarters; $$*), rents kayaks.

MONTE ALTO FOREST RESERVE
506-2659-9347
www.nicoyapeninsula.com/montealto
Central Nicoya, 6 km from Hojancha, between Nicoya and Sámara

High above the stifling summer heat of Central Nicoya is this 346-hectare (855-acre), little-visited nature reserve, which since 1992 has protected the headwaters of the Nosara River. This retreat is home to several animal and plant species, most famously orchids, 67 species of which are visible on a .5-kilometer (.2-mile) nature trail. You could also hike to a waterfall at Cerro Romo, the highest point (833 meters/2,732 feet) in the park. There's also a small museum, sugarcane mill, and very basic **lodge** (montealto92@terra.es; $) that offers dormitory-style accommodations, simple meals, and guided hikes.

MONTEZUMA WATERFALLS
Montezuma, south edge of town
Open: Always
Admission: Free

Montezuma's most famous attraction is this gorgeous tropical cascade with such fabulous form that it's even been a body double for remote Isla del Coco in the movie *Jurassic Park*. And, refreshingly, it's undeveloped and absolutely free-of-charge to anyone willing to make the short, steep, and slippery hike. The main waterfall is more than 20 meters (66 feet) high, and while it's something of a rite of passage to leap fearlessly from the top into the swimming hole below, people have died doing it.

NOSARA BIOLOGICAL RESERVE
506-2682-0035
www.lagarta.com
Nosara, entrance at Lagarta Lodge
Open: 6 AM–4:30 PM, daily
Admission: $6

This small, 35-hectare (90-acre) private nature preserve, which includes a beautiful crescent of beach and about two hours of hiking trails, is protected by Lagarta Lodge. Guided hikes ($12) leave every morning at 6:30 AM, when you'll be more likely to catch a glimpse of some of the 270 bird species, alongside other wildlife. They can also arrange boat tours through the mangroves.

OSTIONAL NATIONAL WILDLIFE REFUGE

506-2682-0470
www.costarica-nationalparks.com/ostionalwildliferefuge.html
Playa Ostional
Open: 8 AM–4 PM, daily
Admission: $15, including guide

Just north of Nosara (and separated by a river impassable to normal cars in rainy season) this gorgeous and isolated 15-kilometer (7-mile) beach may be the most important nesting ground in the world for olive ridley sea turtles. The ladies arrive several times throughout the year, sometime *sola*, but usually as part of truly awe-inspiring *arribadas*, when hundreds—sometimes hundreds of thousands—pile onto the beach day and night for a week of serious nesting.

The largest *arribadas* arrive between June and December, theoretically during the last quarter of a waning moon (though this seems to vary quite a lot). Ostional is the only beach in the world where locals are legally allowed to harvest a portion of the eggs, and they make up for it by chasing away voracious buzzards, and even carrying the little darlings closer to the water. Children will dump a bucketful of babies at your feet, knowing that human nature will dictate that you shield their delicate souls from hovering predators. And those little turtles, endangered but still surviving, will be a part of you forever.

PUNTARENAS AND SOUTHERN NICOYA PENINSULA

CABO BLANCO ABSOLUTE NATURE RESERVE

506-2645-5277, 506-2645-5897
www.caboblancopark.com
7 km south of Montezuma
Open: 8 AM–4 PM, Wed.–Sun.
Admission: $15 ($7 in advance)

Here at the edge of the world is Costa Rica's very first protected area, 1,172 hectares (2,895 acres) of moist tropical forest; cedars, dogwoods and frangipani. Truly unspoiled white-sand beaches can be reached on the wild coastal trail, though the real treasure is offshore, in the wildlife rich 18-hectares (45-acres) of protected sea; hiking and snorkeling trips are arranged from anywhere in the Southern Peninsula. You can camp in the park, or stay in the dorms at San Miguel Biological Station.

There are more comfortable accommodations in tiny Cabuya, next door to the park; the town's Web site (www.caboblancopark.com) has listings. Try Belgian-owned **Hotel Celaje** (506-2642-0374; www.celaje.com; $$*) with lovely teak beachfront bungalows, or much more basic **El Ancla de Oro** (506-2642-0369; caboblancopark.com/ancla; $*), with a solid seafood restaurant. And watch, at low tide, as an ancient stone trail rises from beneath the waves, connecting Cabuya to Cemetery Island, where the indigenous inhabitants once buried their dead.

CURÚ NATIONAL WILDLIFE REFUGE AND ISLA TORTUGA

506-2641-0100
www.curuwildliferefuge.com
5 km from Paquera on the road to Tambor
Open: 7 AM–3 PM, daily
Admission: $8; cabins $16

Declared a national wildlife refuge in 1983, this 1,496-hectare (3,695-acre) park isn't exactly pristine, as it contains farmland and teak orchards slowly returning to nature. But the mangroves, forests, and rampant wildlife are well worth seeing, and few refuges offer such lovely, if basic (and electricity-free), cabins just a stone's throw from the high tide line. Meals are also arranged. The refuge rents horses, kayaks, and snorkel gear, and can arrange all manner of tours, including trips to Tortuga Island, just 3 kilometers (1.8 miles) offshore. The postcard-perfect tropical island, right down to the coconut palms, powdery white beaches, and fantastic snorkeling beneath cobalt water, is also visited by daytrippers from Montezuma, Malpaís, Puntarenas, and Jacó; it can get crowded.

KAREN MOGENSEN FISCHER NATURE RESERVE
506-2650-0607
www.asepaleco.org
Jicaral, office in front of Banco Nacional; reserve accessible by footpath from San Ramón de Río Blanco
Open: 8 AM–3 PM, daily
Admission: Varies; must be arranged as part of tours that include guides, transportation, and lodging

Within this reserve is 84-meter (207-foot) Bridal Veil Falls, famed for being spectacular, though rarely visited, despite being one of Costa Rica's most enduring images. This isolated, 760-hectare (1,877-acre) refuge is accessible only by a steep hike or horseback ride through lush primary forest. You'll stay at Cerro Escondido Lodge, a simple solar-powered spot with fabulous terrace views, which arranges meals and guided tours to the waterfall, local farms, a small museum, and Orquinuñez Orchid Garden, run by a local women's collective.

Adventure Lodges
Buena Vista Lodge (506-2690-1414; www.buenavistalodgecr.com; $$*) With Costa Rica's longest waterslide, hiking trails, a canopy tour, and snake display, this lodge brings in plenty of day trippers. Or stay in plain but pleasant cabins overnight.

★ **Hacienda Guachipelin** (506-2666-8075 lodge; 506-2442-2818 reservations; www .guachipelin.com; 17 km from the InterAmericana on road to Rincón de la Vieja; $$*) Usually arranged as a day trip from area resorts, this relaxed lodge offers hiking trails, hot springs, waterfalls, petroglyphs, a small spa with natural mud baths, and a fairly fabulous, nine-cable canopy tour. Standard rooms are attractive, family-sized, and perhaps a bit worn, but equipped with the usual U.S.-style amenities.

KOKOdrilo Creek (506-2667-0943; Liberia) This new adventure lodge offers passable rooms ($$; "suites" are nicer), but day trips are a better bet, with river floats, horseback riding, and a seven-platform canopy tour.

Boat Tours

VOLCANIC HIGHLANDS
Cata Tours (506-2674-0180; www.catatours.com; Palo Verde National Park, Bebedero, 14 km west of Cañas) Bilingual guided tours on the Tempisque River.

Río Corobicí Float (506-2669-6262; www.riostropicales.com; 5 km north of Cañas on the InterAmericana; $50) Arrange family-friendly floats through Rincón Corobicí Restaurant on the spot (before 3 PM) or make reservations for longer, more challenging Class III and IV white-water rafting treks on the Tenorio and Zapote Rivers.

Meander through searing fumaroles and mud pots at Las Hornillas Volcanic Activity Center.

NORTHERN NICOYA (PAPAGAYO TO PLAYA OCOTAL)

Adventure Tours Charters (506-2848-3252) Luxury 100-foot yacht offers air-conditioned day trips for up to 60, including snorkeling, diving, and kayaking.

Drums of Bora (506-2845-9448; Gulf of Papagayo) All-teak sailing yacht equipped for sportfishing and snorkeling.

Kuna Vela (506-2301-3030; www.kunavela.com; Gulf of Papagayo) This 47-foot sailing vessel offers snorkel tours, sunset cruises, full bar, and dolphin watching.

Tronco Negro (506-2673-0328; $38 per person) Crazy catamaran carved from the trunk of a giant javillo tree, does open-bar party cruises for 40 leaving Playas del Coco at 1 PM, daily.

WESTERN NICOYA (TAMARINDO, NOSARA, SÁMARA)

Blue Dolphin Catamarans (506-2842-3204; www.sailbluedolphin.com; Tamarindo, 100m east of El Pescador Restaurant at Iguana Surf, four hours $60–$75) Cat comes equipped with kayaks, open bar, and fishing gear.

Carrillo Tours (506-2656-0453; www.carrillotours.com; Carrillo Beach, south of Sámara) Half-day kayak trips up the Río Oro.

Nosara Boat Tours (506-2682-0610; www.nosaraboattours.com) See the Río Nosara's mangroves, tours in electric boats.

Lazy Lizard Catamaran Adventures (506-2654-4192; www.sailingcostarica.com; Marina Flamingo; $75) Three-hour sailing tours include snorkels, kayaks, and snacks.

Mandingo Sailing (506-2831-8875; www.tamarindosailing.com; Tamarindo, Restaurant El Pescador; $50–$75) Traditional gaff-rigged replica of a 1800s-era schooner offers sunset tours and more.

Marlin del Rey (506-2653-0114; www.marlindelrey.com; Tamarindo; half-day tours $60–$75) Costa Rica's largest and most luxurious sailing catamaran offers half-day trips including snorkeling, snacks, and drinks.

Tio Tigre Tours (506-2656-0098; samarabeach.com/tiotigre; Samara, 50m east and 100m north of post office) Offers wildlife watching tours in large boats or kayaks, plus snorkeling, turtle tours, and more.

SOUTHERN NICOYA

Montezuma Eco-tours (506-2642-0467; www.montezumaecotours.com) Offers fishing, scuba diving, snorkeling, and treks to Isla Cabuya.

Bay Island Cruises (506-2258-3536; www.bayislandcruises.com) Yacht tours to Isla Tortuga can be arranged from the peninsula or San José, and combined with kayaking, canopy tours, and other adventures.

Canopy Tours and More

Canopy Tour Volcán Miravalles (506-2673-0697; www.volcanoadventuretour.com; Miravalles Volcano, 7 km north of Guayabo; $30) Close to several hot springs resorts, they also organize horseback trips to the top of Miravalles Volcano.

Congo Trail Canopy (506-2666-4422; congotrail@racsa.co.cr; Artola, southeast of Playas del Coco; $55) Two suspended bridges and 11 cables, plus butterfly and snake displays.

Montezuma Canopy Tour (506-2642-0808; www.montezumatraveladventures.com) Packages with the 11-platform, nine-cable canopy can include waterfall hikes and kayak trips.

Tempisque Eco Adventures (506-2687-1212; info@tempisqueecoadventures.com; 4 km south of Puente La Amistad) Seven-cable canopy can be combined with boat tours of Palo Verde National Park.

Wingnuts Canopy Tour (506-2656-0153; Sámara, south end of the beach; admission $55 for adults, $35 for children) Twelve-platform tour offers personalized service and outstanding Pacific views; clients have seen whales breaching offshore.

Diving and Snorkeling

Some of the best diving in Costa Rica, other than Isla del Coco, can be found at sites between Santa Rosa National Park and Catalinas Islands. There are several dive shops in beach towns around Playas del Coco and Tamarindo that arrange trips. Because dives are relatively shallow, less than 25 meters (75 feet), you can usually do three dives per day. Night dives are also offered.

This isn't Belize, and vast amounts of plankton mean relatively low visibility, 9–15 meters (27–45 feet), 20 meters (60 feet) tops, but a huge concentration of life. Popular trips include the Catalinas Islands and Isla Murcielago ("Cats and Bats"), bull sharks at "The Big Scare," and from December through March, migrating manta rays and whale sharks.

Agua Rica Diving Center (506-2653-0094; www.aguarica.net; Tamarindo) Snorkeling and diving trips to the Catalina Islands and Cabo Velas.

Deep Blue Diving Adventures (506-2670-1004; www.deepblue-diving.com; Playas del Coco, next to Hotel Coco Verde) All area dives, plus packages including accommodations.

Diving Safaris Costa Rica (506-2672-1260, 800-779-0055 USA and Canada; www.costa ricadiving.net; Playa Hermosa) Costa Rica's largest, oldest dive shop offers high quality dives, and packages that could include sportfishing and sailing.

Ocotal Dive Shop (506-2670-0321; www.ocotaldiving.com; Playa Ocotal) The gold standard on the Gold Coast, top-flight outfitter offers dozens of dives, group tours, and premium packages through Ocotal Beach Resort.

Pura Vida Dive (506-2656-0643; www.samaradive.com; Sámara) Also arranges sportfishing and sightseeing trips.

Resort Divers (506-2670-0421; www.resortdivers-cr.com; Papagayo Peninsula) Packages with Papagayo resorts.

Rich Coast Diving (506-2670-0176, 800-434-8464 in USA and Canada; www.richcoast diving.com; downtown Playas del Coco) Good deals on great dives.

Summer Salt Dive Center (506-2670-0308, 506-2824-7258; www.summer-salt.com; Playas del Coco, diagonal Capitania del Puerto) All the dives.

Golf

Four Seasons (506-2696-0000; www.fourseasons.com/costarica; Papagayo Peninsula; $250) Atop the spine of the Papagayo Peninsula, this par-72 course, ranked the best in Costa Rica, was designed by Arnold Palmer to maximize incredible views of the Pacific and Gulf.

Hacienda Pinilla Beach Resort (506-2680-7060, 866-294-0466 USA and Canada; Playa Avenella; $40–$100) Resort and residential community sprawls across six beautiful beaches, with splendid Casa Golf Hotel ($$$) sitting right on the 18th hole of the Mike Young–designed golf course.

Arriving at one of Isla del Coco's many waterfalls Photo courtesy of Colin Plant

Papagayo Golf & Country Club (506-2697-0169; www.papagayo-golf.com; $70 for 18 holes with cart) Just 20 minutes from Liberia, this good course has a restaurant, bar, pool, tennis courts, croquet, and boccie ball.

Reserva Conchal Golf Course (506-2654-4000; 800-769-7068 USA and Canada; www.reservaconchal.com; $150) Meticulously crafted by Robert Trent Jones II, this huge (6,341-meter/7,033-yard) course uses lakes, ravines, and views to put a premium on tee shots. Packages can include luxury condo rental, spa services, and tours.

Tango Mar Beach & Golf Resort (506-2683-0001; www.tangomar.com; Playa Tambor, 9 km north of Montezuma; $20 per full day, $30 per cart) Popular, premium, all-inclusive resort overlooks a blue flag beach and offers nine challenging holes, a neatly groomed 2,000-yard executive course perfect for tuning up your short game.

Horseback Riding

Boca Nosara Tours (506-2682-0280; www.bocanosaratours.com; Nosara) Brings horses to your hotel for beach, jungle, and sunset rides.

Casagua Horses (506-2653-8041; www.tamarindo.com/casagua; Tamarindo, across from Monkey Park) Arranges beach and jungle tours throughout the Tamarindo area.

Costa Rica Horse Adventure (506-2640-0672; www.costaricahorseadventure.com; Malpaís) Day trips and multi-day treks throughout the Southern Nicoya.

Haras del Mar (506-2697-1344; www.lomasdelmar.com; 9 km from start of Congo Trail toward Playa Matapalo) Modern equestrian center offers lessons and rides in Ocotal.

Isla del Coco National Park
506-2283-0022
www.costarica-nationalparks.com/cocosislandnationalpark.html
532 km (330 mi.) southeast of Puntarenas

If you're a serious scuba diver, you've already spent weeks, or years, daydreaming about Isla del Coco, called by Jacques Cousteau "the most beautiful island in the world." The enigmatic and isolated UNESCO World Heritage Site is part of all our collective imaginations: This is where Robinson Crusoe was stranded and Jurassic Park founded, with more than 30 waterfalls, dozens of endemic species, untold caches of pirate treasure, and the world's largest concentration of hammerhead sharks.

This is not a place one visits on a whim. There are no accommodations on the island, thus the majority of visitors come on sleep-aboard, expert-only dive trips, some 35 Dramamine-soaked hours from Puntarenas. You'll pay about $3,000 to spend 10 days here, with day trips to the island offered as an option. At least two boats offer the adventure of a lifetime, including **Okeanos Aggressor** (506-2257-0191; 866-653-2667 USA and Canada) and **Undersea Hunter** (506-2228-6613; www.underseahunter.com).

Hot Springs

Both Rincón de la Vieja and Tenorio National Parks are surrounded with hot springs, but the best are on Miravalles Volcano. These have been developed, but there are dozens of family-run springs advertised with hand-lettered signs where you can soak all day for a few dollars.

★ **Las Hornillas** (506-2839-8769; www.lashornillas.com; $30) Not just hot springs, this amazing volcanic wonderland offers short trails through simmering mud pots, steaming fumaroles, and other volcanic activity; there's no lodge, but you can camp for $5.

Thermomania (506-2673-0233; www.thermomania.net; Miravalles Volcano, north of Guayabo; $4 day use) Seven sparkling pools and a warm-water river are set in lush gardens, alongside fun attractions that include a petting zoo, a tiny museum of Tico culture, and a great restaurant/bar. They rent small, rustic rooms with private bath and cute porches ($).

Yökö Hot Springs (506-2673-0410; www.yokotermales.com; Miravalles Volcano, north Guayabo; $5 day use) This pleasant place is geared toward vacationing Ticos, with large cement pools, a sauna, fast waterslide, and the hottest hot spring in Guanacaste. The on-site restaurant is good, the cabins are spacious, simple, and rather romantic ($$*), and the views of Miravalles and Rincón absolutely spectacular.

Other Tours

La Chacará Hacienda & Fiesta Brava (506-2666-8238; www.haciendalachacara.com; 8 km east of Liberia Airport) This working cattle ranch and kid-friendly cultural attraction offers horseback rides, hiking, a small museum and, every Thursday at 5 PM, a *sabanero*-themed, buffet-style dinner show.

Diriá Coffee Tour (506-2659-9130; www.cafediria.com; Hojancha, 24 km south of Nicoya) Guanacaste's only coffee tour can be arranged from anywhere in the Western Nicoya Peninsula, often in conjunction with Palo Verde National Park.

Foto Verde Tours (506-2463-0053; www.fotoverdetours.com) Nature photographer Greg Basco offers photo safaris throughout Guanacaste and Nicoya.

Malpaís Bike Tours (506-2640-0550; www.malpaisbiketours.com; Malpaís) Guided mountain bike trips and rentals will meet you at any Santa Teresa or Malpaís hotel.

Rancho Santa Alicia (506-2671-2543; info@ranchosantaalicia.com; 15 km/8 mi. south of Liberia; open 9 AM–5 PM, daily; free) Demonstration ranch is geared to local families, with bull riding, calf roping, bronco busting, a petting zoo, and horseback riding ($15 per hour), as well as a bar, restaurant, and disco.

Sportfishing

There are scores of operators, many of them independent captains, and any hotel can arrange trips. Most outfits offer half-day excursions including non-alcoholic drinks and fruit or day trips with lunch; boats should have captains with basic first-aid training. Most cost around $75 per hour, three-hour minimum, for four people.

Brindisi (506-2654-5514; www.brindisicr.com; Flamingo Marina) Bertram and Hatteras luxury yachts are fully equipped for sportfishing, and also offer snorkel and sunset tours.

Capullo Sportfishing (506-2653-0048; www.capullo.com; Tamarindo) Uses circle hooks, instead of J hooks, which are easier on billfish.

Costa Rica Deep Sea Sportfishing (506-2670-1062; kingdonsfishing@yahoo.com; Papagayo Gulf) Featuring a 31-foot *Gryphon II*, 37-foot *Predator*, and 52-foot *Gryphon*, fine family-friendly fleet can accommodate groups of four to eight.

Kingfisher Sportfishing (506-2833-7780; www.kingpin-sportfishing.com; Tamarindo; $550 for half day, $850 for full day, each for 5 people) Outfitter also arranges hunting trips.

Tranquilamar (506-2814-0994; tranquilamar.com; Playas del Coco, 300m from beach at Louisiana Bar & Grill) Three 27-foot, 250-horsepower single-prop-engine boats are geared toward small (one- to four-person) groups but capable of handling eight.

Surfing

The tranquil, protected waters of the Northern Nicoya aren't known for their surfing, but you can arrange boats from Playas del Coco to Witch's Rock and Ollie's Point; try **Ruca Bruja Surf Operation** (506-2670-0952; www.costaricasurftrips.com). The rest of the Nicoya coastline, however, is basically one long surfing safari. These are just a sample of the many operators available .

Banana Surf Club (506-2653-1270; www.bananasurfclub.com; Tamarindo, 150m from main street on the road to Langosta) Surf camps, girl's camps, individual lessons, board rentals, and more.

Coconut Harry's (506-2682-0574; www.coconutharrys.com; Nosara, Playa Guiones) "Surf more, work less," truly words to live by. Rent boards, golf carts, cars, hotel rooms, or arrange lessons and packages, Harry's does it all.

C&C Surf Shop (506-2656-0628; www.ticoadventurelodge.com/samara-surf.html; Sámara, 200m from main street on road to Carrillo) School and shop operates out of fun Tico Adventure Lodge ($).

Safari Surf School (506-2682-0573; 866-433-3355 USA and Canada; www.safarisurf school.com) Outfitter offers lessons and packages in Nosara and Malpaís.

Witch's Rock Surf Camp (506-2653-1262; www.witchsrocksurfcamp.com) World-class surf camp offers packages for newbies and pros, with surfin' safaris for everyone.

Wildlife Displays and Rescue Centers

Africa Mía (506-2661-8161; www.africamia.net; 10km south of Liberia on the InterAmericana; open: 8 AM–5 PM, daily; admission $15 per adult, $10 per child; bus $25 per adult, $20 per child; Hummer tour is $65 per adult, $55 per child) "My Africa" really is an African wildlife park in the savannahs of Guanacaste, with cage-free, predator-free enclosures, stocked with giraffes, bongos, giant elands, camels, zebras, ostriches, okapi, and wildebeests, plus a few Costa Rican species who have shown up for the free food. Weird, but fun.

Monkey Park Rescue Center (506-2653-8060; www.monkey-park.org; Portegolpe; open 8 AM–5 PM; admission $15) Accredited center rescues, rehabilitates and releases monkeys that have been abandoned or hurt; 10 monkeys per month are brought here. Guided tours take you through a butterfly enclosure and into the dry tropical forest, where resident howlers, capuchins, deer, and crocodiles reside.

★ **Las Pumas** (506-2669-6044; www.laspumas.com; 5 km north of Cañas; admission $5) This rescue center takes in injured and rescued big cats, then tries to rehabilitate them for release into the wild. Confines are cramped because money is tight, but you can always make a much larger donation to these pudgy pumas, blind ocelots, cute tigrillos adopted as kittens then donated by their increasingly nervous families, and other animals who wouldn't survive in the wild, but have nowhere else to go.

Tempisque Safari (506-2698-1068; www.tempisquesafari.com; Rosario, 33 km southwest of La Amistad Bridge; admission $45) Kid-friendly attraction offers oxcart rides, boat tours, and alligator feedings in their private wildlife refuge next to Palo Verde National Park.

A Central African bongo apparently enjoying the pura vida *lifestyle at Liberia's Africa Mía*

La Selva (506-2305-1610; Playa Carrillo, 6 km south of Sámara; open 8 AM–8 PM) Private animal shelter offers guided tours of their small collection of rescued pizotes, crocodiles, porcupines, jaguarundis, parrots, and other animals; prices include a return visit in the evening, when other animals are active.

Kitesurfing

Bahía Salinas, 68 kilometers (41 miles) north of Liberia, 11 kilometers (7 miles) from the blue-collar town of La Cruz, offers some of the best kitesurfing in Central America, with several spots offering lodging and instruction. Try **Cometa Copal** (506-2676-1192; www.islandsurf-sail.com) or **La Sandía** (506-2676-1045; www.lasandia _costarica.com), which also offers *cabinas* ($). The region's original operation, ★**Blue Dream Kitesurfing School, Hotel & Spa** (506-2676-1042; www.bluedreamhotel .com) can design packages including rentals, lessons, spa treatments, and accommodations at their basic hotel ($), with tiny, tidy rooms. Kayaks, snorkel gear, sportfishing trips, and national park excursions are also on offer.

Though capuchin, or white-faced monkeys, may beg for (or steal) food, human snacks (including bananas) can hurt or kill them.

Yoga

Several hotels listed earlier also offer yoga classes and retreats.

Casa Zen (506-2640-0523; www.zencosta rica.com; Santa Teresa, 1.5 km from Frank's Place) Great budget to midrange hotel offers yoga classes and packages.

Kaya Sol (506-2682-0080; www.kayasol.com; Nosara, 100m south of Minisuper Delicias del Mundo; classes $5 or by donation) Pretty, peaceful hotel ($–$$) with teak rooms and a great vibe, offers community classes at 4 PM in their popular, mostly vegetarian restaurant; donations could include seashells or poems.

Montezuma Yoga (506-2642-0076; www.montezumayoga.com; Montezuma, 250m south of the bus stop at Hotel Los Mangos) Simple but sweet budget hotel ($–$$), offers classes ($12 each, or 10 classes for $100) and retreats.

Nosara Yoga Institute (www.nosarayoga.com; south entrance of Nosara; classes $10) This world-class yoga institute offers single classes and serious long-term instruction on their absolutely gorgeous wooded property.

Rip Jack Inn (506-2653-0480, 800-808-4605; www.ripjackinn.com; Playa Grande; classes $10) Relaxing hotel ($$), with spacious, jewel-toned rooms and a great "healthy gourmet" restaurant ($$–$$$), offers yoga with ocean views, twice daily.

Tamarindo Yoga (506-2653-0294; www.tamarindoyoga.com; Tamarindo, 150m north of the Hotel Capitan Suizo; classes $15) Enjoy classes just minutes from the beach.

Spas

NORTHERN NICOYA (PAPAGAYO TO OCOTAL)

Bahia Azul (506-2670-1098; Playas del Coco, Coco Verde Hotel) Good prices on massages, facials, and more.

Miraval Spa (Punta Cacique, between Playas del Coco and Playa Hermosa) Opening soon, claims it will be one of the best spas in the world.

Nefertitis (506-2670-1554; Playas del Coco) Right on the main drag, this spot offers haircuts, manicures, pedicures, facials, and massages.

Pura Vida Beach Massage (506-2697-0303) Association of physiotherapists will bring tables to any hotel, from Papagayo to Tamarindo; an hour costs about $50.

WESTERN NICOYA (TAMARINDO, SÁMARA, NOSARA)

Damaniti's Day Spa (506-2653-0995; Tamarindo, Zullimar Plaza) Facials, manicures, massages, and package deals.

Essence Day Spa (506-2653-0291; esencedayspa@yahoo.com; Tamarindo, next to Cabinas Coral Reef on the road to Langosta) Massages (including some especially for golf and surf injuries) plus facials, wraps, and a full hair salon.

Spa de Eros (506-2850-4222; 786-866-7039 USA, www.losaltosdeeros.com; 20 minutes east of Tamarindo) One of the world's best hotels offers a $200 spa package, limited to five people per day, which includes four treatments, a healthy lunch, and transportation from Tamarindo.

Tica Massage (506-2682-0096; Nosara, Playa Guiones, across from Casa Toucan) Inexpensive massages and spa services.

SOUTHERN NICOYA PENINSULA

Mi Spa (506-2640-0319; Santa Teresa, Playa Hermosa) Massages, facials, haircuts, manicures, pedicures, as well as yoga classes almost daily.

SHOPPING

Books

Frog Pad (506-2682-4039; www.thefrogpad.com; Nosara, Playa Guiones, 100m south of Gilded Iguana) Sells and trades used books, and rents DVDs, board games, surfboards, and more.

★ **Jaime Peligro** (506-2887-9596; jaimepeligro123@hotmail.com; Tamarindo, Las Olas Center; open 10 AM–8 PM, Mon.–Sat., noon–5 PM, Sun.) Mostly English-language books and guides, plus maps, stamps, postcards, and an excellent music selection collected by the owner, a local music writer.

Librería Topsy (506-2642-0576; Montezuma, downtown) Used books and lots of English-language newspapers and magazines.

Undercover Books (Tamarindo, Plaza Tiquicia Tropical) Offers mostly English-language titles, board games, and more.

Clothing

Casa Natura (506-2811-3611; Playas del Coco main street, across from K-West) Upscale beauty supplies, candles, Bach flower remedies, massage oils, and more.

Dulce (506-2825-5925; Tamarindo, behind Galería Pelicano) Exotic women's clothing, lingerie, linens, lotions, and handmade jewelry.

EK Art Jewelry (ek_jewelry@yahoo.com; Tamarindo) Beautiful handmade jewelry uses shells, fossils, and semiprecious stones.

Papaya con Leche (506-2653-3902; Tamarindo, Shopping Center Diria #9) Ultra-cute beachwear plus custom-made bikinis.

Galleries

Arte de Origen (506-2653-1635; Tamarindo, Plaza Conchal next to Banco San José) Exotic original arts and crafts from across the globe.

Galería Sámara Arte Dragonfly (506-2656-0964; www.samaraarte.com; Sámara, just off the main street) Handmade arts and crafts vary widely in quality, but you'll enjoy rummaging through the psychedelic mess.

Galería Nativa (Nosara, Playa Guiones, minimall) High-quality crafts, in particular woodcarvings, are made by local artists.

Sol y Paz (506-2653-8859; Huacas, Playa Grande–Flamingo intersection) Colorful original art, Mexican and Tico pottery, sculpture, handcrafted furniture, and more.

Malls and Markets

Garden Plaza (www.tamarindoheights.com; 1 km outside Tamarindo) If you're feeling homesick for, say, Irvine, this attractive, modern mall features an upscale Automercado, clothing shops, gym, restaurants, and more.

The Pottery of Guaitíl

About an hour from the Gold Coast, just east of Santa Cruz, is the ceramics center of Guaitíl, population 700, of whom perhaps 200 are professional potters. Using pre-Columbian styles, techniques, and even tools handed down for generations, their heavy, lustrous, and ornate creations are destined for markets all over the country.

Clay is collected from specific spots in surrounding hills, then mixed with other materials, such as sand taken from iguana nests. After mixing, pieces are molded into several designs, painted with natural tints such as the blue-ish *curiol*, and polished to a high sheen using smooth *sukia* stones. The piece is dried outdoors, then carved with a sharp metal tool. Finally, it's baked in a *horno*, or beehive-shaped kiln, at a relatively low heat achieved with firewood.

You can purchase fine pieces anywhere, or drop by one of the many workshops surrounding Guaitíl's central plaza, such as **Tinajitas Pottery** (506-2681-1318), geared for tourists with multilingual guides, or **Coopealianza** (506-2681-1010), operated by a local women's collective that uses only traditional methods.

Mall Plaza Liberia (1 km south of Liberia on the InterAmericana) Small air-conditioned mall offers gourmet groceries, fourplex cinema, department stores, and absolutely spectacular volcano views from the almost abandoned little food court.

Centro Comercial Santa Rosa (southeast corner of Liberia crossroads) Brand-new strip mall has clothing stores; a Jumbo grocer; good Mexican, Italian, and Peruvian restaurants; and the **Outdoor Center** (506-2665-7062), which sells camping and adventure gear.

Plaza Conchal (Tamarindo) Two ATMs, a day spa, several restaurants (including **La Suite** (506-2653-2295; $$$), an upscale wine and salad bar with upscale seafood dishes) and dozens of shops make this rather elegant commercial center a fine place to shop.

EVENTS

Fiestas are a great time to see (and taste) traditional Guanacasteco culture. Expect plenty of marimba music, oxcart parades, *topes* (horse parades), folkloric dancers wearing oversized papier-mâché heads that depict indigenous legends, and *corridos de toros*, Costa Rican—style bullfights, where scores of young men leap into the ring and attempt to touch an irritated bull—the bull is never killed, though human participants occasionally are.

January
San Cruz Cultural Week & National Folkloric Fiestas (January, Santa Cruz) The cradle of Costa Rican Folklore hosts more than 500 artists from Costa Rica and beyond.

Nicoya Fiestas Civicas (Late January, Nicoya) Serious *sabanero* event features *topes*, rodeos, carnival rides, and heavy drinking ending on the feast day of San Blas, Nicoya's patron saint.

February
Mardi Gras (Playa Flamingo) Celebrate Fat Tuesday *pura vida*—style in Playa Flamingo.

March
Papagayo Sailing Regatta (506-2301-3030; www.regattapapagayo.org; last weekend of March) Open to all classifications of vessel, with proceeds going to a new sailing school and scholarship program.

April
Festival of Art & Ecology (last week in April, Playas del Coco) Art exhibitions, live performers, and sand-sculpture contests are fun.

July
Chorotega Ceramic Fair (506-2824-0114; San Vicente, Nicoya) A celebration of indigenous handicrafts and culture with dancing, music, rodeos, and, of course, shopping.

Sea Festival (mid-July, Puntarenas) The port town pays homage to the Virgen del Carmen, patron saint of sailors, with a festive regatta.

Montezuma Music Festival (mid-July, Montezuma) Hipsters hit the beach for this fiesta.

Annexation (Guanacaste) Day (July 25; Guanacaste) Liberia hosts Guanacaste's biggest party, celebrating the 1824 annexation to Costa Rica with concerts, all night disco parties, topes, bullfights, and fireworks at 5 AM every morning. Smaller, but no less enthusiastic, fiestas are held throughout Guanacaste.

September

Vuelta de la Soledad (late September; www.lascoledadmtb.com; Sámara) Serious 83-kilometer (50-mile) mountain bike race through the heart of the peninsula.

August

Tamarindo Jazz & Blues Festival (first weekend in August) Laguna de Cocodrilo brings jazz musicians from all over Costa Rica.

November

Samara Air-Festival (506-2656-8048; www.flyingcrocodile.com) Bring your ultralights to Sámara and take to the air.

Montezuma Film Festival (early November, www.montezumafilmfestival.com) Dozens of venues show films from all over the world

Firewood Festival (12 November; Nicoya) Hundreds of oxcarts, some brightly painted but most daily drivers, arrive in Nicoya laden with firewood for the *Pica de Leña*, a very traditional fiesta with marimba, folkloric dance, and lots of *chirrete*, a mildly alcoholic corn homebrew.

December

La Yegüita (December 12; Nicoya) Since 1531, this Catholic/Chorotega hybrid holiday has celebrated the miracle of the Virgen of Guadelupe conjuring a chestnut mare (*yegüita*) to break up a machete brawl between two brothers; ever since, the Chorotega have been loyal Catholics.

7

CENTRAL PACIFIC COAST
AND THE OSA PENINSULA

Outstanding Waves and Astonishing Biodiversity

This is, perhaps, the Costa Rica of your dreams: Sunny, sprawling beach towns both bohemian and beautiful, separated by long, lonely stretches of sand. Where mountains rise steeply from the crashing surf, then plunge deep into the Pacific, forming the fjords of the sweet Golfo Dulce that frame the untamed Osa Peninsula, which may be the wildest place left on Earth.

The closest real beach town to San José is festive Jacó, the Central Pacific's designated party headquarters. Less than two hours from the capital, this rather rough conglomeration of restaurants, clubs, and hotels brings in Josefinos on weekend jaunts, surfers here for the country's most consistent beach break, and snowbirds basking in the air-conditioned comfort of their high-rise condos, all mixing into a mélange of party people plying the bustling main drag.

Just north is Playa Herradura, home to the plush Marriott Los Sueños, with a fine marina and golf course; Punta Leona, with "Costa Rica's whitest sand"; and wild Carara National Park, perhaps the most easily accessible rain forest wonderland in the country. Jacó's southern neighbor, Playa Hermosa, offers wilder waves and tamer nightlife. Continuing down the coast, you'll pass several beautiful and less touristed beaches, with a few great lodging options in Playa Estilleros and Palo Seco. Isla Damas, just offshore, can be explored in kayaks.

The next destination town is Quepos, an important port since the pre-Columbian era and still home to a serious fishing fleet, just 7 scenic kilometers (4.2 miles), lined with stunning resorts from Manuel Antonio National Park, protecting Costa Rica's most beautiful and visited beaches. The coastal road turns rough and unpaved through the all-important oil palm plantations heading south, passing beautiful beaches including Playa Matapalo, with a blue flag and nesting turtles between July and November.

Then, it's Dominical, another surfers' haven known for its serious waves, surrounded by increasingly fine accommodations. Just 40 kilometers (24 miles) inland, the Tico town of San Isidro del General is the gateway to La Amistad International Park, as well as a chilly alternate route through the cloud forests back to San José.

Continuing south, a sweeping collection of relatively undiscovered beaches are collectively known as la Costa Ballena, the "Whale Coast": Punta Uvita, home to Ballena National Marine Park; Playa Piñuelas, with calm waters for swimming; Playa Ventanas, or Windows

Crossing the Río Rincón on the Osa Peninsula

Beach, with caverns and tunnels carved by waves into the rock; and long, gray Playa Tortuga, at the mouth of the Térraba River, where sea turtles nest in September and October.

Finally, at the nondescript town of Palmar Norte, the Osa Peninsula begins. Take a riverboat ride down Río Sierpe to Drake Bay and utterly untamed Corcovado National Park. Or hike the wild trails between friendly Puerto Jiménez and isolated La Sirena Station, one of the last truly pristine places on Earth.

Across the Golfo Dulce, or "Sweet Gulf," is Golfito, once a bustling banana port and headquarters of powerful United Fruit, today the discount, duty-free shopping capital of Costa Rica (proximity to Panama means low, low prices). Plans are afoot to revitalize the town's tourist potential with a new marina reminiscent of its heady banana-baron heydays. In the meantime, Golfito makes a relaxing stop before heading south to the idyllic surf towns of Playa Zancudo and Pavones.

GETTING AROUND

Air

Sansa (506-2777-0683; www.flysansa.com) offers regular flights between San José and Quepos, with continuing service to Palmar Sur, as well as San José to Drake Bay, Golfito, Palmer Sur, and Puerto Jiménez. **Nature Air** (506-2777-2548; www.natureair.com) offers direct flights between Quepos and Arenal, Liberia, Palmar Sur, Puerto Jiménez, San José, Tamarindo, and Bocas del Toro, Panamá. You can also charter planes to La Sirena Ranger Station, in Corcovado National Park.

CENTRAL PACIFIC

34

San Pablo
de Leon
Cortés
226

LOS SANTOS
FOREST PRESERVE

Quebradas

SURTUBAL
REFUGE

CARARA
NATIONAL
PARK

San Isidro
de El General

CATARATAS
DE CERRO
REDONDO
REFUGE

Rainmaker
Project

Rafiki Lodge

22

243

Pura Vida
Gardens

Río Savegre

Villas
Calletas

Pueblo
Nuevo

34

Marriott
Los Sueños

Mata de
Platano

Quepos

Matapalo

Barú

Dominical

34

Jacó

❶❷

Bejuco

Manuel
Antonio

Platanillo

Escaleras

Isla
Herradura

Quebrada
Amarilla

Esterillos
Oeste

Tamarai Bamboo
Beach Resort

MANUEL
ANTONIO
NATIONAL
PARK

BARÚ DEL
PACIFICO
REFUGE

Cuna de
Angel

N

10 miles

0

10 kilometers

1. Xandari by the Pacific
2. Pélican Hotel
3. Cristal Ballena
4. La Cusinga Ecolodge
5. La Leona Eco-odge,
   Corcovado Lodge Tent Camp
6. Luna Lodge
7. Airport
8. Bosque del Cabo, Encanta
   de Vida Lodge, El Romanso Lodge
9. Lapa Ríos
10. Black Turtle Lodge
11. Köbö Chocolate Tour
12. Danta Corcovado Lodge
13. Osa Wildlife Sanctuary
14. Rainbow Adventures Lodge
15. Playa Nicuesa Lodge
16. Casa Las Orchideas

P A C I F I C

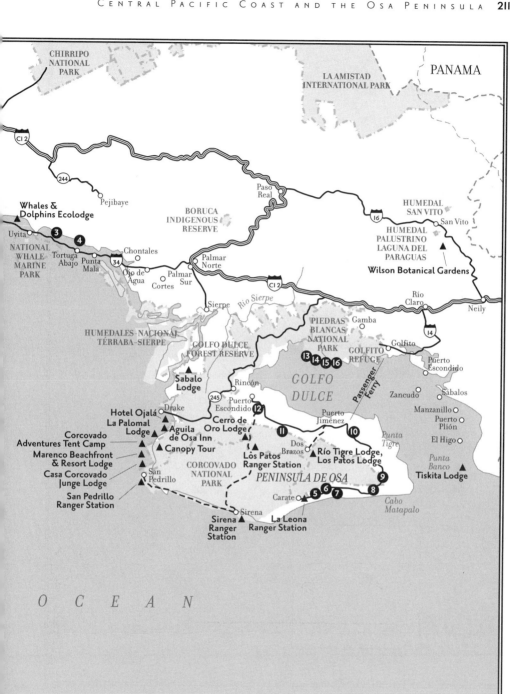

CHIRRIPO NATIONAL PARK

PANAMA

LA AMISTAD INTERNATIONAL PARK

CI 2

244

Pejibaye

Paso Real

HUMEDAL SAN VITO

16

San Vito

Whales & Dolphins Ecolodge

BORUCA INDIGENOUS RESERVE

HUMEDAL PALUSTRINO LAGUNA DEL PARAGUAS

Uvita

❸ ❹

NATIONAL WHALE MARINE PARK

Chontales

Tortuga Abajo
Punta Mala

34

Ojo de Agua
Cortes
Palmar Sur

Palmar Norte

CI 2

Wilson Botanical Gardens

Río Claro

Neily

Sierpe

Río Sierpe

HUMEDALES NACIONAL TÉRRABA-SIERPE

GOLFO DULCE FOREST RESERVE

PIEDRAS BLANCAS NATIONAL PARK

Gamba

Golfito

14

GOLFITO REFUGE

Puerto Escondido

Sabalo Lodge

Rincón

❶❸ ❶❹ ❶❺ ❶❻

GOLFO DULCE

Zancudo

Sabalos

Manzanillo

Puerto Plión

245

Puerto Escondido

Drake

❶❷

Puerto Jiménez

Passenger Ferry

Punta Tigre

El Higo

Hotel Ojalá
La Palomal Lodge

Cerro de Oro Lodge

Aguila de Osa Inn

❶❶

❶❷

Dos Brazos

Río Tigre Lodge, Los Patos Lodge

❶❷

Punta Banco

Corcovado Adventures Tent Camp

Canopy Tour

Los Patos Ranger Station

Tiskita Lodge

Marenco Beachfront & Resort Lodge

CORCOVADO NATIONAL PARK

PENINSULA DE OSA

❾

Casa Corcovado Junge Lodge

San Pedrillo

Carate

❺ ❻ ❼

❽

Cabo Matapalo

San Pedrillo Ranger Station

Sirena

Sirena Ranger Station

La Leona Ranger Station

O C E A N

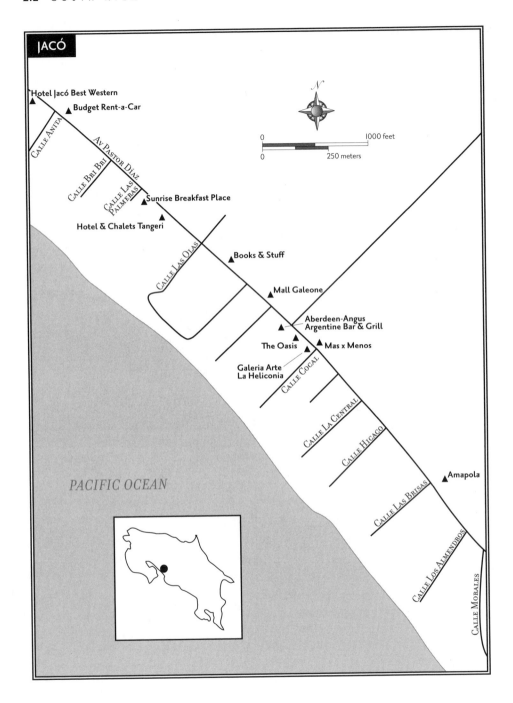

JACÓ

Hotel Jacó Best Western
Budget Rent-a-Car
Calle Anita
Av Pastor Díaz
Calle Bri Bri
Calle Las Palmeras
Sunrise Breakfast Place
Hotel & Chalets Tangeri
Calle Las Olas
Books & Stuff
Mall Galeone
Aberdeen-Angus Argentine Bar & Grill
The Oasis
Mas x Menos
Galeria Arte La Heliconia
Calle Cocal
Calle La Central
Calle Higago
Calle Las Brisas
Amapola
Calle Los Almendros
Calle Morales

PACIFIC OCEAN

1000 feet
250 meters

QUEPOS - MANUEL ANTONIO

See Inset Quepos

Hotel Restaurant
Mono Azul

Hotel &
Restaurant Plimio

To Jacó (70km),
San José (185km)

0   500 feet
0   200 meters

To
Dominical
(45km),
Puerto
Jiménez
(195km)

QUEPOS

1. Estuario Boca Viejo
2. Café Milagro, El Patio Bistro Latino
3. Costa Mar Dreams Sportfishing
4. Galería Zukia
5. El Gran Escape
6. Tropical Sushi
7. Manuel Antonio Divers
8. Best Western Hotel Kamuk
9. Gastronomia L' Angolo
10. Dos Locos
11. Bus Terminal
12. Ríos Tropicales

To Manuel Antonio
National Park (7km)

Hotel Gaia

My Place,
Mi Lugar

B&B La Colina

Café Milagro

Villas Nicolas

Hotel
La Mansíon

Issimo Suites

Hotel
El Parador

Hotel Sí
Como No

Gato Negro

El Avion

Hotel Costa Verde

Marlin
Restaurant

Hotel
Espadilla,
Puerto Escondido
Restaurant

Manuel Antonio
National Park
Entrance

PACIFIC OCEAN

Playa Espadilla

0   1/2 mile
0   1/2 kilometer

Online Resources

Central Pacific Way (www.costaricaway.net) Bilingual, monthly magazine and travel guide for the Central Pacific offers a modest Web site.

El Chunche (www.chunchemag.com) Hip, monthly Jacó-centric magazine has hotel, restaurant, and events listings.

★ **Costa Rica Rainforest Travel** (www.osamap.com) English-language site with maps and links to hotels and other businesses between Dominical and Osa.

Golfito Costa Rica (www.golfito-costa-rica.com) Maps, information, and links for Golfito and the surrounding area.

Playa Herradura (www.playaherradura.info) Guide to the upscale offerings in Playa Herradura, just north of Jacó.

Manuel Antonio.com (www.manuelantonio.com) Links to a handful of excellent hotels, sportfishing operators, and other upscale services.

Osa–Costa Rica (www.osacostarica.com) Spanish-language site with links to hotels, tour operators, and other services.

Puerto Quepos (www.puertoquepos.com) Information and links for hotels, restaurants, tour operators, and much more in Manuel Antonio.

Uvita Information Center (506-2843-7142; www.uvita.info) Books hotels and tours, and runs an outstanding info center at the entrance to Punta Uvita.

Zancudo Times (www.zancudotimes.com) Zancudo news, views, listings, and links.

Bus

There is excellent bus service throughout the region, both along the Coastal Highway and along the InterAmericana, directly from San José to Dominical, then on to points south. Even if you've rented a car, consider taking advantage of public buses ($.30) running between Quepos and Manuel Antonio National Park from 5:45 AM to 7 PM, as parking can be a nightmare, particularly in high season.

Fewer buses serve the Osa Peninsula, thus some people prefer to bus directly to Golfito, then take the passenger ferry across to Puerto Jiménez, with relatively easy access to Corcovado National Park.

Private Shuttle

In addition to the countrywide private shuttle services, which serve Jacó, Manuel Antonio, and Dominical, several local operators offer transportation.

Compatriotas Nicaraguense (506-2828-0858) Private shuttle between Jacó and Nicaragua (Managua, León, and Estelí)

Reyeri Tours (506-2771-6364; www.rayeri.com) Runs shuttles between San José and Dominical, Golfito, Puerto Jiménez, San Isidro del General, San Vito, Sierpe, Uvita, and David, Panama.

Shuttle Osa Runs $35 shuttles between Puerto Jiménez and San José.

Rental Car

Both Jacó and Quepos have several car rental companies. Puerto Jiménez has one, **Solid Car Rental** (506-2335-9441; Café La Onda), with four-wheel-drive vehicles only. Jacó and

Quepos also offer several options for renting scooters and motorcycles; try **Fast Eddie's Scooter Rentals** (506-2777-4127) in Quepos, or **Rent@Me Scooter Rental** (506-2643-1809; Jacó, Main Av near Beatles Bar) in Jacó.

Boat

There are regular boat taxis ($35) between Jacó and Montezuma on the Southern Nicoya; try **Cocozuma Traveler** (506-642-0911; www.cocozumacr.com) and **Montezuma Eco Tours** (506-642-0467; www.montezumaecotours.com). For information on car ferries between Puntarenas and the Southern Nicoya, please see the Guanacaste and Nicoya Peninsula chapter.

Collective taxis (10 AM; $25) and chartered boats run between Sierpe, close to the Palmar Sur airport, to Drake Bay, a scenic 40-kilometer (25-mile) stretch of the protected Río Sierpe wetlands. **Costa Rica Adventures** (506-2788-1016; cradventures@gmail.com); or **Tours Gaviotas de Osa** (506-2788-1212; www.tgaviotas.com), both in "downtown" Sierpe, arrange transportation and tours.

Passenger ferries ($5) connect Puerto Jiménez and Golfito (which has more buses to San José) twice daily. You can also arrange private boat taxis from Puerto Jiménez to Playa Zancudo ($35); try **Toboga Aquatic Tours** (506-2753-53265).

From Golfito, you can get water taxis to Puerto Jiménez, Playa Cacao, Playa Zancudo, and elsewhere. **Association ABOCOP** (506–2775-0712) and several private captains can be found at the docks.

LODGING

The Central Pacific Coast was one of the first regions developed for tourism in Costa Rica, and almost all accessible beaches have good midrange lodging options, often geared to surfers or Tico families. Jacó is home to a wide variety of hotels, but for the most spectacular lodging head north, to Los Sueños or Villas Caletas. South of Jacó, Estilleros and Palo Seco beaches have lovely options as well.

The road between Quepos and Manuel Antonio National Park passes by some of the country's most spectacular resorts; this is honeymoon country. This is also Central America's premier destination for gay and lesbian travelers, and several hotels fly the rainbow flag. If you're looking for solitude, however, try Playa Matapalo, Punta Uvita, and points south. Dominical is still a backpackers' haven, but has a few upscale options as well.

The Osa Peninsula also has its share of upscale lodges and resorts, but as infrastructure becomes less reliable, prices rise, and amenities such as air-conditioning disappear; electricity is often unreliable and all supplies must be shipped in at some cost. Golfito has several good hotels, all of which are filled Friday and Saturday night with excited shoppers; make reservations or plan to stay elsewhere. Nearby Playa Zancudo and Pavones offer mostly budget options, with a few comfortable bungalows and lodges next to those lovely beaches.

Lodging Price Code

Cost of lodging is based on an average per-room, double-occupancy rate at peak season (December through March). Costa Rica's 16.39 percent tax and gratuities are not included. Rates are often reduced during the Green Season (May through November). An asterisk denotes that a full breakfast is included with the room price.

Inexpensive ($)	Up to $50
Moderate ($$)	$50 to $100
Expensive ($$$)	$100 to $200
Very Expensive ($$$$)	Over $200

Hotels

JACÓ

Some of Jacó's best accommodations are listed under Vacation Rentals, later.

LOS SUEÑOS RESORT & MARINA

Manager: Mayela Alfaro
506-2637-8886; 866-865-9759 USA and Canada
www.lossuenosresort.com
info@lossuenosresort.com
Playa Herradura, 800m west of entrance
Price: Very Expensive
Credit Cards: Yes
Handicap Access: Yes

A sweeping Spanish Colonial-style brick lobby, filled with beautiful art, antiques, and fresh flowers, welcomes you to one of the most impressive resorts on the Central Pacific. The top-of-the-line, 201-room Marriott property offers beautiful rooms and top-notch service, exactly what you'd expect. But the architects of holiday dreams have gone even further, building a gorgeous marina, the only one of its size between Acapulco and Venezuela, and the outstanding 18-hole, par-72 championship **La Iguana Golf Course**, with wonderful beach views and plenty of wildlife. Rooms, with tiny balconies opening onto pretty vistas, are furnished with all expected amenities plus little luxuries like hand-painted ceramic tiles, wrought iron detail work, real down pillows and comforters on the wonderful beds, beautiful wood furniture, coffeemakers, work stations with WiFi, and more.

Multiple pools connected by swimmable canals shimmer in the immaculate gardens, where trails lead to a fitness room, tennis courts, casino, spa, and gourmet restaurants, including **Nuevo Latino** (506-630-9000; D; $$$), a fine dining option worth visiting, even if you're not a guest, for inno-

---

Hanging Out in Jacó

Let's face facts: Jacó is more convenient than fabulous, two hours from San José and the international airport, with great waves and a festive party scene. If you're just looking for a comfortable hotel close to the action, rather than some spectacular stay, here are a few fine suggestions.

Best Western Jacó Beach (506-2643-1000; www.bestwesterncostarica.com/locations_jaco.html; Jacó, on the beach; $$$) Resort-style accommodations offer modern rooms with all the expected amenities, including nice pools, tennis courts, tour desk, restaurants, and waves right out back.

Docelunas (506-2643-2211; www.docelunas.com; $$$) Attractive, if isolated spot offers spacious, elegant rooms, a holistic spa, beautiful pool, and good restaurant. You'll have to cross the Coastal Highway to hit the beach, however.

Mar de Luz (506-2643-3259; www.mardeluz.com; Jacó, 150m from the beach; $$*) Appealing hotel tucked away off Jacó's busy strip offers spacious, immaculate rooms, some nicer (with river rock walls) than others, with full kitchens, air-conditioning, and porches overlooking gardens, a barbecue, and clean pools.

Tangerí (506-2643-3001; www.hoteltangeri.com; central Jacó, on the beach; $$$*) Cluster of cute *cabinas* with kitchenettes surrounding flower-filled gardens and a pool, all just steps from the beach, has more charm than most Jacó hotels.

vative pan-Latin cuisine in beautiful surroundings, overlooking a pretty pool and waterfall. Or, walk down to the marina, with many more options, all with ocean views. Marriott also offers villas and condos for longer stays.

VILLA CALETAS

Owner: Denis Roy
506-2637-0505
www.villacaletas.com
reservations@villacaletas.com
8 km (5 mi.) north of Jacó
Price: Expensive to Very Expensive
Credit Cards: Yes
Handicap Access: Yes

Atop the emerald forests of a 350-meter (1,150-foot) bluff, falling steeply to the sea below, this truly stunning hotel echoes a 19th century French estate, with classic columns and elegant archways, stone cherubim, and Romanesque fountains. Ascend the stone pathways lined with tropical flowers, and you'll soon realize that no architectural flourish could match this luxurious property's finest amenity: that view. And you still haven't seen the sun set.

To call the suites "luxuriously appointed" would be an understatement; each is richly adorned with elegant antiques, original art, exotic tapestries, fine Persian rugs, incredible tile work, and other sumptuous extras that simply overwhelm the senses. All rooms have private balconies with sweeping Pacific views. And tastefully tucked away amidst the extravagance are modern amenities including air-conditioning, minibar, coffeemaker, and satellite TV. Better rooms have private pools, while those in the lavish Zephyr Palace, a new addition to the hotel, offer WiFi.

The pricey fine dining restaurant, **El Mirador** (506-2643-0623; open 7 AM–9:30 PM; $$$$) brings in bevies of visitors who come to watch the famed sunsets from the tiny Greek amphitheatre, where musicians sometimes perform.

★ XANDARI BY THE PACIFIC

Owners: Sherrill and Charlene Broudy
506-2778-7070; 866-363-3212 USA and Canada
www.xandari.com
xanpac@xandari.com
Playa Estilleros Este, halfway between Jacó and Quepos
Price: Very Expensive*
Credit Cards: Yes
Handicap Access: Yes

Another fantastic daydream made real by the architect-artist team behind splendid **Xandari Resort in Alajuela** (see chapter 4), this whimsical collection of unique and luxurious villas offers one major improvement over the original property: the Pacific.

You'll fall in love with Xandari's flowing harmony of arched ceilings and gently curving walls, accented with bright tropical colors, cheerful paintings, vibrant tapestries, and fanciful mosaic tiles. The elegant architecture extends to comfortable built-in furniture strewn with throw pillows, and absolutely beautiful bathrooms that open onto private gardens. Behind large, glass French doors, are views over several pools, a Jacuzzi, and that beautiful beach. All the rooms are equipped with air-conditioning, WiFi, CD players, and other amenities, but no TV.

The on-site **restaurant** (B, L, D; $$$$) quite deservedly gets rave reviews for its healthy, gourmet cuisine. An attached spa offers an array of services. Service is excellent, the vibe casual, and the overall experience absolutely perfect.

QUEPOS AND MANUEL ANTONIO
With the highest concentration of divine luxury properties in Costa Rica, this is just a taste of what's available.

ARENAS DEL MAR

Directors: Teri and Glen Jampol
506-2777-2777
www.arenasdelmar.com

Take a break from the rustic at Gaia's sleek restaurant with a view.

info@arenasdelmar.com
Price: Very Expensive*
Credit Cards: Yes
Special: Five CST Leaves

Someone needs to come up with a clever term, a play on "eco" and "luxury," for describing this new wave of sustainable and spectacular hotels. From the moment you arrive, whisked by electric carts to the breezy, open lobby, hung with startlingly fine works of art, you'll realize how easy it is to be green.

The entire property, possessed of an airy openness to nature, was designed to blend into the jungles and beaches, its innovative architecture interspersed with soothing, natural marble, hardwoods, terracotta tiles, bamboo, and rattan. Less expensive rooms are lovely, but rather small; consider upgrading to an ocean-view room or suite, with a half-moon stone Jacuzzi overlooking the Pacific. Linens are the very best quality, showers are solar heated, luxurious toiletries are biodegradable, and wildlife paintings by local artist Ann Laura Vargas may even tempt your attention away from the satellite flat-screen TV and WiFi. The on-site restaurant, **El Mirador** (open B, L, D; $$$$) serves upscale international cuisine made from fresh, local, often organic ingredients.

Arenas del Mar is brand new, and perhaps a bit rough around the edges, but those should soon be polished by directors Teri and Glen Janpol, proprietors of outstanding Finca Blanca in the Central Valley. For instance, one of the nearby beaches,

Playita, was for many years a gay nude beach; while guards are posted to help make sure everything is covered, freer spirits sometimes slip through. Regardless, this fine property represents the best of Costa Rica's new wave of luxuriously sustainable living.

BEST WESTERN KAMUK HOTEL & CASINO

506-2777-0811
www.kamuk.co.cr
info@kamuk.co.cr
Downtown Quepos, Main St.
Price: $$–$$$
Credit Cards: Yes
Handicap Access: Yes

The best hotel in downtown Quepos is absolutely business class, with perfectly acceptable, modern rooms that are just like home, some with views over the water. There's a good pool and third-floor restaurant, **Mira Olas** (6 AM–10 PM, daily; $$–$$$), serving uninspired international cuisine at decent prices over the waves.

Though it lacks some of the Best Western's amenities (and familiarity, which is sometimes comforting), I prefer smaller **Hotel Sirena** (506-2777-0572; www.la sirenahotel.com; downtown Quepos; $–$$), around the corner, with basic, air-conditioned rooms, cable TV, and a very pretty pool.

COSTA VERDE

Managers: Allan Templeton, Rodolfo Muñoz
506-2777-0584, 866-854-7958 USA and Canada
www.costaverde.com
reservations@costaverde.com
Road to Manuel Antonio
Price: Moderate to Expensive
Credit Cards: Yes
Handicap Access: No

A great midrange choice walking distance from the national park (they have their own trail), this hotel may not be beachfront but is absolutely surrounded with lush, wildlife-packed rain forest. From the rustic, open-air lobby and restaurant, with beautifully carved wooden furnishings and chandeliers echoed throughout the property, helpful staff will point you along steep but scenic trails to your choice of rooms. A "family" building has rooms with air-conditioning and television, while the "adult" side has fan-cooled, almost entirely screened-in rooms with no TV. Both have their own pools.

All of the spacious, cleanly tiled rooms have kitchenettes, WiFi, private balconies equipped with Sarchí rocking chairs, and gorgeous hand-carved furnishings throughout. Studios are even larger, with air-conditioning and two beds that are great for families; go for a studio-plus, though, with ocean views. The on-site **restaurant** (B, L, D; $$–$$$$) is fine, but cross the street for an unforgettable dining experience at ★**El Avión** (506-2777-3378; L, D; $$–$$$). In a Fairchild C-123 plane purchased by the Reagan Administration as part of the Iran-Contra Affair, and later abandoned in Guanacaste after the scandal was uncovered, this great spot has a bar in the cockpit, pleasant outdoor seating, and very good seafood.

★ GAIA HOTEL & RESERVE

Manager: Melany Martínez Thomas
506-2777-9797
www.gaiahr.com
reservations@gaiahr.com
Road to Manuel Antonio
Price: Very Expensive*
Credit Cards: Yes
Handicap Access: Yes

Sleek and modern, this exquisite five-star boutique property, a member of the Small Luxury Hotels of the world, is matchless. From the moment you arrive, and are assigned your own personal concierge (there are five employees for every room, a ratio you won't find elsewhere in the region), you'll realize that this is no ordinary hotel. Ascend to the whitewashed restaurant, with outstanding views, afternoon tapas, and a commitment to creative and healthy cuisine. Pause to appreciate the accomplishment: European polish, modern aesthetics and daring architecture, all brilliantly sustainable (of course), conjure an atmosphere of effortless, absolutely luxurious, casual cool.

Each of the 17 refined, Italian-accented rooms and delightfully airy suites is outfitted with the finest amenities, including the impeccable dark-wood and rattan furnishings, 500-thread-count Egyptian cotton linens on the incredibly comfortable beds, and strikingly designed fixtures in the dark sandstone bathrooms. The iPod-ready CD and DVD player is enhanced with Dolby Digital surround sound; private Jacuzzis and pools, resort-wide WiFi, and an unbelievable pool, with multiple waterfalls, put it over the top. The beach is quite a hike (along lovely wilderness trails), thus they thoughtfully offer a complimentary shuttle to the shore. But do you really want to leave? A fully equipped gymnasium, world-class spa, and trails through their private 5-hectare (12-acre) reserve all conspire to keep you here.

ISSIMO SUITES

506-2777-4410; 888-400-1985 USA and Canada
www.issimosuites.com
reservations@issimosuites.com
Off the road to Manuel Antonio
Price: Very Expensive*
Credit Cards: Yes
Handicap Access: Yes

In one of the most majestic locations in Manuel Antonio, overlooking a stunning snorkeling cove beneath the cliffs, this beautiful boutique hotel has been exquis-itely crafted to suit the surroundings, using pale flagstones and cane ceilings to lend a little local flavor to their world-class collection of honeymoon suites.

Spacious and possessed of an understated elegance, each boasts polished wood floors, exquisite furnishings, the finest bedding, and private Jacuzzis (afloat with fresh flowers when you arrive), all overlooking the sea from private patios just beyond entire walls of glass. Every possible desire has been anticipated by the designers, and amenities including DVD players, cable TV, air-conditioning, minibar, microwave, and beautiful bathrooms (with bidets!) are just part of the experience. The on-site spa has relaxing views and an extensive menu. But the real attraction is the top-notch **Restaurant Issimo** (B, L, D; $$$–$$$$), considered the best in Manuel Antonio. Reservations are highly recommended to enjoy the ever-changing menu of creatively presented haute cuisine, served above the surf.

MAKANDA BY THE SEA

Owner: Joe McNichols
506-2777-0442
www.makanda.com
info@makanda.com
Road to Manuel Antonio
Price: Very Expensive
Credit Cards: Yes
Handicap Access: No
Special: Adults only

Isolated and refined, 12 beautiful bungalows have been crafted with a nod to Japanese simplicity from rare tropical hardwoods that frame endless glass-enclosed vistas over the jungle and water. Not all of the villas have ocean views, but each is spacious and air-conditioned, with amenities including CD/DVD players, cable TV, and private patios that at least overlook the gardens and infinity pool.

The property is steeply pitched, making

the walk to your room a challenge for some. The challenging 15-minute trek (wearing shoes) to the quite private beach, small and rocky but secluded, is something like a Stairmaster, but slippery. Happily, they bring breakfast to your room, where you can brew a pot of coffee and enjoy the view and ample wildlife from your hammock or sofas. The on-site ★**Sunspot Poolside Bar & Grill** (reservations required; L, D; $$$$) offers classic upscale cuisine overlooking the pool and gardens. Lovely.

HOTEL SÍ COMO NO
Manager: Russ Jensen
506-2777-0777
www.sicomono.com
information@sicomono.com
Road to Manuel Antonio
Price: Expensive to Very Expensive*
Credit Cards: Yes
Handicap Access: Yes, but much of the property is steps-only
Special: Five CST Leaves

"Yes, of course," is the translation of the name, and the answer to almost any request you might ask the conscientious staff at this Manuel Antonio institution, one of Costa Rica's greenest hotels since 1992. Not just sustainable, however—this remains one of the region's most luxurious properties, perhaps paling against newer resorts but still boasting one of the best views on the strip.

Rooms are delightful (if gently showing their age), with sliding glass doors that open onto stunning views of islets once held sacred. Even the smaller basic rooms (consider upgrading) are air-conditioned and furnished in king-sized beds swathed with fabulous bedding, coffeemakers, live plants, bamboo mirrors, and rattan furniture; the pools are fantastic. There's also a wonderful free theater, a great breakfast buffet, and two excellent restaurants. Upscale **Claro Que Sí** (D; $$$$), with those same stunning views and Caribbean-tinged takes on international cuisine, especially seafood, and more casual **Rico Tico Bar and Grill** (B, L, D; $$$) with international cuisine and live music from the Tres Caciques.

DOMINICAL AND THE COSTA BALLENA
CRISTAL BALLENA
Manager: David Casasola
506-2786-5354
www.cristal-ballena.com
info@cristal-ballena.com
7 km (4 mi.) south of Uvita
Price: Moderate to Very Expensive*
Credit Cards: Yes
Handicap Access: Yes

Clean, spacious, unremarkable luxury rooms overlook the enormous pool and Ballena National Marine Park from the large windows or shared balconies. Furnished with four-poster beds draped in mosquito nets, coffeemakers, WiFi, and other expected amenities, these cool, tiled rooms with wicker furniture and pleasant furnishings make a very comfortable respite from the wonderful out-of-doors. It's a bit of a hike to the beach, but the trails are lovely, and the fine on-site pool is a welcome alternative.

Nearby, elegant **Cuna del Angel** (506-2787-8012; www.cunadelangel.com; 9 km south of Dominical; $$$–$$$$) is a more intimate, but similarly upscale, boutique hotel, with colorful rooms, a heavenly theme, and a world-class spa.

★ LA CUSINGA LODGE
Owners: John Tresemer and Bella Guzmán
506-2770-2549
www.lacusingalodge.com
info@lacusingalodge.com
Punta Uvita, 22 km south of Dominical
Price: Moderate to Expensive*
Credit Cards: Yes
Handicap Access: Challenging

Serene and sustainable family-run eco-lodge set in virgin rain forest above pristine, blue-flag beaches, lets you escape every care in perfect harmony with nature. Take a moment to appreciate the open-air lobby, hewn from locally-farmed wood, raised atop beautiful river-rock floors and walls, framing the spectacular ocean views. Have a seat in a rocking chair; perhaps you'll see a humpback whale breach in the distance. Rooms are tranquil and comfortable, but by no stretch plush: fan cooled, with gorgeous hot showers made with more river rocks (some stones jut out cleverly, for hanging towels), sinks inlaid with shells, huge screened windows, and lovely private porches. Furnishings are comfortable and handmade; and local arts and crafts are the décor. Delicious, reasonably priced organic meals are outstanding.

Descend their private trails to the beaches and rain forest, which you are welcome to explore; one trail leads all the way to Ballena Marine Park. Or indulge in a yoga class or massage on-site.

★ RANCHO PACIFICO

Garison Krause and Silvia Jimenez-Krause
506-2837-2731; 800-621-1975 USA
www.ranchopacifico.com
reservations@ranchopacifico.com
3 km (2 mi.) east of Punta Uvita
Price: Very Expensive
Credit Cards: Yes
Handicap Access: Yes
Special: One CST Leaf

Divine boutique hotel, high above the Whale Tail, offers refined luxury with a view. Villas are flawless, paved in pale flagstone and accented in dark hardwoods, a theme carried through from the wonderful open-air restaurant to the outstanding pool. Huge windows, most screened, open onto the jungle, where you may glimpse the monkeys, coatis, and more than 300 species of birds that inhabit their 100-hectare (250-acre) private reserve. Feel free to explore along trails to waterfalls, swimming holes,

and more incredible *miradores* (overlooks).

Or relax in your villa, some sleeping six, others with kitchens and plunge pools, and all enjoying elegantly understated furnishings, fine balconies, and incredible bathrooms that seem to invite the rain forest indoors. On-site **Spa Tranquila** offers massages in the trees, while the hotel restaurant specializes in healthy, fresh, organic meals, made with many ingredients grown right here. This is a true boutique experience, with 21 employees taking care of a maximum of 24 guests, and concierge service begins the moment you confirm your reservations.

If they're full, and you still want that wonderful Whale Tail view, nearby **Whales and Dolphins** (506-2743-8150; www.whalesanddolphins.net; $$$) is also extremely nice, with attractive rooms and a pricey international **restaurant** (B, L, D; $$$–$$$$) with a view.

VILLAS RÍO MAR

Managers: Christiaan Vijselaar, Sergio Schermel
506-2787-0052
www.villasriomar.com
info@villasriomar.com
800m south of Central Dominical
Price: Moderate
Credit Cards: Yes

Dominical proper lacks any outstanding hotels, but this spot, just south of town, is probably the best, with modern, thatch-roofed cabins scattered around pretty gardens, tennis courts, miniature golf, a semi-private beach, small spa, and nice pool. Rooms are pleasant, air-conditioned, and relaxing, with attractive bamboo furniture, soft lighting, adequate mattresses, and an appealing color scheme; junior suites are much nicer, with Jacuzzis and sitting areas. An on-site restaurant serves pricey international cuisine.

I actually preferred less luxurious

Diuwak Hotel (506-2787-0087; www
.diuwak.com; Dominical, 200m from
beach; $$), right in Dominical, its modern
rooms outfitted with private terraces, air-
conditioning, pretty Sarchí furniture, and
books about Costa Rican politics and his-
tory, edited by owner Orlando Castro M
himself. There's a great pool and lovely,
flagstone-paved **Tu Lui Restaurant** (B, L,
D; $$$), serving Italian-accented interna-
tional cuisine including steak, seafood,
pizza, and pasta alongside one very long
wine list. Diuwak is also home to ★**Green
Iguana Surf Camp** (www.greeniguanasurf
camp.com), and offers package deals.

THE OSO PENINSULA
BOSQUE DEL CABO
Manager: Duarde Avellan
506-2735-5206
www.bosquedelcabo.com
reservations@bosquedelcabo.com
Cabo Matapalo, 22 km (14 mi.) south of
Puerto Jiménez
Price: Expensive*
Credit Cards: Yes
Handicap Access: No

You'll particularly appreciate the balconies
and patios of this plush nature lodge, furnished with hammocks and even sofas.
Because the real luxury offered at this beautiful spot is the wildlife; troupes of both
spider and squirrel monkeys attended my
tour of the property, which finished up with
a flock of macaws, flying beneath a rainbow.

Bungalows are all unique, some wooden,
others whitewashed stucco; many with
kitchens, and others fabulous built-in
couches and furniture. Simple but very
comfortable, all airy and fan cooled, a few
with views over a sharp drop to the Pacific
far below (they'll pick you up at the bottom). The on-site **Bosque del Cabo
Restaurant** (B, L, D; $$$–$$$$) is one of
the region's best, serving an ever-changing
menu of Costa Rican-influenced interna-
tional cuisine. Make reservations.

CABINAS JIMÉNEZ
506-2735-5090
www.cabinasjimenez.com
info@cabinasjimenez.com
Central Puerto Jiménez
Price: Inexpensive to Moderate
Credit Cards: Yes
Handicap Access: Yes

Central Puerto Jiménez has several hotels
(starting at $6 per night), and this is my
favorite, a lovely midrange option right on
the water, with clean, colorful rooms
decked out in Guatemalan fabrics and lots
of hammocks. Air-conditioning, hot-water
showers, and a small pool are also quite
nice. Spend a few extra dollars and get a
room with ocean views and a small refriger-
ator, so worth it.

Other good options in town include
excellent **Cabinas Marcella** (506-2735-
5286; cabmarce@hotmail.com; $), with
tiny, immaculate rooms, some air-condi-
tioned; and much plusher **Parrot Bay Vil-
lage** (866-551-2003 USA and Canada; www
.parrotbayvillage.com; $$$*), catering to
fishers with a group of handsomely
appointed bungalows.

★ **LAPA RIOS**
Owners: Karen and John Lewis
506-2735-5281
www.laparios.com
info@laparios.com
Playa Carbonera, 20 km (12 mi.) south of
Puerto Jiménez
Price: Very Expensive*
Credit Cards: Yes
Handicap Access: Yes
Special: Five CST Leaves

Awaken to the noises of the jungle, a troupe
of curious monkeys perhaps, with the songs
of so many birds behind them that you may
miss the faint crash of waves. But as you rise
from your bamboo bed and gently pull back
the mosquito netting, those panoramic
ocean views, visible just beyond the gardens

Gay Places to Stay and Play

Manuel Antonio has been Central America's premier gay and lesbian destination for years, and offers activities and accommodations aplenty for that colorful crowd. Your hotel can make recommendations for gay-friendly tours and bars (or check out the Web sites listed in the San José chapter), or just stop by the **Barba Roja** on Thursday, or **Tutu Bar**, above El Gato Negro restaurant, anytime (both on the road to Manuel Antonio) for a drink.

Hotel Casa Blanca (506-2777-0253; hotel-casablanca.server1.de; road to Manuel Antonio; $$$) Beautiful location, excellent views, and rooms that could be updated.

Hotel Del Mar (506-2777-0543; www.gohoteldelmar.com; 200m from Manuel Antonio National Park; $$*) Excellent deal on simple, colorful, and very comfy rooms is also straight-friendly.

La Plantación (506-2777-1332; 800-477-7829 USA and Canada; www.bigrubys.com/costarica; $$*) Fabulous bed-and-breakfast, operated by Big Ruby's in Key West, is set in gorgeous gardens with a refreshing infinity pool. Spacious tiled rooms with French doors, DVD players, and other amenities open onto private furnished patios; cabinas are even nicer.

★ **Las Aguas Jungle Lodge** (506-2770-8008; 305-2677-9807; www.lasaguas.com; 40 km/ 25 mi. south of Manuel Antonio, near Dominical; $$–$$$) Happily (for me), this stunningly constructed jungle lodge, surrounded by mountains and waterfalls, is also straight-friendly.

Hotel Villa Roca (506-2777-1349; www.villaroca.com; road to Manuel Antonio; $$$*) Worth it just for the pool, this plush spot has huge, cool, tiled rooms with great beds, all amenities, and original art, though you may prefer that island view from your private porch.

from the screened-in "walls" of your polished private villa, will tune you back in. Have a solar-heated shower in your delightful bathroom, then a cup of organic coffee on your private porch, keeping a sharp eye out for breaching whales and scarlet macaws. Take breakfast in the gorgeous, cane-roofed **Brisa Azul Restaurant** (B, L, D; $$–$$$$), well worth visiting even if you're not a guest. Consider climbing to the *mirador* (overlook) above the *palapas*, as you decide which wonderful tour to take today.

Ranked by *Condé Nast* as the best hotel in Latin America, period, Lapa Rios is more than just a regal retreat into the wilderness. It is a showpiece for sustainable technology (they'll give you a tour) and a model for community involvement. Its 16 bungalows support libraries, schools, and job training programs; they protect more than 400 hectares (1,000 acres) of endangered lowland forest. Not one tree has been sacrificed in its construction, and the

absence of insecticides, chemicals, and amenities including air-conditioning and TV, have helped keep it that way. Make reservations well in advance, and do your part to save the world just by relaxing in absolute paradise.

Bed-and-Breakfasts

AGUILA DE OSA INN

Owner: Brad Johnson
506-2296-2190; 866-924-7722 USA and Canada
www.aguiladeosa.com
info@aguiladeosa.com
San Josecito Beach, Drake Bay
Price: Very Expensive*
Credit Cards: Yes
Handicap Access: No

Rising from the rain forest to sophisticated rooms built from dark, gleaming hardwoods and river rocks, each handcrafted with dozens of mesh windows offering panoramic views of Drake Bay, this is the very definition of elegance in the jungle. Simple and spacious, each of 14 rooms has high ceilings, very comfortable bamboo and rattan furnishings, beautifully tiled bathrooms, and most importantly, private porches with rocking chairs where you'll enjoy an early morning *cafecito* (coffee) while watching the wildlife awake.

CASA SIEMPRE DOMINGO

Owners: Heidi and Greg Norris
506-8820-4709
www.casa-domingo.com
heidi@casa-domingo.com
2 km (1 mi.) south of Pavones
Price: $–$$*
Credit Cards: Yes

Climb into the hills above Pavones (on a four-wheel-drive-only road) to the region's finest bed-and-breakfast, with large, luxuriously appointed rooms, tastefully decorated with beautiful furniture and appealing prints. Amenities include outdoor showers and air-conditioning, but no TV. The lounge and dining area is stunning, with gleaming wood floors and overarching ceilings, opening onto unparalleled views of the Golfo Dulce.

CASCADAS FARRALLAS

Owner: Fatch Kaur Bolívar
506-2787-8378
www.cascadasfarrallas.com
info@farallas.com
5 km (3 mi.) east of Dominical, on road to San Isidro
Price: Expensive to Very Expensive*
Credit Cards: No, but will accept them in the future
Handicap Access: No

Hidden away in the lush jungles above Dominical, this tranquil Balinese-style retreat overlooks a series of cascading waterfalls that give the peaceful property its name. This special spot also offers the opportunity to heal, through massage, meditation, kundalini yoga, and delicious whole foods prepared in accordance with your body's special needs. Detox and strengthening programs can be customized to you.

Designed with the area's natural feng shui in mind, each Asian-accented villa is soothingly aligned with the property's

---

Head for the Mountains

Though the vast majority of visitors prefer Southern Costa Rica's beaches, consider cooling off at one of the region's growing collection of mountain lodges.

Monte Azul (506-2742-5333; www.monteazulcr.com; Rivas, 10km from San Isidro de General; $$$–$$$$*) Artistically decorated retreat offers elegant, tiled rooms, wonderful meals, and hiking trails through the jungle.

Las Cruces Biological Station & Wilson Botanical Garden (506-2524-5774, 919-684-5774 USA; www.threepaths.co.cr; San Vito; $$*; reservations required) Operated by the Organization for Tropical Studies, these incredible tropical gardens showcase more than 1,000 species of tropical plants, which can be visited on day trips, including guided hikes, night tours, and boat trips; or experienced overnight in their relatively plush, polished teak lodge, with large windows, twin beds, and balcony views.

Río Chirripó B&B and Retreat (506-22742-5109; www.riochirripo.com; San Isidro de General; $$*) Close to the Chirripó trailhead, this bohemian bed-and-breakfast, featuring guest rooms and "luxury tents," offers beautiful high-altitude scenery, a cozy fire pit, morning yoga classes, and a gorgeous, slate-tiled hot spring.

The entirely sustainable, hand-built lobby at Danta Corcovado Lodge

ancient trees and dramatically cascading river. Sustainably constructed, each villa is private and airy, lovingly furnished with hand-carved antiques, such as sensuously carved teak tables and comfortable bamboo furniture from Bali, and beautiful mosaic tile work, fabulous bathrooms, flowing tapestries, and flattering lighting, but neither air-conditioning nor television. Why interrupt the music of the river below?

OCEANO CABINAS

Owners: Mark and Stephanie Homer
506-2776-0921
oceanocabinas.com
info@oceanocabinas.com
Playa Zancudo
Price: Moderate*
Credit Cards: Yes
Handicap Access: No

The pristine crescent of Playa Zancudo remains undiscovered territory for the upscale crowd, and most accommodations strung along the wide, pearl-gray beach are geared toward bohemians on a budget. Oceano has that casual vibe, but offers more comfort and style than the rest with two pretty, fan-cooled rooms with white-tiled floors, private hot showers, a cute patio set in pleasant gardens out front, and mosquito nets draped atmospherically across the beds. (*Zancudo*, by the way, is Spanish for "mosquito.") The excellent on-site **Restaurant Oceano** (B, L, D; $$–$$$) is one of the best on the beach, serving great ceviche and other seafood dishes, plus renowned brownies and homemade bread, in festive environs with a full bar.

Other area options include **Cabinas Los Cocos** (506-2776-0012; www.loscocos.com;

$$*), with charming beachfront cabins featuring kitchenettes and cute front porches, including two adorably refurbished banana worker cabins; and **Cabinas Sol y Mar** (506-2776-0014; www.zancudo.com; $), with basic but cute *cabinas* with private hot showers and WiFi; some have porches with beach views. The **restaurant** (B, L, D; $–$$$) is excellent, with big breakfasts and a creative international lunch and dinner menu specializing in barbecue.

Nature Lodges

HACIENDA BARÚ
Owner: Jack Ewing
506-2787-0003
www.haciendabaru.com
info@haciendabaru.com
3 km (1.8 mi.) north of Dominical Bridge
Price: Moderate
Credit Cards: Yes
Handicap Access: No

Adventure lodge sits on 330 hectares (815 acres) of primary rain forest and reforested finca, declared a national wildlife refuge in 1995. Most people visit on a day trip (admission $6 for self-guided tour; guided hikes, canopy tours and other attractions $25 to $35 each), to explore the well-maintained trails and family-friendly attractions, including a butterfly display and orchid garden. Or stay overnight in one of their spacious, beautifully outfitted cabins, designed for families with two bedrooms, screened-in porch and kitchenette, but no air-conditioning. Owner Jack Ewing, who preserved this precious plot of land before the term *ecotourism* had been coined, writes about his experiences and insights in the book *Monkeys Are Made Of Chocolate: Exotic And Unseen Costa Rica*.

CASA CORCOVADO JUNGLE LODGE
Manager: Luis Siles
506-2256-3181; 888-896-6097 USA and Canada
www.casacorcovado.com
info@casacorcovado.com
Río Sierpe
Price: Very Expensive*
Credit Cards: Yes
Handicap Access: No

Located on a 69-hectare (170-acre) private preserve abutting Corcovado National Park, your visit to this all-inclusive remote jungle lodge, with a three-day minimum stay, begins with a trip down the Río Sierpe to their isolated, artfully appointed lodge. Like all accommodations in the region, which lacks reliable 24-hour electricity, conservation is key and amenities like air-conditioning, hair dryers, coffeemakers, and the like simply aren't available. In their stead, you'll be offered fresh flowers, stained glass, colorful Mexican tiles, hammocks, and one of the best backyards in Costa Rica. In addition to the main lodge, two pools, and lovely sunset bar, you'll have access to hiking trails, beaches, waterfalls, and even a bat cave.

★ DANTA CORCOVADO LODGE
Owner: Merlyn Oviedo Sánchez
506-735-1111
www.dantacorcovado.net
info@dantacorcovado.net
Guadalupe (La Palma), well signed from the road to Puerto Jiménez
Price: Moderate*
Credit Cards: No
Handicap Access: No

In the heart of the Osa Peninsula, this fanciful confection of reforested wood has been sculpted into a truly intriguing lodge, with whimsical furniture, rooms, and walkways where you'll coexist with Corcovado's wild inhabitants almost unobstructed. The main building was originally Merlyn's family home, built by his father. Even then they used fallen wood, and made it beautiful; today it is recast with the son's artistic touches: Hanging sinks and mirrors made with polished tree trunks, showers made from river rocks, canopy beds supporting mosquito nets with gleaming limbs. A few *cabinas* are scattered out and about in the wilderness, featuring wonderful porches with the most biodiverse view on Earth.

It's not at all plush—there's no air-conditioning or cable TV, and everything is wide open to the world. But it's comfortable, and more than that, special. It's also relatively easy to access in a rental car, unlike most remote lodges in Osa.

★ LA LUNA LODGE

Owner: Lana Wedmore
506-8380-5036; 888-409-8448 USA and Canada
www.lunalodge.com
information@lunalodge.com
Carate
Price: Expensive to Very Expensive*
Credit Cards: Yes
Handicap Access: No

"Heaven on Earth" was how I'd heard it described, and these luxuriously appointed, *palapa*-topped bungalows ensconced in 30 hectares (75 acres) of privately protected primary rain forest delivered. You have your choice of well-outfitted platform tents on the hillside, standard hacienda-style rooms, or perfect, polished bungalows accessible along flagstone paths through the jungle. With high conical ceilings, private porches, and beautiful furnishings strewn with fresh flowers, these circular, fan-cooled rooms are Carate's finest. You can start the day with a 7 AM yoga class on the stunning hardwood platform above the jungle, then explore the private preserve or book a hiking or scuba diving tour. An on-site spa offers massages and more, while the delightful dining room features healthy and delicious meals seasoned with spices grown right here.

Luxury Tent Camping

With all of this wilderness around, wouldn't you like to go camping? There's no reason to rough it, however, as these wonderful lodges offer comfortable platform tents, some more luxurious than the area's top lodges.

★ **Bahari Beach Bungalows** (506-2787-5014; www.baharibeach.com; Playa Matapalo; $$–$$$) Divinely outfitted tents with pool and beach views offer tiled, private hot-water bathrooms that can be locked; excellent meals are served in the wonderfully rustic lodge.

Corcovado Lodge Tent Camp (506-2257-0766; www.costaricaexpeditions.com; Carate; $$*) A 30-minute hike from the town of Carate, these comfortable, screened-in tents overlooking the sea share cold-water bathrooms and access to Corcovado National Park.

La Leona Eco Lodge (506-2735-5704; www.laleonalodge.com; Carate, Osa Peninsula; $$) Right in Carate, basic but cozy tents have private porches overlooking the spring-fed pool and beach, and shared bath and showers.

★ **Rafiki Safari Lodge** (506-2777-5327; www.rafikisafari.com; Río Savegre Valley, south of Quepos; $$$$*) Stunningly sustainable, effortlessly luxurious, with incredible views of this pristine jungle valley, this collection of tents with polished hardwood floors, beautiful furnishings, and wonderful private porches is flawless. Service is personal and professional, meals incredible, and opportunities to enjoy the wilderness almost endless. The four-wheel-drive-only road into the hills is rough going, but worth it when your South African hosts pour you a glass of wine in the gleaming lodge while the sun sets behind the hills.

NICUESA RAINFOREST LODGE

Owners: Michael and Donna Butler
506-2735-5237; 866-504-8116
www.nicuesalodge.com
North of Golfito, boat access only
Price: Very Expensive*
Credit Cards: Yes
Handicap Access: No

Unspoiled and isolated on a 65-hectare (165-acre) private preserve abutting Piedras Blancas National Park, overlooking a pristine black sand beach, this perfectly executed eco-lodge offers eight divine rooms surrounded by orchards and gardens. Choose either the comfortable Mango Guesthouse or (better) one of the beautiful bungalows rendered sustainably from the rain forest into almost luxurious accommodations, with outdoor showers, private porches, and wraparound views from wide screened windows. All electricity is solar, and candles are provided (lighting pathways through the preserve beneath the starry sky), as are a variety of tours. Don't miss the kayak excursions through the mangroves and into the rarely visited national park, or the complimentary windsurfing out on the bay.

TISKITA LODGE

Owner: Peter Aspinall
506-2296-8125
www.tiskita-lodge.co.cr
1 km north of Pavones
Price: Expensive*
Credit Cards: Yes
Handicap Access: No
Special: Closed mid-September to mid-October

This is one of Costa Rica's original eco-lodges, inhabiting a rambling, *tejas*-topped old farmhouse restored to a colorful grace above 150 hectares (370 acres) of virgin and reforested jungle. Large wooden rooms are basic but tranquil, with fans, large screened windows, and solar-heated showers, some *al fresco*. Fine wooden porches add to the appeal. Tasty typical Tico meals are included and served family style, and the conservationist owner, Peter Aspinall, leads noted guided hikes and tours, which can be enjoyed by non-guests on a day trip. Be sure to see the lodge's collection of more than 100 different tropical fruit trees from all over the world.

Other Hotels

GOLFITO

Golfito lacks exceptional lodging, though **Casa Roland** (casa-roland.com) is currently building a plush boutique hotel in the old United Fruit headquarters.

Banana Bay Marina (506-2775-0838; www.bananabaymarina.com; south Golfito; $$) Geared toward sportfishermen, colorful, comfortable rooms with porches overlooking the docks are great for anyone. The ★**restaurant** (B, L, D; $$–$$$) may be Golfito's best, with excellent seafood, service, and views.

Hotel Las Gaviotas (506-2775-0062; south Golfito; $–$$*) Excellent business-class hotel offers very nice tiled rooms surrounding gardens and a pool, with WiFi, cable TV, and a good seafood restaurant. Great service.

NEILY

Hotel Andrea (506-2783-3784; www.hotelvillabosque.com/andrea_villa_bosque_eng.htm; 100m from the bus station; $) In Ciudad Neily, at an important crossroads close to the Panama border, this cute hotel has modern, tiled rooms with TV and hot showers, as well as nice balconies with rocking chairs outside. The restaurant is great.

PLAYA PIÑUELA

Mar y Selva Ecolodge (506-2786-5670; www.maryselva.com; 29 km south of Dominical; $$*) Lovely, environmentally conscientious bed-and-breakfast caters to

Rafiki Safari Lodge offers the most luxurious "camping" you'll ever enjoy.

health-minded visitors with organic, whole-grain meals, yoga, massages, and a 25-meter (82-foot) lap pool.

PLAYA PALO SECO

Timarai Bamboo Resort (506-770-8355; www.timarai.net; north of Quepos; $$$) It's overpriced and in need of some serious upkeep, but Timarai is still an architectural marvel, constructed almost entirely of bamboo; if you're curious, stop by the beachfront bar, in a colorfully refurbished school bus.

SAN ISIDRO DE EL GENERAL

Hotel Diamante Real (506-2770-6230; www.hoteldiamantereal.com; 100m west of Musoc; $–$$) Bustling San Isidro's best option is a surprisingly nice business-class hotel with generically tasteful, air-condi-

tioned modern rooms with WiFi, cable TV, telephone, and voice mail, plus a pool and nice restaurant downstairs.

SIERPE

Veragua River House (506-2786-7460; Sierpe; $$*) If the handful of acceptable budget hotels clustered in the tiny town of Sierpe doesn't appeal, cross the narrow cable bridge and enjoy this isolated, Italian-owned lodge with wonderful gardens overlooking the river. Simple, eclectically decorated cabins have screened front porches, fresh flowers, and hot showers, but no air-conditioning.

Vacation Rentals

Buena Vista Villas & Casas (506-2777-9081; www.tulemar.com; Manuel Antonio,

Tulemar Beach; $$$$) Premium villas and bungalows with sleek, modern furnishings.

Club del Mar (506-2643-3194, 866-978-5669; www.clubdelmarcostarica.com; south of Jacó, 300m south of Aroyo gas station; $$$–$$$$) A great deal on resort-style amenities; airy, elegant rooms have large sliding glass doors onto private porches and patios overlooking the pool. Nearby, the same California-based real estate company runs similar **Club del Sol** (506-2643-0064; 310-693-4581 USA; www.clubdelsoljaco.com; $$–$$$).

Day Star Properties (506-2643-1290; 800-784-4173 USA and Canada; www.daystar-properties.com) Luxury condominium rentals in and around Jacó, at developments such as **La Paloma Blanca** (www.lapaloma-blanca.com), **Bahia Azul** (www.bahia-azul.com), and **Bahia Encantada** (www.bahia-encantada.com), all with ocean views, swimming pools, WiFi and more.

Vacation Villas Costa Rica (506-2777-5018; 800-2521-4947; www.vacationvillascostarica.com; $$$$) Rents huge, plush, modern villas and homes on the road to Manuel Antonio.

★ **Villas Nicolas** (506-2777-0481; www.villasnicolas.com; road to Manuel Antonio; $$$) Gorgeous, privately-owned condos, some with full kitchens, are all artistically accented and perfectly located between restaurants and views, surrounding a very nice pool and waterfall in the gardens.

Zancudo Rentals (www.zancudo.net) Vacation rentals in a surfing paradise.

RESTAURANTS AND FOOD PURVEYORS

The Pacific Coast is best known for its seafood, often served alongside organic vegetables grown right here, where the sustainable agriculture movement is merging with the country's tradition of family farms.

An enormous variety of tropical fruits are also on offer, just waiting to be blended into a smoothie you'll spend the next decade trying to recreate back home.

Both Jacó and the Manuel Antonio area offer a wide variety of international restaurants, with Manuel Antonio probably taking the fine dining prize, thanks to all the top-notch resorts serving fabulous gourmet cuisine with spectacular views. South of Dominical, however, your options start to thin, and many towns offer only simple *sodas*, surf shacks, and basic seafood restaurants overlooking the ocean.

Restaurant and Food Purveyor Price Code

The following prices are based on the cost of a dinner entrée with a non-alcoholic drink, not including the 13 percent taxes and 10 percent gratuity added to the cost of almost all restaurant meals (except for the very cheapest *sodas*). Menus note whether or not their listed prices include this hefty 23 percent total surcharge, some listing two sets of prices.

Inexpensive ($)	Up to $5
Moderate ($$)	$5 to $10
Expensive ($$$)	$10 to $20
Very Expensive ($$$$)	$20 or more

Restaurants

JACÓ
CALICHE'S WISHBONE
506-2643-3406
Downtown Jacó
Closed: Wed.
Price: Moderate to Expensive
Credit Cards: Yes
Cuisine: Seafood, Mexican
Serving: L, D
Reservations: No

This popular spot is not just your average surf shack, and offers excellent homemade pizzas, filling Mexican dishes, and well-prepared seafood in casual environs catering to surfers (videos of big waves are on continuous rotation). Grab a seat outside on the veranda, and enjoy a great deal on a fabulous meal.

EL HICACO

506-2643-3226
www.elhicaco.net
Central Jacó
Price: Expensive to Very Expensive
Cuisine: Seafood, lobster
Serving: L, D
Credit Cards: Yes
Reservations: Yes

This beachfront landmark is known far and wide for its "Festival of Lobster," each Wednesday from 6 PM–10 PM, with a buffet of crustaceans cooked every which way. But you can get premium-priced seafood, steak, and other dishes (as well as their extravagant signature strawberry daiquiri) any time. Grab one of the open-air seats out under the palms and enjoy some stargazing while you dine.

LEMON ZEST

506-2643-2591
www.lemonzestjaco.com
Jacó, El Jardin Plaza, second floor
Closed: Sun.
Price: Very Expensive
Cuisine: International gourmet
Serving: D
Credit Cards: Yes
Reservations: Yes

The finest dining experience in Jacó proper comes courtesy of Chef Mr. Lemon, a native of the Bahamas trained in New York and Miami, who recently opened this second-floor gourmet eatery to universal accolades. His passion is flavor, wedding different tastes each day. You may begin your meal with a complimentary appetizer; he might whip up a perfectly crisped crab cake with vanilla bean sauce and pineapple salsa. Or try the elegantly presented Hawaiian-style

tuna tartar served with a delicate tower of wonton chips. Creative and colorful salads, perhaps the Portobello mushroom with goat cheese, sun-dried tomatoes, and balsamic vinaigrette could also be a good start the meal.

If you're in the mood, order Mr. Lemon's signature red snapper français, sautéed with white wine and lemon, once hailed by *Zagat* as "the world's best." But why limit yourself? Divine seafood dishes and steaks are served with casual elegance, all overlooking the wild street scene below. Indulge in something from their full bar, with a very good wine list.

POSEIDÓN HOTEL & RESTAURANT

506-2643-1642
www.hotel-poseidon.com
Jacó, north end of town
Price: Moderate to Very Expensive
Cuisine: Asian fusion, Seafood
Serving: B, L, D
Credit Cards: Yes
Reservations: Yes

This simple, open-air wooden restaurant, dressed up with white tablecloths, stemware, and excellent service, presents some of the loveliest, Asian-accented cuisine in town. Start with the tender edamame while perusing the cocktail list. Then move on, perhaps to the coconut curry mahi mahi, or the beef tips in peppercorn-oyster sauce with shitake mushrooms; there's a vegetarian pad Thai as well.

Breakfasts are huge, with great options like the South of Dixie, involving grits, biscuits, and gravy, or the Breakfast Fried Rice, with eggs, bacon, onions, spinach, and rice stir-fried together. **Poseidón** is also a perfectly acceptable midrange **hotel** ($$–$$$*) and home to the **Sky Lounge**, with stiff drinks and sports TV.

PELICAN HOTEL & RESTAURANT

506-2778-8105
www.pelicanhotelcr.com

Playa Estilleros Este, halfway between Jacó and Quepos
Price: Moderate
Credit Cards: Yes
Cuisine: Seafood
Serving: B, L, D
Reservations: No

This rustic, open-air bar and restaurant is right on beautiful Playa Estilleros, making it a popular place for a sunset cocktail, game of pool, or great fresh seafood. The vibe is casual, the jumbo shrimp *al ajillo* (in garlic sauce) great, and the hammocks in the beachfront rancho rather tempting. The attached ★**hotel** ($$) is a great deal on breezy, eclectically furnished rooms, most with air-conditioning and beach views.

★ TACO BAR FISH TACOS
506-2643-0222
www.tacobar.info
Jacó, main drag, in front of El Lagar Hardware Store
Price: Moderate to Expensive
Credit Cards: No
Cuisine: Seafood, Mexican
Serving: L, D
Handicap Access: No
Reservations: No

You might think that the best thing about this popular spot is the seating: On rope swings, surrounding a high bar where you'll mix and mingle with Jacó scenesters and smiling tourists. Order at the window, choosing your favorite fish (ask what's fresh), the type of seasoning (Spicy? Blackened? Garlic?), then whether you want it as a burrito, taco, or perhaps standing alone. Be sure to get a giant smoothie on the side. Each dish is accompanied with a trip to a good little salad bar.

QUEPOS AND MANUEL ANTONIO
EL GRAN ESCAPE
506-2777-0395
www.elgranescape.com
Closed: Tue.

Downtown Quepos
Price: Expensive
Cuisine: Seafood, international
Serving: L, D
Reservations: Yes

This landmark restaurant on the main drag in downtown Quepos is more than just a popular eatery, serving excellently prepared local seafood, from sashimi and bouillabaisse to the "catch of the day," flavorful beef imported from the United States, big burgers, and Mexican classics. This atmospheric spot, hung with fishing lures, stuffed fish, and baseball caps from all over the world is a tradition, where locals and tourists alike gather for cold brew and good grub, to discuss the one that got away.

MAMMA MIA
506-2777-0054
www.mimoshotel.com
Mimos Hotel, road to Manuel Antonio
Price: Expensive
Credit Cards: Yes
Cuisine: Italian
Serving: L, D

Enjoy great Italian cuisine, including wood-fired pizzas, homemade pastas, and traditionally prepared seafood, in an elegant, open-air dining room overlooking this midrange hotel's beautiful pool.

MONCHADOS
506-2777-1972
Downtown Quepos
Price: Moderate
Cuisine: Mexican, Caribbean, and Costa Rican
Serving: D
Credit Cards: Yes
Reservations: No

In a cavernous restaurant in downtown Quepos, decorated with striking Mexican art, gets raves for its pan-Latin preparations, specializing in Caribbean dishes including *rondón*, a slow-cooked seafood soup, and Mexican specialties such as spicy seafood and fajitas. Good *casados* are also on offer. The full bar offers happy hour daily, and there's live music on Tuesday and Saturday.

MONO AZUL
506-2777-2572
www.hotelmonoazul.com
Price: Moderate
Credit Cards: Yes
Cuisine: International
Serving: B, L, D
Handicap Access: Yes
Reservations: Yes

In a landmark budget to midrange hotel, this excellent restaurant dishes up top-flight international cuisine at good prices, including steak, seafood, pasta, Mexican dishes, and salads, all well prepared and served with a smile—or, one of their fancy cocktails. An excellent on-site souvenir shop benefits Kids Saving the Rainforest (www.kidssavingtherainforest.org), which protects a small plot of rain forest and installs "monkey bridges," so tiny *mono titis* (squirrel monkeys) can cross roads.

EL PATIO BISTRO LATINO
506-2777-4982
Central Quepos
Price: Very Expensive
Credit Cards: Yes
Cuisine: Pan-Latin, International
Serving: D
Reservations: Yes

Part of the growing Café Milagro empire, this beautiful restaurant with colorfully painted walls, a lovely little courtyard garden, and elegant cane ceilings, offers a small, ever-changing fine dining menu, based on local ingredients and recipes from throughout the Americas. Presentation is creative, with appetizers such as the plantain tower layering plantains, avocado, fresh tuna, and charred tomato salsa to col-

orful effect. Or try the spicy shrimp ceviche, served with sweet potato cakes. Seafood is always a good bet, and depending on the catch of the day you might find Brazilian-style tuna served with stuffed peppers, or shrimp simmered in a coconut rum sauce. Desserts, in particular baked goods, are fabulous, perfect with a cup of their excellent coffee.

PUERTO ESCONDIDO RESTAURANT
506-2777-0903
www.espadilla.com
Playa Espadilla, close to Manuel Antonio
Price: Expensive
Credit Cards: Yes
Cuisine: International
Serving: L, D
Reservations: Yes

Tucked away on a quiet side street close to Manuel Antonio National Park, this rather elegant restaurant is part of **Hotel Espadilla** ($$$*), a modern midrange hotel with comfortable rooms. The pleasant hotel restaurant has earned a reputation for excellent international cuisine, including steak, seafood, and pasta, served in a rustic outdoor dining room with great service and no pretensions.

RESTAURANT MARLIN
506-2777-1134
Entrance to Manuel Antonio National Park
Price: Moderate
Credit Cards: Yes
Cuisine: Seafood, Costa Rica
Serving: B, L, D
Handicap Access: No
Reservations: Yes

You can quite justifiably bemoan the tragic, not-at-all-sustainable overcrowding that has beset poor Manuel Antonio, and that's how many people spend their entire visit. Or, you could just have fun with it. Pay off the parking mafia, buy a seashell necklace from one of the hippies, and rent an umbrella on the endless white-sand beach (like South Beach, but without the giant high rises!). After you've worn yourself out with sun and surf, get a second floor table above all the gently sunburned action right here, at Restaurant Marlin, which has for years been feeding Ticos and tourists waiting to get into the park five-star *casados* or very fresh seafood. Happy hour starts at 4:30 PM daily, and there's live music on Saturday. There are several other restaurants close to the park entrance, or have **Butch Services**, just one of several beachfront "runners," deliver food (he provides menus) right to your umbrella-shaded beach chair. This is the perfect spot for the game "Where do you think those tourists are from?"

PLIMIO HOTEL & RESTAURANT

506-2777-0055
www.hotelplinio.com
Road to Manuel Antonio
Price: Moderate to Expensive
Credit Cards: Yes
Cuisine: Asian
Serving: L, D
Handicap Access: No
Reservations: Yes

Close to Quepos on the road to Manuel Antonio, this delightful restaurant in forest canopy offers a taste of Asia in a romantically lit, open-air dining room with wine-colored tablecloths and fresh-cut ginger flowers on the wooden tables. The owners, who also operate the attractive attached midrange **hotel** ($$$), grow their own

Café Milagro, Quepos' finest cup of coffee

organic herbs and spices right here, used in specialties such as tom yum sweet and sour soup; chiang mai curried chicken in tamarindo sauce with ginger and peanuts, and even a few Indian options, such as cardamom chicken.

DOMINICAL AND THE SOUTH PACIFIC
COCONUT SPICE
506-2829-8397
Dominical, Plaza Pacifica
Closed: Mon.
Price: Expensive
Credit Cards:
Cuisine: Thai
Serving: D
Reservations: Yes

Ignore the strip mall ambiance (perhaps opting for outdoor seating) and settle into some of the best Thai food in the country, with standbys such as pad Thai, satay, and beautiful soups. Some dishes are more creative, with plenty of seafood and vegetarian options; go for the curry.

★ JADE LUNA
506-2735-5739
www.jadeluna.com
Puerto Jiménez, 500m past airstrip
Closed: Sun.
Price: Expensive to Very Expensive
Credit Cards: Yes
Cuisine: International
Serving: D
Reservations: Yes

It may come as a surprise, as you make your way through lush gardens into the elegant pale archways welcoming you to this open-air restaurant, that this tiny backwater town offers such a fine dining experience. Chef Barbara Burkhardt, a veteran of the New York City culinary scene, uses local ingredients from all over the country—Zarcero cheeses, organic greens from the Central Valley, hormone-free Guanacaste beef, and local seafood—to create an impressive menu featuring flavors and recipes from all over the world. The menu changes according to what's available, but always offers spectacular soups and salads, elegant seafood entrees, and a vegetarian dish (often pasta), as well as her homemade ice creams and sorbets. There's a good wine list.

★ SAN CLEMENTE BAR & GRILL
506-2787-0055
Central Dominical
Price: Moderate to Expensive
Cuisine: International
Serving: B, L, D
Reservations: No

Don't believe that this is the heaviest surf in Costa Rica? Check out all the broken boards suspended from the ceiling of this Dominical institution. Then get your grub on surfer-style with huge breakfasts (don't skip the hot cakes) or some of their Mexican options, including the recommended huevos rancheros, nachos, flautas, and great seafood, all dressed up in the owner's special hot sauce. This is also the local gathering spot for a cold brew, darts, and Ping-Pong any night, but is the place to be on Fridays, when the whole shebang turns into a disco till 2:30 AM.

★ WACHACHÁ RESTAURANT & REGGAE BAR
506-2787-0313
Dominical, 200m from beach
Closed Mon.
Price: Inexpensive to Moderate
Credit Cards: No
Cuisine: Caribbean
Serving: D
Handicap Access: No
Reservations: No

This marvelous little riverfront eatery, with fine views over the estuary from *palapa*-topped cement tables, is home to some of the best Caribbean cooking on this side of the country. Make your way past murals of

Bob Marley and Haile Selassie, perfect with the blasting reggaeton (there's sometimes live music here as well), threading overgrown gardens of heliconias and ginger. The jerk chicken and rice-and-beans are inexpensive and exceptional, or go for one of the coconut milk- and curry-laced seafood dishes.

Food Purveyors

Cafés

Café Café (506-2643-3429; south side of Jacó, on main drag; $$) Cute outdoor café serves up salads, sandwiches, and free WiFi, as well as assorted coffee beverages.

Café de la Suerte (Pavones; B, L; $$) Pleasant café keeps surfers caffeinated and vegetarians happy with their healthy, eclectic menu.

Café La Onda (506-2735-5312; Puerto Jiménez; B, L, closed Sun.; $$) Fiercely air-conditioned café serves coffee, bagels, pastries, and healthy, organic meals.

★ **Café Milagro** (506-2777-0294; www.cafemilagro.com; Downtown Quepos, north end; B, L, D; $–$$$) Adorable eatery is becoming a chain of delightful coffee shops and cafés with its own brew available as beans or in a variety of perfectly executed coffee beverages.

La Petite Provence (506-2643-3995; Pacific Center, across from Cabletica, Jacó; $$) Specialties at this real French bakery and café include sandwiches with imported meats and cheeses, French style pastries.

Solo Bueno (Dominical, north entrance; open 5:30 AM–6 PM; $) Convenient spot for pastries, sandwiches, light meals, and coffee to go.

Pizza

Escalofrío (506-2777-0833; downtown Quepos; L, D; closed Mon.; $$$) Famed for its thin-crust Italian pizzas baked in a wood-fired oven, this cozy, casual spot also serves great antipastis, gelato, espresso beverages, and other homemade Italian specialties.

Il Giardino Ristorante Italiano (Puerto Jiménez) Offers good Italian, vegetarian, and seafood, as well as great pizza.

Los Pibes (506-2643-1146; Jacó, south entrance, 100m south of Soda Hidalgo) Great pizza, plus Argentine empanadas and pies; they also deliver.

★ **Los Vagos de Sierpe** (506-2819-8956; Central Sierpe, Oso Peninsua; L, D; $–$$) This modest Italian-run pizza, pasta, and salad place serves the best food in town.

Sodas

Bar Restaurant Colonial (506-2643-3326; central Jacó; $$–$$$) Huge, *soda*-style landmark restaurant with oxcarts out front serves seafood, steak, and a full range of cocktails; mariachis and calypso bands on weekends.

★ **Exotica** (506-2786-5050; Playa Ojochal, Costa Ballena; L, D; closed Sun.; $–$$$) It looks like a regular *soda*, but this modest spot is the best restaurant on the coast, with gourmet takes on Tico classics and refined world cuisine.

Jacó Rustico (506-2643-2117; Jacó; $) On a side street close to El Hicaco, "the best *soda* in Jacó" has a great steam table buffet.

★ **Mi Lugar Restaurante Mirador Ronny's Place** (506-2777-5120; road to Manuel Antonio, turnoff at Amigos del Río Rafting; $$$) With outstanding views and great seafood, grilled meats, Tico classics, and a full bar, this open-air eatery is so highly recom-

View from Ronny's Place in Manuel Antonio

mended by my parents that they might disown me if I didn't list it. Ronny is great, and helped them spot toucans over lobster and sangria.

★ **Restaurant Carolina** (506-2735-5185; Central Puerto Jiménez; B, L, D; $$) Delightful *soda* is Puerto Jimenéz' most popular, serving good typical and seafood, cold beer, and good street views.

Restaurant Las Vegas (506-2788-1082; lasvegassierpe.com; Central Sierpe; B, L, D; $$) Mega-*soda* right by the Sierpe docks serves perfectly acceptable Tico classics and seafood, and is also a great place to organize fishing trips and boat tours.

Specialty Foods and Delis

American Market 24/7 (506-2643-2344; Jacó, next to Beatle Bar) U.S. brands and junk food, open till 3 AM.

Jimmy T's Provisions & Gourmet Foods (506-2673-8636; www.jimmytsprovisions.com; Playa Herradura, Los Sueños Marina) Stock the yacht (or rental car) with imported meats, cheeses, liquors, and other items, including five kinds of caviar.

Ristorante L'Angulo (506-2777-9502; downtown Quepos) Well-stocked Italian deli serves imported meats, cheeses, olives, and deli items, as well as sandwiches, salads, and other light meals.

Sushi

The Lighthouse (506-2643-3083; 24 hours; north entrance of Jacó; $$$) This steakhouse and sushi bar is open round the clock.

Tropical Sushi (506-2777-1710; downtown Quepos, close to Gran Escape; D; Closed Tue.; $$$$) The region's most authentic sushi is served around a tiny garden; 5 PM–7 PM, daily is all-you-can-eat sushi.

Tsunami Sushi (506-2643-1638; central Jacó L, D; $$$) Despite the location—the second floor of El Galeone strip mall—this is the real deal, a Japanese-style sushi restaurant with elegant furnishings, sakis, and top notch sushi, plus other Japanese cuisine.

Grocery Stores

Mas x Menos (506-2643-3611; mjacoe@csu.co.cr; Central Jacó) The biggest grocery store in Jacó delivers.

Super Joseth (506-2777-1095; road to Manuel Antonio) Halfway between Quepos and Manuel Antonio, this well-stocked little shop also delivers.

Super Mas (506-2777-1162; downtown Quepos) Manuel Antonio's biggest grocer is a good place to get supplies before heading toward the park and resorts.

CULTURE

Until very recently, most of this resource-poor region, without the rich volcanic soils of the Central Valley and points north, was isolated from the rest of the country. Even during the indigenous era, these were a people apart, trading more often with the sailing tribes of North and South America (who stopped to trade in the calm Golfo Dulce) than the rest of the country.

The most important settlement, at the time of the Spanish conquest, was at Quepos, where "the most beautiful people in the Americas" according to Spanish chroniclers, greeted conquistadors with jeers and threats. Pearl divers, skilled fishers, and turtle hunters, these were skilled fighters (even the women were trained warriors) and wove fine fabrics dyed purple using sea mollusks, prized by European royalty. The islands off Manuel Antonio National Park were spiritual centers, with what's now Isla Bruja the site of indigenous religious ceremonies, while Isla Larga (more commonly called Breadloaf) was home to Costa Rica's first mission, San Bernardino, founded 1571. You can see ruins left behind by both cultures on various tours.

In the late 1800s, United Fruit brought agribusiness and infrastructure to the region, and from Quepos south it was one swath of banana plantations. After a blight leveled the fields, however, the fincas were replanted with oil palms, still one of the region's most important economic activities.

By the 1960s, a road connected Quepos to San José; this was the end of the line. A few tourists, mostly Ticos, began arriving, and by the mid-1970s businesses like Barba Roja were catering to an increasingly international crowd. Today, this is one of the most visited spots in Costa Rica, the hub for the entire South and Central Pacific regions.

Museums

BORUCA INDIGENOUS MUSEUM

506-2771-2533
Buenos Aires, Boruca Reserve
Open: 9 AM–5 PM, Mon.–Fri.
Admission: Free

A fine excuse to visit the Boruca Indigenous reserve is this small, *palapa*-topped museum, with displays about traditional culture and handicrafts, in particular the masks used for the Baile de los Diablitos, or Dance of the Little Devils, a ceremonial dance re-enacting resistance to the Spanish Conquest. This is Costa Rica's only indigenous group still producing so many traditional crafts, including graceful bows and arrows made from pejibaye wood, and small sculptures, often armadillos or turtles, made from jícaro gourds and balsa wood. All of these are on sale at several private homes and shops in the reserve.

TÉRRABA INDIGENOUS MUSEUM
506-2771-0511
Buenos Aires, Térraba Indigenous Reserve
Open: 9 AM–5 PM, Mon.–Fri.
Admission: Free

This tiny museum has displays on Térraba culture, including a traditional home and kitchen, plus tools and weapons.

Music and Nightlife

JACÓ
Jacó isn't just *a* party town, Jacó is *the* party town. The vibe is invigoratingly seedy, side streets not at all safe (leave your camera and credit cards at the hotel), and the whole thing one great night out, though you might not remember much of it.

Beatle Bar (Central Jacó) The local...ahem...gentlemen's club.

Monkey Bar (506-2643-2357; Central Jacó) Outfits are skimpy and floor space is packed at this very popular bar and meat market. Watch your wallet.

Rioasis (506-2643-3354; Central Jacó) Garden seating, cheap beer, pizza, and Mexican food make this a winner; also delivers.

Wahoos (506-2643-1876; Central Jacó, across from Beatle Bar) Rockin' little joint serves seafood, has serious happy hours, and karaoke Wednesday.

QUEPOS AND MANUEL ANTONIO
Bambú Jam (506-2777-3369; road to Manuel Antonio) At the Hotel Mirador del Pacifico, has live music and Latin dance throughout the week, plus good world cuisine.

Barba Roja (506-2777-0331; www.barbaroja.co.cr; road to Manuel Antonio; B, L, D; $$$) Manuel Antonio institution and gathering place has a full bar, fabulous sunsets, solid seafood, and Tex-Mex cuisine.

Dos Locos (506-2777-1526; Central Quepos; B, L, D; $$$) Quepos institution keeps 'em coming back with good Mexican food, better margaritas, and a mean *guaro* sours. There's live music on Wednesday and Friday, and good people watching.

DOMINICAL
Maracatu (Central Dominical) Pretty spot surrounded by gardens serves healthy, organic, and mostly vegetarian typical Costa Rican food, and has live music most nights.

Tortilla Flats Restaurant & Bar (506-2770-0033; www.tortillaflatsdominical.com; on the beach; B, L, D; $$) Basic budget hotel ($) is the only beachfront bar in town, serving seafood, subs, and sunsets over beer and cocktails to a sandy, sunburned crowd. Ladies get free shots on Thursday.

OSA PENINSULA AND GOLFO DULCE

Juanita's Mexican Bar & Grill (506-2735-5056; downtown Puerto Jiménez; open 6 AM–2 AM) This popular spot serves cold beer and good Mexican food almost around the clock.

8° Latitude (506-2775-0235; Golfito) Popular expatriate bar has good food, imported liquor, and very friendly young ladies keeping the sportfishermen hooked.

RECREATION

Parks and Preserves

CENTRAL PACIFIC

BALLENA NATIONAL MARINE PARK

506-2743-8236

www.costarica-nationalparks.com/ballenanationalmarinepark.html

Punta Uvita

Open: 8 AM–4 PM

Admission: $6

In one of those remarkable coincidences of *la naturaleza* that gives even staunch atheists pause, the focal point of this national park is a perfect, crescent peninsula, cupped toward the sunset, and attached to the mainland by a slender stretch of golden sand. The "Whale Tail," as this coral reef-wrapped formation is known, marks the warm waters of a humpback whale nursery, one of the few places on Earth that these gentle giants will trust with their young.

Pods of whales arrive from cooler climes each August, and winter here until mid-March, until their tiny (4-meter/13-foot) babes are ready for the wide world. Sea turtles, olive ridleys, and occasionally rare hawksbills, also come here to nest between May and November. Tourists, however, rarely visit, and despite the fine beaches and intensity of life, you may have this place to yourself. You can snorkel the reefs right offshore, with 18 species of coral and untold numbers of fish; any dive operator on the Central Pacific can arrange trips.

CARARA NATIONAL PARK

506-2383-9953

www.costarica-nationalparks.com/cararanationalpark.html

22 km (14 mi.) north of Jacó

Open: 7 AM–4 PM, daily

Admission: $8, $15 with guide

Preserving that important juncture along the Pacific Coast, where the humid tropical forests of the lush and rainy south meet the dry tropical forests of Guanacaste, this 5,242-hectare (13,397-acre) park is both incredibly biodiverse and convenient to visit, between Jacó and San José. Book a tour anywhere, or just show up, as bilingual guides are waiting to show you around Carara's steamy marshes, lagoons, primary forests, and the Río Grande de Tárcoles, with the country's highest concentration of crocodiles, including 6-meter (18-foot) long monsters with names like "Osama bin Laden" and "Tornado."

About 4 kilometers (2 miles) before the ranger station, you'll cross the Tárcoles Bridge, with the famed Mirador de Cocodrilos (Crocodile Viewpoint), a top spot for photos of the cute critters. It's also a prime spot for camera snatching and car break-ins, so be alert.

The ranger station has potable water and access to two hiking trails, a family-friendly 1-kilometer (.6-mile) nature loop, and a 4.5-kilometer (2.7-mile) Araceas Nature Trail, which follows the river and around the lagoons and marshes. There's also a wheelchair accessible loop. But most people go on a boat tour from nearby Tárcoles, where several companies offer guided tours.

Crocodile Man Tour (506-2637-0771; www.crocodilemantour.com; Tárcoles) Two-hour riverboat and wildlife-watching tour, with a crocodile feeding, plus horseback riding, diving, sportfishing, and other tours.

Jungle Crocodile Safari (506-2236-6473; www.junglecrocodilesadari.com; Tárcoles) Two-hour boat tour, with crocodile feedings.

Vic-Tours (506-645-1015; www.victourscr.com; Villa Bijagua) Runs croc tours, guided hikes into Carara, and tours of Bijagual Waterfall and Manuel Antonio as well.

MANUEL ANTONIO NATIONAL PARK

www.costarica-nationalparks.com/manuelantonionationalpark.html
506-2777-5185
Open: 7 AM–4 PM, Tue.–Sun. (Closed Mon.)
Admission: $10

While waiting to enter Manuel Antonio National Park, why not rent an umbrella and relax right outside?

Considered Costa Rica's most aesthetically perfect collection of beaches, this tiny (1,980-hectare/4,890-acre) national park is Costa Rica's second-most-visited attraction (after Poás), hosting some 200,000 sun lovers annually on its postcard-perfect shores. And, if you want that idyllic shot—coconut palms, crashing waves, white sand, and nothing else—arrive at 7 AM when the gates open, and rush past Beach One and Beach Two, which are already lost causes, in high season at least. Then start shooting. Because the gamboling hordes of adorable families, love-struck honeymooners, and khaki clad photographers are right behind you, and will soon fan out across the beaches and jungle, climbing to craggy and volcanic 72-meter (236-foot) Cathedral Point (star of many "Visit Costa Rica" advertisements), and lounging on the powdery white sand.

Despite the crowds, this spot is gorgeous, with wonderful hiking and snorkeling, surrounded by some of the finest resorts in the country. There's a 600-person limit in the park Tuesday through Friday, and an 800-person limit Saturday and Sunday, which helps a bit, though late risers may end up waiting outside the park, on a packed stretch of sand where you can rent beachside umbrellas.

South Pacific
LA AMISTAD INTERNATIONAL PARK
506-2200-5355
www.costarica-nationalparks.com/laamistadinternationalpark.html
Southern Costa Rica and Western Panama
Open: 8 AM–4 PM
Admission: $7

This cooperative effort between Costa Rica and Panama preserves the southern Talamanca, as an enormous (400,929-hectare/990,717-acre) UNESCO World Heritage Site. Reaching 3,549 meters (11,644 feet) at Cerro Kamuk and containing at least 12 separate life zones, this park is home to ⅔ of the species in Costa Rica, including 450 different birds, all 6 neotropical cats, and more than 200 reptiles and amphibians. Unfortunately, roads and trails are poorly maintained; guides are highly recommended for any serious exploration. There are three main Costa Rican entrances to the park, with stations that offer potable water and camping ($5).

The northernmost access point is at the **Ujarrás Station**, near Buenos Aires; short trails lead to hot springs and viewpoints, longer ones across the park for a week-long trek to the Caribbean. You can organize guides through park rangers, or try **Durika Biological Reserve** (506-2730-0675; www.durika.org; $*) a 8,500-hectare (21,000-acre) private preserve, organic farm, and basic lodge close to Ujarrá.

Heading south, park headquarters is at **Altamira Station** (506-2200-5355), accessible on a four-wheel-drive-only road from the tiny town of Guacíma. It has an excellent campground, with electricity, showers, and a TV lounge, and several trails, including the multiday trek ascending Cerro Kamuk. Find guides through **Tres Colinas** (506-8814-0889) or nearby **Finca Palo Alto** (506-2743-1063; www.hotelfincapaloalto.com; $*), with basic cabins and horses.

The southernmost entrance, accessible from the cute mountain town of San Vito, is at **Pittier Station** (506-2773-4060) with basic camping and trails; guides can be arranged through **Hacienda La Amistad** (506-7289-7667; www.laamistad.com; $$$*), with small wooden cabins, a coffee finca, guided hikes, and horseback rides.

Dominical is one of the few beaches with lifeguards, watching over the heavy surf.

CAÑO ISLAND BIOLOGICAL RESERVE

www.costarica-nationalparks.com/canoislandbiologicalreserve.html
20 km off the northern Osa Peninsula
Open: 8 AM–4 PM, daily
Admission: $10

This idyllic tropical island is as fascinating for its historic significance as its natural abundance. This is where Sir Francis Drake supposedly landed in 1579 on his round-the-world pirating adventure, leaving behind his name and buried treasure, which you can look for along a well-maintained trail into the jungle. Archaeologists have also unearthed tombs and perfectly rounded granite spheres.

But the real treasures are offshore. The island is surrounded by five coral reefs among the steep 25-meter (80-foot) cliffs of dark volcanic rock, boasting 19 species of coral and an incredible variety of marine life, including sea turtles, dolphins, whales, white-tip sharks, rays, and huge snapper and grouper. Dive operations in Manuel Antonio and Osa organize excursions to what's becoming known as the best diving in the country, while every Drake Bay outfitter offers inexpensive snorkeling and hiking trips.

★ CORCOVADO NATIONAL PARK

506-2735-5036; 506-2735-5580

www.costarica-nationalparks.com/corcovadonationalpark.html
Osa Peninsula
Open: Ranger stations open 8 AM–4 PM
Admission: $10

There simply is no other place like this left on Earth. Long protected from progress by its isolation at the end of the peninsula, and world; and legally in 1975, this rare and valuable swath of lowland tropical forest still cradles its heritage of remarkable biodiversity. More than 80 percent of the Osa Peninsula is preserved in some way, as part of the **Osa Conservation Area** (www.costarica-nationalparks.com/osaconservationarea.html). Together, they protect 2 percent of the world's genetic library, including herds of white-lipped peccary, all four Costa Rican monkey species, flocks of scarlet macaws, and lots of big cats. Wear sunscreen, repellant, and boots when you explore, as there are also some 10,000 species of insects and several poisonous snakes. It can be fiercely hot and muggy, when there's not a downpour; the region gets up to 600 centimeters/236 inches of rain annually, with regular showers even in the dry season (February through April).

This is not an easy or inexpensive place to visit. The main service towns surrounding the park—Puerto Jiménez, La Palma, and Agujitas (Drake Bay)—are remote, with access via rough roads, boats, or planes. Tours can be easily arranged from Drake Bay, Puerto Jiménez, and Sierpe (several companies also offer all-inclusive tours from San José). Or visit on foot—the enormous park is connected by a network of well-maintained trails, which can get steep in the volcanic and mountainous heart, and be cut off at high tide along the steaming beach trails; check tidal charts with your hotel in Drake Bay or the **Oficina de Area de Conservación Osa** (506-2735-5580; Puerto Jiménez) in Puerto Jiménez.

There are three park entrances, all with camping ($5), dorm-style accommodations ($10), and meals ($8–$11), which must be arranged well in advance through AMBCOR (see below). **La Leona** is next to Carate, 42 kilometers (26 miles) on a good dirt road with several river crossings from Puerto Jiménez; **Los Patos**, 11 kilometers (7 miles) from La Palma, is the most remote; and **San Pedrillo** is accessible from Drake Bay. Trails connect all three, converging at **La Sirena Ranger Station**, the park headquarters, with basic accommodations, meals, and an almost mythic significance to biologists. You can charter a plane or boat if the walk seems too much.

If you're planning to visit Corcovado on a package tour, or on day trips arranged through an area lodge or tour operator, they'll take care of almost everything. But if you hope to do some independent exploration, these sites offer important information about trails, transportation, lodging, and all that biodiversity.

AMBCOR (Environment, Biology, and Research in Corcovado; www.corcovado.org) Comprehensive online park guide, with maps, travel tips, and information about the animals and environment; this is also where you reserve food, campsites, and dorms one month in advance.

Corcovado Expeditions (506-8818-9962; www.corcovadoexpeditions.net; Drake Bay) Excellent outfitter organizes everything from day hikes to all-inclusive, multi-day packages in and around the park.

Corcovado Info (www.corcovadoinfo.com) Commercial site offers maps, information, and links to area hotels.

Fundación Corcovado (506-2297-3013; www.corcovadofoundation.org) Grassroots preservation group offers a great English-language park guide for tourists.

PIEDRAS BLANCAS NATIONAL PARK
www.costarica-nationalparks.com/piedrasblancasnationalpark.html
Osa Peninsula

Extending the Osa Conservation Zone around Golfo Dulce, this undeveloped park boasts rugged mountains, stunning beaches, and the highest diversity of plant life, meter for meter, in Costa Rica. Though there are no ranger stations or official trails, it's relatively easy to visit through any Golfito-area hotel, or through Austrian-operated eco-lodge **Esquinas Lodge** (506-2741 8001; www.esquinaslodge.com; La Gamba; $$$*; three CST Leaves) with delightful cabins surrounding a gorgeous, spring-fed pool in paradise.

TÉRRABA-SIERPE NATIONAL WETLANDS
www.costarica-nationalparks.com/terrabasierpenationalwetlands.html
Osa Peninsula

Though there are no facilities or trails in this important wetland reserve, most famous for its huge flocks of pelicans (the "Costa Rican Air Force"), it is relatively easy to visit on a riverboat trip between tiny Sierpe, with road access from the mainland, and isolated Drake Bay. Any hotel or tour outfitter in either town can arrange birding, fishing, and nature tours through estuaries lined with eight species of mangrove, and tiny green islets where egrets, herons, kingfishers, and other birds frolic. Or you can stay can stay at a handful of nature lodges, geared toward sportfishers and nature lovers, including **La Florida** (506-2788-1016; www.lafloridacostarica.com; $$$*, including all meals and transportation from Palmar Sur), with comfortable wooden bungalows and fishing packages; and more modest **Río Sierpe Lodge** (506-2253-5203; www.riosierpelodge.com; $$*), with fishing, diving, and birding packages.

Agricultural Tours
★ **Köbö Farm** (506-2398-7604; www.fincakobo.com; Osa Peninsula, on road from Chacarita to Puerto Jiménez) This 20-hectare (50-acre) farm with more than 30 tropical crops, operated by the Guaymi Indigenous Reserve, will show you how fresh chocolate is grown and processed the old-fashioned way. They also offer guided hikes and kayak trips through their farmland and primary rain forest, plus cute, basic **rooms** ($) with private showers in a six-room wooden lodge.

Villa Vanilla Botanical Garden and Spice Tour (506-2779-1155; www.rainforestspices .com; 17 km east of Quepos; tours 9 AM and 1 PM, Mon.–Sat.; admission $40) Spice farm uses biodynamics (www.biodynamics.com) to grow organic vanilla, cinnamon, black pepper, allspice, and many other plants; also offers large, rustic cabins ($) with full kitchens and 3 kilometers (1.8 miles) of hiking trails through the woods.

Boat Tours
This is just a small sample of the many, many boats and tours available.

JACÓ

Bay Island Cruises (506-2258-3536; www.bayislandcruises.com) Tortuga Island tour could include transfers between Jacó and San José.

Kayak Jacó (506-2643-1233; www.kayakjaco.com; Playa Agujas, 14 km/9 mi. north of Jacó) Paddle to more secluded beaches in sea kayaks or outrigger canoes.

Parasailing Adventures (506-2637-8425; Los Sueños Marina, Playa Herradura) Just north of Jacó, offers parasailing.

QUEPOS

★ **Calypso Cruises** (506-2256-2727; 866-978-5177; www.calypsocruises.com; Puntarenas) Island tours (Cedros, Guayabo, Negritos, Tortuga) in the Nicoya Gulf on a luxury catamaran include transport from Quepos or Manuel Antonio, and a beach barbecue.

Costa Rica Flying Boat Tours (506-2368-1426; www.flyingboatcostarica.com; Quepos) You read that right—flying boat tours. Fly from Estuary Boca Vieja over Manuel Antonio, Isla Damas, and Dominical, in a contraption that looks like a sturdy inflatable dinghy attached to a hang glider with a motorcycle motor. I'd do it.

Safari Mangrove Tours (506-2777-3557; www.safarimangrove.com; Quepos) Estuary tours in flat-bottomed boats or kayaks, including the canals to Damas Island.

Samantha's Paradise Tours (506-2774-0258; www.samanthatours.com; Quepos) Snorkeling, sightseeing, and sportfishing tours; Web site has a good rundown on area fishing.

Sunset Sails Tours (506-2777-1304; www.sunsettours.com; Quepos) Enjoy sunset over a gourmet dinner on this beautiful wooden sailing yacht.

DOMINICAL AND BAHÍA BALLENA

Dolphin Tours (506-2743-8013; www.dolphintourcostarica.com; Punta Uvita) Yacht and

Dropping anchor in Puerto Jiménez

If you break your board in Dominical's whitewater, the San Clemente will give you a free taco and beer. Righteous.

kayak tours of Bahía Ballena, Corcovado, and Caño Island; also sportfishing.

Southern Expeditions (506-2787-0100; www.southernexpeditionscr.com; Dominical, across from soccer field) Sea kayaking, snorkeling, diving, sportfishing, and Caño Island.

Punta Uvita (506-2743-8047; Punta Uvita) Family run operation offers tours of Ballena, Corcovado, and Isla del Caño, as well as sportfishing.

OSA AND GOLFO DULCE

Gaviotas de Osa (506-2778-1212; www.tgaviotas.com; Sierpe) Dolphin tours, sightseeing in Corcovado, and sportfishing.

Zancudo Boat Tours (506-2776-0012; www.loscocos.com) Rents kayaks and surfboards, and runs guided kayak tours.

Canopy Tours and More

Canopy Adventure Jacó (506-2643-3271; www.adventurecanopy.com; Jacó) Serious 13-platform, 3-kilometer (1.8-mile) canopy offers night tours with reservations.

Corcovado Canopy Tour (506-2810-8908; www.corcovadocanopytour.com; Drake Bay) ICT certified canopy flights through the world's most biodiverse treetops.

Chiclets Tree Tour (506-2643-1880; www.jacowave.com; Jacó) thirteen-platform tour is close to town and gets raves.

★ **Rainforest Arial Tram Pacific** (506-257-5961; www.rainforestrams.com; Jacó) Takes in two rare tropical wildernesses, its quiet open trams soaring silently through dry forest and rain forest on a two-hour guided tour. They also offer guided hikes, heliconia and medicinal plant gardens, and a snake exhibition.

Titi Canopy (506-2777-3130; www.titicanopytours.com; Manuel Antonio) Fly through primary rain forest on 16-platform tour.

Diving and Snorkeling

Bill Beard's Diving Safaris (506-2453-5004, 877-853-0538 USA; www.billbeardcostarica .com; Manuel Antonio) Arranges dive packages that could include sportfishing, jungle tours, and more.

Costa Rica Adventure Divers (506-2231-5806, 866-553-7073; www.costaricadiving.com; Drake Bay) Based at delightful **Jinetes de Osa Lodge** ($$*) this operation offers diving, snorkeling, and kayak trips to Caño Island, Golfo Dulce, and beyond.

Herradura Divers (506-2637-7123; www.harraduradivers.com; Playa Herradura) PADI courses just north of Jacó.

Manuel Antonio Divers (506-2777-3483; www.manuelantoniodivers.com; Quepos, next to Hotel Malinche) Professional dive operator offers PADI certification, dive trips, and snorkel tours to Caño Island in a sweet catamaran.

Mystic Dive Center (506-2788-8636; www.mysticdivecenter.com; Playa Ventanas) Offers diving and snorkel tours of Ballena National Marine Park and Caño Island.

Oceans Unlimited Scuba Diving (506-2777-3171; www.oceansunlimitedcr.com; Quepos, at the beginning of the road to Manuel Antonio) Similar dives and prices as Manuel Antonio Divers.

Guided Hikes

Barú Falls Tree of Life Tours (506-2787-8133; www.treeoflifetours.com; Dominical) Adventure lodge offers day trips and overnights in the waterfall-strewn wilderness, with options for hiking, horseback riding, rappelling, and swimming.

★ **The Bug Lady** (506-8382-1619; www.thenighttour.com; Drake Bay) Join biologist Tracie the "Bug Lady" for a fascinating two-hour night tour through the jungle.

Pura Vida Gardens & Waterfalls (506-2645-1001; www.puravidagardensandwaterfalls .com; Tárcoles, 12 km north of Jacó; admission $15) Manicured gardens, rampant wildlife, and views of Costa Rica's tallest waterfall, just 10 minutes from the car.

Rainmaker Conservation Project (506-2777-3565; www.rainmakercostarica.org; signed 10 km (6 mi.) south of Parrita) Private, 607-hectare (1,500-acre) preserve is also a family-friendly destination with a 3.5 kilometer (2 mile) trail past waterfalls and swimming holes, complete with six suspension bridges.

Rancho La Merced (506-2771-4582; www.rancholamerced.com; Punta Uvita; hikes $25, horseback rides $35) Next to Ballena Marine Park, this 500-hectare (1250-acre) private wildlife refuge protects more than 300 bird species and other wildlife, with trails through the wilderness and along the river; an old farmhouse offers basic lodging ($$*).

Horseback Riding

Bella Vista Lodge (506-2787-8069; www.bellavistalodge.com; 3 km south of Dominical; $$) Simple but comfortable hardwood lodge and cabins, plus excellent horseback riding tours to Baru Waterfall and area beaches.

Brisas del Nara (506-2779-1235; www.horsebacktour.com; Quepos) Day trips to waterfalls and swimming holes.

Discover Horseback Riding Tour (506-2241-1853; www.crocodilecostarica.com; Tárcoles) Adrenaline junkies can combine horseback rides and crocodile spotting.

Finca Valmy Tours (506-2779-1118; www.valmytours.com; Quepos) Group, private, and overnight treks on horseback.

★ **Nauyaca Waterfalls** (506-2787-8013; www.cataratasnauyaca.com; 10 km from Dominical on the road to San Isidro de Pérez Zeledón; tours 8 AM–2 PM, close Sun.; admission $45, reservations required) A great day trip from Dominical, take a 2.5 hour ride to these 65-meter (213-foot) falls cascading into such scenic swimming holes, where a picnic lunch is served.

Rancho Savegre (506-7779-9016; www.ranchosavegre.com; Playa Palo Seco, between Jacó and Quepos) Beach trips on quality horses are perfect for beginners; they also offer lessons and weddings.

Other Tours

Birding Tours of Costa Rica (506-2643-1938; www.costaricabirdingjourneys.org) Arranges serious birding hikes, including two-week trips ($1,900–$2,600) into the rain forest.

Estrella Tour (506-2777-1286; Quepos, spinning gym in front of Escuela de Corea) Day trips on mountain bikes.

Fourtrax Adventures (506-2643-2373 Jacó; 506-2777-1829 Quepos; www.fourtrax adventure.com) There are several ATV-tour outfits in the region; this one operated in both Jacó and Quepos.

Friends of the Osa (506-2735-5756; www.osaconservation.org; Puerto Jiménez) In addition to other conservation-based activities, offers one-week ($300) volunteer opportunities to help protect the sea turtles.

Hang Glide Costa Rica (506-2353-5514; www.hangglidecostarica.com; 10 km/6 mi. south of Jacó) Tandem hang gliding flights; also offers tours in an ultralight "designed for *National Geographic*."

★ **El Silencio** (506-2380-5581; www.geocities.com/coopsilencio/albergue.htm; between Quepos and Dominical, follow Río Savegre signs from coastal road) Historic community tourism cooperative offers guided hikes, community tours, horseback rides, and basic lodging ($).

Sportfishing

Central Pacific

Karahé Sport Fishing (506-2777-0170; 877-623-3198 USA; www.karahe.com; Manuel Antonio Beach; $$$*) Perfectly acceptable hotel is entirely dedicated to sportfishing; or just sample the sea's bounty at the on-site restaurant, **El Canto del Mar** (506-2777-0170; B, L, D; $$$–$$$$), serving great cocktails by the sea.

Costa Rica Dreams Sport Fishing (Playa Herradura)

King Tours (506-2643-2441; 800-213-7091 USA; www.kingtours.com; Los Sueños Marina Resort) Fleet of top-notch yachts.

Rich Coast Charters (506-2777-4444; 877-450-9927 USA; www.costaricafishing.co.cr; downtown Quepos) Established outfitter offers all-inclusive sportfishing trips.

Though the nation has no military, many Costa Ricans refer to their endangered pelicans as the "Costa Rican Air Force."

SOUTH PACIFIC

Banana Bay Marina (506-2775-0838; www.bananabaymarina.com; Golfito) Arranges fishing trips and all-inclusive vacations.

Crocodile Bay (506-2735-5631; www.crocodilebay.com; Puerto Jimenez; $$$$*) Resort lodge offers deluxe fishing, spa, and adventure packages.

Sportfishing Charters (506-2364-4499, 610-306-1970 USA; www.sportfishinggolfito .com; Golfito, Las Gaviotas Resort) Arranges packages with a good choice of area hotels, and also runs tours from Puerto Jiménez.

Sportfishing Unlimited (506–2776-0036; www.sportfishing.co.cr; Golfito) Serious sport-fishing and package deals with different area hotels.

Zancudo Lodge (506-2776-0008; 800-854-8791 USA; www.thezancudolodge.com; Zan-cudo; $$$$*) Premium fishing lodge offers good rooms, great boats, and the chance to add to their list of 60 I.G.F.A world records.

Surfing

Del Mar Surf Camp (506-2385-8535; www.costaricasurfingchicas.com; Playa Hermosa, 4 km south of Jacó) Ladies' surf camp offers packages including, massages, canopy tours, and more.

★ **Green Iguana Surf Camp** (506-2825-1381; www.greeniguanasurfcamp.com; Domini-cal) Very professional outfit starts you off at mellower beaches if Dominical's famously heavy surf is too much.

Jacó Surf School (506-2829-4697; www.jacosurfschool.com; Jacó, on the beach) Costa Rican Surf Team alumni Gustavo Castillo promises your money back if you don't stand up on the board.

Manuel Antonio Surf School (506-2777-4842; www.masurfschool.com; Manuel Antonio Beach) Lessons, tours to area breaks, and packages.

Roxy Costa Rica Surfaris (www.roxycostarica.com; Playa Hermosa and Jacó) Women's surf camp offers trips all over the country, plus packages like the mother-daughter surfari.

Tropical Surf School (506-2774-0001; www.tropicalsurfschool.com; Manuel Antonio) Lessons and guided tours.

Uvita Surf School (506-2743-8022; uvitasurfschool@hotmail.com) Learn to surf in a national park with this locally owned operation.

Wildlife Displays and Rescue Centers

Fincas Naturales Butterfly Botanical Gardens (506-2777-0973; www.butterflygardens.co .cr; between Quepos and Manuel Antonio, across from Si Como No; admission varies, $15–$30 per adult, $8–$25 per child) Great spot for family fun on 12 hectares (30 acres) of rain forest, with guided hikes, night tours, botanical gardens, and butterfly, reptile, and amphibian displays.

Neo Fauna (506-2643-1904; www.neofauna.com; La Mona, near Jacó; open 7 AM–5 PM, daily) Eco-project offers guided tours of their big butterfly gardens, snake, and frog displays.

Getting ready for white-water rafting on the Río Savegre

Osa Sea Turtle Conservation Program (506-2838-9171; www.osaseaturtles.com) Volunteer to help protect sea turtles from poachers.

Reptilandia Park (506-2787-8007; www.crreptiles.com; 7 km from Dominical on road to San Isidro; open 9 AM–4 PM; admission $10) Probably the most impressive snake exhibition in the country, with more than 200 species of snakes plus komodo dragons, crocodiles, turtles, and other cold-blooded critters, and Friday is feeding day!

White-Water Rafting

Amigos del Río (506-2777-0082; www.amigosdelrio.net; road from Quepos to Manuel Antonio) Great operation offers Class III rapids on the Río Savegre and more challenging Río Naranjo, plus ocean and estuary kayak trips.

Ce-Os Turbolencias (506-2787-8328; ceosturbolencias@yahoo.com; Dominical) Tico outfitter offers Class I family floats to serious, 25-kilometer (15-mile) treks with Class IV+ rapids, on several beautiful jungle rapids.

Quepoa Expeditions (506-2777-0058; quepoaexpeditions@yahoo.com) White-water rafting, kayak, and snorkel tours around Manuel Antonio and Isla Damas.

Ríos Tropicales (506-2777-4092; www.adventurash2o.com; just south of Quepos on road to Manuel Antonio) Costa Rica's biggest outfitter offers white-water treks on the Naranjo and Savegre, as well as ocean kayaking and mangrove tours.

Spas

JACÓ

Aolani Holistic Center (506-8820-4059; Jacó, south entrance, next to Hotel Amapola) Massages, Chinese medicine, dance therapy, and yoga.

Blossom Ayurvedic Spa & Holistic Center (506-2643-2211; Jacó, Doce Lunas Hotel) Yoga, meditation, raw foods, and other natural therapies, at pretty Doce Lunas.

Luz Massage (506-2354-8491; Jacó, next to Hotel Balcón del Mar) Massages right on the beach, or call for room service.

Serenity Spa (506-2643-1624; www.serenityspacr.com; Central Jacó, behind Zuma Rent-a-Car) Offers massages, wraps, facials, and packages; more luxurious locations at Villa Calletas and Si Como No hotels.

QUEPOS AND MANUEL ANTONIO

Spa Uno (506-2777-2607; www.spauno.com; off Quepos-Manuel Antonio road) Beautiful day spa offers pricey premium spa services.

Raindrop Spa (506-2777-2880; www.raindropspa.com; 1 km (.6 mi.) south of Quepos on road to Manuel Antonio) Gorgeous teak-and-flagstone spa in the jungle has top-of-the-line selection of wraps, massages, facials, yoga classes, and other treatments.

Sivana Yoga & Massage (506-2777-5268; www.sivanayoga.com; road to Manuel Antonio) Ultra plush yoga studio and retreat (offering three stunning bungalows and meals, perhaps part of multi-day yoga retreats) also offers massages.

SOUTH PACIFIC

Guaria de Osa (www.guariadeosa.com; San Josecito Beach, Drake Bay; $$$$*) Yoga, tai chi, and wellness retreat has nice rooms and platform tents, your choice.

Mango Tree Spa (506-2786-5300; www.themangotreespa.com; Tres Ríos de Coronado, 40 km/25 mi. south of Dominical) Secluded jungle spa offers meditation, breathing and yoga classes, high-tech facials, and lots of massages. They have four pretty villas on-site.

Wooden church on the Osa Peninsula

SHOPPING

Books

Books 2 Go (506-2777-1754; downtown Quepos, two shops down from Cabinas Hellen) Book exchange and inexpensive tours.

Books & Stuff (506-2643-2508; downtown Jacó) Excellent bookstore offers lots of English-language books, travel and wildlife guides, newspapers and magazines, maps, and music.

La Buena Nota (506-2777-1002; www.labuenanota.com; road to Manuel Antonio, next to Karahe) Souvenirs and beachwear, plus used books, magazines, and newspapers.

Clothes

Galería La Heliconia (506-2643-3613; central Jacó) Art gallery specializes in stunning handmade jewelry.

Guacamole (506-2643-1120; www.guacamoleonline.com; Multicentro, Costa Brava; Jacó) Hippie fashion plates must check out the beautifully batiked, 100 percent handmade, all-original clothing designs.

Namaste (506-2643-2936; Jacó; Paseo Las Americas Local #1) Groovy imports from India and Asia, including clothes, décor, and souvenir-sized coolness.

Galleries

Felix Murillo Artista Costarricense (506-2643-1539; www.felixmurillo.com; Jacó, next to Amapola Hotel) Colorful modern art is both figurative and fish-urative.

Osa Arts Fine Art Gallery (506-2735-5426; downtown Puerto Jiménez) Local artists do mainly wildlife themes.

Osa Pulchra (506-2365-3848; Puerto Jiménez, Osa) Handmade souvenirs from area indigenous and rural artisans, plus pretty gardens out back.

Regalame (506-2777-0777; www.regalameart.com; road to Manuel Antonio) At Sí Como No hotel, this fine art gallery offers fine original painting, sculpture, ceramics, and more from local artists.

EVENTS

February

Quepos Civic Fiestas (mid-February)

San Isidro de el General Civic Fiestas (mid-February)

Jacó Beach Music Festival (early February; www.jaco2008.com) Four stages, 30 artists, and lots of parties.

March

Los Sueños Signature Billfish Tournament (www.costaricaclassic.com; www.ls tournaments.com; Playa Herradura) This catch-and-release classic raises money to fight cystic fibrosis.

November

Reef Classic Latin Pro (www.alaslatintour.com; Jacó) The hemisphere's best surfers battle it out in Jacó.

Ruta de Conquistadores (www.adventurerace.com) The world's toughest bike race traces the path of Spanish settlers.

December

Festival de los Diablitos (December 30; Boruca Indigenous Preserve) "Little Devils" wearing Boruca masks give out food and *chicha* (corn beer) and re-enact the Spanish conquest.

For humans, it's all in the wrist when artisanal fishing; for egrets, in the neck.

8

THE CARIBBEAN COAST

Lush Tropical Rhythms

Luxuriously green in a way that the rest of Costa Rica can only aspire to, the jungle-carpeted Caribbean Coast is so thick with life that the wholly wild realm north of the provincial capital, Puerto Limón, is accessible only by boat or plane. This is no inconvenience, at least not one you will begrudge, not after your boat begins its voyage through the living tunnels of endangered flora and fauna that comprise this dreamscape of rivers and canals.

Long isolated by these once impenetrable rain forests, which still blanket Braulio Carrillo National Park and the Talamanca Mountains (2,000 meters/6,560 feet) with life, the Caribbean Coast is very different from the rest of Costa Rica not only in its climate, but in its character. This culture was created, not by Spanish settlers, but by a heady mix of Afro-Caribbeans, British pirates, and American entrepreneurs who eventually linked the coast with the capital of San José, building a railroad at almost unfathomable cost through the malaria-ridden jungles.

Today the road is smoothly paved through the partially tamed forests, to beaches where visitors are welcomed with a West Indian lilt and reggae soundtrack. Your first sight of the sea is from Puerto Limón, the railway's old terminus and most important port in Costa Rica. This gritty port city's fascinating history and architecture aside, there's little here for international visitors save a sweet central park with sloths in the trees, and transportation to the rest of the coast. At press time, however, the World Bank had just granted Costa Rica a $72.5 million loan to clean up and modernize the provincial capital; perhaps one day less adventurous explorers will have good reason to spend more time here.

Just north of Limón is Playa Bonita, the widest beach on the Caribbean Coast, framed with coral reefs that rose from the water during a 1991 earthquake. Its handful of hotels are geared more toward Ticos, with international visitors continuing 7 kilometers (4 miles) north to Moín, for boats into the swampy coastal lowlands. Tiny Parismina is only just becoming known for its excellent fishing and nesting sea turtles, and even boasts a small, grassroots turtle protection program. Much more touristy Tortuguero offers many more hotels and fabulous lodges, as well as a national park and the world's first sea turtle conservation project. Farther north along the canals is isolated Barra del Colorado, with a few fishing lodges catering to those who come for the world's best tarpon fishing.

Most visitors head south from Puerto Limón, however, along the paved coastal road, to towns that still cater primarily to the dreadlock-and-tattoo set. Cahuita is more mellow, a relaxed outpost of Caribbean culture with great food and music. Lodging is more limited, but offers easy access to beautiful Cahuita National Park, a jungle headland fringed with

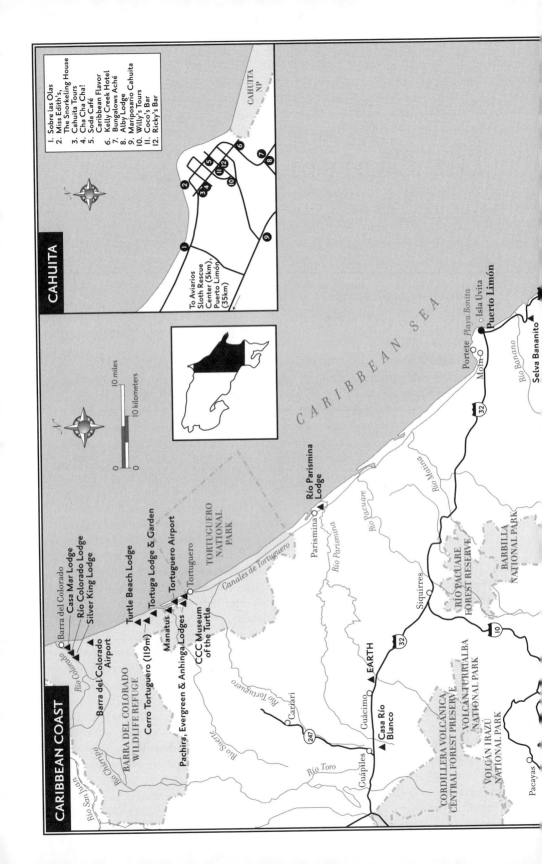

CARIBBEAN COAST

Barra del Colorado
Casa Mar Lodge
Río Colorado Lodge
Silver King Lodge

Barra del Colorado Airport

BARRA DEL COLORADO
WILDLIFE REFUGE

Turtle Beach Lodge

Cerro Tortuguero (119m)

Tortuga Lodge & Garden

Manatus

Tortuguero Airport

Pachira, Evergreen & Anhinga Lodges

CCC Museum
of the Turtle

Tortuguero

TORTUGUERO
NATIONAL PARK

Canales de Tortuguero

Río Colorado

Río Chirripó

Río San Juan

Río Tortuguero

Río Suerte

Río Parismina

Parismina

Río Parismina
Lodge

CARIBBEAN SEA

Guápiles

Río Toro

Guácimo

EARTH

Casa Río
Blanco

Capiari

247

32

Siquirres

10

RÍO PACUARE
FOREST RESERVE

Río Pacuare

Río Matina

BARBILLA
NATIONAL PARK

Pacayas

Portete Playa Bonita
Moín   Isla Uvita
        Puerto Limón

32

Río Banano

Selva Bananito

CORDILLERA VOLCÁNICA
CENTRAL FOREST PRESERVE

VOLCÁN IRAZÚ
NATIONAL PARK

VOLCÁN TURRIALBA
NATIONAL PARK

0   10 miles
0   10 kilometers

CAHUITA

To Aviarios
Sloth Rescue
Center (5km),
Puerto Limón
(35km)

CAHUITA NP

1. Sobre las Olas
2. Miss Edith's,
   The Snorkeling House
3. Cahuita Tours
4. Cha Cha Cha!
5. Soda Café
   Caribbean Flavor
6. Kelly Creek Hotel
7. Bungalows Aché
8. Alby Lodge
9. Mariposario Cahuita
10. Willy's Tours
11. Coco's Bar
12. Ricky's Bar

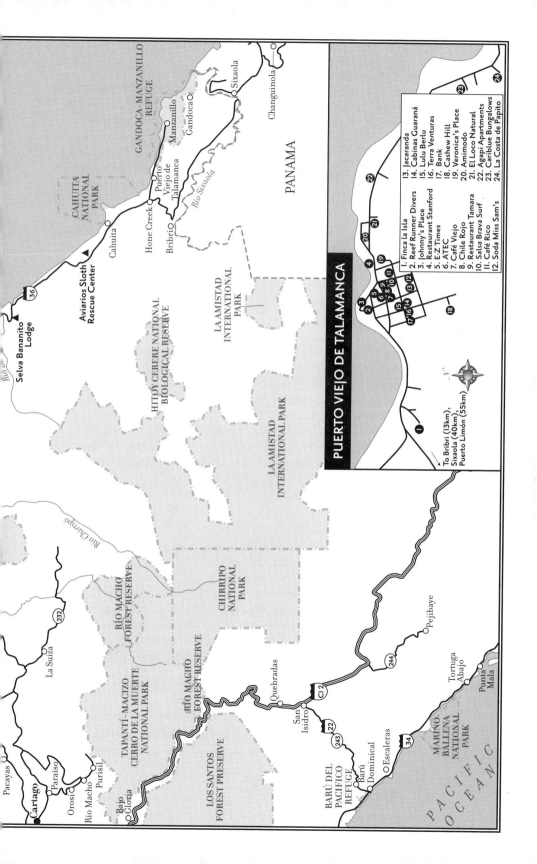

PUERTO VIEJO DE TALAMANCA

To Bribri (13km),
Sixaola (40km),
Puerto Limón (55km)

1. Finca la Isla
2. Reef Runner Divers
3. Johnny's Place
4. Restaurant Stanford
5. E-Z Times
6. ATEC
7. Café Viejo
8. Chile Rojo
9. Restaurant Tamara
10. Salsa Brava Surf
11. Café Rico
12. Soda Miss Sam's
13. Jacaranda
14. Cabinas Guaraná
15. Lulu Berlu
16. Terra Venturas
17. Bank
18. Cashew Hill
19. Veronica's Place
20. Amimodo
21. El Loco Natural
22. Agapi Apartments
23. Cariblue Bungalows
24. La Costa de Papito

coconut palms, white-sand beaches, and Costa Rica's largest coral reef.

Continue south to Puerto Viejo de Talamanca (not to be confused with Puerto Viejo de Sarapiquí, in the Northern Zone), the Caribbean Coast's official party town, with the best nightlife and restaurant scene in the country. Luxury and nature lovers can find endless options for solitude, comfort, and blue-flag beaches on the 12-kilometer (7-mile) road south to the village of Manzanillo, actually inside the Gandoca-Manzanillo National Wildlife Refuge.

On the other side of the refuge, tiny Gandoca has a few very basic lodges and a renowned organic farm. Nearby Bribri is home to an indigenous reserve with waterfalls, craft stores, and an iguana farm you can visit on tours arranged in Puerto Viejo and Cahuita. Just beyond is the tiny border town of Sixaola, with access to Bocas del Toro, Panama.

Note that Caribbean weather is mild but humid, with rainfall well above the Costa Rican average year round; it gets wetter the farther north you go. Though it's drier from January through March, and perhaps in late August and early September (the "mini dry season"), bring an umbrella.

SAFETY

The Caribbean Coast has a reputation for crime, primarily because of violence between competing narco-traffickers, who stay well away from tourists. (Small-time drug dealers may approach you, however, and should be avoided, as they often work with police to entrap tourists). Puerto Limón can be sketchy, particularly at night: Park your car in a guarded lot, and stick to the well-lit tourist areas around Parque Vargas after dark.

Cahuita and Puerto Viejo (and to a lesser extent, Tortuguero) are touristy, with their share of drug dealers, pickpockets, and muggers, all of whom are under increasing pressure from a recently ramped up police presence. Crime rates have fallen dramatically, but stay alert and take big-city precautions.

GETTING AROUND

It's a quick and easy jaunt to the beaches south of Limón, but heading into the wild north requires some planning.

Air

Limón International Airport (LIO), which had its runway paved in 2006, has regular Nature Air flights from San José and Bocas del Toro, Panama. Sansa offers flights from San José.

Tortuguero Airport (TTQ) hosts Nature Air flights from San José daily, with one morning flight continuing to **Barra del Colorado** (BCL). Sansa also serves Tortuguero and Barra del Colorado airports.

Car

It's a smooth and scenic 140 kilometers (88 miles) from San José to Puerto Limón on Highway 32, an important shipping route usually packed with trucks. You'll pass the agricultural centers of Guápiles (with access to the river port in Cariari), Guácimo, and Siquirres before reaching the coast. It's another 20 kilometers (35 miles) south to Puerto Viejo on the paved but potholed coastal road.

Poás (800-607-POAS; www.carrentals.com) is the only Caribbean rental car company, important if you want to drop your car off before heading to Tortuguero or Panama. There are offices in Guápiles (506-2710-4380) at the Hotel Suerre, where they'll help you arrange transport to Tortuguero; and at Hone Creek (506-2750-0400), halfway between Cahuita and Puerto Viejo.

Bus

All Caribbean-bound buses from San José leave from the **Gran Terminal del Caribe** (506-2222-0610; Calle Central, Avs 13 & 15).

Private Shuttle

Several private shuttle companies serve the Caribbean Coast. Ask at your hotel or any tour office, or try **Interbus** (506-2283-5573; www.interbusonline.com), **Grayline Fantasy Bus** (506-2232-3681; www.graylinecostarica.com), or **Shuttle Me** (506-2294-7670; www.shuttleme.co.cr).

Boat

There are no real roads into the northern Caribbean, which means you'll either fly or ply the sultry jungle lowlands by boat; I highly recommend the latter, at least one way. There are three main ports: Moín, 7 kilometers (4.2 miles) north of Puerto Limón; Cariari, with two private docks (Pavona and La Geech), north of Guápiles; and Caño Negro, near Siquirres, with boat taxis to Parismina. You can also arrange more expensive private boats from Puerto Viejo de Sarapiquí, covered in the Northern Zone chapter. It's easier to make reservations through a hotel or tour office, but you can certainly arrange boats at the dock.

In Cariari, drivers can park at Hotel Central, where they'll help arrange boats. Buses to Cariari leave San José at 9 AM daily, and are met by touts from companies including **Bananero** (506-2709-8005), ★**Pura Vida Tours** (506-2479-9045), ★**Clic Clic** (506-2844-0463), and **Coopetraca** (506-2767-7137), most with offices in Cariari's old bus terminal (five blocks from the San José terminal where you arrive). Collective boats to Tortuguero cost about $10 each way.

Moín, a $6 taxi from downtown Puerto Limón, has regular boat service throughout the day to Tortuguero ($30); boats can stop in Parismina by advance arrangement. Try **Tropical Wind** (506-2798-6059) or **Mayron Knight Tours** (506-2758-3981). Water taxis from Caño Negro to Parismina cost $15 each way.

Barra del Colorado does not have regular boat service, which means you'll either arrange transportation through your lodge, or hire a private boat from Moín or Tortuguero.

LODGING

Accommodations on the Caribbean Coast are less expensive than on the Pacific Coast, but visitors looking for the full five-star resort experience will be disappointed. Don't despair! There are several very comfortable options, most along the divine coastline stretching between Puerto Viejo and Manzanillo; and on the canal north of Tortuguero. This is just a sample of what's available; check out **Costa Rica Hotels** (www.hotels.co.cr/caribbeancoast.html) for more options.

Note that very few hotels on the Caribbean Coast have air-conditioning in all their rooms; units burn out quickly in this humidity. If you can't go without, be sure to ask if they have a room or two with climate control.

Lodging Price Code

Cost of lodging is based on an average per-room, double-occupancy rate at peak season (December through March). Costa Rica's 16.39 percent tax and gratuities are not included. Rates are often reduced during the Green Season (May through November). An asterisk denotes that a full breakfast is included with the room price.

Inexpensive ($)	Up to $50
Moderate ($$)	$50 to $100
Expensive ($$$)	$100 to $200
Very Expensive ($$$$)	Over $200

Hotels

PUERTO LIMÓN AND AROUND
HOTEL MARIBÚ CARIBE
506-2795-2543
www.vacationcity.com/costa-rica/hotel
/maribu-caribe/
Puerto Limón, Playa Bonita, 5km north of town
Price: Moderate*
Credit Cards: Yes
Handicap Access: No

The nicest property overlooking broad Playa Bonita (but without easy beach access) is this three-star collection of clean but basic whitewashed bungalows. Circular, *palenque*-style villas are spacious duplexes with wooden floors and furniture, clean and air-conditioned, scattered around pleasant gardens with a small pool. Breakfast is included, and serves traditional Caribbean cuisine at other meals. The staff speaks some English and will happily arrange tours and transportation.

HOTEL & COUNTRY CLUB SUERRE
Manager: Katty Comacho
506-2710-7551
www.suerre.com
info@suerre.com
Guápiles, 1 km from Santa Clara gas station
Price: Moderate to Expensive
Credit Cards: Yes
Handicap Access: Yes

Halfway between San José and Puerto Limón, and just half an hour from Cariari, this friendly little resort property caters mainly to wealthy Tico families. Clean, tiled rooms with dark wood furniture are large, modern, and comfortable, and come with air-conditioning, cable TV, telephones, and other amenities you'd expect at a business-class U.S. hotel. The real draws are all the activities, including two pools (one Olympic-sized) and a Jacuzzi, a good-sized gym, tennis courts, volleyball courts, Ping-Pong tables, a large playground, and much more.

PARK HOTEL
Owner: Oscar Zen
506-2798-0555
parkhotelcostarica.com
info@parkhotel.com
Downtown Puerto Limón, 100m north and 25m west of Parque Vargas
Price: Inexpensive to Moderate*
Credit Cards: Yes
Handicap Access: Yes

This is easily the finest accommodation in the City of Limón, where few international tourists opt to stay the night—their loss, by my reckoning, as I rather like Limón's sultry yet down-to-earth ambiance. Petite but cheerfully painted rooms have high ceilings, cable TV, telephones, air-conditioning, great beds and furnishings, and, for a few extra dollars, small balconies with big ocean views. The restaurant is very good, and the location just perfect, just steps from the sea wall, and one block from delightfully dilapidated Parque Vargas and its contingent of greenish sloths.

NORTH OF PUERTO LIMÓN

Most accommodations in the Northern Caribbean are either expensive, all-inclusive nature lodges, or basic budget backpacker spots, with little in between. In addition to listed lodges and bed-and-breakfasts, comfortable options in Tortuguero include **Miss Miriam's** (506-2709-8002; across from the soccer field; $–$$) and **Miss Junie's** (506-2709-8029; north end of town; $), both with great restaurants; and **La Casona** (506-2709-8092; near the dock; $), which accepts credit cards. Visitors to Parismina can find comprehensive hotel listings and homestays on www.parismina .com.

MANATÚS HOTEL

506-2709-8197
www.manatushotel.com
info@manatushotel.com
Tortuguero, 3.5 km north of village
Price: Very Expensive*
Credit Cards: Yes
Handicap Access: Yes

For years, even the most upscale accommodations in Tortuguero brought you close to nature—a little too close to some, who would have preferred air-conditioning as part of their remote tropical rain forest experience. Enter Manatús, a stylish new entry on the canal, with beautifully constructed Caribbean-style bungalows and what's been acclaimed as the best fine-dining restaurant in the Northern Caribbean (not that there's a lot of competition). There's even an on-site spa and canopy tour.

In addition to that refreshing climate control, your beautiful little bungalow, with wraparound porch and soothing canal views, comes equipped with cable TV, Internet access, minibar, and beautiful jungle-chic furnishing where you can relax without quite escaping from it all. Which is sometimes more relaxing. And just wait until you see that pool.

SOUTH OF PUERTO LIMÓN

ALMONDS & CORALS

Owners: Aurora Gámez and Marco Odio
506-2271-3000
www.almondsandcorals.com
info@almondsandcorals.com
Manzanillo, 12 km (8 mi.) south of Puerto Viejo
Price: Expensive to Very Expensive
Credit Cards: Yes
Handicap Access: Yes
Special: Five CST Leaves

This remarkable escape into the heart of the Caribbean wilderness, within primary jungles protected by the Gandoca-Manzanillo Wildlife Refuge, is just steps away from an isolated blue-flag beach—and minutes by taxi or bicycle from Puerto Viejo's festive scene. Despite the price, this isn't a full-service resort, it's more of an eco-lodge, albeit a very comfortable, and easily accessible place to commune with nature. Luxurious and completely sustainable villas in the forests have no "walls," per se; they are instead screened in, hung with gauzy curtains, but otherwise wide open to wild nature, including troupes of howler monkeys who will act as your alarm clock. Inside each *palapa*-topped daydream are most of the quality amenities you'd expect at an upscale hotel (other than air-conditioning), with rustic but very comfortable furnishings (including hammocks), nice lighting, and modern hot-water bathrooms with hairdryers and all the organic toiletries you'll need.

Follow the raised wooden pathways through the wild jungle (there are hiking trails throughout the property), and you'll find a covered outdoor Jacuzzi, as well as the restaurant where you'll enjoy your included breakfast and dinner. You're about 3 kilometers (1.8 miles) from the tiny town of Manzanillo.

HOTEL ATLANTIDA

Manager: Domingo Seco
505-2755-0115
www.atlantida.co.cr
atlantis@racsa.co.cr
600m north of Cahuita on beachfront road
Price: Moderate to Expensive
Credit Cards: Yes
Handicap Access: No

Since 1979, this lusciously overgrown property has offered comfortable accommodations to visitors in love with Cahuita, but not the sandy *cabina* scene. The sprawling gardens are home to lots of tiny, colorful frogs, as well as 32 comfortably equipped rooms fronted with appealing bamboo porches. All of the gently aging rooms are agreeably furnished, with paintings by local artists and cane ceilings that bring the jungle ambiance indoors, polished rattan furniture, subdued lighting, and fresh flowers. Suites are much nicer, and include Jacuzzis, but no air-conditioning.

Also on the grounds is a slightly rusty but fully functional gymnasium, a good restaurant serving fairly upscale Caribbean and international cuisine, and a fine pool fronted with a bar and open grill. The attentive staff arranges massages and all manner of tours.

★ CARIBLUE BUNGALOWS

Owner: Sandra Cernielli
506-2750-0035, 506-2750-0518
www.cariblue.com
cariblu@racsa.co.cr
Playa Cocles
Price: Expensive*
Credit Cards: Yes
Handicap Access: No

Beautifully constructed bungalows were built with polished attention to detail, from the charming, *palapa*-style exteriors, brightly painted to match the jungle flowers, to the exquisitely crafted and colorful interiors, with mosaic tile work, original art, and other elegant if not extravagant extras. Furnishings are simple but delightful, from the gorgeous bamboo beds softly lit by hand-carved lamps, to the hammocks on each covered teak porch overlooking the impressive gardens, which come alive with singing frogs every evening. Most sleep four to six people, and they also rent a fully-equipped, two-bedroom, two-bathroom house.

Though rooms are simple, the lobby and lounge area, with the same artistic architectural detail, is equipped free WiFi and a TV with DVD player, as well as books, games, billiards, and Ping-Pong. The pool is an absolute masterpiece, as is the on-site gourmet restaurant ($$$), serving excellent seafood and traditional Italian cuisine.

LA DIOSA

Owners: Jaqueline Bürkler and Marcela Ruiz
506-2755-0055
www.hotelladiosa.net
reservation@hotelladiosa.net
Cahuita, 2 km north of center on the beach, Black's Beach entrance
Price: Moderate*
Credit Cards: Yes
Handicap Access: Yes

"The Goddess" Hotel welcomes you with

celestial statues of the world's great feminine archetypes arranged throughout the exuberant gardens. Trails lead past their sometimes serene, sometimes flirtatious countenances, as well as tiny waterfalls, enormous flowers, and the rather spectacular raised pool, to the blue-flag beach just beyond. A healthy breakfast is served beneath a quiet *palapa*, and there's a meditation and yoga platform as well, where you can arrange classes or just find your own space.

The bungalows—named for goddesses as well, Aphrodite, Isis, Pachamama—are lovely inside and out, with lots of exposed dark rock, polished wood, and large windows, all delightfully painted with beautiful tiles, large bathrooms, and tasteful, elegant furnishings in bamboo and wood. Most rooms come with air-conditioning and a few with large Jacuzzis.

At the time of research, the proprietors were about to open an all-inclusive yoga retreat, the **Goddess Garden** (www.the goddessgarden.com) with a full-service Caribbean vegetarian restaurant and Ayurvedic spa.

JACARANDA
Owner: Vera Kahn
506-2750-0069
www.cabinasjacaranda.net
veragarden@yahoo.ca
Central Puerto Viejo, 300m west of the beach
Price: Inexpensive
Credit Cards: Yes
Handicap Access: Yes

Unfortunately, there are no truly luxurious hotels in downtown Puerto Viejo, but this very comfortable midrange option is one of my favorite hotels in all Costa Rica. Vera has put her heart and soul into this place, cultivating the lavish gardens with flowers and fruit trees that curl above paved pathways and strategically placed hammocks in a kaleidoscope of color. Rooms are simple, romantic, and unique, with comfortable beds, in-room safes, hot showers, and wonderful art, all custom designed right down to the hand-wrought curlicue bars on each window, both beautiful and functional. Only two have television and air-conditioning, so far; reserve those well in advance. There's yoga every Thursday, if you're feeling a bit stiff.

Another excellent option in downtown Puerto Viejo is cozy **Cabinas Guaraná** (506-750-0244; www.hotelguarana.com; $), with artsy, fan-cooled rooms around a quiet courtyard.

Sea turtles get all the attention, but Tortuguero's canals have plenty of river turtles, too.

KELLY CREEK HOTEL

Owner: Andrés Alcala
www.hotelkellycreek.com
kellycr@racsa.co.cr
Entrance of Cahuita National Park
Price: Inexpensive to Moderate
Credit Cards: Yes
Handicap Access: No

This good hotel has the best location in Cahuita, facing the sugary white-sand beaches just outside the national park, where birds, sloths, monkeys, and other local wildlife like to congregate. The Spanish owners are no slouches when it comes to keeping the four cavernous wooden rooms in tip-top shape, and every piece of furniture is polished to the same rich luster as the teak from which the hotel was constructed. Decent bathrooms, better beds, and huge closets (perfect for a multi-day stay) are all accented by very nice paintings by the hotel's owner.

Breakfast is not included, but is served every morning in their fabulous little Spanish restaurant overlooking the sea. At dinner, the specialty is paella (order in advance; there's a two-person minimum), with other Spanish dishes on offer.

MAGELLAN INN

Owner: Terry Newton
506-2755-0035
www.hotelmagellininn.com
hotelmagellininn@yahoo.com
Cahuita, north end of village near Playa Negra
Price: Moderate to Expensive*
Credit Cards: Yes
Handicap Access: Challenging

For many years, this was the absolute paragon of elegance in Cahuita, and though the classic three-star property may be showing its age, that somehow adds to the sweet languorous luxury imbuing each elegant detail. Make your way through the sumptuous gardens and across ornate Persian rugs to the restaurant and lobby, with a refined ambiance in classic cane furnishings and fresh flowers beneath the fans, the perfect place to relax as evening rolls in.

Rooms are attractive, with more fine carpets and rich tapestries, as well as good beds and furnishings; for a few dollars you'll even get air-conditioning. But just beyond those fine French doors, your private terrace beckons with comfy chairs and perhaps a hammock hanging in the gardens that surround the fine pool just beyond. Some rooms even have WiFi. The French-Caribbean restaurant, **Casa Creole**, is considered one of the region's best.

★ SHAWANDHA LODGE

Manager: Jaqueline Maho-Diaz and Nicolas Bufille
506-2750-0018
www.shawandhalodge.com
shawandha@racsa.co.cr
Playa Chiquita, 4.5 km south of Puerto Viejo
Price: Moderate to Expensive*
Credit Cards: Yes
Handicap Access: No

These upscale, wooden-framed, thatch-roofed villas on stilts were designed to look like a primitive village, scattered throughout the jungle. But as soon as you cross the palm-fringed porch (furnished with a sofa and hammock, should you want to while away a rainy day relaxing to the tempo of the raindrops), all illusions of a primitive existence evaporate. Cozy and colorful, with lots of polished teak, each fan-cooled bungalow comes complete with a king-sized bed, beautiful furnishings, and lots of lovely original art, including indigenous pottery. Step down into the sunken bathrooms for the piece de resistance, artistically tiled bathrooms, each of them fabulous and unique.

★ TREE HOUSE LODGE

Owner: Edsart Besier
506-2750-0706

www.costaricatreehouse.com
info@costaricatreehouse.com
Punta Uva, 5 km south of Puerto Viejo
Price: Expensive to Very Expensive
Credit Cards: No
Handicap Access: No

These absolutely unbelievable bungalows, snuggled into the protected solitude of Punta Uva's blue-flag coastline, are among my absolute favorites in the country. Surrounded by jungle, these "tree houses" are built almost entirely from sustainable materials, such as fallen trees hauled here in oxcarts from deep in the jungle. Every detail is inspired, from the subtle play of light and color upon each fine-grained polished wooden floor, to more lighthearted extras, like the toilet enthroned within a living tree. The Beach Suite has one of the world's truly awesome bathrooms, part spacecraft, part Garden of Eden, where a sparkling serpent will tempt you into staying very clean.

Each of the houses is unique; one sleeps six and all come equipped with either a kitchenette or full kitchen. All are luxuriously outfitted with original art, sculptural furniture, psychedelic tilework, and all the amenities except air-conditioning, but those ocean breezes are rolling in from only 150 yards away. Edsart, the friendly owner, also operates the Iguana Conservation Tour, which means you'll be able to enjoy lots of rescued iguanas hanging out in the trees.

Bed-and-Breakfasts

NORTH OF PUERTO LIMÓN (TORTUGUERO, PARISMINA, AND BARRA COLORADO)

★ CASA MARBELLA
Manager: Daryl Loth
506-833-0827
casamarbella.tripod.com
safari@racsa.co.cr
Tortuguero Village, across from Catholic church
Price: Inexpensive*

Credit Cards: No
Handicap Access: No

The second-best thing about this adorable inn is its fine wooden dock, lazing right over the river where you can watch iguanas, bats, birds, and perhaps a Jesus lizard or two race across the water as it turns sunset violet at the end of the day. What's the best thing? Your host, Daryl Loth, perhaps the region's best naturalist guide, who organizes the very best hikes, boat trips, and any trek into the squishy and spectacular rain forest.

The rooms themselves are simple, immaculately clean, and whitewashed, with high ceilings, fans, and private hot showers with skylights. There's a community kitchen, and big breakfasts are included. And the third best thing about Casa Marbella? Why, the location. Unlike the isolated lodges accessible only by boat, you're in the adorable little fishing village of Tortuguero, with yummy Caribbean restaurants and a pretty (if not exactly swimmable) beach.

SOUTH OF PUERTO LIMÓN
★ EL ENCANTO B&B INN
Owners: Pierre-Léon Tetreault and Patricia Kim
506-2755-0113
www.elencantobedandbreakfast.com
info@elencantobedandbreakfast.com
Cahuita, 400m north of town
Price: Moderate to Expensive*
Credit Cards: Yes
Handicap Access: Yes

A refined and delightful oasis of comfort in Cahuita, this absolutely perfect bed-and-breakfast is also an excellent value. Five minutes south of town on the shady beachfront road, you won't miss the elegant efflorescence of the manicured garden, into which a glistening pool, yoga pavilion, and serene stone statues are secreted. A Spanish mission-style monument of sweeping adobe arches, the main building houses the relaxing lounge area, where fruit, fresh bread, omelets, and other goodies are served every morning.

Rooms and *cabinas*, one with a kitchenette, are cool and immaculate, where expertly crafted gleaming wood and pale adobe architecture come together, accented with high quality furnishing. There are nods to Cahuita's hippie heart and soul in some of the international fabrics and artwork inside, but these tastefully bohemian touches merely make this bed-and-breakfast's exceptional quality stand out even more.

Nature Lodges

North of Puerto Limón
ARCHIE FIELD'S
RÍO COLORADO LODGE
Owner: Dan Wise
506-2232-8610; 800-243-9777 USA and Canada
www.riocoloradolodge.com
tarpon@racsa.co.cr
Barra del Colorado
Price: Very Expensive*
Credit Cards: Yes
Handicap Access: Yes

One of Costa Rica's premier fishing lodges, isolated in the undeveloped Barra del Colorado National Wildlife Refuge and legendary for tarpon that average 35 kilograms (80 pounds), but regularly break 80 kilograms (200 pounds); and world-class snook that range from 10 to 20 kilograms (22 to 45 pounds). Most people book all-inclusive packages that include two-day guided trips on their fleet of 23-foot fiberglass boats equipped with every possible necessity and amenity, including all tackle and a fully stocked cooler. Not enough? Feel free to fish for *guapote*, *mojarra*, and *machaca* from the dock.

The whole place is built on stilts, including a recreation room with a pool table, full bar, and satellite TV, and several covered outdoor lounging areas. There's even a small zoo and animal rehabilitation center inherited from the previous owners. Rooms are huge, air-conditioned, and basic, not fancy but good enough for star anglers like Orlando Wilson. If you're here to enjoy the non-edible wildlife, they'll certainly arrange all sorts of nature tours; one of the best involves a fabulous riverboat trip from Puerto Viejo de Sarapiquí. Also check out nearby **Silver King Lodge** (506-711-0708; www.silverkinglodge.net; $$$$*) and **Casa Mar Lodge** (800-543-0282; www.casamarlodge.com; $$$$*), with similar rates, amenities, and monster tarpon.

PACHIRA LODGE (INCLUDING EVERGREEN AND ANHINGA LODGES)
Owner: Guillermo Ortiz Acuña
506-2256-7080
www.pachiralodge.com
info@pachiralodge.com
Tortuguero, 2 km north of village on canal
Price: Expensive to Very Expensive, all-inclusive
Credit Cards: Yes
Handicap Access: Yes

Just across the canal from the village of Tortuguero, this is actually three fabulous lodges in one. Pachira, the flagship property, is a modern and architecturally interesting family-style lodge burnished to a high sheen, with excellent service and very comfortable, fan-cooled rooms, with lots of windows and attractive furnishings surrounding a turtle-shaped pool. (The head is actually the whirlpool—nice.) Buffet meals are included, including wine at dinner, as well as turtle tours, sportfishing trips, and other excursions throughout the region.

Across the causeway, they've built more rustic, and less expensive, Evergreen Lodge, with 16 little fan-cooled cabins on stilts with private hot-water baths. The vibe is much more "in the jungle," and will appeal to those having a Tarzan-and-Jane moment. If you're looking for something a bit more comfortable, try the brand new Anhinga Hotel & Spa, which will have even nicer accommodations and amenities, including a full-service spa, than the Pachira.

RÍO PARISMINA LODGE

Owner: Judy Heidt
800-338-5688 toll-free international line
www.riop.com
fish@riop.com
Parismina, halfway between Puerto Limón and Tortuguero
Price: Very Expensive*
Credit Cards: Yes
Handicap Access: No

This deluxe, all-inclusive fishing lodge is also the best hotel in Parismina, with rates that include daily fishing trips into the fertile mouth of the Río Parismina, where voracious schools of huge silvery tarpon, snook, tuna, mackerel, *guapote*, *mojarra*, snapper, and even bull sharks are just waiting to be pulled out of the water. Spacious, fan-cooled wooden rooms are comfortable but basic, with large windows and a few pieces of furniture set around fabulous gardens with covered hammocks, a pool, and Jacuzzi. They also arrange all sorts of nature tours, including nighttime crocodile tours and nesting turtle excursions in season.

Two other Parismina fishing lodges offer similar amenities, **Caribbean Expedition Lodge** (506-232-8118; www.costaricasportfishing.com; $$$$*) and **Jungle Tarpon Lodge** (800-544-2261; www.jungletarpon.com).

★ TORTUGA LODGE & GARDENS

Manager: Valentin Corral
506-2257-0766
www.costaricaexpeditions.com
costaric@expeditions.co.cr
Tortuguero, across from the airstrip
Price: Moderate to Expensive*

Credit Cards: Yes
Handicap Access: Yes

Operated by the always-outstanding Costa Rica Expeditions, this great jungle lodge is an even better value as part of an all-inclusive package, including all meals, a guided park tour, and transportation from San José; take the canals at least one way. In between, you'll relax in this sprawling wooden structure overlooking the river. It's very comfortable, if not exactly luxurious, with large, fan-cooled rooms with pleasant color schemes, huge screened windows, and acceptable décor. It's worth another $50 for the palatial penthouse suite, upstairs, with better mattresses and views, nice wicker-furnished seating areas, and a bigger bathroom.

They arrange all sorts of tours, including fishing trips on the *Bull Shark*, a beautifully built, flat-bottomed fishing boat custom-designed to maneuver the canals by the lodge's original owner and former National Tarpon Fishing Champion, Eddie Brown.

SOUTH OF PUERTO LIMÓN

PUNTA MONA CENTER FOR SUSTAINABLE LIVING AND EDUCATION

Grandfather and President: Padi
Mother: Tiffany
506-2222-0135, 506-2222-4568
www.puntamona.org
info@puntamona.org
6 km south of Manzanillo, 10 km north of Gandoca
Price: Inexpensive*
Credit Cards: No
Handicap Access: No
Special: Reservations required

In the heart of the Gandoca-Manzanillo Wildlife Refuge, accessible only by a swampy but scenic hike (guide recommended) or shuttle boat ($15, three-person minimum), a tribe of idealists both Tico and international are hoping to construct a clean and sustainable world. The basic lodge, including a yoga studio and dock, is built with fallen wood and sustainable materials. Electricity comes from solar panels; drinking water from a sand-filtered rain cache. Your meals, all included, are mostly grown here; organic vegetables, herbs, and more than 100 tropical fruits, including organic bananas that you may have already paid a few cents extra for at Wholefoods back home (an excellent investment in our collective future; thanks!). It's not flawless, but if you'd like to learn more about how humans might possibly thrive without destroying so much that we cherish, this might be a great place for you. They also offer day trips, including lunch and boat transport from Manzanillo, for $65.

SELVA BANANITO LODGE

Owner: Jürgen Stein
506-2253-8118
www.selvabananito.com
reserves@selvabananito.com
About 25 km (15 mi.) southwest of Puerto Limón
Price: Very Expensive*
Credit Cards: Yes
Handicap Access: No

Getting there is half the fun, and it's done in a high-clearance four-wheel-drive (transport provided as part of a package deal), as you'll need to cross four fairly serious streams. Then relax and let your cynicism about ecotourism evaporate into the 850 hectares (2,000 acres) of primary highland rain forest bordering La Amistad National Park. Cabins, made with lumber that could not have been sold, are rustic but pretty, with ceramic-tiled floors stretching from spacious bedrooms out onto private porches overlooking the rain forest. Beds are comfortable and the showers are solar heated, but there's no electricity; lighting is by candle or lantern.

Bananito takes ecotourism seriously, with blackwater treatment in all-natural ponds (with flowers!); biodegradable toi-

letries; and even offers a three-night "carbon neutral" package to help offset your flight here. Other packages, with your choice of "hard" or "soft" adventure, are a bit less esoteric. Mostly organic meals are included, and they can accommodate vegetarians.

Other Hotels

CARIARI

Hotel Central (506-2767-6890; central Cariari; $) You're probably spending the night in this hard-working banana town because you want to take the wildlife packed morning boat to Tortuguero. Patricia, the lovely proprietress of this rather basic budget spot caters to international tourists, with simple but spotless rooms with shared bath, guarded parking, luggage storage, and travel arrangements.

GANDOCA

Cabinas Orquideas (506-2754-2392; central Gandoca; $) The best of a handful of very basic budget lodges in this almost undeveloped village, Orquideas even has some clean, wooden rooms with private cold-water showers. All meals are included for just $5 more.

GUÁPILES

★ **Casa Río Blanco** (506-2710-4124; www.casarioblanco.com; Río Blanco, 7 km south of Guápiles, 1 km south of the bridge; $$*) There are several decent budget hotels in central Guápiles, but this wonderful option, perched atop a 20-meter (60-foot) cliff overlooking burbling Río Blanco and stunning rain forest canopy, offers simple, tin-roofed wooden cabins with private hot showers, wonderful art, and amazing porches, as well as a swimming hole just a short hike away.

SIXAOLA

Hotel Imperio (506-2754-2289; across from police checkpoint; $) If you get stuck in Sixaola, this is the safest, cleanest

Puerto Viejo de Talamanca's nightlife is as mellow, or as festive, as you want.

option, where very basic wooden rooms come with private cold baths.

Vacation Rentals

★ **Agapi Apartments** (506-2750-0446; www.agapisite.com; 1 km south of Puerto Viejo; $*) Huge, teak, beachfront apartments, some with full kitchens, can also be rented nightly.

Aguas Claras (506-2750-0131; www.aguas claras-cr.com; Playa Chiquita, 5 km south of Puerto Viejo; $$–$$$) Absolutely adorable gingerbread bungalows so photogenic that they appeared in the movie *Caribe*, come fully equipped for two to eight people.

Caribe Sur Real Estate (506-2759-9138; www.caribesur-realestate.com) A wide range of vacation rentals all over the southern Caribbean.

★ **Cashew Hill** (506-2750-0256; www.cashewhilllodge.co.cr; Puerto Viejo; $$–$$$) Above Puerto Viejo, this creative, col-orful collection of cleverly decorated casitas come fully equipped for free spirits.

Finca Chica (506-2750-1919; www.finca chica.com) Fine houses for rent on Playa Cocles.

★ **Pachamama** (506-2759-9196; pacha mamacaribe.com; Punta Uva; $$) Flawless houses and bungalows come with bikes.

RESTAURANTS AND FOOD PURVEYORS

Perhaps the best reason to visit the Caribbean Coast is the cuisine, undeniably Costa Rica's finest. Nothing against the *casado*, but Caribbean dishes are seasoned so subtly with coconut milk, ginger, fresh pepper, and West Indian curry that there simply is no comparison.

The classic dish is called (even by Spanish speakers) "rice-n-beans," like a *gallo pinto* slowly simmered in coconut milk and spices. Try it with spicy, slow cooked jerk chicken, so tender it falls off the bone, or whole fried fish, often served in ginger or curry sauce. *Patacones* are Caribbean-style plantains; instead of the soft, sweet versions you'll get on the Spanish side of the country, these are cooked green and hard fried, sometimes with cheese on top. *Pati*, or spicy meat-and-vegetable fried pies, are sold everywhere, as is *pan de coco*, bread made with coconut milk. The most famous dish, which you really must try, is *rondón*, a slow-cooked stew of fish, lobster, root vegetables, coconut milk, and anything else the chef could "run down."

For dessert, try regional sweets such as the gingery *pan bon*, laden with candied fruit, *ginyaqué* (ginger cookies) and *plantintó*, a festival candy made from plantains and brightly colored for effect.

Puerto Viejo and Cahuita are also home to scores of Italian, French, American, and other immigrants, who serve up a wide variety of international cuisine.

Restaurant and Food Purveyor Price Code

The following prices are based on the cost of a dinner entrée with a non-alcoholic drink, not including the 13 percent taxes and 10 percent gratuity added to the cost of almost all restaurant meals (except for the very cheapest *sodas*). Menus note whether or not their listed prices include this hefty 23 percent total surcharge, some listing two sets of prices.

Inexpensive ($)	Up to $5
Moderate ($$)	$5 to $10
Expensive ($$$)	$10 to $20
Very Expensive ($$$$)	$20 or more

Restaurants

PUERTO LIMÓN
★ RESTAURANT BRISAS DE CARIBE
506-2758-0138
Puerto Limón, across from Parque Vargas
Price: Inexpensive to Moderate

Credit Cards: Yes
Cuisine: Caribbean, Costa Rican
Serving: B, L, D
Reservations: No
Handicap Access: Yes

A fine excuse to stop and enjoy Puerto Limón is this lovely little restaurant in the city center, which opens right onto Parque Vargas, sometime pitched as the "prettiest city park in Costa Rica." That's probably an overstatement, but this urban jungle of towering trees, some with sloths (pay one of the enterprising children 100 colones to point one out), presided over by a grand gazebo painted in peeling pastels, is a fine place to sit or stroll.

Stretch your legs for a moment and take a look out over the sea wall to see Isla Uvita, where Christopher Columbus once stood and named this land Costa Rica, the "Rich Coast." Then, kick back at an outdoor table at Brisas de Caribe, "Breezes of the Caribbean." It's several steps above a *soda*, with a solid steam table buffet at lunch and great Limonese-style typical food all day. It's not really anything special, except that it is.

NORTH OF PUERTO LIMÓN
Pickings are slim in the tiny villages of Parismina and Barra del Colorado, where you'll choose between the all-inclusive lodges or very basic *sodas*. Tortuguero has a few more options in the village: Try **Miss Miriam's** (506-2709-8002; $–$$), with fantastic Caribbean cuisine at great prices; or more upscale ★**Miss Junie's** (506-2709-8029; $$–$$$), where it's best to order your food early in the day so she'll have time to let it simmer.

SOUTH OF PUERTO LIMÓN
AMIMODO
506-2750-0257
300m south of Puerto Viejo, Punta Salsa Brava
Price: Expensive to Very Expensive
Credit Cards: Yes

Cuisine: Italian, Seafood
Serving D; L on weekends
Handicap Access: Yes
Reservations: Yes

Begin with the fresh fish prosciutto, the catch of the day thinly sliced and prepared Italian style, perfect with some special vintage from the wine list. This is a romantic place, where the ecotourists and expats wear their carefully casual bohemian best. You can eat inside, at the friendly full bar, where there's live music, often salsa and merengue, every Friday at least. More romantic are the candlelit tables outside, right on the sandy beach.

Everything on the menu is delicious, but try the tropical ravioli, homemade pasta stuffed with shrimp, pineapple, curry, and coconut sautéed in a white wine reduction sauce. Or go high-end, with the *parillada mixta*, an impressive seafood platter for two.

CASA CREOLE

506-2755-0035
www.hotelmagellininn.com
Cahuita, 2 km south at Playa Negra, in the Magellan Inn
Closed: Sun.
Price: Moderate to Expensive
Credit Cards: Yes
Cuisine: French Caribbean
Serving: D
Reservations: Yes
Handicap Access: Challenging

Pure candle-lit elegance in the lush tropics, this longstanding French-Caribbean restaurant is considered one of the region's best. Start with a shrimp cocktail, flavored with coconut and pineapple, or *acras*, a spicy and very traditional Caribbean fried fish appetizer. Mains change regularly, but the quintessential French-Caribbean dish is lobster thermidor, in which lobster meat is mixed with a rich sauce with hints of brandy and mustard, then browned inside the shell. Desserts are the specialty of the house, with such delights raspberry *coulis*, *profiteroles*, and crème brûlée.

CHA CHA CHA!

506-2394-4153
Cahuita, main road, 200m inland
Open: 2 PM–10 PM, Tue.–Sun.
Price: Expensive
Credit Cards: Yes
Cuisine: International
Serving: D
Reservations: Recommended
Handicap Access: No

Everyone loves this fun spot in a freshly painted wooden bungalow. The menu is eclectic and international, always starting with top quality meats and very fresh seafood. Just add great service, music, and flavor from all over the world, and you've got a recipe for one of the most popular places in town. From Caribbean cuisine to Italian pastas and spicy Thai salads, there's something for everyone. This probably isn't the place for folks in a hurry, however; everything is cooked fresh and served to order, so it might take a while for your meal to arrive.

CHILE ROJO

506-2750-0319
Puerto Viejo, city center
Closed: Wed.
Price: Moderate
Credit Cards: No
Cuisine: Asian
Reservations: No
Handicap Access: No

This small Asian-fusion restaurant is one of Puerto Viejo's most popular restaurants, with good reason: Great prices, great service, and food that transcends 99.9 percent of all the greasy Chinese takeout available elsewhere in the country. Thursday is sushi night, where $10 buys all you can eat; the place gets packed. Or come anytime for favorites including the deliciously spiced Thai green curry, or the Chile Rojo cheeseburgers, with chipotle aioli. Vegetarians will rejoice at their choices, not just the stir-fries and curries; the veggie combo platter includes samosas, falafel, hummus, tabbouleh, olives, and cheese.

E-Z TIMES
506-2750-0663
Puerto Viejo, city center
Price: Moderate
Credit Cards: Yes
Cuisine: Seafood, International
Serving: L, D
Reservations: No
Handicap Access: No

A relaxing way to end your day is at this mellow eatery just steps from the sea, with lots of colorful Indian- and Asian-print pillows that make the long community tables that much more comfortable. The music is great and the scene friendly, centered on a wood-fired oven, where pizza and other dishes are made. There is a friendly bar, serving a host of festive cocktails. The fish tacos are rumored to be the best on the coast, but I opted for the Nicaraguan fish soup: Absolutely exquisite.

EL LOCO NATURAL
506-2750-0263
Puerto Viejo, 400m south of town
Closed: Wed. in slow season
Price: Inexpensive to Moderate
Credit Cards: No
Cuisine: International, vegetarian
Serving: D
Handicap Access: Yes

This Puerto Viejo institution just relocated from its funky upstairs, downtown digs to a newer, bigger spot by the beach, even better for showing off your new dreadlocks. You've got choices: Pick your entrée (beef, chicken, fish, vegetarian, vegan, and so on), your veggies, and one of several exotic

sauces, such as green madras curries, spicy coconut Caribbean style, or smoky chipotle cream sauce. Then let them do their thing. Shake it out with the live acoustic music appearing onstage at least twice a week, almost nightly in high season. There's also a full bar.

★ MAXI'S
506-2759-9073
Manzanillo, 13 km south of Puerto Viejo
Price: Moderate to Expensive
Credit Cards: Yes
Cuisine: Caribbean
Serving: L, D
Handicap Access: No
Reservations: No

At the end of the road from Puerto Viejo, just before the Gandoca-Manzanillo Wildlife Refuge becomes tangled jungle, rises this landmark, two-story wooden restaurant and bar, where everyone in town gathers for a cold beer, fabulous seafood, maybe some live music, and a tall tale or two.

Maxi's is most famous for its amazing *rondón*, but try the whole fried fish (or lobster, in season) served with rice, beans, *patacones*, and love. The vibe is a little bit wild and the service can be uneven, but those fine beach views and rain forest hues with exotic flavors and reggae thumping in the background will make this a memory you'll hold dear.

★ MISS EDITH'S
506-2755-0248
Cahuita, 110m northeast of the police station
Price: Moderate to Very Expensive
Credit Cards: No
Cuisine: Caribbean, Costa Rican
Serving L, D
Reservations: No

This is the quintessential Caribbean dining experience. Hidden away in the southeast corner of Cahuita, you'll find this humble wooden restaurant just above the waves, surrounded by coconut palms and fishing boats, some perhaps used to catch the incredible meal you're about to enjoy.

Pull up a wooden chair and peruse the simple menu, offering what one well-traveled friend calls "the best jerk chicken in Costa Rica." I've always opted for the fresh fish (lobster, chicken, and vegetarian choices are also available), served whole in coconut sauces, Caribbean curries, and other traditional preparations. Fish in ginger curry arrives whole and sizzling on an oversized plate, topped by a mountain of onions and swimming in the remarkably rich sauce, which you can sop up with the bobo rice, a yellow grain cooked with cassava and carrot, and root vegetables served on the side. Vegetarians must try Miss Edith's meatless *rondón*, almost as good as the real thing.

QUE RICO PAPITO

506-2750-7045
www.lacostadepapito.com
Playa Cocles, 1.5 km (1 mi.) south of Puerto Viejo
Price: Moderate to Expensive
Credit Cards: Yes
Cuisine: International
Serving: B, L, D
Handicap Access: Yes
Reservations: Yes

At La Costa de Papito, a fine little midrange hotel with cute bungalows ($$*) across from the fabulous blue-flag surfing beach of Playa Cocles, this rustic restaurant serves what Chef Walter Bustos calls "biodegradable" cuisine. Start with one of their wonderful salads, served (and this is a rarity in Costa Rica) with your choice of several dressings. Then it's your choice of appetizers, including ceviche served inside carved-out red peppers, or perhaps some Peruvian *causa* (mashed yuca and potatoes layered with seafood and rich sauces). Thai

chicken, Caribbean coconut soup, or even lobster in a light wine and lemon sauce could be your appetizer; choices change with the day's catch and harvest. There's often live music, including jazz and world music, a solid wine list, and lots of cocktails served at their popular Sloth Society Bar.

PECORA NERA

506-2750-0490
pecoranera@racsa.co.cr
Playa Cocles, 2 km south of Puerto Viejo
Price: Moderate to Very Expensive
Cuisine: Italian
Serving: L, D
Credit Cards: Yes
Reservations: Recommended

Puerto Viejo is quite the Italian outpost, and you'll notice the endearingly lilted Spanish and spectacular cuisine all over the area. There must be a dozen great Italian restaurants in town, but ask anyone where they'd like you to take them to dinner. This polished teak-and-flagstone restaurant, with white tablecloths and candles, will be the answer.

There is, indeed, a menu, and everything on it shines. But the key to enjoying your evening to its fullest is placing your faith in the tastes of the owner-chef, who comes up with a few fresh flavors every evening as a special. Seafood, homemade pastas and gnocchis, and delicious desserts are always worth a try.

SOBRE LAS OLAS

506-2755-0109
Cahuita, 200m north on the beachfront road
Closed: Tue.
Price: Expensive
Cuisine: Seafood, Italian
Serving L, D
Credit Cards: Yes
Reservations: Yes

The name means "Over the Waves," and

that's where you'll dine at this rustic and romantic spot just above the surf. The specialty is seafood, with either Italian or Caribbean flair: Will you be having the garlic shrimp, with more Mediterranean flavor, or perhaps the locally inspired snapper in coconut sauce? The beef is also outstanding, or opt for a plate of fresh pasta. Presentation is divine, as befits a place benefiting from such views, and often involves fresh herbs. There's a good wine list and hammocks on the patio outside.

Food Purveyors

Bakeries

Bread and Chocolate (506-2750-0723; central Puerto Viejo) Great breakfasts are served with your own French press, but come back for the famed truffles and fabulous brownies.

Dorling's Bakery (506-2709-8132; Tortuguero Village) Best bakery in the canals also offers fancy espresso beverages and light meals.

Cafés

Buddha Café (506-2709-8084; Tortuguero Village; open 9 AM–9 PM) Mostly vegetarian menu includes pizzas, sandwiches, crêpes and more.

Café Rico (506-750-0510; Puerto Viejo, 100m south and 100m east) Combination Laundromat-café has fabulous breakfasts, Britt coffee, and fruit drinks made with honey instead of refined sugar. Free movies are shown here regularly.

Mate Latte (Playa Chiquita, 5 km south of Puerto Viejo; open 10 AM–6 PM, Mon.–Sat., 2 PM–5 PM, Sun.) Cute café on Playa Chiquita specializes in organic coffee drinks and "frosties," blended frozen fruit. Light meals include the Silk Road Plate, with hummus and carrot paté.

★ **Miss Holly's Kitchen** (506-2750-0131; Playa Chiquita, 5 km south of Puerto Viejo; $) Great coffee, free WiFi, and excellent food—try their famed fish Cariburger. Chef Flory Campos had just won the 2007 "Best Chef in Puerto Viejo," in a major upset, so they may expand the menu.

Pan Pay (506-2750-0081; central Puerto Viejo) Great breakfasts, a beachfront location, and an excellent $7 set lunch featuring Spanish cuisine, make this a popular spot.

Pizza

Cactus (506-2302-0542; Cahuita, 50m inland from Sobre Las Olas; $–$$) Open every evening except Monday with great pizza, pasta, and seafood.

★ **Café Viejo** (506-2750-0817; Puerto Viejo downtown; $$$) Probably the most popular bar/restaurant in Puerto Viejo (which is saying something), this sleek and relatively upscale evening out should most definitely include the divine thin-crust pizza.

Sodas

Bionatura (506-2758-0423; Puerto Limón, behind the cathedral) *Soda* serves Costa Rican *típico* and Caribbean classics, without the meat.

Restaurante Tamara (506-2750-0148; Puerto Viejo downtown) For 25 years, this simple *soda* presided over by Bob Marley and Haile Selassie has been offering great prices on excellent Caribbean-style typical food, along with a very full bar.

Bob Marley's words and wisdom echo along Costa Rica's Caribbean Coast.

Selvyn's (Punta Uva, 5 km south of Puerto Viejo) Local favorite serves two typical main dishes every night, and stays open till they're gone.

Grocery Stores

★ **El Duende Gourmet** (Playa Chiquita, open 7:30 AM–7 PM) Great little gourmet grocer has interesting international brands (including imported liquor) and good prices on local products.

Mas x Menos (Puerto Limón, across from the market) Convenient place to get groceries before heading south.

CULTURE

The Caribbean Coast is as connected, culturally, with Jamaica and the West Indies as it is with the rest of Costa Rica. Long separated from the Central Valley by the steep, muddy, and malaria-infested Talamanca Mountain Range, the trip from coast to coast was once a quest undertaken only by the foolhardy and desperate, such as the indigenous peoples who took refuge here after their more arable lands in the Central Valley were appropriated by Spanish settlers.

Instead, this coast was the province of British pirates like Henry Morgan, and their Miskito Indian allies (themselves a mix of African, British, and indigenous blood), who swashbuckled and plundered up and down the coast, sacking unwary Spanish homesteads and founding their own, including Cahuita (Miskito for "sanguillo tree"), a favorite seasonal hunting spot. Only once did the Spaniards make any real effort to interfere in this other world, organizing a military strike in 1709. They were beaten back by indigenous leader Pablo Presbere, and never returned.

Until 1871, when President Tomás Guardia, buoyed by coffee profits, proposed constructing a railroad that would connect San José with Puerto Limón, allowing him to ship the "golden bean" abroad much more efficiently. He contracted U.S. entrepreneur Minor C. Keith to construct the 166-kilometer (103-mile) track through uncharted jungle; more than 4,000 workers, including two of Keith's brothers, died. Locals soon stopped applying for the treacherous job, so Keith brought in contract workers, first convicts from the United States, then indentured workers from China; all succumbed to tropical diseases. Finally, Afro-Caribbeans from Jamaica and Barbados arrived, and thrived. The railroad was finally completed on June 23, 1910, but many of the workers never went home, instead staying on to participate in Keith's next venture, a little banana company that would eventually become United Fruit. By the time he died in 1929, Keith's holdings had multiplied across the Americas, the term "Banana Republic" was already a cliché, and he was one of the richest and most powerful men in the world.

Today, the descendants of his workforce, many of whom still speak English, form the backbone of the Caribbean Coast's culture. Although Limón remains Costa Rica's poorest province, thanks to tourism and shipping it is finally catching up with the rest of the country. And the rest of the country turns out for Limón's biggest party, Carnaval, which begins October 8.

Museums

CCC MUSEUM OF THE TURTLE
506-2709-8091
Tortuguero, north end of the village
Open: 10 AM–noon and 2 PM–5:30 PM, daily (closed Sun. morning)
Admission: $1

Since 1954, the Caribbean Conservation Corporation has been studying sea turtles along this 35-kilometer (22-mile) stretch of black sand beach, discovering most of what we curious humans know about the mysterious creatures. The CCC's conservation model—developing ecotourism opportunities for area residents and providing an alternative income to that provided by harvesting the turtles and eggs, rather than just policing the nests—has been so successful that it's now employed throughout Costa Rica and the world. You can learn more about sea turtles and the CCC at this small, informative, and kid-friendly museum. The CCC also offers basic, dorm-style lodging and organizes pricey volunteer opportunities.

MUSEO ETHNOHISTÓRICO DE LIMÓN
506-2758-2130
Puerto Limón, 100m south of Parque Vargas
Open: 9 AM–noon and 1 PM–4 PM, Mon.–Fri.
Admission: Free

This small museum on the second floor of the post office will theoretically be open by the time this book hits the stands, featuring exhibits of Limón's history and ethnography.

Music and Nightlife

Nightlife, in particular live music, in Puerto Limón is legendary, but unless you know some Spanish and can handle yourself in potentially spirited situations (read: drugs, guns, and alcohol), it's probably best to stick to the tourist quarter close to Parque Vargas. Cevichito, 50m inland from the park, has a film noir vibe and great food.

In the sparsely populated North Caribbean, it's usually your choice of a drink at the lodge, or boozing it up with the fisherman at very basic bars. South of Limón, however, Cahuita and Puerto Viejo offer two of Costa Rica's best nightlife scenes. Here are just a few of your options; be sure to hit Maxi's (see Restaurants, earlier) at least once.

Baba Yaga (506-2388-4359; 50m west of Hot Rocks) Decent Caribbean restaurant has a popular Ladies' Night every Tuesday and Reggae Night, with live DJs, on Tuesday and Sunday.

El Dorado (506-2750-0604; Puerto Viejo, downtown) Slightly divey and very popular restaurant/bar has a pool table, happy hour, and OK food.

Hot Rocks (Puerto Viejo, downtown; open 3 PM–2:30 AM; $$) Under the big red tent, serves cold brews, cocktails, great food, and three free movies each night at 6:30 PM, 7:45 PM, and 9:45 PM.

Johnny's Place (downtown Puerto Viejo) The place to dance Thursday through Saturday starts up the reggae at 10 PM.

Restaurant Stanford (506-2750-0016; 200m south of Puerto Viejo) Classic drinking spot has been remodeled, but still serves great seafood, music, and awesome views of Salsa Brava.

RECREATION

Parks and Preserves

There are more than 40 parks and protected areas on the Caribbean Coast, most of them poorly developed for visitors. For complete listings, check out Costa Rica National Parks Web site (www.costarica-nationalparks.com); area tour offices can probably arrange guided trips to any of them.

NORTH OF PUERTO LIMÓN
BARRA DEL COLORADO NATIONAL WILDLIFE REFUGE
www.costarica-nationalparks.com/barradelcoloradowildliferefuge.html
Northern Limón
Open: Ranger station open 8 AM–4 PM
Admission: $7.25

One of the world's wettest places, Costa Rica's largest wildlife refuge is an 81,000-hectare (200,070-acre) maze of canals, rivers, and seasonal swampland choked with lush and overgrown jungle. Accessible only by boat or plane, this unbelievably wildlife-rich protected area is most famous for huge tarpon. Almost inaccessible otherwise, the only easy way to see the jaguars, tapirs, manatees, and innumerable waterfowl in its freshwater, saltwater, and mangrove ecosystems is by booking one of the all-inclusive fishing lodges at the mouth of the Río Colorado, all of which will happily arrange nature tours.

The park itself is undeveloped and almost unprotected; only six park guards patrol this swampy expanse, versus a small army of hunters, loggers, narco-traffickers, and *hueveros* (sea turtle egg harvesters). For this, it's sometimes called a "paper park," protected legally, but in reality wide open to exploitation. There's only one way this is likely change, tourism. So drop by.

TORTUGUERO NATIONAL PARK

506-2710-2929, 506-2710-2939
www.costarica-nationalparks.com/tortugueronationalpark.html
Northern Limón Province
Open: 8 AM–4 PM, daily
Admission: $10

One of Costa Rica's most popular and important parks, the "mini-Amazon" is accessible only by boat, along canals of slow-moving dark water threading 19,000 hectares (77,032 acres) of otherwise impenetrable wilderness. It's home to more than 450 species of birds—more than in all of Europe—as well as some 60 mammals and almost 200 reptiles and amphibians, including the water-walking Jesus lizard.

Tortuguero's most famous visitors drop by between June and October, some 30,000 green sea turtles who haul their graceful bulk from the saltwater to nest right here, as they have for millennia. Several hundred leatherbacks visit November through May, a number that continues to drop. Only a handful of the incredibly endangered hawksbills still make their way here, as they are cruelly harvested, and not even for meat; their shells are used to make that tacky jewelry that looks like cheap Chinese plastic. Loggerheads also drop by.

Most park visitors stay in Tortuguero Village or one of the nearby all-inclusive lodges, where they can arrange guided riverboat tours, explore the park in canoes, or climb Cerro Tortuguero, a 119-meter (390-foot) volcanic hill with panoramic views over lowlands. During turtle season, every hotel room in Tortuguero fills up, so make reservations. Turtle tours ($10) are arranged at the ranger station or through your hotel. Only 400 guests are allowed on the beaches at one time, so make reservations.

SOUTH OF PUERTO LIMÓN
CAHUITA NATIONAL PARK

506-2755-0461, 506-2755-0060
www.costarica-nationalparks.com/cahuitanationalpark.html
Cahuita, 100m south of town center
Open: 8 AM–4 PM, daily
Admission: $10 at Puerto Vargas Ranger Station, by donation at Kelly Creek in Cahuita

This beautiful and easily visited national park, home to muddy trails that access 14 kilometers (8 miles) of some of the sweetest sugary white beaches you've ever seen, is actually more important for what lies offshore. Its 22,000 marine hectares (54,340 acres) protect the only fully developed coral reef in Costa Rica, which wraps around the end of the peninsula. This surreal concentration of wildlife, which locals claim is the most biodiverse place in the world, meter for meter, boasts some 35 species of coral, 128 seaweeds, 140 molluscs, 44 crustaceans, and more than 125 fish, including the parrot fish, queen angel fish, isabelita, manta ray, and three types of shark, as well as sea urchins, white shrimp, and marine sponges, all frolicking among the elkhorn, brain coral, and venus sea fans. At the mouth of the Río Perezoso (Sloth River), there's even a shipwrecked slave boat from the mid-1700s. Unfortunately, the reef is dying, so please treat it carefully.

Several tour outfitters in Cahuita organize snorkel tours and hiking trips throughout the park, as well as sea turtle tours during nesting season. The park has two entrances, Kelly Creek, conveniently right in Cahuita; and Puerto Vargas, just south of town, which has access to the park's best swimming beaches (the reef and currents make swimming diffi-cult and/or dangerous elsewhere). You can hike the 7-kilometer (4.2-mile) trail connecting the two, then easily catch a bus back to town.

GANDOCA-MANZANILLO NATIONAL WILDLIFE REFUGE

506-2759-9100
www.costarica-nationalparks.com/gandocamanzanillowildliferefuge.html
Limón Province, 100m south of Manzanillo
Open: 8 AM–4 PM, daily
Admission: $7

Indigenous Reserves

Several tour operators visit area indigenous reserves, including the **Talamanca-Bribrí Indigenous Reserve**, boasting several tours and trails, but most famously 30-meter (100-foot) Volio Waterfall; the **Keköldi-Bribrí Reserve**, with an iguana farm, herb garden, and craft stores; **Talamanca-Cabecar Indigenous Reserve**, which is just beginning to accept tourists into their communities, by reservation only; and the **Yorkin Indigenous Reserve** on the Panama border, which offers *cayuko* (canoe) trips, hikes to Cerro Buena Vista, and overnight adventures in their very basic lodge.

These indigenous reservations were set aside in 1977, and have basically autonomous governments that theoretically base their economies on rational use of resources, though in reality, many people work grueling hours in the banana plantations for a few dollars a day. Ecotourism has proven prof-itable, particularly for Keköldi Reserve, which is closest to Puerto Viejo. Other groups are now gradu-ally accommodating visitors with tours, souvenirs, and even lodging. Still, many residents have rather conflicted feelings toward the camera-snapping tourists visiting their relatively poor communities in growing numbers. (Wouldn't you?) So please be respectful, and see what you can learn from these people who have lived so differently from you. Operators offering tours include:

ATEC (Ecotourism and Conservation Association of Talamanca; 506-2750-0191; www.greencoast .com/atec.htm; Downtown Puerto Viejo) Grassroots, non-profit federation of tour guides and concerned locals focuses on small-scale, locally-owned, sustainable tourism, and can arrange great tours to any of the reserves.

Talamanca Network for Community Ecotourism (506-2756-8136; www.actuarcostarica.com; Hone Creek, between Cahuita and Puerto Viejo) Offers community conscious guided hikes and overnight tours throughout the area, usually staying at very basic lodges in campesino or indige-nous villages.

Willie's Tours (506-2843-4700; www.willies-costarica-tours.com; central Cahuita) This feisty, Eng-lish-speaking operator doesn't bother with being quite so politically correct, he just gives great tours to the Keköldi Reservation. His office also offers the fastest Internet access on the Caribbean.

Stretching from Punta Uva south to the tiny town of Gandoca, this 9,449-hectare (23,332-acre) refuge is multi-use. About 90 percent of the park is still privately owned, including the town of Manzanillo, where you'll find the MINAE office where you can pay the entrance fee and organize guides, if the rangers are there.

There are several trails through the park, most of them muddy and poorly marked; you're better off hiring a guide here or through any of the tour operators in and around Puerto Viejo. I like **ATEC** (506-2750-0191; www.greencoast.com/atec.htm), with several options for tours, or try the **Association de Guías de Manzanillo** (505-2759-9064; 506-2759-9043; crlocalguide@hotmail.com) offering set prices for hikes by accredited guides, including specialists in bird-watching, snake-watching, medicinal plants, and more.

There is much to do in this still rather disorganized refuge. Coral reefs close to Punta Uva, Punta Mona, and Manzanillo are visited by several operators offer snorkeling and diving trips, often in conjunction with dolphin tours or trips to Gandoca Lagoon (home to the rare and tiny freshwater tucuxí dolphin).

Or hike into the mountains, carpeted with rich rain forest characterized by the massive cativo tree, so dense that light rarely reaches the understory. Or head to the beaches, fringed with coconut palms and almonds, perfect for sunbathing, but because of fierce currents and sharp coral, not so great for swimming. The refuge is also home to at least 350 bird species, three types of monkeys, jaguarundis, ocelots, caimans, manatees, several different dart frogs, and 35 nesting couples of the endangered green macaw. Punta Mona (see Accommodations, earlier) offers simple lodging and tours right in the heart of it all.

LA CEIBA PRIVATE RESERVE
506-2750-0275
www.rpceiba.com
From Punta Uva, 8km south of Puerto Viejo toward Manzanillo, 2km after signed turnoff
Open: By reservation
Admission: $30

Adjacent to Gandoca-Manzanillo Wildlife Refuge, this 42-hectare (104-acre) private reserve protects another important piece of tropical humid rain forest that's home to vibrant quantities of Caribbean life, including several remarkable ceiba trees. Guided tours should be arranged in advance, and prices include lunch and a naturalist guide; a boat tour can be added on. The reserve also rents three remarkable, fully equipped teak villas ($$–$$$*) with stunning views over the jungle.

Agriculture Tours
Las Cusingas (506-2382-5805; turnoff 2 km east of Guápiles, from there 4 km on 4WD road; $5, including guide) Botanical garden and research station focuses on edible and medicinal plants, offering tours and horseback rides.

Costa Flores (506-2716-7645; north of Guácimo; open by appointment; $12) Tours of this enormous flower farm, with more than 500 varieties on 120 hectares (300 acres), are geared to the cruise ship crowd, but can be seen independently with advance notice.

EARTH (506-2713-0000; www.earth.ac.cr; Pocoro Guácimo) International non-profit university offers programs in sustainable agriculture and natural resource management, develops eco-friendly crops, has a great souvenir shop, and can arrange tours ($10–$20) and lodging.

★ **Finca La Isla** (506-2750-0046; www.greencoast.com/garden.htm; Black Beach, 500m north of Puerto Viejo; open 10 AM–4 PM, daily; admission $5, with tour $10) The Caribbean Coast's most extensive botanical garden includes more than 60 types of tropical fruits; crops including pepper, cinnamon, ginger, vanilla, and chocolate; and scores of flowering plants. Beautiful.

Standard Fruit Banana Tour (506-2768-8683; www.bananatourcostarica.com) Dole's parent company offers group tours, by appointment, at three plantations near Siquirres.

Boat Tours

Victor Barrantos (506-2709-8055; 506-2709-8015; www.tortugueroinfocr.com; Tortuguero Village) Boat tours through Tortuguero National Park and canals.

Cahuita Tours (506-2755-0000, 506-2755-0101; www.cahuitatours.com; cahuitatours@yahoo.com) Antonio Mora offers excellent tours of Cahuita national park, including hiking, snorkeling, and even trips through the coral reef in a glass-bottomed boat.

Jungle Jessie's (506-2711-0939; jessie@junglejessietours.com; Parismina) Riverboat tours and fishing trips around Parismina; also offers guided hikes and boogie board rentals.

★ **Daryl Loth** (506-2833-0827; casamarbella.tripod.com; Tortuguero Village, scross from Catholic church) Biologist and renowned naturalist guide offers great prices on top-notch three-hour boat tours ($15), two-hour turtle tours in season and several guided hikes, including up 119-meter (390-foot) Tortuguero Hill ($15, including boat transport).

Canopy Tours and More

Brisas de la Jungla (506-2797-1291; www.junglebreeze.com) Just 15 kilometers (9 miles) from Puerto Limón and geared to the cruise ship crowd, this canopy tour comprises 12 cables, a 2.4-kilometer (1.5-mile) horseback ride and a guided 1-kilometer (.6-mile) hike.

Terraventuras Canyoning (506-2750-0750; www.terraventuras.com; Puerto Viejo) This serious canopy delivers, with 23 decks and 2,760 meters (2,990 yards) of cables, and can be combined with canyoning (rappelling down a waterfall) or several other tours.

Tortuguero Canopy (506-2256-7080; www.pachiralodge.com; $25) Rates for this respectable eight-platform, 11-bridge canopy include boat transport from your hotel.

Chocolate Tours

If you love chocolate, you'll particularly enjoy these tours offering the opportunity to see it grown, ground, and simmered into the sweet treat you've always adored—and you'll finally get to try fresh cocoa fruit.

Cacao Trails Chocolate Tour (506-2756-8186; www.cacaotrails.com; 10 km south of Cahuita across from the Tree House Hotel; admission $20, guide $5) More than just a chocolate tour, this labor of love includes a Chocolate Museum, with antique machinery, old photos, and informative displays; an Indian Museum, with Bribri crafts; organic gardens, with different fruits, veggies, and flowers; and even the option of a canoe tour through area waterways.

ChocoArt Tour (506-2750-0075; chocoart@racsa.co.cr; Playa Chiquita; $15, four person minimum) Make reservations for this Swiss-run chocolate tour.

Petromila Nalenga, of Tsiru úe Cacao House, extracts beans from the cacao fruit.

★ **Tsiru úe Cacao House** (Puerto Viejo, 5.5 km south on road to Bribrí; $5) Petromila Nalengana, who grew up in an isolated Bribri village, offers this sometimes funny and always sweet tour of her jungle gardens and traditional home, where you'll watch her prepare chocolate from scratch, mixed with natural flavorings such as coffee, coconut, and vanilla.

Diving and Snorkeling

Aquamor (506-2759-9612; www.greencoast.com/aquamor2.htm; aquamor1@racsa.co.cr; Manzanillo) Dive operator offers a variety of dives and snorkel tours, as well as resort courses and Gandoca Lagoon dives, all with an educational bent.

Reef Runner Divers (506-2750-0480, 506-8879-1537 cell; www.reefrunnerdivers.com; on the beach next to the police station, Puerto Viejo) Offers several different dives, certification courses, multi-day package deals, rentals, snorkeling, and other options, including nude diving and dolphin tours.

The Snorkeling House (506-2361-1924; www.centralelements.com/tanostours, Cahuita, at Miss Edith's) Offers all the snorkeling tours with one delightful bonus: breakfast and/or lunch at Miss Edith's restaurant.

Other Activities

Caribbean Costa Ricans (506-2798-2203; www.caribbeancostaricans.citymax.com; Puerto Limón, next to the docks) Geared to the cruise ship crowd but ready for anything, offers a Limón walking tour, plantation visits, and other tours.

Centro Turistico Brigitte (506-2755-0053; www.brigittecahuita.com; Cahuita, Playa Negra) Full-service tour operator specializes in horseback rides and guided hikes, but can arrange almost anything.

Danta Salvaje (506-2750-0012; www.ladantasalvaje.com; $210 all-inclusive, three-night tour) Adventurers in good physical condition can make the climb to this very basic wooden lodge in an idyllic Eden above unspoiled Braulio Carrillo National Park.

Dragon Scooter Rentals (506-2750-0728; Cahuita, next to Cabinas Los Almendros; open daily 8 AM till late) Rents scooters.

Seahorse Stables (506-2859-6435, 506-2750-0468; www.horsebackridingincostarica .com) Argentine-run operation offers several day trips and multi-day treks through the region.

Surfing

Though Salsa Brava in Puerto Viejo is the most famous wave, there are great beach breaks better for beginners up and down the coast.

Salsa Brava (salsabravasurfshop@hotmail.com; next to Hotel Puerto Viejo; open 9 AM–6:30 PM, Thu.–Tue.) On the main strip in Puerto Viejo, this surf shop offers everything you need: swimsuits, rash guards, and surf lessons ($50 per person for two hours), and buys, rents, and sells surfboards.

Lucas Surf School (506-2756-8224; next to Bread & Chocolate Restaurant, Puerto Viejo) Rents surfboards, and offers lessons and tours.

Uvita Surf (506-2758-1016; www.uvitasurf.com; Puerto Limón) Runs surf trips to Isla Uvita, just off Puerto Limón.

Turtle Tours

Ladies love the Caribbean Coast, and four species of sea turtle come here to nest: Leatherbacks (February through July, peaking in April and May); green turtles (July to October); hawksbills (March to October); and rarely, loggerheads.

ASTOP (Salvemos las Tortugas de Parismina; 506-2710-7703; www.parisminaturtles.org; Parismina) Homegrown operator arranges lodging, tours, and volunteer opportunities. Make reservations by phone between 2 PM and 4 PM Monday, Wednesday, and Friday.

Caribbean Conservation Corporation (CCC; 506-2709-8091; www.cccturtle.org; Tortuguero, north end of village) Costa Rica's first sea turtle conservation organization organizes great tours and pricey volunteer opportunities.

Widecoast (506-2261-3814; www.latinamericanseaturtles.org) Network of Cahuita, Manzanillo, and Gandoca guides and conservationists organizes tours and volunteer opportunities on the South Caribbean coast.

Save the Turtles (707-2538-8084; www.costaricaturtles.com; Parismina) Another great Parismina-based organization can arrange basic lodging (including home stays) and guided tours.

Wildlife Displays and Rescue Centers

★ **Aviarios Sloth Rescue Center** (506-2750-0775; www.slothrescue.com; 11 km/7 mi. north of Cahuita on the main road; admission $25 per person; open Mon.–Sat.) Meet Buttercup, the cuddliest sloth in Cahuita, at this important sloth rescue and rehabilitation facility The tour includes a screening of *Hardly a Deadly Sin*, a movie about the sloth's plight; a one-hour canoe ride through the sanctuary's estuary, where you'll probably see former residents hanging out in the trees; and a lecture about sloths. They also offer seven comfortable, modern rooms ($$$*, including tour) with air-conditioning, cool tiles, and cute furnishings, some of which are set up like suites sleeping six.

Butterfly Garden (506-2750-0086; Punta Uva, 7 km south of Puerto Viejo; open 8 AM–4 PM, daily; admission $5, kids under 12 free) Butterfly garden and farm offers educational tours, and also raises and releases eyelash pit vipers into the wild. Aw.

Iguana Conservation Tour (506-2750-0706; www.iguanaconservationtour.com; $15) Since 2000, Edsart has been raising green iguanas and releasing them into the Gandoca-Manzanillo wildlife refuge, where they have been hunted to scarcity by locals (who consider them delicious). There's also a botanical garden, art gallery, and an "adopt an iguana" program.

White-Water Rafting

Exploradores Outdoors (506-2222-6262; www.exploradoresoutdoors.com) Offers Río Pacuare rafting trips that could include transfers to San José and La Fortuna. They also arrange inexpensive treks to Tortuguero.

Juppy y Tino (506-2750-0621; juppytinoadventures@yahoo.com) Rents kayaks and leads river kayak tours on Río Sixaola; also does waterfall tours, snorkel trips, hiking and bird-watching trips, dolphin tours, and Kekoldi Reserve tours.

Ríos Tropicales (506-2233-6455; www.riostropicales.com) The biggest white-water rafting company in Costa Rica offers Río Pacuare and other rafting trips.

Anhinga sunning itself on the way to Tortuguero

Spas

Anhinga Hotel & Spa (506-2257-2242; Tortuguero, just north of park entrance) Massages and other spa treatments in the jungle.

Jardín Escondido (506-2340-8889; jardinescondido@hotmail.com; Puerto Viejo, 1 km east of Cabinas Monte del Sol; open noon–6 PM, Tue.–Fri.) Massages, herbal baths, aromatherapy, and other holistic treatments.

Pure Jungle Spa (506-2750-0080; www.lacostapapito; Playa Cocles) At La Costa de Papito, this place embraces the jungle theme with Bribri clay mud masks, banana and chocolate wraps, and lots of other treatments.

Shopping

★ **Muebles de Bamboo** (506-2710-1958; www.brieri.com; Guápiles, 5 km south in Río Blanco; by appointment) Brian Erickson's amazing bamboo furniture is on display here. Nearby, his wife Patricia's home gallery (506-2711-0823) is open by appointment, and filled with her flowing and figurative Caribbean paintings.

Echo Books (summermusic303@yahoo.com; 2 km south of Puerto Viejo; open 11 AM–6 PM, Fri.–Tue.) It's worth the trek to visit this charming air-conditioned bookstore and café with new and used books.

Tribal Market (506-2869-2109; tribalmarket2@yahoo.com; Playa Chiquita, 6 km south of Puerto Viejo; open 10 AM–5:30 PM, Wed.–Sun.) This interesting outlet features high quality handicrafts from Southeast Asia, India, Africa, and all over Latin America.

EVENTS

March

South Caribbean Music Festival (506-2750-0062; www.playachiquitalodge.com; Playa Chiquita, 5 km/3 mi. south of Puerto Viejo) Performers from all over the Caribbean, Costa Rica, and beyond, jam the reggae, dancehall, soca, calypso, and jazz for crowds on Playa Chiquita.

September

Arte Viva Festival (Puerto Viejo) The last weekend of September brings out the artists, artisans, musicians, and *fiesteros* (party people).

Arrival of Christopher Columbus to Costa Rica (September 25) A re-enactment of the iconic event takes place every year in Cariari.

October

Limón Carnaval (Puerto Limón and throughout Costa Rica) Beginning October 8 with the crowning of Carnaval Queen, the Caribbean Coast's biggest party means music, dancing, parades, fireworks, floats, and other festivities, peaking on October 10, Cultures Day, and October 12, Día de la Raza or Columbus Day. Make reservations well in advance.

December

Carnavalitos Cahuita (Cahuita) A smaller, week-long version of Limón's Carnaval brings the musicians and party people to this much more mellow venue.

9

Great Side Trips in Nicaragua & Panama

Though Costa Rica gets most of the press, the neighboring nations of Nicaragua and Panama have plenty to offer the more intrepid tourist. I've chosen four of my favorite destinations just beyond Costa Rica's borders, all perfect for a few days' exploration, or perhaps your 72-hour "visa vacation" (which automatically renews your 90-day Costa Rican tourist visa).

Granada and Southwest Nicaragua, convenient from Guanacaste and Liberia, is centered on the Spanish Colonial gem of Granada, among the hemisphere's oldest European cities. From here, you can arrange tours to handicraft markets, volcanoes both active and dormant, lake islands, and the surfing stronghold of San Juan del Sur. The **Río San Juan**, accessible from Arenal/La Fortuna and Sarapiquí, is a liquid world of riverboat rides through the wilderness to island art colonies and ancient Spanish fortresses.

In Panama's Caribbean Coast, **Bocas del Toro**, just south of Puerto Viejo de Talamanca, is an archipelago of islands surrounded by white-sand beaches, celestial blue water, and lovely coral reefs. The marvelous mountain town of **Boquete**, with delightful high-altitude hiking, excellent rafting, and a fine collection of rather upscale accommodations and restaurants, can be reached over land from the Central Pacific Coast and Osa Peninsula, or more conveniently by plane from San José and elsewhere in Costa Rica.

Nicaragua

Though Nicaragua is currently one of the poorest countries in the hemisphere, it wasn't always so. Spanish colonists once grew wealthy off Nicaragua's unparalleled natural resources—enormous Lake Nicaragua and its stunning islands; the San Juan River, once the shortest route between the Atlantic and Pacific Oceans—and invested their earnings in magnificent churches and buildings, with truly fine examples still standing in gorgeous Granada. The economic situation is improving, in part thanks to tourism, but the country remains much less expensive than Costa Rica.

Though travelers of a certain age may still associate Nicaragua with the Contra War of the 1980s (and President Daniel Ortega, the Sandinista leader of that era, was recently re-elected, which did little to encourage foreign investment), the nation is now a stable, peaceful democracy, and actually has a lower crime rate than Costa Rica. President Ortega remains on surprisingly good terms with the U.S. government, and Nicaragua continues to offer travelers the very best deals in Central America.

At Mi Jardín es Su Jardín, you'll understand why they call Boquete the "City of Flowers."

Nicaragua's currency is the *cordoba*, but dollars are widely accepted, and it's easy to change Costa Rican colones in the regions covered.

Granada and Southwest Nicaragua

Strategically located on the shores of Lake Nicaragua, less than 40 kilometers (24 miles) from the Pacific Ocean, Granada has been a commercial, political, and cultural hub since it was founded in 1524. Nicknamed La Gran Sultana, in honor of the old Moorish stronghold in Spain, it has in recent years become a tourist Mecca, thanks to its impeccably restored architecture and fine collection of restaurants, hotels, churches, and museums. A must for architecture and photography buffs, this Colonial jewel also makes a comfortable base for seeing the rest of this incredible region.

To the southwest, close to the Costa Rican border, is the surf town of San Juan del Sur (SJDS), offering breaks up and down the Pacific; with a wide range of wonderful accommodations, eateries, and tour outfitters, it too is a great base for exploring Southwest Nicaragua. Just offshore in Lake Nicaragua are several islands, including the Zapatera Archipelago, with its wealth of archaeological treasures, protected as a national park; and spectacular Isla Ometepe, formed by two volcanoes connected by a slender, sandy isthmus, currently being considered for one of the World's Seven Natural Wonders.

To the north and east of Granada are two volcanic national parks, cloud-forested Mombacho Volcano and very active Masaya Volcano; after visiting, you could swim in Laguna de Apoyo, a cool crater lake just east of town. Masaya is also home to one of Central America's best handicrafts markets, the perfect spot to finish your souvenir shopping.

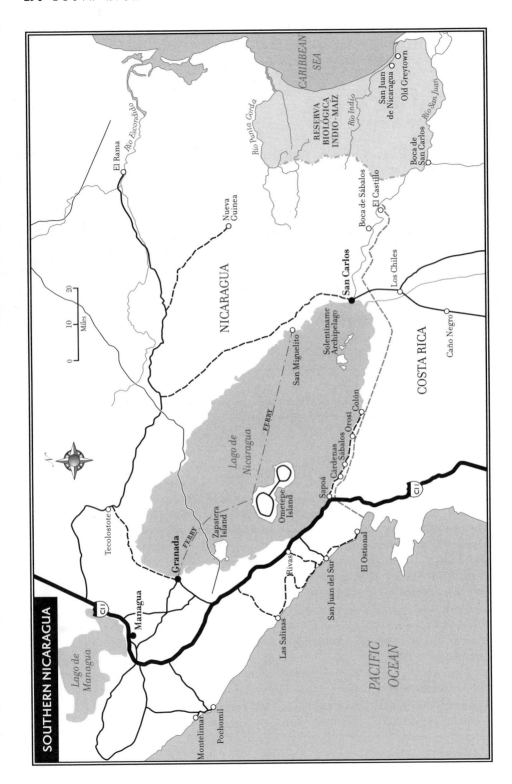

SOUTHERN NICARAGUA

Online Resources Nicaragua

Anda Ya! (www.andayanicaragua.com) Monthly, Granada-centric "tourist directory" has bilingual information online.

Between the Waves (www.wavesnicaragua.com) Saucy magazine and Web site has up-to-date articles and destination information.

Find It Granada (www.finditgranada.com) Directory includes services for tourists (including vacation rentals) and expatriates.

Granada (www.granada.com.ni) Listings and links.

INTUR (www.intur.gob.ni; www.visitanicaragua.com) The Nicaraguan Tourism Board has two great Web sites in Spanish.

★ **Manfut** (www.manfut.org) Huge, sloppy, amazing site has photos and articles (most in Spanish) concerning every corner of Nicaragua.

San Juan del Sur Guide (www.sanjuandelsurguide.com) Comprehensive listings and a free, downloadable, printable guidebook to SJDS and the surrounding area. Also check out **San Juan del Sur** (www.sanjuandelsur.org.ni) and **San Juan del Sur Newsletter** (www.san-juan-del-sur.com).

★ **Vianica** (www.vianica.com) Huge English-language site with lots of information about hotels, restaurants, and activities for every major Nicaraguan destination.

Visit Río San Juan (www.visitriosanjuan.com) CANTUR, the local tourist bureau, puts out a free "guidebook," available at their kiosk in San Carlos or online.

GETTING AROUND

The diminutive Granada Airport, about 3 kilometers (1.8 miles) from town, was briefly served by Nature Air (www.natureair.com) with flights from San José and Liberia, Costa Rica, but international flights have been suspended until a permanent customs desk can be set up; check online to see if they've resumed. The closest international airport is in the capital city of Managua, **International Airport Augusto C. Sandino** (MGA; www.eaai.com.ni), about 50 kilometers (31 miles) from Granada, with regular but pricey flights from San José. Your hotel can arrange airport transfers.

The easiest way to come overland from Costa Rica is to book a comfortable, air-conditioned international bus from either San José (nine hours) or Liberia (five hours): **King Quality** (505-222-3065 Nicaragua, 506-2258-8832 Costa Rica; www.kingqualityca.com; $22); **Tica Bus** (505-222-3031 Nicaragua; 506-2248-9636 San José; 506-2665-1616 Liberia; www.ticabus.com; $15); and **Transnica** (505-277-2104 Nicaragua; 506-2223-4242; www.transnica.com; $15). Buses can drop you off in Granada (recommended), while more adventurous travelers can ask to be dropped in Rivas, with cabs to San Juan del Sur or the ferry terminal of San Jorge, which offers boat service to Ometepe Island (see sidebar). You can also ask international buses to leave you at the border, where you can catch cabs to San Juan del Sur.

There are several car rental places in Granada, including **Alamo** (505-277-1117; www.alamonicaragua.com; Hotel Colonial, northwest corner of the park), **Avis** (505-467-4780; www.avis.com.ni); and **Budget** (505-552-2323; 800-758-9586; www.budget.com.ni), which also has offices on either side of the border. The region is quite drivable, with better roads and signage than Costa Rica, but this book is not a sufficient driving guide for the casual tourist. For most short-term visitors, I recommend sticking to taxis, tours, and public transportation. Recommended tour operators are listed under Activities, later, or your hotel can take care of everything.

Pick up free maps at many Granada and SJSD hotels and tour offices, or try Granada's **INTUR** (Nicaraguan Tourism Institute; 505-552-6858; www.visitanicaragua.com; diagonal from Convento San Francisco; open 8 AM–12:30 PM and 2 PM–5 PM, Mon.–Fri., 8:30 AM–12:30 PM, Sat.) which also has flyers, a help desk, and booklets filled with information about the area. There are several maps online, including Nicaragua (www.lib.utexas.edu /maps/americas/nicaragua_rel_97.pdf), and this interactive satellite map (www.maplandia .com/nicaragua/granada). **Bosawas** (bosawas.com/maps/granada) has a great online map of Granada. **Anda Ya!** (www.andayanicaragua.com) has good maps of Granada and San Juan del Sur (click on the city under "mapas," in the right-hand column).

Although Rivas is the public transportation hub, it's easier to arrange private transportation throughout Southwest Nicaragua from Granada. **Paxeos Shuttle Services** (505-465-1090; www.paxeos.com; Central Plaza, next to the cathedral) offers convenient and inexpensive direct service between your hotel and the Managua airport, San Juan del Sur, and San Jorge, where you catch the ferry to Ometepe.

Granada streets are organized in a classic Spanish grid, built around a central plaza presided over by the cathedral. Most hotels, restaurants, museums, and shops are within three blocks. The major road heading east 2 kilometers (1.2 miles) toward Lake Nicaragua, Calle La Calzada, is being turned into a pedestrian mall. South of the city center on Calle Atravesada are the market, and buses to Rivas. West, on Real Xalteva, are several churches and Fortaleza Polvera.

San Juan del Sur sprawls along the Pacific, with access to quieter beaches and communities along a four-wheel-drive-only coastal road. Ometepe's hourglass shape is almost entirely circumnavigated by a single road between the two major cities of Altagracia and Moyogalpa. Regular buses and private shuttles ply the road.

LODGING

Granada's most recent tourism boom has resulted in some of the city's most exquisite Colonial mansions being remodeled into lovely hotels. These are just a few of the finest.

GRANADA

Hotel Alhambra (505-552-4486; www.hotelalhambra.com.ni; west side of Central Park; $$–$$$) The sentimental favorite, this elegant property right on the plaza has housed VIP visitors to Granada since long before the tourist boom. Though modern amenities including air-conditioning, cable, and WiFi have been added, rooms—which vary widely in size and design—don't quite live up to the fabulous lobby's promise. Spring for an upstairs room with a tiny balcony overlooking the plaza.

Casa Merced (505-552-2744, 305-395-7021 USA; www.casalamerced.com; Calle Real Xalteva, across from Merced Church; $$*) This absolute gem has only seven spacious, beautifully tiled and painted rooms, decorated with antiques, religious art, and Guatemalan bedspreads, including WiFi and air-conditioning, all wrapped around a flower-filled courtyard.

★ **Casa San Francisco** (505-552-8235; www.csf-hotel-granada.com; Calle Corral #207, around the corner from Convento San Francisco; $$*) A fabulous hotel offering Spanish Colonial styling with artsy and elegant furnishings, including lots of wrought iron curlicues and huge hand-tiled bathrooms, original art from all over the world, private balconies and patios, a small pool, and one of the best restaurants in town, **Los Chocoyos** (505-552-8513; L, D; $–$$), serving mostly organic Latin-fusion cuisine with lots of vegetarian options; there's usually live music on weekends. They also offer a Laguna de Apoyo guesthouse for day-trippers ($10 including round-trip transportation) and overnight guests ($$*).

Hotel Colonial (505-552-7581; www.hotelcolonialgranada.com; 25m north of Central Park; $$) Excellent option off the plaza offers spacious, gem-toned rooms with attractive, modern furnishings, great bathrooms, amenities including WiFi, and a great outdoor pool with swim-up bar. On-site **Euro Café** (505-552-2146; B, L, D) serves coffee, gelato, homemade pastries, and light meals with lots of vegetarian options (including hummus and pasta dishes), plus two awesome extras: **Mockingbird Books**, with lots of new and used English-language titles; and **Seeing Hands Blind Massage** (see Spas, below).

★ **Hotel Darío** (505-552-3400; www.hoteldario.com; Calle La Calzada, 200m toward lake from Central Park; $$$*) Named for Nicaragua's most famous poet, this fine new option occupies a 19th-century neoclassical landmark that has been completely refurbished in fine woodwork with Moorish echoes surrounding a beautiful courtyard garden and pool. Rooms are small but flawlessly designed and decorated, with elegantly hand-carved doors, bathtubs in the marble-lined bathrooms, Direct TV, WiFi, and wonderful art and furnishings. There's a pool and gym on-site, as well as two restaurants, **El Tranvía** (L, D; $$$), serving gourmet international cuisine, and the less formal **Cafetería Chocolate** (B, L, D; $), with a deli that also serves breakfast and salads.

La Casona de los Estrada (505-552-7393; www.casonalosestrada.com; Calle El Arsenal; $$*) Bed-and-breakfast-style inn offers great value on "luxuriously rustic," Colonial-

Schoolchildren heading to class in Spanish Colonial Granada

style rooms, with air-conditioning, telephones, cable TV, and great, personalized service. Displayed art and pottery is for sale.

Gran Francia (505-552-6000; www.lagranfrancia.com; southwest corner of central park; $$$*) Granada's most historic hotel, this grandly restored mansion was once home to President William Walker, the U.S.-backed mercenary who tried to conquer Central America. Though this is certainly the city's most exclusive address, remember that classic Colonial styling means smallish, dark singles as well as considerably nicer doubles and suites, with wonderful balconies. Antique-style furniture, hand-painted Spanish tiles, and an indoor pool have been enhanced with air-conditioning, telephones, and WiFi. Even if you choose not to stay, stop by their second-story restaurant and bar, **El Arcángel**, for drinks with a view.

★ **Patio El Malinche** (505-552-2235; www.patiodelmalinche.com; Calle El Caimito, 250m from the Alcaldía, toward the lake; $$*) Classic Colonial hotel offers immaculate, modern, air-conditioned rooms with big windows, cable TV, and WiFi, surrounding a lovely pool. Very nice.

SAN JUAN DEL SUR

★ **Morgan's Rock** (505-232-6449; www.morgansrock.com; Ocotal Beach; $$$*) This is considered the best hotel in Nicaragua, and I wholeheartedly agree. With absolutely flawless bungalows scattered through the primary rain forest, hewn from rich, sustainably-harvested hardwood, creatively and luxuriously furnished, all overlooking a pristine beach (furnished with architecturally interesting *palapas*), this would be a fine spot even without their commitment to community development and ecosystems preserva-

Perhaps the best way to see Granada is in one of the horse-drawn taxis waiting at the central park.

tion. World-class service, top-notch tours, and a divine restaurant serving Latin fusion cuisine complete the most perfect package in the country.

El Nido B&B (505862-5344; www.elnidobedandbreakfast.com; north of SJDS, near Maderas Beach; $$*) Appealing bed-and-breakfast offers two pretty, air-conditioned rooms with flagstone accents around the sparkling pool, pretty gardens, and sunbathing platform. Views are outstanding, the owners sweet, and breakfast is cooked to order.

Park Avenue Villas (505-837-0582; www.parkavenuevillas.com; central San Juan del Sur, 100m above the beach; $$–$$$) Modern, fully-equipped condo-style suites are tastefully outfitted in creams and taupes, plus plenty of wicker and ceramic to complement the views over Nicaragua's best beach town. Suites featuring one or two bedrooms also include full kitchens, maid service, WiFi, and a chlorine-free pool.

Parque Maritime el Coco (505-892-0124; www.playaelcoco.com.ni; 18 km south of SJDS, 4WD recommended; $$–$$$$) Fully-equipped cottages in all shapes and sizes are designed for families and are located just steps from a gorgeous but isolated beach. Hammocks, outdoor grills, full kitchens, and nice furnishings are great, as is the beachfront restaurant, **Puesto del Sol** ($$–$$$$) with seafood, international, and Nica cuisine, and as the name implies, fine sunsets.

La Posada Azul (505-568-2524; www.laposadaazul.com; central San Juan del Sur; $$$*) Painstakingly renovated historic wooden home has character to spare, with clean, spacious rooms, simply but thoughtfully furnished, and a lovely second-floor balcony just a block from the ocean, though there's a fabulous pool right here. Breakfast, with homemade scones and muffins, gets raves.

★ **Hotel Pelican Eyes Piedras y Olas** (505-568-2110, 866-350-0555; www.piedrasyolas .com; 150m east of the church; $$$–$$$$*) Flowing, organic architecture that understands adobe's potential is meshed with cane, polished raw wood, and ceramic elements, earning these hilltop bungalows numerous accolades. The infinity pools are stunning, especially at sunset, and service is outstanding, though empathic types may be more rewarded by their numerous community programs. **La Cascada Restaurant** (B, L, D; $$–$$$$) with those same outstanding views, is arguably SJDS's finest dining, with exquisitely prepared seafood and steak, served alongside often-organic accompaniments.

Vacation Rentals

Casa Granada Property Management (505-552-0407; casagranadarentals@yahoo.com; Casa San Francisco) Homes in and around Granada.

Details Management (505-432-4724; mavericks_granada@yahoo.ca; 104 Calle El Arsenal) Vacation rentals, plus advice and aid for expatriates and those considering the big move.

Granada Property Services (www.gpsnicaragua.com) Apartments and homes, some quite luxurious.

Nicaragua Vacation Rental (505-568-2498; 323-908-6730 USA; www.vacationrentals nicaragua.com) Rentals in and around San Juan del Sur.

DINING

Granada and San Juan del Sur offer the widest variety of international cuisine and fine dining in Nicaragua (outside Managua, the capital). Less touristed destinations, including

Granada's Independence Plaza is a colorful confection of incredible architecture.

Masaya, Ometepe Island, and Rivas, offer mostly small, family-run restaurants serving typical Nicaraguan cuisine.

Granada Restaurants

The very best spot to sample Granada's signature dish, *vigarón*, is at one of the kiosks in the Central Park. Boiled yuca topped with a spicy slaw and pork rind, it is best complemented with a glass of *chicha*, a sweet corn drink.

Asia Latina (Thai-Latin Fusion; 505-552-4672; Calle La Libertad, 100m *al lago* from the Central Park; $–$$) Popular spot with sidewalk seating and great local art offers unusual fusion dishes such as a special pad Thai, made with local ingredients, a Malaysian-style fish in a coconut milk, cilantro, and ginger sauce, and a spicy version of *ropa vieja*, or Cuban-style shredded beef, just perfect with one of their renowned *mojitos*. They also rent midrange rooms and organize tours.

Charly's (German; 505-552-4452; near Old Hospital; L, D; $–$$) German-themed, *palapa*-topped restaurant serves sausages, grilled meats, and other traditional Saxon cuisine, plus plenty of Nica and veggie options, and giant glass boots for holding your beer.

El Jardín de Orión (French; 505-552-1220; next to Casa El Recodo; L, D, closed Mon. and Tue.; $$) Brand-new garden restaurant is a beautiful spot to enjoy French cuisine.

★ **Mediterreneo** (Spanish; 505-552-6764; Calle El Caimito, 150m toward the lake from the Alcaldía; $$–$$$) Granada's oldest, and still one of the best restaurants embodies casual elegance in an old mansion. They offer outstanding Spanish classics such as tapas, gazpacho, and paella, as well as more creative entrees including curried chicken with caramelized pineapple, and mussels in marinara sauce.

Mona Lisa (Italian; 505-552-8187; Granada, Calle la Calzada; L, D, closed Wed.; $–$$) Creative, wood-fired pizzas, homemade pastas, and a comfortable atmosphere.

Nuestra Casa (Barbecue; 505-552-8115; Calle Consulado; L, D; $–$$$) Alabama native serves the best baby back ribs in Central America, plus plenty of other grilled specialties.

Tercer Ojo (International; 506-552-6451; Calle El Arsenal, across from Convent San Francisco; L, D; $–$$) French-owned eatery is lovingly draped in romantic bohemian-style, where you can relax and enjoy an eclectic menu including excellent sushi, great Spanish tapas, authentic French crêpes, and a variety of vegetarian options, as well as books, board games, and a gourmet deli in front.

★ **El Zaguán** (Nicaraguan; 506-552-2522; behind cathedral; L, D; $$–$$$) Popular spot specializes in grilled meats and fresh fish dishes, served in a cozy dining area where dueling mariachi bands ask for requests.

Granada Cafés

Café DecArte (505-552-6461; Calle La Calzada; open 11 AM–4 PM, closed Tue.; $$) Elegant café, art gallery, and community gathering place offers organic salads, light meals, and great desserts by day, becoming **Pasta Pasta** (D, closed Tue.; $$) at night, with yummy homemade pastas, lasagnas, and a solid wine list.

Café Melba (Calle El Marririo, 50m north of La Calzada at Zoom Bar; B, L, D, closed Mon.; $–$$) Vegetarian café offers meat-free quiches, burgers, and typical food.

★ **Kathy's Waffle House** (505-552-7488; across from El Convento; B, L; $) Enjoy big breakfasts, friendly service, and chatty expatriates with the best view in town: the celestial blue façade of El Covento.

Garden Café (505-552-8582; Calle Libertad, 100m east of Central Park; B, L; $) In an exquisite Colonial mansion with great garden seating, serves big salads, beautiful pastries, and creative sandwiches.

★ **Nica Buffet** (Calle Estrada; B; $) This Dutch-owned, full-service restaurant offers arguably the best breakfasts in town, with excellent local coffee.

San Juan del Sur Restaurants

The shoreline is fringed with several fabulous seafood restaurants including **Buen Gusto** (505-568-2304; Calle Costera; $$), always a solid bet, though **El Timón** (505-815-3247; Calle Costera; $$–$$$), with outstanding seafood and several types of ceviche, is the traditional favorite.

Big Wave Dave's (505-568-2110; www.bigwavedaves.net; B, L, D; $$) Great grub and good company at this landmark spot, with comfort food and a full bar.

El Colibrí (505-863-8612; behind Catholic church; D, Wed.–Sun.; $$) Enjoy top-notch Mediterranean cuisine including pastas, steaks, kebabs, and vegetarian choices in gorgeous gardens.

El Pozo (el-pozo.com; 100m south of central park; D, Wed.–Mon.; $$$) Offers eclectic international cuisine made with fresh, local ingredients and served with flair.

CULTURE

Granada, founded in 1524, claims the title of "Oldest Spanish City in the Americas (Still on the Same Spot)," which is probably true. The city has, however, been sacked by pirates and burned to the ground on several occasions, most completely in 1856 by U.S.-backed mercenary William Walker.

But because most buildings are constructed primarily of adobe, the city's floor plans and basic structures have probably remained true to their 16th-century architectural splendor, and buildings have since been rebuilt to Colonial specifications. Climb to the top of the Church of Merced and enjoy the *tejas*-topped view of Spanish Colonial homes, built for a strong defense and a beautiful life, with high walls surrounding interior gardens.

Architecture

Architecture buffs disappointed that Costa Rica couldn't offer the classic Colonial construction so common in Mexico or Guatemala, will be delighted to see the sun rise over Granada's Spanish central park, surrounded by beautiful buildings. Presiding over the plaza is the 1583 **Cathedral of Granada**, rebuilt to an elegant neoclassical façade in 1915, and renovated to its current glory in 2006. On the southeast corner of the park, the **Hotel Gran Francia** (see Lodging, above) is the exquisitely remodeled former home of William Walker. Head north to the adjoining Plaza of Independence, marked by an obelisk memorializing the 1821 struggle for independence from Spain. To the right is the **Fundación Casa Los Tres Mundos** (505-552-4176; www.c3mundos.org) a cultural center that often shows movies and has other activities, boasting the 1720s stone **Portico de los Leones**, the only remnant of the original building to survive Walker's rage.

At the end of the plaza, make a right on Calle Arsenal to reach sky blue 1585 **Convento y Museo San Francisco** (Museums, below), rebuilt in 1868 and restored in 1989. Other important churches include the 1655 **Iglesia de la Merced** (Calle Real Xalteva), a beautiful baroque church with a simple 1862 interior dedicated to the Virgins of Merced and Fatima; climb to the top ($1) for incredible views over the city. Other interesting churches include nearby **La Capilla María Auxiliadora** (Calle Real Xalteva) with its wonderfully painted interior, and pleasant 19th century **Xalteva Church** (Calle Real Xalteva), on the site of the original indigenous city of Xalteva.

Museums

Fortaleza la Polvera (Calle Real Xalteva; admission $0.70; open 7 AM–5 PM) This 1748 fortress and jail has been transformed into an art school and tourist attraction; knock on the door and they'll let you roam the grounds and ascend the old guard towers, with views to the lake.

★ **Mi Museo** (505-552-7614; www.granadacollection.org; Calle Atravesada 505, across from Bancentro; open 8 AM–5 PM; admission free, gratuities appreciated) Excellent private museum, housed in a gorgeous Colonial mansion, displays 5,223 of Nicaragua's finest pre-Columbian pottery and artifacts. English-speaking guides will show you around for a tip.

Museo Casa Natal Sor María Romero (505-552-6069; Iglesia Xalteva, 100m al lago, 100m sur, Calle Estrada; open 8 AM–noon and 2 PM–5 PM, Tue.–Sun.; admission free) The renovated childhood home of a revered nun (1902–1977) who set up girls' schools, health clinics, and aid ministries in Costa Rica.

Museo de Antropología (505-563-3708; Rivas, 250m from the Escuela Internacional de Agricultura; open 9 AM–noon and 2 PM–5 PM, Mon.–Sat.; $1) If you have an hour to spend in Rivas, grab a horse-drawn carriage and visit this excellent little museum, housed in another of William Walker's headquarters. Features include archaeological artifacts, historic murals, creative taxidermy, and other mementos from Rivas' past.

★ **Museo Convento San Francisco** (505-552-5535; open 8 AM–5 PM, Mon.–Fri., 9 AM–4 PM, Sat. and Sun.; admission $2) Excellent museum inhabiting a restored 1585 mansion offers an incredible model of the city, fine art, and several other displays, including an important collection of ancient basalt statues depicting creatures that seem half-animal, half-man, probably carved between 800 and 1200 A.D. on Isla Zapatera.

Nightlife

Café Nuit (505-552-7376; Calle La Libertad) Live music, usually from house band Clave del Sol, plus a dance floor, bar, and good food.

Centro Turistico (Lakeshore) The lakefront park, 2 kilometers (1.2 miles) east of the city center, has several discos; be sure to take taxis at night!

★ **El Club** (505-552-4245; www.elclub-nicaragua.com; Calle La Libertad and Av Barricada; B, L, D; $–$$) Sophisticated spot offers exotic cocktails and excellent international cuisine in the sleek interior or atmospheric garden bar. They also rent really cool, modern rooms ($).

Enoteca (505-552-8514; www.enotecavinosymas.com; north side of Central Park) Granada's finest selection of wines.

Zoom Bar (505-643-5655; www.nicazoombar.com; Calle Calzada, 300m east of park) Expatriate hangout has excellent burgers, WiFi, a very full bar, and NFL in season.

RECREATION

Southwest Nicaragua offers endless options for recreation and entertainment; this is just a taste of what's offered. Ask at your hotel or any local tour operator about other activities.

Isla Ometepe, A World Apart

Rising from Lake Nicaragua, once known as Cocibolca or the "Sweet Sea," Isla Ometepe's hourglass figure is formed by twin volcanoes: active and symmetrical Concepción, perhaps smoking; and relaxed and cloud-forested Maderas, topped with a muddy but refreshing crater lake. Any hotel can arrange guided climbs up either, or try ★**Exploring Ometepe** (505-647-5179; www.exploring ometepe.com) located by the main ferry dock in Moyogalpa.

There is so much more to do in this remarkable wonder of nature; **Visit Ometepe** (www.visita ometepe.com) offers excellent maps, hotel listings, transportation, and tour information, just to get you started. Other hikes lead to impressive waterfalls and cool swimming holes, or just around the island, with several small, sandy beaches. Horseback treks, kayak trips, kiteboarding excursions, and more will exercise your body; two tiny archaeological museums in the major towns of Altagracia and Moyogalpa will fascinate your mind.

The island lacks any truly plush hotels, but **Hotel Villa Paraiso** (505-563-4675; www.villaparaiso .com.ni; Playa Santo Domingo; $$) is quite nice, with comfortable, air-conditioned cabinas overlooking a sandy beach, fronted by private porches with hammocks. Next door, **Finca Santo Domingo** (505-654-1594; hotel_santo_domingo@yahoo.com; Playa Santo Domingo; $–$$) is almost as comfortable, with several sizes of pleasantly decorated rooms. Also check out **Hotel Charco Verde** (505-887-9302; www.charcoverde.com.ni; $–$$), with private, air-conditioned cabins and a good restaurant next to a beautiful gray-sand beach.

Though ferries run from Granada to Altagracia twice weekly (a four-hour trip; departing 3 PM, Mon. and Thu., returning 11 PM, Tue. and Fri.), it's much more convenient to take a bus or taxi to San Jorge, on the lakeshore close to Rivas, with ferries (a one-hour trip; $2) running to Moyogalpa almost hourly. Buses and taxis meet every boat, no matter what time you arrive.

Parks and Preserves

La Flor Wildlife Refuge (505-458-2514, 505-563-4264; fcdeje@ibw.com.ni; 22 km south of SJDS; admission $12) Around seven times between July and January each year, olive ridley sea turtles arrive in *arribadas*, or mass nestings, to this scenic stretch of beach just south of San Juan del Sur. Tour operators in Granada and SJDS arrange night trips; call the refuge to find out if an arribada is occurring. Solitary turtles nest year-round. Camping ($30) is allowed.

★ **Laguna de Apoyo Nature Reserve** (www.lagunadeapoyonicaragua.com; 10 km/6 mi. west of Granada) This newly-protected and stunning crater lake is perhaps the deepest and cleanest body of water in Central America. Just minutes from Granada, this quiet pool is cloaked in dry tropical forest inhabited by troupes of howler monkeys. It is also home to a growing number of hotels and restaurants where you can relax as you swim, kayak, sailboard, or just watch the world drift by. Several hotels in Granada offer day-trips and overnights at a handful of lakefront "beach clubs," including **San Simian Lakeside Bungalows Café & Bar** (505-813-6866; $*), operated by Casa San Francisco. Or try luxurious **Norome Resort & Villa** (505-883-9093; www.noromevillas.com; $$–$), with plush, cavernous bungalows built into the steep and jungled crater walls.

★ **Masaya Volcano National Park** (505-522-5415; Masaya, 28 km/17 mi. northwest of Granada; open 9 AM–4:45 PM; admission $4.50) The world's most heavily venting volcano (and yes, you can walk to the lip of the crater and peer down to the lava bubbling deep inside) was once thought to be the entryway to hell; a cross placed at the rim in 1528 (though this isn't the original) may very well keep its demons inside. The excellent park also offers 20 kilometers (12 miles) of hiking trails beginning at the natural history museum at the entrance.

Mombacho Volcano Natural Reserve (505-552-5858; www.mombacho.org; open 8 AM–5 PM, Thu.–Sun., to groups with reservations Tue. and Wed; admission $6) Defining the Granada skyline, this volcano topped with a cloud forest has hiking trails that thread its ragged bulk, past fumaroles, a wealth of wildlife, and incredible views over Granada and the lake. Tours are easily arranged, and guides are available at the bottom of the mountain. From the parking area, you'll need to take a special truck to the top, leaving at 8:30 AM, 10 AM, 1 PM, and 3 PM.

Zapatera Archipelago National Park (Lake Nicaragua, about 20 km/12 mi. south of Granada) Archipelago of 13 islands includes inhabited Zapatera, historically considered Ometepe's male counterpart, and Isla el Muerto (Isle of Death), where the fearsome statues displayed at Convento San Francisco were originally found. Scores of petroglyphs remain on several islands. There's not really any public transport, thus it's best to arrange tours from Granada. Try **Zapatera Tours** (505-842-2587; www.zapateratours .com), with a very nice lodge for day-trippers and overnight guests; or **Sonzapote Campesino Cooperative** (505-899-2927; www.ucatierrayagua.org), a community tourism operator offering unique tours and basic lodging.

Boat Tours

Granada's signature trip sends boats cruising through the 365 volcanic **Isletas de Granada**, scattered in a loose crescent just offshore in Lake Nicaragua. Thrown from Mombacho Volcano perhaps 12,000 years ago, today these wildlife rich islands are home to beautiful mansions, ancient fishing communities, and even a Spanish fortress. Any hotel or tour desk can

Mombacho Volcano and the cathedral dominate the Granada skyline.

arrange a tour, or take a taxi to Puerto Asese, where you can hire covered, motorized canoes to make the trip for around $15 per hour. **Marina Cocibolca** (505-228-2073; www.marina cocibolca.net) can arrange trips all over the lake. You could even stay on the isletas overnight, at **El Roble Nicaragua Descanso** (505-894-6217; www.nicadescanso.com; $$$*), with pleasant but basic rooms and a restaurant, or new **Hotel La Ceiba** (505–882-6723; nir@nicaraolake.com.ni; $$$*). You can also rent kayaks to explore the isles at **Inuit Kayak** (506-614-0813; Centro Turistico, on the lake) and **Mombotours** (see Tours, below).

San Juan del Sur has several yacht tours, including fishing trips and sunset cruises. Try **Aida Sailing Tours** (505-568-2287; congosprod@hotmail.com; Calle Central), with good prices, or ★**Sailing Adventures Pelican Eyes** (505-568-2110; www.piedrasyolas.com; Pelican Eyes Hotel), boasting a graceful sailing yacht.

Canopy Tours and More

Da Flying Frog Canopy (505-568-2351; SJDS, Carretera a Marsella; $25) Nicaragua's longest, fastest, and arguably prettiest canopy tour combines 2.5 kilometers (1.6 miles) of zip lines with horseback rides ($10 per hour) and a massive petroglyph.

Senderos Los Monos Canopy Tour (Ometepe, Playa Santo Domingo; open 9 AM–5 PM; admission $8) Small four-cable, six-platform tour on Ometepe is perfect for folks looking for a shorter ride.

Diving and Snorkeling

Scuba Dive Laguna de Apoyo (505-882-3992; www.gaianicaragua.org; Laguna de Apoyo) Freshwater fish aren't particularly exciting, but that steep and creepy crater-lake dropoff, to 250 meters (820 feet) at the center, is something else.

Scuba Shack (www.scubashack-nicaragua.com; San Juan del Sur) PADI certification, diving, and surf tours.

Other Tours and Activities

Blue Mountain (505-552-5323; www.bluemountainnicaragua.com; Granada, Calle Real Xalteva) Offers horseback riding trips in Mombacho Reserve, through the White Towns, and around Masaya.

NicaYoga (505-400-0255; www.nicayoga.com; 3 km east of SJDS) Nicaragua's first yoga community offers classes, packages, and retreats.

Spanish Schools

It's considerably cheaper to learn Spanish in Nicaragua than Costa Rica, and Granada has several schools, including **Casa Xalteva** (505-552-2436; www.casaxalteva.com); **Nicaragua Mía** (505-552-2755; www.nicaragua-mia-spanishschool.com); and **One on One** (505-552-6771; www.spanish1on1.net). Beach lovers could try **San Juan del Sur Spanish School** (www.sjdsspanish.com) or **Nicaspanish Language School** (505-832-4668; www.nica spanish.com), both in SJDS. Or, learn Spanish inside a volcanic crater at **Apoyo Intensive Spanish School** (505-882-3992 www.gaianicaragua.org).

Sportfishing

Salt Water Fishing (505-608-3646; Granada, Centro Turistico) Fishing trips in fast motorboats on Lake Nicaragua and the Pacific.

Superfly Sportfishing (505-884-8444, 443-451-4300; www.superflynica.com; SJSD) Recommended operator works with the finest hotels to organize plush packages in San Juan del Sur and around the country.

Surfing

SJSD is Nicaragua's surfing stronghold, though the best beach breaks are about 10 kilometers (6 miles) north.

Arena Caliente Surf Camp (505-815-3247; www.arenalcaliente.com; SJDS; 50m north of Mercado) Lessons, boards, and tours to secret waves.

Chica Brava (505-894-2842; 832-519-0253 USA; www.chicabrava.com) Nicaragua's first surf camp for the ladies offers fairly plush accommodations overlooking the bay.

Dale Dagger Surf Tours (www.nicasurf.com) Nicaragua's original operator offers tours and packages.

Nicaragua Surf Report (www.nicaraguasurfreport.com) Online surf report also has information on surf tours, lessons, beach rentals, and more.

Tours

Granada is an excellent base from which to arrange tours throughout the region and country; these are just a few of the many operators available.

★ **DeTöur** (505-837-0559; www.detour-nicaragua.com; Calle Caimito, 150m east Alcaldia) Community-oriented outfitter offers adventuresome versions of all the usual tours, often including bicycles, kayaks, and/or horses, plus guided trips into Nicaragua's wild and difficult-to-access interior.

Gray Line (505-266-6134; www.graylinenicaragua.com) Runs tours all over Nicaragua and Costa Rica, and can customize packages to see both.

★ **Mombotour** (505-552-4548; www.mombotour.com; Centro Comercial Granada) Excel-

Relaxing on the beach in San Juan del Sur

lent adventure operator offers a canopy tour, private wildlife preserve (with petro-glyphs!), guided hikes, kayak tours, horseback rides, coffee tours, and more.

Tierra Tour (505-862-9580; www.tierratour.com; Cathedral 200m toward the lake, Calle La Calzada) Longstanding Granada operator offers city tours, trips to area parks and attractions, guided hikes, and daily shuttle service to León and San Juan del Sur.

Va Pues Tours (505-606-2276; www.vapues.com; central park) Excellent countrywide operator specializes in trips to León and Northern Nicaragua.

Spas

Almazen (505-418-7965; almazen.nicaragua@gmail.com; Granada, 150m south of cathedral) Massages, facials, and yoga classes.

Luna Bella Day Spa (505-803-8196; www.lunabella.org; SJDS, 100m south of Restaurant

Nicaragua produces some of the world's finest cigars, and Doña Elba's are among the best.

Colibrí; by appointment only) Enjoy a massage, facial, and other beauty treatments by the beach.

★ **Seeing Hands Blind Massage** (Euro Café, next to Hotel Colonial, northwest corner of the Central Park) Unique social program has trained blind Granadinos to give great massages for about $13 per hour.

Shopping

Granada has scores of stores selling souvenirs and handicrafts, but serious shoppers should visit the nearby town of Masaya and its 1888 **Antiguo Mercado de Masaya**, a Gothic castle-like structure housing some 200 handicraft vendors with merchandise made all over the country. Thursday night, they offer free folkloric dance shows.

Books

El Gato Negro (505-809-1108; www.elgatonegronica.com; central SJDS, 100m east of El Timón) Excellent English-language bookstore stocks intriguing titles and guides, and has a café.

★ **Maverick's** (505-432-4724; Calle El Arsenal; open 9 AM–6 PM, Tue.–Sat., 10 AM–noon,

Sun.) Good selection of English-language magazines and books, plus sustainable and community-conscious souvenirs, tourist information, great coffee, and many other services (vacation rentals, Spanish school, piercing studio) for tourists and expatriates alike.

Galleries and Souvenirs

★ **Claro Oscuro** (505-871-0627; across from Merced Church) Showcases the region's best primitivist, surrealist, and other modern artists, as well as as the colorful work of owner Ricardo Maya.

Donde JansZen (505-626-0451; 100m south Gran Francia) In addition to handmade clothes, bags, lamps, and jewelry, also offers Reiki massage and tarot readings.

Doña Elba Cigars (505-860-6715; elbacigar@cablenet.com.ni; 50m west of Xalteva Church; open 8 AM–8 PM, daily) Nicaragua produces some of the world's finest cigars, regularly beating Cuban stogies. Watch as Granada's best are hand-rolled right here, then admire photos of Arnold Schwarzenegger, George Tenet, and others smoking up with the owners.

El Recodo (505-552-0901; www.casaelrecodo.com; between Calles La Libertad y El Consulado) The "oldest house in Granada," probably built in the mid-1700s is indeed a Colonial gem, and co-starred in the mildly hallucinogenic *Walker* (1989), depicting the life of William Walker, as told by the director of *Sid and Nancy*. Really. Today, the house is packed to the brim with antiques and unusual handicrafts.

Events

International Poetry Festival (February; Granada; www.festivalpoesianicaragua.org.ni) Nicaragua has poetry in its soul, and its writers, such as Rubén Darío, Gioconda Belli, and Ernesto Cardenal are its heroes; this is where they are celebrated.

Procession of the Virgin of Carmen (July 16; SJDS) The patron saint of fishers blesses SJDS boats.

Río San Juan and Solentiname Archipelago

This side trip is taken on boats along the mighty San Juan River that connects Lake Nicaragua to the Atlantic Ocean, forming the border between Costa Rica and Nicaragua. It can be done independently, but may be more suited to adventurous travelers who speak a bit of Spanish. That's just not you? Arrange a guided tour, of perhaps several days, in La Fortuna and Sarapiquí, both covered in the Northern Zone chapter.

The steaming city of San Carlos is the regional capital, with boat connections to the border town of Los Chiles, Costa Rica, where you can catch a boat across the border, and throughout the region. Few people linger in the blue-collar port town, with little to do beyond visiting the small Spanish fortress. Instead, visitors might head west to the idyllic ★Solentiname Islands, with a few hotels and attractions, including a beautiful church, museums, and a world-famous, Sandinista-era artists collective known for detailed, primitivist paintings and colorful balsawood sculptures.

Or, tourists take the classic riverboat trip down the Río San Juan, stopping in either gritty **Boca de Sábalo**, with a few good lodges, or lovely ★**El Castillo**, a car-free collection of cute wooden buildings right on the river, topped off by the finest Spanish fortress in Nicaragua, pictured on the 50-cordoba note. A very few intrepid travelers continue all the way to the Atlantic Coast and San Juan de Nicaragua (formerly San Juan del Norte), perhaps the rainiest spot in North America, with spectacular fishing and the ruins of Greytown, founded in 1848 and destroyed during the Contra War.

Getting Around

Muggy San Carlos is the region's transportation hub. **La Costeña Air** (505-263-2142; www .tacaregional.com/costena/index.html) offers at least one flight daily from Managua to **San Carlos Airport** (NCR); get tickets well in advance. There are no flights to Costa Rica. Buses make the 10-hour trip between San Carlos and Managua six times daily.

The overland (or rather, over water) trip from Los Chiles, Costa Rica, may be Central America's most scenic border crossing. Three blocks before the Los Chiles docks, have your passport stamped at customs, across from Hotel Tulipán. Pay a $1 municipal tax at the docks, where you'll find a small restaurant and covered seating. Public boat schedules change often, but there is at least one boat daily ($10) at around 1:30 PM, which meets the 5:30 AM bus from San José (Transportes San Carlos; 506-460-5032; San José, Av 7 & Calle 12; 5-hour trip; $3). After a 1.5-hour boat trip, Nicaraguan customs in San Carlos will stamp your passport ($7). At press time, public boats returned to Costa Rica at 10:30 AM and 12:30 PM daily; it costs $2 to leave Nicaragua.

Boats leave from San Carlos to destinations throughout the region. For boats down the Río San Juan, to Sábalo, El Castillo, and San Juan de Nicaragua, make a right and walk 300m to the port; public boats leave at least four times daily to Boca de Sábalo (2.5-hour trip; $4) and El Castillo (3-hour; $4), and three times weekly to San Juan de Nicaragua (10-hour trip; $12). This is also where you catch the ferry to Granada (15-hour trip; 3 PM, Mon. and Thu., returning 3 PM, Tue. and Fri.).

The border crossing from Los Chiles, Costa Rica, to San Carlos, Nicaragua, begins on beautiful Río Frío.

For boats to Solentiname, make a left from customs and walk about 1.5 blocks to the CANTUR tourist information kiosk, right by the Solentiname docks. Boats leave Tuesday and Friday midday. There are no ATMs in the Río San Juan, and one local bank in San Carlos; bring cash. Dollars, Costa Rican colones, and of course Nicaraguan cordobas are all widely accepted and changed. Credit cards are accepted at some hotels and restaurants.

LODGING

RÍO SAN JUAN

★ **Hotel Posada del Río** (505-850-7581, 505-552-7581 reservations; El Castillo; $–$$) Wonderful new option and arguably the Río San Juan's finest lodging also boasts El Castillo's best location, right above the rapids. Enjoy the view, and sound, from gorgeous, air-conditioned, gem-toned rooms with real hot-water showers (and rain-forest showerheads), huge windows, private porches, cable TV, great mattresses, and other amenities you won't find anywhere else. It's run by Hotel Colonial in Granada, which can make reservations.

Río Indio Lodge (506-296-3338; 866-593-3176 USA; www.rioindiolodge.com; San Juan de Nicaragua; $$$$*) Deluxe, all-inclusive fishing lodge offers plush wooden rooms, great food, and package deals that could include transportation from Barra de Colorado, Costa Rica.

Hotel Sábalos (505-892-0176; Boca de Sábalo; www.hotelsabalos.com.ni; $) Immaculate wooden rooms with fans get a lovely breeze off the river in this lovely lodge, which also boasts an excellent restaurant.

★ **Sábalo Lodge** (505-583-0046, 505-278-1405; www.sabaloslodge.com; Boca de Sábalo; $–$$*) Unique lodge offers basic, open-air bamboo *cabinas* with hammock-strung porches and private cold showers. Multi-day package deals include tours, fishing trips, and meals.

Hotel Victoria (505-583-0188; hotelvictoria01@yahoo.es; El Castillo; $*) Friendly hotel and restaurant has small, clean rooms, most with Direct TV, air-conditioning, and private hot-water baths; rates include your choice of full breakfast. A great deal.

Montecristo Lodge (505-583-0197; www.montecristoriver.com; east of Boca de Sábalo; $–$$) Riverfront lodge has nice cabins with private hot showers, hiking trails, and horses, and organizes all sorts of fishing, wildlife, and community tours.

SAN CARLOS

Most lodging in the city proper is very basic, but a step above are **Hotel Cabinas Leyko** (505-583-0354; leyko@ibw.com.ni; 200m west Casa Cural; $*) offering tidy rooms, some with air-conditioning and private bath; or **Carlhys Hotel** (505-583-1121; 50m south of Catholic Church; $) with slightly better tiled rooms. **La Esquina del Lago** (505-823-5233; www.nicaraguafishing.com; $$$$*), across the Río Frio from San Carlos, offers multi-day sportfishing packages.

SOLENTINAME

Albergue Celentiname (506-377-4299; San Fernando Island; $*) Comfortable, fan-cooled cabins, one sleeping six, are surrounded by beautiful gardens with hiking trails and a petroglyph.

Hotel Cabañas Paraiso (506-301-0809; gsolentiname@amnet.com.ni; San Fernando

Island; $*) Simple rooms in paradise offer stunning views over the archipelago.

Hotel Mancarrón (506-393-9612; hmancarrun@ibw.com.ni; Mancarrón Islands; $*)
Basic, whitewashed rooms in El Refugio, heart of the art colony.

DINING

The region's big culinary draw is the famed Río San Juan shrimp, larger than many lobsters
and available at any restaurant worth its deep fryer.

RÍO SAN JUAN

El Cofalito (505-583-0185; El Castillo, by the dock; B, L, D; $–$$) Outdoor seating with a
view of the El Castillo port; also offers canoe and kayak rentals and tours.

Koma Rico (505-892-0176; Boca de Sábalo; B, L, D; $–$$) Offers great typical food and
local information (in Spanish) right by the Sábalo docks.

★ **Restaurant Vanessa** (505-583-1212; El Castillo; B, L, D; $–$$) Top-notch typical food,
including perfectly prepared river shrimp, is served right above the rapids.

SAN CARLOS

El Granadino (505-641-3812; San Carlos, above docks; L, D; $–$$) Great food, festive
ambiance, full bar, and dancing after dark.

Restaurant Mirador (505-583-0377; San Carlos, 150m south of church; L, D; $–$$) Typical
food with great view from an old Spanish lookout, with old cannons.

CULTURE

Even before the fabled connection between the Atlantic Ocean and Lake Nicaragua was discovered by Spanish conquistadors in 1525, authorities were discussing the construction of a
transoceanic canal. It would be centuries until such a project was undertaken.

Regardless, the San Juan River immediately became an all-important trade route,
attracting merchants, tourists, and pirates, who occasionally fought their way through
"Devil's Rapids" to sack Granada. In 1675, Spain built the fortress at El Castillo above the
rapids, where one of the most famous battles in Nicaraguan history was won by 19-year-old
Rafaela Herrera. After her father, the fortress commander, was killed at the onset of a 1762
pirate attack, she manned one of the cannons herself, inspiring her father's troops to vic-
tory. By the mid-1800s, the entire region had grown wealthy off U.S. settlers and gold rush-
ers taking the fastest, safest route to California. After the Panama Canal opened its locks in
1914, however, the region became an isolated and impoverished backwater. The Contra War
devastated the area, with major battles at El Castillo and the Solentiname islands killing
hundreds and destroying local infrastructure. Today, however, with help from the Spanish
government, the area is experiencing something of a renaissance, thanks in part to tourists
who are trickling into the region.

Museums

★ **El Castillo Fortress** (El Castillo; open 8 AM–noon and 1 PM–5 PM; admission $2, camera
fee $1.50, video fee $3) More properly called the Forteleza de la Limpia Pura y Immacu-
lada Concepción, this magnificent 1666 stronghold above El Castillo has been thoughtfully restored with interpretive plaques and a great museum.

The lounge at the Sábalo Lodge is right over the Río San Juan.

Museum of the Solentiname Archipelago (San Fernando Island; open 8 AM–noon and 1 PM–5 PM; admission $2) Excellent museum includes samples of the area's ancient petroglyphs, natural history displays, and lots of local art.

San Carlos Fortress (San Carlos, 100m above the plaza; open 24 hours; admission free). This 1724 edifice is now a cultural center with stunning views of the river meeting the lake.

Solentiname Library & Archaeological Salon (Mancarrón Island, open 8 AM–noon and 1 PM–5 PM, Mon.–Sat.) Community library displays the islanders' original primitivist paintings and a few ancient artifacts. It's close to ★**Nuestra Señora de Solentiname**, a historic church decorated with the simple artwork of the islands.

RECREATION

Parks and Preserves

Los Guatusos Wildlife Refuge (south of Lake Nicaragua) Enormous 430-square-kilometer (166-square-mile) reserve preserves Lake Nicaragua's southern shore, and can be reached by boat ($50–$80) from Solentiname or San Carlos. Most tours visit the **Ecological Center** (505-270-5434; www.fundar.org.ni) with guided hikes, horseback rides, canoe tours, and dorm-style lodging ($*), or **Esperanza Verde** (505-583-0354; leyko@ibw.com.ni; $$*), with simple rooms, hiking trails, and tours.

Indio-Maíz Biological Reserve (north of the Río San Juan between El Castillo and San Juan de Nicaragua) Important wildlife preserve is mostly inaccessible, but you can arrange trips to adjacent **El Quebracho Private Wildlife** Reserve (505-583-0035; fdrio@ibw.com.ni; Boca de Sábalo), with guided hikes and basic lodging; and **Refugio Bartola** (505-880-8754; www.refugiobartola.com; 3 km east of El Castillo; $*) an isolated river lodge geared toward groups, with hiking trails and guided tours.

Boat Tours

Several operators offer boat tours, including trips through the Solentiname Islands' museums, workshops, and petroglyphs. Private tours to Guatusos Wildlife Refuge, and sportfishing trips, are also offered by most outfitters. Try **Transportes Turistico San Miguel** (505-828-6136; San Carlos); **Tropic Tours** (505-583-0010; tropictours@tropictours.net; San Carlos); **Viajes Turisticos Ortíz** (505-583-0039; San Carlos, close to boats for Solentiname); or **Guatuzy Sport Fishing** (505-843-7583; www.guatuzy.com) with pricey packages in both Costa Rica and Nicaragua.

Several operators offer canoe and kayak tours; try **El Cofolito** or **Minisuper San Antonio** (505-690-0681), both in El Castillo.

Other Tours and Activities

El Castillo Butterfly Garden (El Castillo; admission $2) Women's collective runs this small *mariposario*.

The Río San Juan is one of Nicaragua's most precious and closely guarded treasures.

Guías Turísticos Río San Juan (El Castillo and Boca de Sábalo) Professional guide collective (ask your hotel to make reservations) offers tours of area parks and preserves, Spanish fortress tours, arduous treks to area hot springs, and horseback rides, among many other offerings.

Shopping

The Solentiname Archipelago is home to a world-famous artists collective, renowned for its detailed, jewel-toned primitivist paintings and colorfully painted balsawood sculptures. San Fernando Island boasts the **Union of Painters and Artisans of Solentiname "Elvis Chavarría"** (505-277-0939), selling top-of-the-line examples of both, as well as a handful of private workshop galleries. The tiny town of El Refugio on Mancarrón Island also has about 25 family workshops.

Events

International Tarpon & Bass Tournament (mid-September, San Carlos) Fishers from Nicaragua and around the world try to land record-breaking *sábalo*.
Lagunero Tournament (May, Solentiname) Annual competition to catch big fish.
San Carlos Civic Fiestas (November 4, San Carlos) Special masses and a canoe rally between San Carlos and El Castillo.

Panama

Though Panama is most famous for the Panama Canal (www.pancanal.com), it is also an up-and-coming ecotourism destination, and has preserved some 25 percent of its territory, which actually protects more biodiversity than Costa Rica. Add a rich indigenous heritage, world-class surfing, incredible hiking, quetzals flitting through the cloud forests, extensive coral reefs, 1,518 islands, and 2,850 kilometers (1,767 miles) of shoreline, and Panama is finally getting the international crowds' attention.

Panama's official currency is the U.S. dollar (and please note that Costa Rican colones are difficult to exchange once you cross the border). Tourist visas are generally good for only 30 days.

Bocas del Toro

This laid-back tropical paradise is the Caribbean of your daydreams: Sapphire-blue water, spreading coral reefs, powdery white sand, stunning jungle scenery rising behind the coconut-palm fringed beaches, and dolphins frolicking just offshore. Bocas consists of 9 islands and 52 keys, with some 250 scenic islets scattered between them, offering enough sunbathing, swimming, snorkeling, surfing, hiking, and hammock testing to keep you "busy" for weeks.

The main island is Isla Colón, home to Bocas Town, the area's urban and transportation center. From here you can arrange boats, bikes, or car taxis to several beautiful beaches, including Bluff, with surfing, and Boca del Drago, offering great snorkeling. Tiny Isla Caranero, right offshore, has a few lodging options and more fine beaches. Massive Bastimentos Island, with the tiny, car-free village of ★Old Bank, offers real Caribbean flavor and the region's best hiking and beaches, including Wizard Beach, with surfing; Playa Largo, with nesting sea turtles May through December; and Red Frog Beach, with thousands of strawberry-sized red poison dart frogs. Much of the island is protected as part of Bastimentos National Marine Park. There are several other islands and beaches, some home to lovely hotels, which can be visited on tours or by renting private boats.

GETTING AROUND

Bocas del Toro International Airport (BOC) is five blocks from the waterfront of central Bocas Town, and is served by **Nature Air** (506-299-6000; www.natureair.com), with daily flights from San José and Puerto Limón, Costa Rica; **Aeroperlas** (507-757-9341; www.aeroperlas.com), with daily service to Panama City, and to David three times a week (45 minutes from Boquete); and **Air Panama** (507-316-9000; www.flyairpanama.com) with regular flights to San José and Panama City.

Getting here overland from Puerto Viejo de Limón or Cahuita, Costa Rica, takes around three hours. Buses and taxis run 53 kilometers (33 miles) south of Puerto Viejo to the border crossing in somewhat scruffy Sixaola, with extremely basic lodging and dining. Get stamped out of Costa Rica just before the rickety trestle bridge, which you will cross on foot; make way for trucks and buses. Panamanian customs is on the other side of the bridge; you'll have to buy a $5 "tourist card." No one changes colones to dollars at the border, and colones are rarely accepted, so bring dollars! There's one bank and ATM in Bocas Town.

Collective taxis then take you 20 kilometers (12 miles; $6) to the port town of Chaguinola or (depending on tides), 35 kilometers (22 miles; $10) to the larger, busier port town of Almirante. Close to the Almirante docks is a terminal with buses to David (4-hour trip; $7) and Panama City (10-hour trip; $23). There's one direct bus daily between San José, Costa Rica, and Changuinola (Transportes Bocatoreño; 506-2222-2666; 10-hour trip; $10; departs at 10 AM daily).

Online Resources
Bocas del Toro, Panama (www.bocas-del-toro.org) Well-organized site with links and information.
Bocas del Toro Portal (www.bocas.com) Comprehensive portal with hotels, vacation rentals, tour operators, and real estate agents.
Boquete Times (www.theboquetetimes.com) Arts and culture magazine offers articles and links.
Boquete.org (www.boquete.org) Comprehensive listings geared to expatriates.
Boquete Guide (www.boqueteguide.com) Blog-style coverage of Boquete.
Panama Live (www.mypanamalive.com) Online tourism magazine with cool videos, plus news, information, and links.
★ **Panama Tour Planner** (www.panamainfo.com) Free online guidebook to the country, with links.
★ **Republic of Panama** (www.republic-of-panama.com) Nuts and bolts info you need to know before you go.
Virtual Panama (www.virtualpanama.com) Well-written descriptions of Panama's attractions and services.

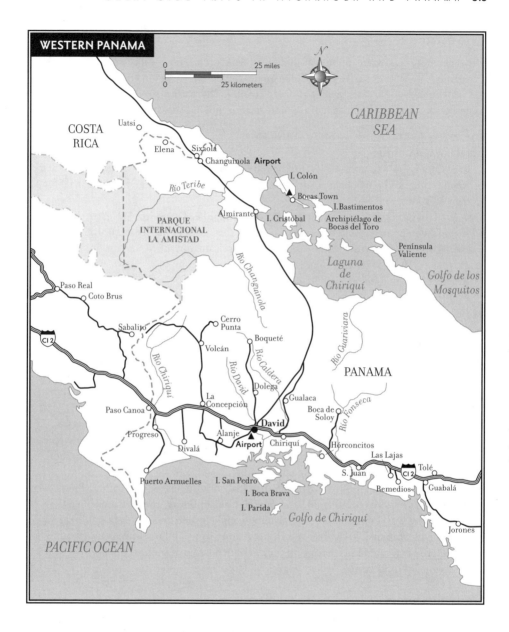

Collective boat taxis run from Changuinola ($6) and Almirante ($4) to Bocas Town, with the airport and most hotels, restaurants, and services. From here, you can arrange private boat taxis to Carenero ($1), Bastimentos ($2.50), and more remote island beaches. Car taxis can take you to the Smithsonian ($.50), Bluff Beach ($8), or Boca de Drago ($14).

Several maps are available online, including **Bocas Portal** (www.bocas.com/btistown .htm) with maps of the archipelago and Bocas Town; and **Bocas Marine Tours** (www.bocas marinetours.com) also shows boat taxi routes. Free maps are available at the **IPAT Tourism Office** (507-322-1338; www.visitpanama.com; Bocas Town, Calle 1 & Av D; open 8:30 AM–4:30 PM, Mon.–Fri.), or purchase a *Ruta de Aventura Bocas Del Toro* ($3.50) at area shops.

Lodging

The recent tourism explosion means that there are scores of hotels accommodating every price range, most in Bocas Town, but also on nearby Carenero and in Old Bank, Bastimentos, which make up the archipelago's "urban" center. There are also several lodges, many quite upscale, scattered across more remote islands and beaches on the archipelago.

Bocas Town, Carenero, and Old Bank Hotels

Hotel Bocas del Toro (507-757-9771; www.hotelbocasdeltoro.com; Bocas Town, Calle 1 & 3; $$$) Century-old boutique hotel on the water offers Caribbean styling, small polished-wood rooms, and plush details such as 400-thread count sheets, and WiFi. Spring for a balcony room, well worth it.

Casa Acuario (507-757-9565; joberg1301@cwp.net.pa; Isla Carenero; $$) With a bed-and-breakfast ambiance (though breakfast is extra) this guest house has appealing wooden rooms over the water, air-conditioning, gorgeous cane furniture, and original art.

★ **Eclypse de Mar** (507-6430-4730; www.eclypsedemar.com; Bastimentos Island; $$$*) Argentine-owned luxurious polished hardwood, thatch-roofed bungalows are arranged over the water, next to 2.5 hectares (6 acres) of private rain forest. Elegant furnishings include built-in glass "tables" that let you see into the water, plus lots of louvered wood shutters that open your fan-cooled oasis to the tropical breezes, and private porches with hammocks.

Hotel El Limbo (507-757-9062; www.ellimbo.com; Calle 1 & 3; $$–$$$*) Well-maintained, historic Victorian offers pretty, air-conditioned rooms; those with ocean views are larger and nicer. The **restaurant** (B, L, D; $$) is top notch, with great pizza. They have a secluded lodge on Bastimentos ($$–$$$*).

Hotel Swan's Cay (507-757-9090; www.swanscayhotel.com; Calle 2; Bocas Town; $$$) Bocas Town's long-standing luxury option now boasts a nice pool and oceanfront terrace two blocks from the hotel, as well as a plush lobby with lots of teak and antiques, but rooms are somewhat cramped and outdated.

★ **Tropical Suites** (507-6689-9394; www.tropical-suites.com; Bocas Town, Calle 1; $$$–$$$$) The most comfortable accommodations in Bocas Town are modern rather than quaint, with lots of taupe, ivory, bamboo, and chrome decorating large and airy suites. Full kitchens, WiFi, air-conditioning, and dining and work areas are great, though you may spend more time on your private porch overlooking the bay. There are discounts for long-term stays.

Outlying Hotels

Casa Cayuco (www.casacayuco.com; Bastimentos Island, 45 minutes from Bocas Town; $$$$*) Surrounded by the national park, this jungle-enshrouded, all-inclusive retreat overlooking quiet coral reefs offers three deluxe wooden bungalows, fan cooled and breezy with solar-heated showers, fine furnishings, and indigenous handicrafts as décor.

★ **Dolphin Bay Hideaway** (507-6618-2020; www.dolphinbayhideaway.com; Bocorito, San Cristóbal Island, 20 minutes from Bocas Town; $$–$$$*) This attractive bed-and-breakfast is far from the crowds and close to nature, offering three cheerfully painted and comfortably furnished rooms, with fine porches, and a menagerie of wildlife. It's remote, so water and electricity may be in short supply, though there is WiFi. A great deal.

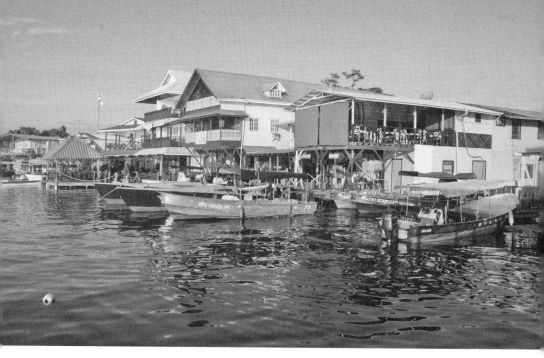

Bocas Town, on Isla Colón, has hotels and restaurants built out over the calm Caribbean waters.

Hacienda del Toro (507-757-9158; www.haciendadeltoro.com; Bocarito, San Cristóbal Island, 20 minutes south of Bocas Town; $$$*) More modern option in Bocorito offers nicely decorated cabins with WiFi, hot water, and private porches overlooking the pool.

La Loma Lodge & Butterfly Farm (507-6619-5364; www.thejunglelodge.com; Bastimentos, Bahía Honda, 15 minutes from Bocas Town; $$$$*) Spacious, airy cabins with romantically dressed beds, simple furnishings, and relaxing porches open onto hilltop views over a deep bay and Isla Solarte. All meals, transport, and tours of the butterfly farm are included.

Punta Caracol (507-757-9718; www.puntacaracol.com; Isla Colón, 20 minutes from Bocas Town; $$$$*) Stretched along an arc of slender bridges across a shallow Caribbean reef, these beautifully constructed thatch-roofed bungalows with modern, almost minimalist décor and some of the best hammocks anywhere, offer a secluded paradise.

⭑ **Tranquilo Bay** (507-380-0721, 713-589-6952 USA; www.tranquilobay.com; Isla Bastimentos; $$$$*) The plushest lodge in Bocas del Toro offers all the luxuries (including air conditioning) in large, modern cabins overlooking the bay. Cool white tiles, hardwood accents, small sitting areas, and large hammock-festooned porches; close to an indigenous village that you're welcome to visit on one of the many tours.

DINING

The region's best grocery stores (still quite basic) are in Bocas Town; stock up before heading to other islands. **Super Gourmet** (507-757-9357; end of Calle 3 beside Hotel Bahía, Bocas Town) has a deli with sandwiches and salads, and also carries a nice selection of upscale international groceries, including organic chocolate bars from the **Caribbean Chocolate Company** (www.caribbean-chocolate-company.com).

International

Casbah (507-6647-4727; Bocas Town; Av G north; D, closed Sun. $$–$$$) Mediterranean and Middle Eastern specialties, including kebabs and several vegetarian-friendly salads, served in rather romantic environs.

Cosmic Crab Café (507-757-9157; www.careeningcay.com; Caranero Island; L, D, closed Mon.; $$–$$$$) The specialty is Caribbean king crab claws, served with lime garlic butter sauce. But fresh fish is delivered daily, then perhaps steamed in a banana leaf, made into seafood lasagna, blackened, or sesame seared with wasabi ginger sauce. Chicken, steak, and vegetarian food are also available, but at least start with the crab cakes, and finish with the key lime pie.

Guari Guari (507-6627-1825; Isla Colón, Playa Itsmito, 2 kilometers from Bocas Town; D, closed Wed.; $$–$$$) Make reservations to enjoy this Spanish and German-owned restaurant offering an ever-changing menu of gourmet Continental cuisine, with Mediterranean, Asian, and Latin influences. Go for the full six-course dinner ($14).

Lemongrass Bar & Restaurant (507-6721-6445; kepaho@hotmail.com; Bocas Town; L, D; $$–$$$) On a relatively elegantly decorated porch overlooking the bay, this spot offers great (if less than authentic) Thai food, such as chimichanga spring rolls (fried!), spicy coconut soups, and Asian-accented seafood specials every night. Lunch is less expensive, with creative sandwiches and wraps; try the curried chicken.

Om Café (Calle 5 & Av G; open B, D; $$) Polished second-floor spot does acceptable Indian cuisine, most of it vegetarian, with quite a bit of flourish and excellent service.

Último Refugio (507-6640-1878; Bocas Town, Av Sur, at end of Calle 3; D, closed Mon.; $$–$$$) Ramshackle shotgun shack extending out over the water does surprisingly sophisticated cuisine, such as sesame seared tuna steak, Asian shrimp soup, and vegetarian options. There's often live music.

The town of Old Bank, on Bastimentos Island, is the heart of Bocas del Toro's Caribbean soul.

Caribbean and Panamanian Cuisine

Caribbean Delights (Parque Bolivar; L, D; $) Grab a fresh fruit shake (dozens of fruits on offer) and a snack at this stand next to Bocas Town's central park.

★ **Doña Mara** (507-757-9551; www.donamara.com; Carenero Island; B, L, D; $$–$$$$) Tidy, unassuming bed-and-breakfast offers modern, air-conditioned rooms with antique furnishings and cable TV ($$*), as well as one of the best Caribbean-style seafood joints on the islands, with great burgers and salads as well.

Lili's Café (507-6560-8777; www.kodiakbocas.com/lilis; Bocas Town, Calle 1; B, L; $–$$) Do breakfast right, watching the sunrise drape every bayfront Victorian curlicue and column with ribbons of gold. Lili serves up sandwiches, pastas, soups, homemade bread, and more alongside her signature "Killin' Me Man" pepper sauce.

Le Pirate (Bocas Town; Calle 1 & Av D; L, D; $$–$$$) Get your buccaneer on at this local favorite, serving Caribbean style seafood right by the water taxi docks.

★ **Roots** (507-6626-3340; Old Bank; L, D, closed Tue.; $) Bastimentos landmark serves the best Caribbean cuisine in the archipelago—ceviche, pork chops, chicken, fresh seafood dishes, all served with rice and beans simmered in coconut milk—above the water in a simple, open-air wooden dining room.

Bakeries and Cafés

Panadería y Dulcería Aleman (507-757-9436; Calle 5 & Av G; $) European breads and delicious pastries, plus breakfast and sandwiches throughout the day.

Starfish Coffee (507-6621-4108; Calle 3, Av A & B; open B, L, D, closed Sun.; $$) Cool community-oriented coffee shop over the water offers coffee, pastries, sushi after 5 PM, and tapas throughout the day.

CULTURE

Though Christopher Columbus stopped here in 1502, the Spanish never successfully settled the region, leaving the Guaymí Indians, today known as the Ngöbe-Buglé, to retain their culture and land, more or less. Instead, the first foreign settlers were British and Afro-Antillean pirates, who attempted to settle Boca del Drago in the 1700s, and in 1826, founded Bocas Town, building many of the village's pretty gingerbread Victorians, classic examples of Caribbean architecture.

Free, English-speaking Afro-Antilleans began arriving in the late 1800s to work the banana plantations in what was becoming Panama's wealthiest region. After a banana blight destroyed the crops and economy in the 1920s, however, the region fell into poverty and isolation, developing its own language, a Creole called Guari-Guari, and relying on subsistence agriculture and fishing. When Chiquita returned to the area with disease-resistant bananas, wages were much lower and failed to revive Bocas.

Then in the early 2000s, international tourists began flooding Bocas from across the border, creating an economic boom for which the islanders were rather unprepared. Panama does not protect citizens and national parks from foreign investors as well as Costa Rica does, so please try to patronize locally owned businesses, and avoid properties that put the national park or reefs at risk.

In addition to enjoying the local Caribbean culture, you can also visit indigenous-operated ecotourism projects such as such as **Bahia Honda** (507-6669-6269; www.bocas.com

/indians/bahiahonda.htm; Bastimentos; reservations required) with guided jungle hikes, handicrafts, and a restaurant serving Ngöbe and international food over the water.

Nightlife

Barco Hundido (Bocas Town, Calle 2) Young crowd, dancing, and a sunken ship right off-shore.

★ **La Feria** (Bastimentos) Also known as Blue Monday, classic wooden bar right on the water offers cheap beer, live music, and a great Caribbean vibe.

Iguana Bar & Surf Club (www.bocas.com/laiguana.htm; Bocas Town, Calle 1) Live DJs, great reggae, a full bar, and surf videos—what else do you need?

Mondo Taitu (507-757-9425; Bocas Town) Backpacker hostel also hosts the most hopping happy hour in town.

Pickled Parrot (507-757-9853; bocasbluemarlin.com; Isla Carenero; $$–$$$) Boisterous restaurant and bar above the water has burgers, great ceviche, and karaoke on Wednesday. They also rent guest rooms.

RECREATION

Parks and Preserves

Bastimentos Island National Marine Park (507-758-8967; Bastimentos Island and Zapatillos Key; open 8 am–6 pm; admission $10) Established in 1988 as Panama's first national marine park, this 13,226-hectare (32,668-acre) preserve stretches from tiny Zapatillos Key across the center of Bastimentos Island, protecting Playa Larga, where four species of sea turtle nest between May and September. You can camp ($5) at either Playa Larga or Zapatillos with permission from **ANAM** (507-757-9442; Calle 1), in Bocas Town.

The coral reefs off Zapatillos Key have the best diving and snorkeling in the region, with fairly healthy coral, underwater caves, and nurse sharks. Visibility is low after it rains. You can also hike around the Bastimentos section of the park; guides hang out in Old Bank.

Bicycles

Isla Colón's best beaches can be reached by bicycle. Ask at your hotel, or try **Bocas Rent-a-Bike** (507-6446-0787; Calle 1 & Av D).

Boat Tours

In general, boat tours are full-day affairs that take in three or four beaches and snorkel areas at a time; tours may also include visits to a dolphin breeding ground and/or bat cave.

Agua Azul (507-6604-6559; www.aguaazulbocas.com; Bocas Town; $250 per full day, $450 per half day) Luxury charters include food, fishing and snorkel equipment, CD player, E-Tek 175, and GPS.

Bocas Marine & Tours (507-757-9033; www.bocasmarinetours.com; Bocas Town, Main St.) Taxi service and tours.

Boteros Bocatoreños Unidos (507-757-9760; boterosbocas@yahoo.com; Bocas Town, Calle 3) Taxi service and tours.

Catamaran Sailing (507-757-9710; www.bocassailing.com; Bocas Town, next to Hotel Dos Palmas) Snorkel tours on a sailboat.

The fiercely independent Kuna people sell their remarkable molas, *traditional reverse appliqué textiles, in Bocas Town.*

El Jaguar Tours (507-757-9383, 507-6633-5036; Old Bank, Bastimentos) Bastimentos operation offers all the tours with bilingual guides.

Diving and Snorkeling

Calm, often clear waters make this a fine place to dive, but visibility is low after it rains; be patient. Zapatillos, inside the marine park, and Hospital Point, with a serious wall, are the best dive sites. Most hotels have snorkel equipment to lend or rent.

Bocas Water Sports (507-757-9541; www.bocaswatersports.com) Dive trips, plus kayak and boat tours.

La Buga Dive Center (507-757-9534; www.labugapanama.com; Bocas Town, nest to El Último Refugio) Certification and custom trips.

The Dutch Pirate (507-757-1414; www.thedutchpirate.com; Bastimentos) Bastimentos operator.

★ **Starfleet Diving** (507-757-9642; www.starfleetscuba.com; Calle 1 & Av 3) Diving and snorkel tours, PADI certification, massages, and package deals.

Other Tours and Activities

Ancon Expeditions (www.anconexpeditions.com) Renowned adventure outfitter offers tours and lodging in Bocas and beyond.

Bocas Butterfly Garden (507-757-9008; open 9 AM–3 PM, Wed.–Mon.; Isla Caranero, $5) Small *mariposario* has Panamanian species.

Finca Los Monos (507-757-9461; www.bocasdeltorobotanicalgarden.com; Isla Colón, north of Bocas Town, just past Smithsonian; open 1 PM, Mon. and 8:30 AM, Fri.; admission $10) Botanical gardens feature dozens of species of heliconia, ginger, palm, and other tropical plants.

SOPOSO Rainforest Adventure (507-6631-2222; www.soposo.com; Changuinola) Unusual operator offers guided day trips ($90) into the rain forest, including visits to indigenous villages. Or, stay overnight in their basic lodge.

Smithsonian Tropical Research Institute (www.stri.org; 2 km north of Bocas Town) Free tours of this tropical-ecosystems research facility are offered every Friday and Saturday at 3 PM.

★ **Spanish by the Sea** (507-757-9518; www.spanishbythesea.com; Calle 4 & Av A) Spanish school also has campuses in Boquete, Panama, and Turrialba, Costa Rica.

Surfing

Bocas has some excellent and uncrowded surfing, particularly from December through March. On Isla Colón, Paunch is good for less experienced surfers, with a sandy bottom and three peaks; while Bluff Beach has a long, powerful break; and Dump, a coral bottom and short, tubular ride. Carenero Island has a reef break on the northern tip, with long tubes. Hire a boat to Silverbacks, with insane waves that can reach 7 meters (25 feet). On Bastimentos, Wizard Beach and neighboring Second Beach both get good beach breaks.

Bocas Surf School (www.bocassurfschool.com) Conveniently located at **Lula's B&B** (507-757-9057; www.lulabb.com; Calle 6 & Av G, across from Cocomo; $$*), with tidy, air-conditioned rooms featuring WiFi and great beds, this surf school offers day classes and packages.

Del Toro Surf (507-6570-8277; deltorosurf@yahoo.com.ar; Isla Colón) Arranges lessons and surf tours.

Spas

Estetic Island Relax (507-6688-4303; islandrelax@hotmail.com; Calle 10 & Av G, across from the hospital) Day spa offers massages, wraps, facials, and waxes.

SHOPPING

Kuna Indians sell remarkable handicrafts at stands all over town, including their spectacular beadwork and reverse-appliqué textiles called *molas*, amazing pieces of art that cost between $10 and $60, depending on quality. Learn more before you buy at **Panama Art** (www.panart.com/molainfo.htm).

Up In the Hill (Bastimentos Island) Steep, sometimes muddy, 15-minute hike from Old Bank rewards you with this bohemian outpost selling lovely and inexpensive organic lotions, creams, soaps, and more.

EVENTS

May Day (May 1) A Caribbean tradition, the Palo de Mayo (Maypole Dance) takes place every Labor Day.

Bocas Town Civic Fiestas (November 16) Parties and parades mark Bocas' founding.

Bastimentos Civic Fiestas (November 23) Bastimentos takes over as party host, with live music, dance parties, and more parades.

Boquete

Spring is always in the air in this high-altitude (1,057-meter/3,477-foot) escape from Panama's Pacific heat, perfumed with flowers. Surrounded by brilliant green mountains, including Panama's only major volcano, Barú (3,475 meters/11,398 feet), this has long been a mountain retreat for the country's wealthy. It is fast becoming an international destination, with lovely lodging and dining options in the *bahareque*, a floating, misty sort of rain that doesn't really get you wet but rather refracts the light into multiple rainbows. The agricultural region is also famed for its oversized vegetables, honey-sweet oranges, and fine coffee, including one of the world's top brews, La Esmeralda Especial Geisha (www.hacienda esmeralda.com), which sells for as much as $130 per pound.

GETTING AROUND

The major regional hub, 40 kilometers (24 miles) south of Boquete, is David, Panama's third largest city, capital of Chiriquí Province, and home to **Enrique Malek International Airport** (DAV; airport.u.nu/DAV). It's served by Air Panama (www.flyairpanama.com), flying to Panama City daily, and San José, Costa Rica, three times weekly; and Aeroperlas (www.aeroperlas.com), with daily service to Panama City and flights to Bocas del Toro three times per week. From the airport, **Boquete Shuttle Service** (507-720-1635; www.adventurist .com; Los Establos Plaza on Boquete's Main St; $10), runs between the airport and Boquete hotels. If you stay overnight, David's best hotel is the **Gran Hotel Nacional** (507-775-2221; hotelnacionalpanama.com; Calle Central; $$–$$$), with large, air-conditioned, slightly outdated business-class rooms and suites, two great restaurants, a fairly fabulous pool, and a casino.

Taxis charge about $3 to make the 5-kilometer (3-mile) run from the airport to the bus terminal, where buses make the 45-minute trip for $1.50 between David and Boquete every half hour. You can also get buses from David to Almirante (4-hour trip; $7), where you can catch boat taxis to Bocas del Toro; Panama City (8-hour trip; $15); and direct to San José (Tracopa; 8-hour trip; $15) once daily at 7:30 AM. The border crossing at Paso Canoas is easy to navigate, but time consuming; allow two hours. Entering Panama costs $5, leaving $1.

Taxis congregate at Boquete's Central Plaza. Central Boquete is extremely strollable, with most restaurants and hotels within a few blocks, but several hotels and restaurants are far from town. Pick up a free regional map provided by Casa Solution, a local real estate company, or purchase a *Rutas de Aventuras Boquete Map* ($3.50; www.rutasdeaventura.com). The official tourist office, **IPAT** (507-526-7000; 1.5 km/1 mi. south of Boquete; open 9 AM–6 PM, Mon.–Fri.) has maps and information, or try **Cacique Souvenirs**, open daily on the southwest corner of the central plaza, with maps and free tourist information in English.

LODGING

These are just a few of the many, many options available.

Hotels

Boquete Garden Inn (507-720-2376; www.boquetegardeninn.com; Palo Alto, just north of Boquete; $$*) With views over Boquete and the mountains, this appealing inn offers several spacious, warmly (if simply) decorated *cabinas* furnished with full kitchenettes and set in lovely gardens.

★ **Isla Verde** (507-720-2533; islaverdepanama.com; 200m west of Banco Nacional; $$– $$$) Quiet cluster of architecturally outstanding "roundhouses"—spacious, colorful, two-story, fully-equipped apartments with every amenity—are based on Indian design, and tastefully decorated with bright European sensibilities, cheerful Panamanian hand-icrafts, and comfortable, artsy furniture, all with impeccable style. Breakfast is available, or you may cook it yourself in the full kitchen. Suites have private balconies with views.

Panamonte Inn & Spa (507-720-1324; www.panamonte.com; 200m north of Catholic church; $$$) Handsome wooden inn has hosted Boquete's VIP visitors since 1914, and still radiates an old world grace among the gorgeous gardens, appealing spa, absolutely beautiful ★**hotel bar**, and the excellent **restaurant** (L, D; $$$) serving upscale Pana-manian fusion cuisine. Rooms, however, are on the small side (suites are a bit better) and despite modern amenities, could use an overhaul.

Valle Escondido (507-720-2454; www.valleescondido.biz; well-signed 600m west of Main St; $$$$*) Boquete's most luxurious option is at Valle Escondido, a gated, Mediter-ranean-esque residential community of luxurious villas overlooking a nine-hole golf course. The hotel is cleverly designed like an Italian village, complete with cobbled walkways. Rooms and suites are appointed with rich fabrics, leather and wicker furnish-ings, Persian rugs, and all modern amenities, from flat-screened TVs to hairdryers. There's an on-site spa, pool with a solarium, full gym, three good restaurants, and sta-bles.

Bed-and-Breakfasts

Hotel Los Establos (507-720-2685; www.losestablos.net; north of Boquete; $$$*) Small, Mission-Revival style hotel, all sweeping arches and ancient *tejas*, has cozy, comfortable rooms with wood and wicker furnishings, a saloon festooned with cowboy hats, and splendid volcano views.

Finca Lerida (507-720-2285; www.fincalerida.com; 9 km/5 mi. north of Boquete; $$–$$$*) Built in the 1910s to Scandinavian specs by a Norse architect who had worked on the canal, this cozy clutch of quaint cabins and fairly basic wooden rooms, all tidy and cheerfully decorated, are surrounded by a coffee plantation and private cloud forest.

La Montaña y el Valle Coffee Estate Inn (507-720-2211; www.coffeeestateinn.com; Calle Jaramillo Alto; $$$*) Romantic mountaintop inn has three generously sized bungalows, comfortably furnished with excellent beds, bright indoor sitting areas, and private porches, hidden among beautiful gardens within a coffee plantation. Breakfast, with homemade scones and sweet oranges, as well as the optional gourmet candlelit dinners, can be served en suite.

★ **Palo Alto Riverside Hotel** (507-720-1076; www.paloaltoriverside.com; Palo Alto, north

Valle Escondido is one of Boquete's best hotels.

of Boquete; \$\$\$–\$\$\$\$*) Absolutely stunning inn overlooking the river offers six divinely inspired rooms with large windows (some with entire walls of glass), slate floors, and excellent bathrooms with Italian fixtures, French toiletries, and bathtubs. Graceful teak furnishings imported from Bali, Egyptian cotton sheets, WiFi, plasma TVs, and other elegant amenities make this a winner. The ★**restaurant** (B, L, D; \$\$–\$\$\$) serves beautifully presented Panamanian and international cuisine (the specialty is trout) overlooking the river.

DINING

The international expatriate set is discovering Boquete, and both opening and enjoying a fine collection of elegant eateries.

International Restaurants

Al Zaraya (Middle Eastern; 507-720-2707; 200m west of Los Establos Plaza; L, D; \$\$\$) In an oddly out-of-place Moroccan fortress, enjoy Middle Eastern and Mediterranean cuisine, a full bar, and belly dancing Saturday night.

★ **Art Café la Crepe** (French; 507-6769-6090; 150m north of the Catholic church; L, D;

closed Mon.; $$) Vibrant décor, including original art, and exquisite crêpes, such as shrimp in white wine sauce, or fried apple with rum flambé, make this excellent little restaurant with a respectable wine list a winner.

Bistro Boquete (International; 507-720-1017; B, L, D; closed Mon.; $$–$$$) Elegantly rustic environs—a historic building, wooden bar and tables, indigenous fabrics, and awesome murals—make a fine backdrop to knockout international cuisine, including perfectly prepared steak, creative trout dishes, pastas, and vegetarian offerings.

Hibiscus (French; 507-720-2652; Alto Lino; B, L, D; closed Thu. and Sun.; $$$–$$$$) Though Boquete's favorite French eatery has moved to new, more scenic environs up Alto Lino road, the ever-changing menu of classic Continental cuisine made with the freshest Panamanian ingredients remains one of the region's highlights.

★ **Il Pianista Trottaria** (Italian; 507-720-2728; L, D; closed Mon.; $$–$$$) Everyone loves this outstanding spot for upscale Italian classics, wood-fired pizzas, real Caesar salads, and huge calzones all served in an old log and flagstone cabin next to a waterfall. Don't skip the creative seafood cocktails.

★ **Machu Pichu** (Peruvian; 507-720-1502; behind Banco Nacional; L, D; $$) Tucked away in a strip mall, this serves absolutely top-of-the-line, attentively presented ceviches, and other traditional Peruvian cuisine. Try the *corvine del chef* in lobster salsa, or the *arroz marinera*, rice with shellfish, known for its invigorating properties.

Panamanian Restaurants

Central Park Café (507-6482-2777; behind Central Plaza Park, next to the Farmer's Market; open 6 AM–9 PM; $) Inexpensive typical food and set plates close to the park.

★ **Restaurant Sabrosón** (507-720-2147; Main St, across from Deli Barú; B, L, D; $) No matter how wealthy or refined you are, don't miss this excellent steam-table buffet, serving Panamanian classics like fresh trout and *sancocho*, a spicy chicken-and-vegetable soup.

Roxane's Grill (507-6675-7508; L, D, closed Mon.; $$–$$$) Relaxing spot overlooking the river offers grilled meats and fish, roasted chicken, and baby back ribs.

Bakeries and Cafés

Café Kotowa (507-720-3852; Main St, Los Establos Plaza; open 8:30 AM–4:30 PM) Great Panamanian coffee, Starbucks strip-mall ambiance, and an on-site tour operator that rents cars.

★ **Café Ruiz** (www.caferuiz.com; toward Mi Jardín Es Su Jardín; open 7 AM–6 PM, Mon.–Sat., 10 AM–6 PM, Sun.) For almost 90 years, this classic Boquete coffee shop has been caffeinating clients on their way to the gardens.

Lerida Estate Café (507-6611-8062; open 7 AM–9 PM) High atop Boquete—take the left fork before Panamonte Inn, then a left at the next fork—café offers beautiful mountain views, delicious traditional and international cuisine, and a decent wine list.

Punto de Encuentro (507-720-2123; 50m off Main St, close to Boquete Country Inn; B; $) Boquete's best breakfast amidst beautiful gardens.

Sugar & Spice (just north of "Y," make a left at La Huaca; B, L; $) Sean and Ada of the local Vegetarian Society run this friendly spot, serving muffins, fruit-filled empanadas, enchiladas, and more.

Grocery Stores and Delis

There are several small grocery stores in town, including **Romero** (behind Central Plaza Park; open 24/7) and **Bruna Supermercado** (Main St, kitty-corner from Bistro Boquete). For large, U.S.-style grocers, you'll need to visit David.

Deli Barú (507-720-2619; main road; open 9 AM–8 PM; $) Brands from the United States, Europe, and beyond, plus sandwiches and snacks.

Farmer's Market (across from Romero; open 7 AM–3 PM, Mon.–Sat.) Inexpensive produce straight from the farm.

CULTURE

Until 1916 Boquete was just another remote agricultural village, where descendents of Spanish settlers and Guayarí Indians gleaned a living from the rich volcanic soil. That's until the railroad rolled through. Overnight, Boquete was tied to the national, and international economy, and began growing export crops—vegetables, navel oranges, flowers, and coffee. Though the collapse of coffee prices in the 1990s hit the town hard, the growing tourist industry kept the economy from collapsing altogether. Recently named one of the world's most desirable retirement spots, the expatriate industry continues to expand, driving land prices straight up.

Boquete is also an important trade town for the Ngöbe and Buglé (collectively known as the Guaymí) people, who augment their subsistence economy by working the coffee plantations and selling high quality handicrafts, available all over town. Gentlemen usually wear modern Western clothes, while ladies still swirl through the City of Flowers in brightly colored, hand-appliquéd dresses.

Nightlife

Amigos (506-720-2714; on Central Park; open 7:30 AM–whenever) Casual pub with great cheeseburgers, pool tables, NFL in season, and garden seating.

Bar La Huaca (100m north of Zanzibar; open Thu.–Sun.) Popular disco gets packed on Friday for ladies night, with DJs other nights.

La Cabaña (507-720-2433; across the river from downtown Boquete; opens 5 PM, Tue.–Sat.) Live music and international cocktails in a log cabin overlooking the river.

Panamonte Garden Bar (507-720-1327; 100m north of town; open noon–11:30 PM) Gorgeous bar with sofas, easy chairs, and a fireplace overlooks the lovely gardens of this historic hotel.

Zanzibar Jazz Club (507-720-1699; www.barzanzibar.com; end of Main St; open Wed.–Mon., 4 PM–midnight) Greek-owned with African décor, international liquors, and a jazz soundtrack (live music on weekends), this is the hippest spot in town for a tipple.

RECREATION

Parks and Preserves

Barú Volcano National Park (507-775-2055; 11 km west of Boquete; admission $3) Cloudforested Volcán Barú (3,475 meters/11,398 feet), Panama's only active volcano and highest point, offers excellent hiking through the mist. The 8-kilometer (5-mile) Quetzal Trail connects Boquete to the town of Cerro Punta; most hikers take a bus one way; it's uphill from Boquete. You could stay in Cerro Punta at ★**Los Quetzales Lodge** (507-771-2182; www.losquetzales.com; Guadalupe; $$$*), featuring fully-equipped wooden *cabinas* with WiFi and kitchens on a private, 312-hectare (770-acre) reserve inside the national park. Alternately, ranger stations offer very basic dorm beds and camping ($). Dress warmly, as it can get down below 8°C (45°F) at night. You can also summit Barú, a serious, 10 to 12-hour guided hike; some companies do part of the trail in a four-wheel-drive. It will probably rain, so come prepared.

Botanical Gardens

Paradise Gardens (507-6615-6618; paradisegardensboquete.com; Bajo Volcanicito; open 9 AM–1 PM, Tue.–Fri., 10 AM–4 PM, Sat. and Sun.; admission $5) Botanical garden and wildlife sanctuary displays birds, monkeys, big cats, a friendly kinkajou, and other rescued animals, also boasts the biggest butterfly garden in Panama.

★ **Mi Jardín es Su Jardín** (My Garden in Your Garden; just north of town, make a left at La Huaca; open 9 AM–5 PM; admission free) Spry nonagenarian Eduardo González Jované has opened his spectacular gardens, with more than 50 types of flowers, plus sculptures, bridges, slides, and a small chapel, to the (nonsmoking) public, free of charge. And that's Panamanian hospitality.

Coffee Tours

Café Ruiz (507-720-3852; north of town, toward Mi Jardín Es Su Jardín; www.caferuiz.com; $22.50) Make reservations for pickup at their cute mountainside café to tour the coffee plantation and roasting plant.

Kotowa Coffee (507-720-3852; www.coffeeadventures.net; entrance of Boquete Valley; tours weekends, by reservation) See Kotowa's coffee plantation.

Golf

Cielo Paraiso (507-720-2431; www.cieloparaiso.com) Residential community plans to have Boquete's first 18-hole course open by late 2008.

Valle Escondido Golf (507-720-2454; www.valleescondido.biz; well-signed 600m west of Main St; $34, cart $25) Nine-hole executive course.

Guided Hikes

Several guides offer a variety of hikes, including the Quetzal Trail (6 hours, $30–$80); Barú Volcano (10 hours, $70–$100), with tours starting well before sunrise; Caldera Hot Springs and Petroglyphs (4 hours; $20–$30); and across La Amistad International Park to Bocas del Toro (5 days). Camping can almost always be arranged.

Feliciano Gonzalez (507-6624-9940; www.geocities.com/boquete_tours)

Panama Expeditions (507-6462-9584; panama.tours@yahoo.es) Also offers hikes in nearby Cerro Punta, Veraguas, Barrilles Archaeological Park, and the Chiriquí coast.

Eduardo Serrano (507-6601-6479; eduardo_serrano_quiel@hotmail.com) Specializes in birding.

Other Activities

Boquete Tree Trek (507-720-1635; www.canopypanama.com; office at Los Establos Plaza, Main St; admission $60) Fly through the clouds on this 3-kilometer (1.8-mile), 13-platform canopy tour, with Tarzan swing. They also arrange biking, hiking, and other tours.

Boquete Mountain Safari Tours (507-6742-6614; www.boquetemountainsafaritours.com; $35–75) Jeep tours through the mountains.

Habla Ya Spanish School (507-720-1294; www.hablayapanama.com; Los Establos Plaza, Main St.) Spanish courses, community tours, volunteer opportunities, and homestays.

White-Water Rafting

These well-watered mountains offer top-notch rafting, from family-friendly Class I floats to wilder Class III–IV rides year-round, morphing into serious Class V expert white water in rainy season. There are two excellent operators located on Main St: ★**Chiriquí River Rafting** (507-720-1505; www.panama_rafting.com) and **Panama Rafters** (507-6633-4313; www.panamarafters.com), with similar prices ($70–$100) and services.

Spas

The Haven (507–720-1327 Panamonte Inn; 507-720-1943 Valle Escondido; www.thehaven spa.com) Located at two of Boquete's best hotels, offers massages, facials, and pedicures, plus laser and holistic therapies.

SHOPPING

Boutiques and galleries are gaining a foothold in this increasingly upmarket village, but for malls and department stores, you'll need to visit David.

Cacique Souvenirs (507-720-2217; southwest of Central Plaza) Good souvenir shop also sells English-language books and offers tourist information.

Estilo Campo (507-720-1390; north of Catholic church) Cute yellow cottage houses artisans painting adorable birdhouses with flowers; they also sell strawberry marmalade and homemade ices, called *duros* in Panama.

Folklorica (507-720-1212; north of Catholic church) Great souvenirs, beautiful antiques, and used English-language books. Next door, **Puente del Mundo** offers traditional Panamanian handicrafts, including indigenous masks and clothing.

Read & Relax Boquete (507-202-2158; Plaza Los Establos, Main St.) Cozy bookstore with lots of English-language titles.

EVENTS

Flower and Coffee Fair (January) The City of Flowers blooms for two weeks as Boquete displays beautiful bouquets.

Boquete Jazz Festival (mid-February) Live jazz from national and international musicians at venues all over town.

Orchid Fair (April) The riverside fairgrounds are once again filled with flowers.

Fascinating tiger-herons enjoy the Pacific Coast.

Outdoor Adventures

You know the statistics: More than 28 percent of this stunning country is protected, and despite its small size contains some 4 percent of the planet's genetic library, boasting more biodiversity than entire continents. Moreover, this greenest of nations has also protected much of its 1,290 kilometers (800 miles) of coastline, washed by both the Pacific and Caribbean, to guarantee that their jungle-enshrouded beaches will still welcome nesting sea turtles as well as blissed-out surfers. And then there are those dozens of volcanoes, presided over by ever-erupting Arenal, and the uncounted rivers and waterfalls pouring from the misty highlands into the hot, fertile valleys below.

Until the past decade or so, discovering the vast wealth of the "Rich Coast" required quite a workout, thus the first waves of visitors to crash on Costa Rica's beaches were surfers and scientists, climbers and birders, active people for whom some sweat was just part of the adventure. Such invigorating opportunities for exploration still exist, and you could spend days or weeks criss-crossing the country on foot, horseback, or canoe.

But Costa Ricans, so eager to show off all they have accomplished, have created new ways into the rain forests (sustainably, of course), which they call "soft adventure." Canopy tours, aerial trams, and hanging bridges take you into the treetops, while white-water rafting excursions and slow family-friendly riverboat floats guide you through the wetlands. Five-star hotels let you lounge in luxury along scalloped, white-sand beaches, and ecologically designed golf courses house toucans and spider monkeys in the rough. And after all this, you can even soak in soothing hot springs cascading through paradise.

Adventure Lodges

Wrapped in rain forest, these lodges offer comfortable if rustic accommodations, plus a variety of family-friendly tours including canopies, guided hikes, swimming holes, hot springs, water slides, riverboat floats, wildlife displays, and much more. You can stay overnight, or indulge in day passes and package deals that might include transportation from San José or the beaches.

Buena Vista Lodge (506-690-1414; www.buenavistalodgecr.com; Guanacaste) Canopy tour, waterslide, and cute cabins.

Hacienda Barú (Dominical; 506-787-0003; www.haciendabaru.com; Central Pacific) Wildlife refuge has cabins, zip lines, and tree climbs.

★ **Hacienda Guachipelin** (506-442-2818; www.guachipelin.com; Guanacaste) Next to Rincón de la Vieja National Park, has hot springs, canopies, and more.

Pozo Azule (877-810-6903; www.pozoazul.com; Sarapiquí) Rafting, canopies, butterflies, guided hikes, and very comfy camping, as well as a "jungle lodge."

★ **Sueño Azul** (506-764-1000; www.suenoazulresort.com; Sarapiquí) Upscale hotel offers floats, canopy, and yoga retreats.

Canopy Tours and other Aerial Adventures

The moniker "canopy tour" is a bit euphemistic: Also called zip lines, they whiz through the treetops at such speeds that you might not even notice the wildlife. There are more than 70 canopy tours in Costa Rica, and they can be arranged by almost any hotel or tour desk, often including lunch and transportation. The best include auxiliary adventures such as horse-back rides, guided hikes, wildlife displays, hanging bridges through the trees (from which you're more likely to spot wildlife, as you'll be moving more slowly and quietly) and even aerial trams. Many can also arrange bungee jumps and canyoning (rappelling down water-falls). Favorites include:

Puentes Colgantes de Arenal (506-479-9686; www.puentescolgantes.com; Northern Zone) Fabulous hanging bridges, with waterfalls, in the shadow of Arenal Volcano.

Rainforest Arial Tram (506-257-5961; www.rfat.com) Glide through the trees on amazing trams, one next to Braulio Carrillo National Park between San José and the Caribbean, the other on the Central Pacific Coast.

Selvatura (506-645-5929; www.selvatura.com; Monteverde) Great cloud-forest attraction offers bridges, hikes, wildlife displays, a canopy, and much more.

SkyTrek & Sky Walk (506-645-6003; www.skytram.net; Northern Zone) In both Arenal and Monteverde, offers trams, bridges, and top-notch canopies.

Turu Ba Ri (506-250-0705; www.tububari.com; Central Valley) All sorts of adventures just outside San José.

There are more than 100 species of heliconia, closely related to the banana.

Caving

Costa Rica is riddled with wonderful cave systems, but only two are easily accessible to tourists. Barra Honda National Park (Guanacaste), close to Liberia and the beach towns of the Nicoya Peninsula, offer tours of 2 of more than 40 caverns. From La Fortuna and the Arenal area, you can also arrange trips to muddy and mar-velous Venado Cavern (Northern Zone).

Diving and Snorkeling

With the exception of Isla del Coco, an isolated, expen-sive-to-visit Pacific island famed for huge schools of hammerhead sharks, Costa Rica is rarely considered a top diving and snorkeling destination. This is because its incredibly wildlife-rich waters thrive on the bounty of plankton welling up from the depths, a cloud of life that limits visibility on the Pacific to a paltry 9–15 meters (27–45 feet), 20 meters (60 feet) tops (decreasing during rainy season, May–December), with the Caribbean side only a bit clearer.

But divers come here precisely because of all that

life: As you ply the undersea mist of this rich coast, you may see, swimming serenely up through the opacity, entire *arribadas* of sea turtles arriving to nest, several species of dolphins, sharks, rays, and whales (including the enormous whale shark), as well as puffer fish, eels, starfish, sea horses, cortez angelfish, hogfish, parrotfish, clown shrimp, octopi, different corals, and so much more.

Diving in Costa Rica is reasonably priced, not as inexpensive as Honduras' Bay Islands, but significantly less than such premium locations as the Cayman Islands or Bahamas. Most shops offer resort dives for the uncertified and curious, as well as PADI certification if you'd like to see more. Most dives are relatively shallow, under 25 meters (75 feet), so you can usually do three dives per day, and shops often offer sunset, night, and even nude dives (though you'll probably want a 3 millimeter suit for most excursions) to spice things up.

ATVs aren't just for fun on Costa Rica's unpaved back roads—they're the best means of transportation.

Snorkel rentals and guided tours can be arranged in almost any coastal town, and most tour boats keep snorkel equipment on board.

GUANACASTE AND THE NICOYA PENINSULA

Home to Costa Rica's best diving, particularly during June and July, this region has several shops, most in the Northern Nicoya (from the Papagayo Peninsula south to Ocotal) and Tamarindo. Some sites are for experienced divers, such as The Big Scare, known for its serious currents and plethora of bull sharks, or Punta Gorda, near Ocotal, where thousands of eagle rays swirl in impossibly tall columns. Plenty are fine for beginners, however.

The most popular trip is the "Cats and Bats," a day trip to Catalina and Murciélago Islands (*murciélago* is Spanish for "bat"). The rocky outcroppings of these idyllic islands attract all manner of life, including sharks and huge Pacific rays, with wingspans of up to 7 meters (24 feet) and weighing some 1,350 kilograms (almost 3,000 pounds). They congregate here because the water is cooler; wear a full 3 to 5 millimeter wetsuit for this dive.

The Southern Nicoya Peninsula still lacks dive operators, but you can still get some snorkeling in. Arrange trips to Bahía Gigante, home to several islands including Isla Tortuga, from Montezuma, Puntarenas, or Jacó.

CENTRAL PACIFIC AND OSA PENINSULA

The Central Pacific, in particular Drake's Bay, Manuel Antonio, and Caño Island, offers some of the clearest diving in Costa Rica. The most famous site is Bajo del Diablo (Devil's

Red torch flower is among the loveliest in the ginger family.

Canyon), with visibility that can top 30 meters (100 feet) under peak conditions, allowing you to explore the undersea mountainscape, alive with schools of manta rays between February and April, and all manner of wildlife throughout the year.

Twenty kilometers (12 miles) south of Drake's Bay, Caño Island is a great site for divers and snorkelers, with schools of fish so intense that they block the sunlight. Dive trips are usually arranged from Manuel Antonio or Drake's Bay, as are snorkel treks to Caño Negro.

The Caribbean

Cahuita and Manzanillo preserve Costa Rica's only major living reef systems, with some 35 species of coral and 400 species of fish, dolphins, sharks, and whales. The best time to visit is February through April, and late September through October, when the Caribbean's dry(er) season allows more visibility offshore.

Outfitters visit about 20 sites, including shallow dives into the coral gardens that extend some 500 meters (1,640 feet) from Cahuita Point in Cahuita National Park, with sea fans, giant elkhorn, sea turtles, and huge schools of fish, as well as a fine collection of sunken ships—perfect for beginners. Deeper dives take you to amazing underwater vertical walls, home to hundreds of species of fish.

You can snorkel right offshore in several spots, including Cahuita National Park and Gandoca-Manzanillo National Wildlife Refuge, as well as Punta Uva, right in front of

Arrecife Restaurant; many hotels and tour operators rent equipment or arrange guided snorkel tours.

Golf

As Costa Rica goes upscale, this green and well-watered country is opening some of Latin America's finest golf courses. Though the first courses were built in the Central Valley, newer and more fabulous options, designed by Arnold Palmer, George Fazio, and Ted Robinson Jr., among others, have been built along the sunny Pacific, most in Guanacaste. Golf is gaining in popularity, not just among visitors, but also Costa Rican businesspeople and members of the diplomatic community, who tend to be friendly and bilingual, and happy to invite solo foreigners along.

Several specialty operators offer advice and arrange tours; visit **Golf Costa Rica** (www.golfcostarica.com), offering customized luxury tours to different greens and great hotels, with packages that could include sportfishing and national park visits; **Costa Rica Adventure Golf** (877-2258-2688; www.golfcr.com) with lots of information and tours; **Golf in Costa Rica** (www.golfincostarica.com) with a nifty newsletter; or Landy and Susan Blank at the **Cariari Country Club Pro Shop** (888-2672-2057; landy22@racsa.co.cr), who have been helping golfers putt their way through paradise for years.

Several new golfing greens are being developed, including two new world-class courses on the Papagayo Peninsula that should open while this book is on the shelves.

Cariari Country Club (506-2293-3211; www.clubcariari.com) Opened in 1974, this George Fazio-designed, par-71 course was once considered Costa Rica golfing's crown jewel, traditional, elegant, and challenging. You must be a guest at Herradura Resort and Conference Center, or know a member.

Costa Rican Country Club (www.costaricacountryclub.com; Escazú) Short, nine-hole executive course, originally built in 1944, has one of the most beautiful clubhouses in Central America. You'll need to go with a member, but some North American clubs offer reciprocity.

Four Seasons Papagayo (506-2696-0000; www.fourseasons.com/costarica; Guanacaste) This Arnold Palmer-designed par-72 course is ranked the best in Costa Rica, maximizing the Papagayo Peninsula's incredible views.

La Iguana Golf Course (506-2630-9000; www.marriott.com; Central Pacific) Swanky Marriott Los Sueños Resort, just north of Jacó, offers the excellent par-72 Ted Robinson Jr. course with rain forest and river views.

Hacienda Pinilla Beach Resort (506-2680-7060, 866-294-0466 USA and Canada; Guanacaste) Plush golfing resort near Tamarindo lets you sleep on the 18th hole of its Mike Young-designed golf course.

Papagayo Golf & Country Club (506-2697-0169; www.papagayo-golf.com; Guanacaste) Just 20 minutes from Liberia, this relaxed course with a family-friendly clubhouse is a great deal.

Parque Valle del Sol (506-2282-9222; www.vallesol.com; Central Valley) Cool and convenient spot in Santa Ana's rolling hills make this mature 18-hole course, originally designed in the 1970s and recently revamped by Tracy May, a great place to golf.

Reserva Conchal Golf Course (506-2654-4000; 800-769-7068 USA and Canada; www.reservaconchal.com; Guanacaste) Huge, Robert Trent Jones II course offers lakes, ravines, and views galore.

Los Reyes (506-2438-0858; www.losreyescr.com; Central Valley) Close to the Alajuela airport, this nine-hole, par-70 course is perfect for your last round in Costa Rica.

Tango Mar Beach & Golf Resort (506-2683-0001; www.tangomar.com; South Nicoya) Just north of Montezuma, Tango Mar offers a neat nine-hole executive course overlooking a blue-flag beach.

Hiking

The very best way to explore Costa Rica's remarkable wildlife is on foot, and there are literally hundreds of hikes to be had. Though a few are accessible only to serious hikers willing to rough the blister brigade for days on end, there are plenty of less strenuous options where almost anyone can see huge waterfalls, bubbling volcanic mud pots, natural hot springs, and all sorts of wildlife without straining themselves. And of course, there are lots of trails catering to everyone in between.

Costa Rica's mild climate lends itself to outdoor exploration, but there are considerations to keep in mind. The cloud forests are often cloudy, which means you might not be able to see that wet wildlife lurking out in the mists. They can also be quite chilly; wear layers that will stay warm when wet. The rain forests carpeting the Caribbean, Northern Zone, Central Pacific, and Osa Peninsula are hot, humid, and often rainy, and even during dry season you'll want to waterproof the essentials (eg., your camera) and perhaps bring a poncho. Rubber boots work wonderfully in these muddy regions, and can usually be rented wherever they're needed. If your feet are size 44 or larger (U.S. men's 10), consider bringing your own. There's usually no need for boots in the dry tropical forests of Guanacaste and the Nicoya Peninsula, but these hikes get hot and offer little shade in dry season, when trees drop their leaves.

Dehydration and sunstroke are the two greatest dangers all hikers in Costa Rica face. Bring water, sunscreen, and a brimmed hat, and don't forget to stop and rest; that's probably when you'll see the most wildlife, anyway. And, speaking of wildlife, be aware that there are poisonous snakes and biting insects in those woods; watch where you put your hands. Stores in San José, La Fortuna, and Liberia carry hiking and camping equipment, but prices are usually much higher than in the United States or Europe.

It's almost always worth hiring a guide for your hike. He or she can point out wildlife you would have otherwise missed, and they usually carry cell phones and first-aid kits, always reassuring. Any hotel or tour desk can arrange guides, some of whom specialize in birds, medicinal plants, geology, and more, so ask. Often, independent guides are waiting around at the ranger station. Dozens of general tour companies include, or can add, guided hikes as part of a package.

This is just a sample of what Costa Rica has to offer by way of trails:

Arenal National Park (Northern Zone) Centered on spectacular, erupting Arenal Volcano (which cannot be climbed), this national park offers 4 kilometers (2.5 miles) of trails past still steaming lava flows from the 1992 eruption, as well as a *mirador* (viewpoint) of all the action. More strenuous hikes lead to Arenal's dormant, lake-topped twin, Cerro Chato, or try the short, steep (think of the return trip as 15 minutes on a very scenic Stairmaster) hike to La Fortuna Waterfall.

Cahuita National Park (Caribbean Coast) Thoughtfully maintained, this 7-kilometer (4.3-mile) coastal trail traces white Caribbean beaches fringed with wild jungle and coconut palms, and connects two park entrances with easy bus transportation in between.

Toucans are common throughout the Central Pacific and Osa Peninsula.

Chirripó National Park (Central Valley) It's even snowed atop Mount Chirripó (3820 meters/12,530 feet), Costa Rica's highest mountain, a two-day, 16-kilometer (10-mile), steep but non-technical hike from San Gerardo de Rivas.

Corcovado National Park (Osa Peninsula) This is the jungle primeval, probably the most biodiverse place on Earth, famously crossed by an iconic, two-day trek. Or opt for shorter guided hikes through some smaller but no less wondrous corner of Corcovado, arranged anywhere.

Manuel Antonio National Park (Central Pacific) Costa Rica's most popular park offers little solitude in high season, but if you don't mind the crowds (or would rather visit in the rain), you can hike through some of the most beautiful shoreline ever preserved.

Monteverde Cloud Forest Preserve (Northern Zone) With 24 kilometers (15 miles) of well-maintained trails around the misty "Green Mountain," this is one of the most popular hiking parks in Central America. Too popular? Neighboring **Santa Elena Cloud Forest Reserve** has 12 kilometers (7 miles) of excellent hiking.

Rincón de la Vieja National Park (Guanacaste) Offers some 25 kilometers (16 miles) of well-maintained hiking trails through dry tropical forest, including a relatively flat, 4-kilometer (2.5-mile) loop that rewards hikers with a variety of volcanic activity, while longer trails access waterfalls, hot springs, and the simmering volcanic crater, all less than an hour from Liberia.

Despite their fearsome roar, howler monkeys are usually quite shy.

Tirimbina Rainforest Center & La Selva Biological Station (Northern Zone) Both of these
private preserves have networks of trails through the Sarapiquí wilderness, open to day
hikers. Explore on your own, or make reservations for a naturalist-guided tour.

Horseback Riding

Horses are still widely used as transportation throughout Costa Rica, and almost any tour
desk can find horses and guides. Some hotels may arrange horses through friends and family, which is usually just fine, although guides might not be fully bilingual, or may assume
you already have equestrian experience. Beginners will probably feel more comfortable
with established outfitters, who usually offer English-speaking guides. They often have
larger horses as well, a consideration if you weigh more than 100 kilograms (220 pounds).

Top spots for arranging horseback riding tours include Monteverde and the Arenal
region (adventurous and experienced horseback riders can even ride between the two),
while almost every major beach town offers outfitters galore.

Kayaking and Canoeing

There are excellent opportunities for kayak and canoe trips throughout the country. Sea
kayak rentals and tours are plentiful on both coasts, often involving excursions into rivers
and mangrove-lined estuaries. On the Caribbean, top spots include Cahuita and Puerto
Viejo de Talamanca, where in addition to sea kayaks, you can arrange kayak and canoe tours
in area rivers and estuaries. The endless canal system surrounding Tortuguero National
Park can also be explored in both canoes and kayaks, offered by several tour companies, as
well as independent local guides, in Tortuguero.

There are plenty of rivers waiting to be run inland, as well. Many rafting operators offer the option of riding the white water in sea kayaks, but they're a specialty in the tiny town of La Virgen de Sarapiquí, in the Northern Zone.

Sportfishing

Costa Rica's world-famous sportfishing is mostly catch and release, as big billfish are protected by law. But there are still varieties, such as tuna and dorado, which you can keep, and have cooked to order at a lodge or some restaurants. You must have a Costa Rican fishing license ($30), which is rarely included in "all-inclusive" package tours. All major coastal towns are served by boats completely equipped for sportfishing excursions, perhaps including lunch, a full bar, and/or snorkel equipment, that can be rented for around $300 per day, for four people.

The Nicoya Peninsula is well known for enormous tuna, plentiful year round. Marlin can be caught November to March, while May through August is prime time for sailfish, wahoo, and dorado. Outfitters are plentiful in Playas del Coco, Tamarindo, Ocotal, Sámara, and Carrillo.

Farther south, tuna are a bit smaller, but this is the top spot for roosterfish and snook. Marlin can be caught from September to November, with sailfish plentiful from December through April. Dorado and yellowfish peak in late May. Although there are outfitters in Puntarenas and Jacó, Quepos is the star of the show, with operators who'll organize fishing trips all over the country.

The Osa Peninsula, particularly Golfo Dulce, is famed for its large tuna and roosterfish year round, marlin August through September, and sailfish December through March. Operators are concentrated in Golfito and Playa Zancudo, with great snook fishing.

The Caribbean side is most famous for absolutely enormous tarpon and snook, and luxury-fishing lodges can be found in Barra del Colorado, Tortuguero, and Parismina. The Caribbean side offers a steep drop-off just one mile from land, so you won't need to travel as far to find roosterfish, amberjack, grouper, wahoo, and record-breaking snappers.

Inland, Lake Arenal is plied by several boats in search of *guapote* (rainbow bass), while farther north, Caño Negro Wildlife Refuge protects top stocks of tarpon, snook, *mojarra*, and *guapote*. Or, if you speak some Spanish, do like the Ticos do and fish for stocked trout (in the mountains) or tilapia (almost anywhere) at very basic lodge/restaurants signed from every major road. Get the latest on what's biting at www.ticotimes.net/fishingforum.

Surfing

Costa Rica is one of the world's top surfing destinations, and you could fill an entire book with information about the different waves, tours, schools, and shops available. Happily, a few fine writers have already done that: Check out Mike Parise's ★*The Surfers Guide to Costa Rica & SW Nicaragua*, the classic, and regularly updated, guide to more than 80 breaks on both coasts. Available in Costa Rica, *The Tiquicia Surf Map Guide* by Alvaro Solano, a local championship surfer, has more abbreviated information, plus a great map to the breaks.

Guanacaste and the Nicoya Peninsula have world-class breaks centered on the rapidly gentrifying town of Tamarindo, star of *Endless Summer II*. With a great beach break right in front of town, and just north in less-crowded Playa Grande, plus massive reef breaks just south in Playas Avellanas and Negra, you'll never be bored. You can also arrange boats to Ollie's Point and Witch's Rock, off Santa Rosa National Park.

Continuing south around the coast, Sámara has good swells, though most serious surfers

338 C O S T A   R I C A

continue north to Nosara's Playa Guiones. Malpaís and Santa Teresa, in South Nicoya, also offer great waves.

On the Central Pacific Coast, the grungy-but-fun surf town of Jacó, along with neighboring Playa Hermosa, have excellent, regular waves and lots of surf schools, making this a great destination for beginners. Continuing south, less crowded waves can be found at Estilleros Oeste, Playa Bejuco, Playa Palo Seco, Isla Damas, and even Manuel Antonio National Park. Dominical is the next surf town south, legendary for its hip vibe and some of the heaviest surf in the country, not really for beginners; local surf schools start you out at neighboring beaches. There are several breaks around the Osa Peninsula, in particular Playa Zancudo and Playa Pavones, with some of the world's best waves.

The Caribbean Coast also has some excellent breaks, including a world-class left at Isla Uvita, just off the coast of Puerto Limón (there are good waves on the beaches just north of the port town as well). Cahuita has a few good surfing beaches, but the most famous wave on the Caribbean is in Puerto Viejo, Salsa Brava. It's for experienced surfers only, but plenty of other beaches south to Manzanillo offer excellent breaks for every skill level.

Surf Schools

There are dozens of surf schools in Costa Rica, most offering package deals that could include accommodations, meals, yoga, guided tours, and even Spanish classes. These are just a few:

Coconut Harry's Surf Shop (506-2682-0574; www.coconutharry's.com; Nosara) Work less and surf more here, where they rent boards and arrange lessons and tours.

Del Mar Surf Camp (506-2385-8535; www.costaricasurfingchicas.com; Playa Hermosa) This one's for the ladies, with massages, manicures, pedicures, hiking, and plenty of surfing.

Green Iguana Surf Camp (506-2825-1381; www.greeniguanasurfcamp.com; Dominical) Excellent, professional school and camp offers accommodations, tours, and starts you off at mellower beaches if Dominical's famously heavy surf is too much.

Manuel Antonio Surf School (506-2777-4842; www.masurfschool.com; Manuel Antonio) Lessons, expeditions to neighboring beaches, and a fabulous amenity: Award-winning board-shaper Mauricio "Tule" Jimenez will make a board to your specs and have it waiting.

Roxy Costa Rica Surfaris (www.roxycostarica.com; Playa Hermosa and Jacó) Women's surf camp offers trips all over the country, plus packages like the mother-daughter surfari.

Tropical Surf School (www.tropicalsurfschool.com; Manuel Antonio) Instructors are national champions, who offer lessons, private guided tours, and board rentals.

Vista Guapa (506-2643-3242; www.vistaguapa.com; Jacó) Champion wave rider Alvaro Solano offers a bed-and-breakfast-style surf camp and yoga studio with lessons and tours.

White-Water Rafting

Heavy rains, high mountains, and exquisite river scenery all add up to one thing: Some of the world's best white-water rafting. There are several companies offering white-water tours, including several great local guides and large operators with runs all over the country: **Exploradores Outdoors** (506-2222-6262; www.exploradoresoutdoors.com) and **Ríos Tropicales** (506-2233-6455; www.riostropicales.com), which can include transportation

Turtle Tours

One of the most magical evenings you'll ever experience begins on a dark, protected beach awaiting the commencement of a 130 million-year-old passion play. Mother turtles, so graceful in the waves, haul themselves heavily onshore to lay hundreds of eggs, amidst discomfort and danger, so that their species might survive. This arduous journey is now more important now than ever, as their numbers dwindle toward extinction due to shrinking habitats and food supplies, increasing pollution, careless fishing, beachfront developments (light lures the fragile babies inland, to their death), and the continued harvest of turtles and eggs. Four of the world's seven species of sea turtle nest here, along both coasts.

Olive ridleys, called *tortuga lora* for their parrot-like beaks, arrive on Pacific beaches from June to December, sometimes solo, but more often as part of huge *arribadas*, mass nestings in which thousands of turtles cover the sands night and day. Arribadas arrive year round, most often June through December, to protected Playa Ostional, Playa Nancite in Santa Rosa National Park, and most recently at Playa Camaronal, protected just a few years ago and now hosting wonderful waves of life once again, for the first time in decades. Olive ridleys also come along Playa Caletas, Esterillos, Playa Hermosa, Nosara, and Matapalo, all on the Pacific side.

Green turtles, though protected by international convention, remain widely harvested for their meat and eggs. Here, their rights are better respected, and they have started nesting in increasing numbers between September and March on several Nicoya beaches, including Playa Caletas, Playa Naranjo, Cabuyal, Carate, and Río Oro, and on the Caribbean Coast from February through July.

Mother hawksbill turtles, however, return less and less often to the gray sands where they were born, as they have been hunted almost to extinction for their shells, still used to make jewelry. The few who still come, more beautiful than any bracelet, nest along both coasts between May and January.

The leatherback, or *baula*, was once considered sacred, and remains the biggest, fastest, and deepest-diving sea turtle, as well as the largest reptile, on the planet. They patrol every ocean, from the frozen poles to the steaming tropics, in search of their only food, jellyfish. Despite increased protection worldwide, their numbers are plummeting, even here at their most important nesting ground, Las Baulas National Marine Park in Playa Grande. If you're lucky, you may see them here between September and March, or along the Caribbean between February and July.

"Turtle Tours" are arranged at almost all of these beaches, and you must go with a guide. Sightings are not guaranteed, but if you do attend one of the lovely lady's labors, please don't touch her or expose her to light (flash photography requires a hard-to-get permit), or ask the guide to do so. These creatures, who live some 70 years and have complex social lives, are probably more intelligent and sensitive than most give them credit for. If you miss the blessed event, come back to the beach at daybreak, when babies push up out of the sand and scurry clumsily out to sea. Only one in a thousand of these cuties will make it to maturity.

If you'd like to learn more, there are two tiny turtle museums worth a visit: El Mundo de la Tortuga (World of the Turtle) in Las Baulas National Marine Park in Playa Grande, Guanacaste, and the Caribbean Conservation Corporation (CCC) Museum of the Turtle in Tortuguero, on the Caribbean Coast. The CCC also arranges volunteer opportunities (506-2709-8091; www.cccturtle.org), which give visitors the opportunity to help monitor and protect nesting turtles. Many other volunteer programs are available; check the Caribbean Coast, and Central Pacific and Osa Peninsula chapters for listings.

Urracas *(magpie jays), common throughout Guanacaste, are social and inquisitive.*

between major tourist destinations as part of the package, convenient if you don't rent a car.

Río Corobicí (Guanacaste) Arrange a mellow, family-friendly Class I or II float on the spot at their headquarters, an hour from the Liberia airport; or make reservations for wilder rides on nearby Tenorio and Zapote Rivers.

Río Naranjo (Central Pacific) Quepos' best-kept secret offers serious Class IV action.

Río Pacuare (Central Valley) Famously ranked among the world's most beautiful rivers by *National Geographic Traveler*, the lush Pacuare offers Class III and Class IV rapids that can be experienced on a day trip or, better, with an overnight at a remote jungle lodge.

Reventazón (Central Valley) The roughest white water in Costa Rica offers monster Class IV and Class V rapids; some experience is required.

Río Savegre (Central Pacific) In the stunning Saavegre Valley, this view-packed trek offers Class II and III rapids for beginners and kids, plus Class IV sections sure to get you wet.

Sarapiquí (Northern Zone) Class III rapids are perfect for active families and beginners, or arrange even calmer floats through the rain forest.

11

Suggested Reading

Costa Rica has inspired an incredible range of writers to expound on their favorite aspects of Tico history, culture, and wildlife. This is just a sample of what's available. Stop into one of Costa Rica's many English-language bookstores for even more.

Children's Books

Kids love rain forest critters, so get them excited about your trip.

Collard, Sneed B., and Michael Rothman. *The Forest in the Clouds*. Watertown, MA: Charlesbridge Publishing. 2000. $7.95. Take an illustrated journey through the misty cloud forests, where you'll find such denizens as the resplendent quetzal, two-toed sloth, and many more.

Deady, Kathleen W. *Costa Rica*. New York, New York: Children's Press. 2005. $6.95. Read about Costa's Rica's road to democracy, as well as volcanoes, oxcarts, and efforts to protect the environment.

Katz Cooper, Sharon, and Allan Eitzen. *Costa Rica ABCs: A Book About the People and Places of Costa Rica*. Mankato, Minnesota: Picture Window Books. 2007. $25.26. The country's unique animals, plants, and customs in an illustrated ABC book for young children.

Witte, Anna. *The Parrot Tico Tango*. Cambridge, Massachusetts: Barefoot Books. 2005. $6.99. Illustrations created from fabric, paint, and paper tell the story of Tico Tango and his quest for brightly colored objects and exotic fruits in the jungle.

Cookbooks

Can't get enough of that *gallo pinto*? You'll find the recipe right here.

Ramírez Carrera de Aragón, Juana. *Cocina Costarricense*. San José, Costa Rica: University of Costa Rica SA. 2007. $5. Costa Rica's very first cookbook, originally published in 1903, has been re-released including 700 very traditional recipes, half of which are desserts.

Urbina Castro. *My Kitchen: Costa Rican Typical Recipes*. San José, Costa Rica: Litografia e Imprenta Bentacourt Costa Rica. 1996. $10. Definitive English-language collection of traditional Tico cuisine.

Culture

Biesanz, Richard, Karen Zubris Biesanz, Mavis Hiltunen Biesanz. *The Costa Ricans*. Long Grove, Illinois: Waveland Press, Inc. 1988. $15.50. Insight to the character and customs of the Costa Rican people, with a look at Tico cultural, economic, and social change.

Biesanz, Richard, Karen Zubris Biesanz, and Mavis Hiltunen Biesanz. *The Ticos: Culture and*

Social Change in Costa Rica. Boulder, Colorado: Lynne Rienner Publishers. 1998. $20.00. A study of a country with more teachers than soldiers, higher standards of living and literacy rates, and better health care than its Central American neighbors.

Booth, John A. *Costa Rica: Quest For Democracy*. Boulder, Colorado: Westview Press. 1999. $38.00. Traces democratic development through the schools, churches, and politics of Costa Rica.

Cruz, Consuelo. *Political Culture and Institutional Development in Costa Rica and Nicaragua: World-making in the Tropics*. Cambridge, England: Cambridge University Press. 2005. $85. Serious academic tome examines original documents to understand why these two neighboring nations, the wealthiest and poorest in Central America respectively, have taken such different paths.

Palmer, Paula. *Taking Care of Sibo's Gifts*. San José, Costa Rica: Editorama S.A. 1993. $12. An environmental treatise based on the beliefs and experiences of Costa Rica's Keköldi people.

Palmer, Paula. *What Happen? A Folk-History of Costa Rica's Talamanca Coast*. San José, Costa Rica: Zona Tropical. 2005. $12.95. The Caribbean Coast's fascinating history and traditions, as told by the people themselves.

Wallerstein, Claire. *Culture Shock! Costa Rica: A Survival Guide to Customs and Etiquette*. Singapore: Marshall Cavendish Corporation. 2007. $11.00. Teaches the reader to "live, work, and play like a Tico."

Fiction

Gagini, Carlos. *Redemptions: A Costa Rican Novel*. San Diego, California: San Diego State University Press. 1918. $35.00. A symbolic tale that takes place in San José at the turn of the 20th century, as U.S. economic, political, military, and cultural influence was growing throughout Central America.

Jaramillo Levi, Enrique (Editor). *When New Flowers Bloomed: Short Stories by Women Writers from Costa Rica and Panama*. Pittsburgh, Pennsylvania: Latin American Literary Review Press. 1991. $10. Anthology of 31 stories by women authors, offering the reader an alternative perspective on the history and culture of Central America.

Ras, Barbara (Editor). Arias, Oscar (Author). *Costa Rica: A Traveler's Literary Companion*. Berkeley: California Whereabouts Press. 1993. $10.00. Twenty-six fictional stories of life reveal the real story.

Guides

Several specialty guidebooks can help you find your passion.

Eudy, Lee. *Chasing Jaguars: The Complete Guide to Costa Rican Whitewater*. Chapel Hill, North Carolina: Earthbound Sports Inc. 2003. $30.50. Details 40 of Costa Rica's best whitewater runs, and throws in a few of the best surfing beaches for good measure.

Greenspan, Eliot. *The Tico Times Restaurant Guide to Costa Rica*. San José, Costa Rica: The Tico Times SA. 2007. $10. Updated, bilingual restaurant reviews tell you where to eat all over Costa Rica, in particular San José and the Central Valley.

Mitchell, Sam. *Waterfalls and Hot Springs of Costa Rica*. Cincinnati, Ohio: Menasha Ridge Press. 1995. Melt your cares away in one of Costa Rica's hidden hot springs, or jump into a refreshing swimming hole.

Parise, Mike. *The Surfer's Guide to Costa Rica*. SurfPress Publishing. 2006. $21.95. The definitive surf guide to Costa Rica. With more than 30 years of research and in its sixth edition, this is the definitive book on surfing in Costa Rica.

History

Allen, William. *Green Phoenix: Restoring the Tropical Forests of Guanacaste, Costa Rica*. New York, New York: Oxford University Press. 2001. Immensely readable success story of two scientists who overcame financial, scientific, cultural, and political (Iran-Contra anyone?) hurdles to reforest Guanacaste Province.

Evans, Sterling. *The Green Republic: A Conservation History of Costa Rica*. Austin, Texas: University of Texas Press. 1999. $18.00. History and context for the emergence of conservation in Costa Rica.

Longley, Kyle. *Sparrow and the Hawk: Costa Rica and the United States during the Rise of José Figueres*. Tuscaloosa, Alabama: University Alabama Press. 1997. $30.00. Profiles the development of U.S.–Costa Rica relations following the 1948 civil war José Figueres' rise to power.

Molina, Iván. *The Costa Rica Reader: History, Culture, Politics*. Durham, North Carolina: Duke University Press. 2004. $24.00. Using words and art, this book focuses on the sociological evolution of the country.

Real Estate

Left your heart in Tamarindo? Consider joining the thousands of North Americans and Europeans who have moved here for good. But be aware, there's plenty of hype out there: It's not as cheap or easy as real estate agents may say. These guides give you the real story.

Howard, Christopher. *The New Golden Door to Retirement and Living in Costa Rica*. San José, Costa Rica: Costa Rica Books. 2007. $26.95. Long-time resident and relocation expert updates this guide to navigating Costa Rica's wild real estate market; his Web site (www.costaricabooks.com) lists more of his books, including the great *Guide to Costa Rican Spanish*, and information.

Maranon, Jon. *The Gringo's Hawk*. Eugene, Oregon: Kenneth Group. 2001. $25.00. Engaging memoir of the author's journey from 21-year-old tourist to landowner and conservationist in the Pacific town of Morita.

Oliver, Scott. *How to Buy Costa Rica Real Estate without Losing Your Camisa*. San José, Costa Rica: Consultores Britanicos S.A. 2005. $14.95. Good resource for those investing and/or purchasing real estate in Costa Rica.

Van Rheenen, Erin. *Living Abroad in Costa Rica*. Berkeley, CA: Avalon Travel Publishing. $19.95. 2007. Well-written guide to finding a home, a job, residency, and how to fit in once you're settled.

Wildlife Watching

There are dozens of books detailing Costa Rica's wonderful wildlife, including these.

Beletsky, Les. *Costa Rica: The Ecotravellers' Wildlife Guide*. Burlington, Massachusetts: Academic Press. 1998. $6.00. Endorsed by the Wildlife Conservation Society, this primer provides an introduction to the flora, fauna, and principles of ecotourism in Costa Rica.

Carr, Archie. *The Windward Road*. Gainesville, Florida: University of Florida Press. 1979. $16.95. Founder of the world's first sea turtle conservation program recalls wanderings that led him to Tortuguero.

Dressler, Robert L. *Field Guide to the Orchids of Costa Rica and Panama*. Ithaca, New York: Cornell University Press. 1993. $28. Excellent photography and illustrations allow orchid lovers to make specific identifications.

Forsyth, Adrian. *How Monkeys Make Chocolate: Unlocking the Mysteries of the Rain Forest*. Toronto, Canada: Maple Tree Press. 2006. $9.95. Through intelligent text and amazing photos, learn the secret ingredients in many familiar products like chocolate, aspirin, and rubber.

Fogden, Michael. *Hummingbirds of Costa Rica*. Tonawanda, New York: Firefly Books. 2006. $49.95. Fabulously illustrated guide to the hummingbirds of Costa Rica from one of its most revered photographers.

Frankie, Gordon W., Alfonso Mata, and S. Bradleigh Vinson. *Biodiversity Conservation in Costa Rica (Learning the Lessons in a Seasonal Dry Forest)*. Berkeley, California: University of California Press. 2004. $34.95. Comprehensive and academic look at the ecology, biodiversity, and conservation status of the region.

Guyer, Craig and Maureen Donnelly. *Amphibians and Reptiles of La Selva, Costa Rica, and the Caribbean Slope: A Comprehensive Guide*. Berkeley, California: University of California Press. 2004. $24.95. Authoritative and convenient resource for finding and identifying amphibians and reptiles of the Caribbean lowlands.

Kavanagh, James. *Costa Rica Butterflies & Moths: An Introduction to Familiar Species*. Phoenix, Arizona: Waterford Press. 2007. $5.95. Make the most of your search for Costa Rica's array of butterflies and moths.

Kavanagh, James. *Monteverde Birds: An Introduction to Familiar Species of the Monteverde Cloud Forest*. Phoenix, Arizona: Waterford Press. 2007. $5.95. Pocket guide with illustrations of the birds found in the Monteverde Cloud Forest.

Miyata, Ken. *Tropical Nature: Life and Death in the Rain Forests of Central and South America*. New York, New York: Touchstone. 1987. $14. Vast amount of information about the rain forests with a focus on evolutionary principles.

Garrigues, Richard. *The Birds of Costa Rica: A Field Guide*. San José, Costa Rica: Zona Tropical. 2006. $29.95. An excellent, well-illustrated guide to Costa Rica's bird species.

Janzen, Daniel H. *Costa Rican Natural History*. Chicago, Illinois: University of Chicago Press. 1983. $40.00. Hefty compendium of all things natural in Costa Rica is 20 years old, but remains the top-rated guide for travelers and academics interested in the land.

Miller, Jeffrey C., Daniel H. Janzen, and Winifred Hallwachs. *100 Caterpillars: Portraits from the Tropical Forests of Costa Rica*. Harvard, Massachusetts: Belknap Press. 2007. $39.95. The hidden lives of pre-butterflies captured in all their spiny, squishy, and spectacular glory.

Savage, Jay M. *The Amphibians and Reptiles of Costa Rica: A Herpetofauna between Two Continents, between Two Seas*. Chicago, Illinois: University of Chicago Press. 2005. $47.50. Spells it out for amphibian and reptile lovers.

Stiles, F. Gary, and Alexander F. Skutch. *A Guide to the Birds of Costa Rica*. Ithaca, New York: Cornell University Press. 1990. $26.00. Hefty book is the bible for bird lovers.

Zuchowski, Willow. *Guide to Tropical Plants of Costa Rica*. San José, Costa Rica: Zona Tropical. 2006. $20. Comprehensive guide with more than 540 photos is designed for the amateur botanist, with English, Costa Rican, and scientific names for cross-referencing.

General Index

Lodging by Price

Dining by Price

Dining by Cuisine